The Talcott Parsons Reader

BLACKWELL READERS

In a number of disciplines, across a number of decades, and in a number of languages, writers and texts have emerged which require the attention of students and scholars around the world. United only by a concern with radical ideas, Blackwell Readers collect and introduce the works of pre-eminent theorists. Often translating works for the first time (Levinas, Irigaray, Lyotard, Blanchot, Kristeva), or presenting material previously inaccessible (C. L. R. James, Fanon, Elias), each volume in the series introduces and represents work which is now fundamental to study in the humanities and social sciences.

The Lyotard Reader
Edited by Andrew Benjamin

The Irigaray Reader
Edited by Margaret Whitford

The Kristeva Reader
Edited by Toril Moi

The Levinas Reader
Edited by Sean Hand

The C. L. R. James Reader
Edited by Anna Grimshaw

The Wittgenstein Reader
Edited by Anthony Kenny

The Blanchot Reader
Edited by Michael Holland

The Elias Reader
Edited by S. Mennell

The Lukács Reader
Edited by Arpad Kardakay

The Cavell Reader
Edited by Stephen Mulhall

The Guattari Reader
Edited by Garry Genosko

The Bataille Reader
Edited by Fred Botting and Scott
   Wilson

The Eagleton Reader
Edited by Stephen Regan

The Castoriadis Reader
Edited by David Ames Curtis

The Goffman Reader
Edited by Charles Lemert and Ann
   Branaman

The Frege Reader
Edited by Michael Beaney

The Virilio Reader
Edited by James Der Derian

The Hegel Reader
Edited by Stephen Houlgate

The Angela Y. Davis Reader
Edited by Joy James

The Stanley Fish Reader
Edited by H. Aram Veeser

The Žižek Reader
Edited by Elizabeth Wright and
   Edmond Wright

The Talcott Parsons Reader
Edited by Bryan S. Turner

Forthcoming:
The Bauman Reader
Edited by Peter Beilharz

The Talcott Parsons Reader

Edited by

Bryan S. Turner

University of Cambridge

BLACKWELL
Publishers

First published 1999

2 4 6 8 10 9 7 5 3 1

Blackwell Publishers Inc.
350 Main Street
Malden, Massachusetts 02148
USA

Blackwell Publishers Ltd
108 Cowley Road
Oxford OX4 1JF
UK

Library of Congress Cataloging-in-Publication Data

Parsons, Talcott, 1902–
   [Selections. 1999]
   The Talcott Parsons reader / edited by Bryan S. Turner.
      p. cm. — (Blackwell readers)
   Includes bibliographical references and index.
   ISBN 1–55786–543–4 (hardcover : alk. paper). — ISBN 1–55786–544–2
(pbk. : alk. paper)
   1. Sociology. 2. United States—Social conditions. I. Turner,
Bryan S. II. Title. III. Series.
   HM585.P372 1999
   301—dc21
                                         99–25740
                                              CIP

British Library Cataloguing in Publication Data

A CIP catalogue record for this book is available from the British Library.

This book is printed on acid-free paper.

Contents

Acknowledgments

The editor and publisher gratefully acknowledge the following for permission to reproduce copyright material:

"Christianity and Modern Industrial Society" (1962), from Edward A. Tiryakian (ed.), *Sociological Theory, Values and Sociocultural Change: Essays in Honor of Pitrim A. Sorokin* (Free Press, New York, 1963; reprinted by permission of Simon & Schuster, New York, 1999).

"Belief, Unbelief, and Disbelief" (1971), from R. Caporale and A. Grumelli (eds), *The Culture of Unbelief: Studies and Proceedings from the First International Symposium on Belief* (University of California Press, Berkeley. Copyright © 1971 The Regents of the University of California).

"Religious Symbolization and Death" (1973), from A. Eister (ed.), *Changing Perspectives in the Scientific Study of Religion* (Wiley-Interscience, New York, 1973. Copyright © 1973 John Wiley & Sons. Reprinted by permission of John Wiley & Sons, Inc.).

"The Symbolic Environment of Modern Economies" (1979), *Social Research* vol. 46 (3), 1979.

"Illness and the Role of the Physician: A Sociological Perspective" (1951), *American Journal of Orthopsychiatry*, vol. 21, 1951.

"Toward a Healthy Maturity" (1960), *Journal of Health and Human Behavior*, vol. 1 (Fall), 1960.

"The 'Gift of Life' and Its Reciprocation" (co-authored with R. C. Fox and V. M. Lidz) (1972), *Social Research*, vol. 39 (3), 1972.

"Evolutionary Universals in Society" (1964), *American Sociological Review*, vol. 29 (3), June 1964 (reprinted by permission of the American Sociological Association, Washington D.C.).

"Pattern Variables Revisited: A Response to Robert Dubin" (1960), *American Sociological Review*, vol. 25 (4), August 1960.

"Social Strains in America" (1955), from D. Bell (ed.), *The New American Right* (Criterion Books, New York, 1955).

"The Distribution of Power in American Society" (1957), *World Politics*, vol. 10 (October), pp. 123–43 (© 1957 Center of International Studies, Princeton University. Reprinted by permission of the Johns Hopkins University Press).

"Order and Community in the International Social System" (1961), from J. N. Rosenau (ed.), *International Politics and Foreign Policy* (Free Press, New York, 1961; reprinted by permission of Simon & Schuster, New York, 1999).

"Polarization of the World and International Order" (1961), from Q. Wright, W. M. Evan and M. Deutsch (eds), *Preventing World War III* (Simon & Schuster, New York, 1961).

"Youth in the Context of American Society" (1962), *Daedalus*, vol. 91 (1) (Winter). Reprinted by permission of *Daedalus*, Journal of the American Academy of Arts and Sciences, from the issue entitled: "Youth: Change and Challenge", Winter 1962, vol. 91, no. 1.

"Death in American Society" (co-authored with V. M. Lidz) (1963), *American Behavioral Scientist*, vol. 6 (9), pp. 61–5 (copyright © 1963 by Sage Publications Inc., Thousand Oaks. Reprinted by permission of Sage Publications Inc.).

"Religion in Postindustrial America: The Problem of Secularization" (1974), *Social Research*, vol. 41, 1974.

Introduction: The Contribution of Talcott Parsons to the Study of Modernity

Parsons and Modernity

These selections from the sociology of Talcott Parsons are based on a number of fundamental assumptions, which have guided my decision as to which elements of Parsons's extensive *oeuvre* might be included. Parsons was a prolific writer, whose academic career stretched over more than half a century. In addition, he contributed to a broad range of issues in contemporary sociology. In making this selection, my aim has been to uncover the "essential Parsons," and thus many articles and chapters, which are in themselves of interest, have not been included in so far as they do not address what I believe are the constitutive issues of his sociology. That his work continues to evoke robust responses, ranging from praise to outright hostility, leads me to believe that a short but effective collection of his work will find a sympathetic reception in the academic community.

His sociology remains academically important and controversial, because Parsons's work is an explicit defence of modernity in terms of its cultural values, political system, and moral authority. Against the contemporary interest in the implications of postmodernism, Parsons presents us with an unambiguous celebration of modernity. Parsons's sociology does not exhibit any subtle feelings for the ambiguities or ambivalence of modernity. By contrast with conservative traditionalism and reactionary politics, Parsons's commitment to liberal democracy, industrial capitalism, and secular values of achievement and universalism remains undiluted and largely unquestioned. Radical critics of modern society have often been committed implicitly to a nostalgic or romantic defense of tradition and community (Turner, 1987). Conservative critics of modern technological civilization such as Martin Heidegger lamented the negative impact of technology on man's place in the world (Heidegger, 1977). Radical critics of contemporary capitalism such as Theodor Adorno attacked the alienation of human beings under conditions of capitalist exploitation, but implicitly defended aristocratic notions of academic authenticity (Stauth and Turner, 1988).

In contemporary sociology and philosophy, there is often a yearning for communal stability and authentic values, which has been expressed through various forms of communitarianism. Émile Durkheim's attack on egoistic individualism in *Professional Ethics and Civic Morals* (1992) established a sociological perspective on communal solutions to utilitarian individualism and promoted the importance of intermediary groups in regulating the market. By contrast, Parsons believed that the process of modernization improved the capacity of society to respond effectively to new challenges through the division of labor and institutional upgrading. Modern values of activism and individualism were to be embraced as positive responses to modern conditions. In his political sociology, Parsons believed that liberal values (such as individual freedoms and personal autonomy) would triumph over authoritarian political regimes. While critics condemned modernity because it was seen to erode the meaningfulness of human existence, Parsons saw it as the fulfillment of a positive trend in western history. For Parsons, the seed beds of modernity were in Greek democracy and Christian ethical teaching, and the outcome of modernization were the secular values of universalism, activism, and individualism. Parsons remained opposed to what he called the "ideological pessimism" about modern societies which was prevalent in his time (Parsons, 1971: 142).

Parsons defended modern society, but he was specifically the champion of the American version of liberal capitalism (Robertson and Turner, 1991). Radical critics from C. Wright Mills to Alvin Gouldner attacked American society as an aggressive capitalist system, which was imperialist in its foreign relations and exploitative internally through the class system and the caste-like hierarchy of racial groups. For Parsons, despite these obvious patterns of inequality and exploitation, American society and its values were the summation of a process of secular enlightenment, which started in the seventeenth-century Puritan sects and culminated in American denominationalism. Parsons's vision of secular social reality could be described as Weberian, but without the overwhelming sense of melancholy which saturates Weber's world-view (Goldman, 1992).

Parsons's secular liberalism has been unfashionable in post-war social theory. One reason for this critical attitude towards Parsons is the intellectual dominance of post-humanism as the legacy of Nietzsche and Heidegger. This legacy has been profoundly influential in the critique of subjectivity in the work of Foucault and Derrida (Renaut, 1997). Parsons's later work was specifically concerned with the human condition, with death and the problem of religion in late modernity; his stance has been clearly out of tune with the prevailing fashion. However, one can anticipate a reaction against the anti-humanism of structuralist and post-structuralist social theory, because there is a need for a robust theory of democracy and human rights in the modern world. The question of human rights has become more rather than less urgent in late twentieth-century politics. In French social theory, one can see such a reaction in contemporary discussions of human rights in the work of Luc Ferry and Alain Renaut, who have also conducted a critical engagement with Heidegger's orientation to technological modernity (Ferry and Renaut, 1990). One can detect similar re-appraisals of democratic theory in reactions to the legacy of J. F. Lyotard (Rojek and Turner, 1998).

Whether or not one accepts Parsons's version of American secular triumphalism, it is important to read Parsons in order to grasp, in its unexpurgated form, the essence of cultural modernity. Francois Bourricaud's *The Sociology of Talcott Parsons* (1981) is one of the few studies of Parsonian sociology to grasp fully the centrality of cultural values to Parsons's understanding of modernity, especially the so-called "pattern variables." Bourricaud's study was first published in French as *L'individualisme institutionnel* in 1977. This title captures Parsons's notion that social actors must make choices between a fixed range of alternative courses of action. The voluntaristic theory of action pays attention to both the normative and material determination of the social relations and the voluntaristic nature of social action. The pattern variables describe this phenomenon of institutionalized individualism. The variables articulate a number of dichotomies that define the nature of choice between different courses of action: universalism versus particularism, diffuseness versus specificity, affective neutrality versus affectivity, achievement versus ascription (later described as performance versus quality).

In the pattern variables, modernity is a set of values which inscribe universalism, affective neutrality, role specificity, and performance into the central institutions and culture of a modern society. Modernization is that social process which brings about the dominance of these secular values of achievement, universalism, and neutrality. Finally, this process of modernization can be detected in a broad range of systematic changes in the contemporary world. These changes include the professionalization of the occupational system with a growing emphasis on the credentialization of specific, affectively neutral, and universalistic services. In the growth of a mass education system, especially at the tertiary level, Parsons saw new opportunities for the extension of democracy on the basis of a secular ethic which embraced universalism and achievement. In Parsons's terms, the final wave of modern citizenship after the welfare state was the educational revolution. Modernization also involved the secularization of religion and the transformation of the Protestant ethic into a democratic value system.

Reading Parsons

In order to understand the grand narrative of progressive modernization, of which postmodern theory is the critique, one should read Parsons carefully and thoughtfully. But how is this reading to be accomplished, given the apparent complexity of his argument, and what is to be read, given the obvious diversity of his writing? In trying to answer that question, there are broadly six principles of selection on which this essential collection has been made. The first obviously is that Talcott Parsons's work has, towards the close of the twentieth century, a major significance and value for sociology, and more widely for the social sciences. His sociology has both scope and depth as a general approach to the social sciences. Parsonian sociology, especially in *The Social System* (1951), is an attempt to construct a general theory of social action, which will integrate the separate disciplines of the social sciences. Its scope and complexity are daunting. At the same time, his social theory, especially *The Structure of Social Action* (1937), represents a profound criticism of utilitarianism, and in the modern period provides us with a compelling criticism of economic rationalism as a platform for social policy. In addition, he has made specific and lasting contributions to various fields within general sociology such as the sociology of religion (Parsons, 1962), medical sociology (1975), and economic sociology (Parsons and Smelser, 1956). He was also responsible for introducing the work of Max Weber to the English-speaking academic community through his translation of Weber's *The Protestant Ethic and the Spirit of Capitalism* (1930). He contributed more widely to the creation of a sense of "classical sociology" through his commentaries on the work of Émile Durkheim and Vilfredo Pareto. In short, Parsons offers a general but systematic framework for the analysis of modernity.

Second, Parsons played an important role politically as a critic of fascism. Although Parsons retained a deep respect for German culture and scholarship, he was highly critical of National Socialism in Germany and he campaigned to get the government of the United States committed to American involvement in the Second World War. Parsons subsequently wrote a series of insightful and important sociological essays on the social origins of fascism. Parsons's criticism of fascism has not been fully appreciated by sociologists, who, following the critical evaluation of Parsons's functionalism by Alvin Gouldner (1970) in *The Coming Crisis of Western Sociology*, regarded Parsons as either intellectually apathetic or politically reactionary. The appreciation of Parsons's critical analysis of fascism was not fully established until the publication of Uta Gerhardt's *Talcott Parsons on National Socialism* (1993). It is true that Parsons's objection to fascism was part of a wider criticism of authoritarian regimes. He was thus equally critical in his later years of communism. His political orientation was that of a liberal reaction to various forms of authoritarianism, and thus we can analyze Parsons's political sociology as an expression of his commitment to the principles of modern citizenship, as presented in the work of T. H. Marshall (1964).

Third, it is difficult to read Parsons without being impressed by the importance of religion in his understanding of modern society. Parsons rejected the secularization thesis. In the post-war period, sociologists typically embraced a naive theory of modernization which stipulated an inevitable secularization of religious institutions and values. The continuing importance of Protestantism in mainstream American life, the vitality of Judaism, the centrality of Hinduism to Indian politics, and the world-wide importance of fundamentalism have obviously thrown doubt on the secularization thesis. Islam in particular appears to have survived long periods of secular nationalism, communism, and western commercialism (Turner, 1994b). However, Parsons's sociology of religion does not involve the proposition simply that religion can survive industrialization. Because he followed in the footsteps of Durkheim's sociology of religion (1954), Parsons had a subtle understanding of the contribution of religious values to cultural systems, and how religion as "the serious life" in Durkheim's terms was an underpinning of the human condition as such. Parsons does not share the pessimism of Alasdair MacIntyre's post-Catholic criticism of modernity (MacIntyre, 1981) or the optimism of those sociologists who treat the American civil religion in its commercial forms as evidence of the human need for religion.

Parsons's argument was that with secularization many aspects of Protestant culture are both transferred and transformed into pluralism, activism, and individualism.

Fourth, Parsons is a founder of medical sociology. He studied many facets of this issue, which was set within a sociology of the professions, and many aspects of the importance of health and illness. These sociological interests brought him directly into contact with a number of key existential issues such as sex, aging, sickness, and death. His concept of the sick role has been criticized (Turner, 1995), but it provided an original insight into sickness as a social condition. His work on Freudian issues in the doctor–patient relationship also provided a provocative framework for the development of sociological analysis of professional roles. Parsons also contributed to the notion that medicine is one of the basic institutions of modern society, and that it is impossible to understand the emphasis on activism in American culture without a recognition of the ways in which medical values shape and inform modern culture.

Fifth, he also had a very practical involvement in and concern for sociology as a discipline (Parsons, 1950). His involvement in the interdisciplinary program at Harvard in the Department of Social Relations gave Parsons an important insight into the place of sociology within theories of social action. Parsons had a very clear idea of the importance of general theory to the survival of sociology in the university. His theory of the social system was also an attempt to understand sociology in relation to the issues of integration and motivation of social actors. Parsons's account of the allocative and integrative problems of any society produced an important defense of sociology as that science which attempts to analyze the contribution of shared values to the creation of an integrated social system.

Sixth, his writings can be seen as broadly a reflection on the role of American society in relation to the emerging world order. Parsons's sociology has relevance to the growing importance of globalism, difference, and social complexity, and hence by stressing the importance of Parsons as a theorist of modernity, I obliquely point forward to the development of postmodern theory. Parsons's work on global politics and international relations has been somewhat neglected by commentators.

In terms of these principles of selection, these readings attempt to correct the view that Parsons's sociology was so abstract that he could make no real contribution to the study of contemporary society. These essential readings note Parsons's contribution to the study of international relations, political sociology, and the study of economics. These selections also attempt to recognize the importance of Parsons's medical sociology where his analysis of the doctor–patient relationship played an important part in the development of the sociological study of the professions and professional practice. Parsons's medical sociology also embraced the study of death in modern societies, the process of aging, and the values which inform our understanding of the human condition. For this reason, one should not artificially separate Parsons's work on the impact of religion on secular society. In making that connection between religion and secular values, Parsons remained aware of his intellectual debt to the classics. Hence I have selected work to represent his deep understanding of the cumulative nature of sociological theory. Finally, Parsons remained committed to the defense of American liberal democracy. This attachment to American civilization remains controversial. Its positive side was the defense of citizenship as a framework for liberty, for example in his work on race relations in America. Its negative side was American triumphalism and a blindness to cultural differences.

Criticism and Re-appraisal

There has clearly been since the 1980s a major re-evaluation of the sociology of Talcott Parsons and an extensive assessment of his legacy. Since Parsons's death in 1979, there have been a number of important contributions to the systematic overview of his work (Adriaansens, 1980; Alexander, 1984; Buxton, 1985; Holton and Turner, 1986; Munch, 1981). This re-appraisal of Parsonian sociology is often associated with the neo-functionalist revival (Alexander, 1985, 1988a). In this introduction, I wish to contribute to this re-assessment through an examination of a frequent criticism of Parsons's functionalism, namely its inability to provide a valid framework for the analysis of historical processes and social change. In order to give this discussion a specific focus, I shall consider a critical comparison between the figurational or process model of sociology in the work of Norbert Elias (1978a) and Parsons's structural functionalism. This comparison with Elias is relevant because they have both been criticized for their conservatism, they have both drawn heavily from Weber and Freud, and they were both influenced by the Weber legacy at Heidelberg in the 1920s (Bogner, 1986, 1987).

There are broadly three (somewhat repetitive) criticisms of Parsonian sociology. First, by its emphasis on value integration and social equilibrium, it could not account for social conflict, dysfunction, or the collapse of equilibrium (Dahrendorf, 1968). Second, and related to the first type of criticism, it is claimed that Parsons's sociology could never grasp specific historical processes, and was in any case evolutionary and teleological in its treatment of such processes as differentiation (Gouldner, 1970). Finally, Parsons's sociology was typically too abstract and general to cope with the real and empirical issues of politics, social conflict, and social change (Mills, 1959).

It is interesting to note that, while neo-functionalism is often broadly regarded as a defense of the legacy of Parsonian sociology, it has generally accepted the legitimacy and validity of these three criticisms of Parsons's sociology. Alexander (1985: 15) recognizes the need for a greater emphasis on conflict, interests, and contingent social change in the neo-functionalist critiques of Parsons. Elsewhere Alexander (1987: 375) has argued that "Sociological theory today is no longer engaged in the effort to dethrone Parsons. It is post Parsonian, not anti." The implication is that modern sociology, having digested the critique of Parsons, can now proceed to achieve the kind of synthesis which Parsons had hoped to establish in his general theory of action. Alexander's recent work *Action and Its Environments* (1988b) offers a promising development of this post-Parsonian synthesis.

While I am sympathetic to Alexander's project (and more generally to the neo-functionalist paradigm), I do not fully accept these conventional criticisms of Parsons and Parsonian sociology. Furthermore, I do not accept the idea that Parsons's approach was antipathetic to historical analysis. I want to sketch out briefly an alternative interpretation of the general thrust of Parsons's sociology by reflecting on the parallel between German *Lebensphilosophie* and Parsonian action theory.

However, in order to focus on this debate, I turn first to a contribution from Johan Goudsblom who, in a defense of Elias's analysis of the civilizing process (Elias, 1978a, 1982), offers a highly negative evaluation of Parsons as a sociologist. Goudsblom (1987: 327–31) argues that there are three crucial differences between the sociological work of Parsons and Elias. The first difference is that, while Parsons "worked as a theorist," Elias is concerned with the "interplay between theoretical and empirical investigation." Second, in his theory of social systems, Parsons employed "static and disjunctive" elements, while Elias has always retained a major commitment to understanding "the processual character of the social world." Finally, while Parsons always "focussed on the problem of normative order," Elias has maintained a clear interest in "the part played by conflicts and power in the dynamics of societies." Although these criticisms of Parsons are by no means original (see, for comparison, Cancian, 1960; Nagel, 1956), they provide a useful summary, and the comparison drawn between Elias and Parsons is prima facie interesting.

To suggest that Parsons was a "theorist" who was not concerned to analyze the interplay between theoretical and empirical inquiry is to make a general charge against Parsons which is palpably false. The entire purpose of Parsonian sociology was to develop a general theory of action (which would be common to all social sciences) as the foundation for theoretically informed social investigation. More importantly, Goudsblom's accusation ignores, for example, Parsons's specific application of his approach in his essays on German social structure (Parsons, 1942), the sick role (1951), the urban family (Parsons and Fox, 1953) or aging, youth, and social structure (Parsons, 1964). Goudsblom appears to take Parsons's claim that *The Structure of Social Action* was an empirical inquiry as the principal ground for describing Parsons as a "theorist." Parsons's own position was that *The Structure of Social Action* was not an exercise in formal theory construction, but rather developed a voluntaristic theory of action through an empirical inquiry into the collapse of various types of positivism in European social theory. In my view, *The Structure of Social Action* remains the principal sociological challenge to the rationalist and specifically utilitarian models of action which inform economic theory and which more broadly underpin collective rational action theory. A rather more appropriate criticism is that the empirical discussions of social processes which are contained in Parsons's essays are not linked systematically with the type of theory contained in, for example, *The Social System*.

Second, Goudsblom argues that Parsons was primarily concerned with the juxtaposition of static, disjunctive elements. In particular, it is suggested that Parsons's development of the dichotomy of *Gemeinschaft* and *Gesellschaft* into the rigid ahistorical system of the pattern variables is the classical illustration of

Parsons's propensity for reducing the complexity of social processes into static theoretical contrasts. Of course, we should note that not only was Parsons concerned to understand the social conditions (for example in the historical development of Christianity) which promote varying combinations of the pattern variables (Parsons, 1962), but he was also committed to the use of the pattern variables as a heuristic device for comparative sociology (between, for example, Japan and the United States) in his analyses of activism as a value. Parsons also employed the pattern variables to understand comparatively and historically the relation between expert and client in the development of the professions (Parsons, 1960).

Goudsblom further illustrates the allegedly stationary character of Parsonian theory by claiming that Parsons operated with a rigid, ahistorical contrast between personality and the social system, which was merely a sociological reflection on the common-sense contrast between "individual" and "society." I offer three counter-arguments against this position. In the first instance, Parsons always examined, theoretically and empirically, the interpenetrations of "culture," "social system," and "personality" in the notion of "double contingency"; there was also a constant emphasis on culture as the critical feature of the integration of personality and social role. Second, Parsons had a clear appreciation of the historical development and specificity of "the individual" in the western tradition. Third, Parsons's view of the personality was profoundly influenced by the psychoanalytic theories of Sigmund Freud (Parsons, 1959) and by the developmental theories of Jean Piaget (Lidz and Lidz, 1976); he had a clear view not only of the tensions between "individual" and "society," but also of the tensions in "the personality" between ego, superego, and id.

Finally, Goudsblom criticizes Parsons for an emphasis on normative integration, while applauding Elias's focus on the role of conflict and power in social life. Of course, Parsons had responded to this critique in his own lifetime in his essays on power, influence, and authority (Parsons, 1967). He was clearly aware of the contradictions and conflicts in modern social systems, especially in terms of conflicts over equality and citizenship. These are issues which are reflected in his essays on the black American (Parsons and Clark, 1966). Parsons recognized that the establishment of procedural rules of democracy created a framework for the management of conflict rather than the eradication of conflict. In this respect, Parsons was obviously influenced by the work of American philosophers of law such as Lon L. Fuller, whose analysis of common law attempted to identify the procedural agreements necessary for social order (Sciulli, 1992).

I do not wish, in defending Parsons's sociology from these critical assessments, to pretend that Parsons was not fundamentally interested in the conditions of social integration and normative order. Of course, he was, but two issues should be observed in this respect. First, while David Lockwood's distinction between social and system integration (1992) is useful, Parsons never saw social (as opposed to system) integration as complete. Second, to argue that conflict and power are crucial to social life is a banality. A theory of conflict is never adequate in itself as a theory of society.

M+F Paper?

One of the persistent issues in functionalist sociology has been the relationship between causal analysis and functional descriptions of system needs. The distinction between these two approaches was clearly recognized by Durkheim (1958), who argued that the search for the antecedent causes of social phenomena was quite separate from the question of the function of social structures in relation to social requirements. It can be argued that the analysis of system needs was the defining characteristic of functionalism and that functionalism never resolved the logical relationship between function and cause. Furthermore, the fact that neo-functionalism does not address the question of functional prerequisites and system needs signifies that it is not a form of functionalism.

This characterization of the problem of the relationship between traditional functionalism and neo-functionalism is useful in pinpointing the criticism of Parsonian functionalism as an ahistorical mode of analysis. In Parson's sociology, we clearly find both types of analysis. The studies of the evolutionary importance of Christianity for the emergence of modern citizenship belong to causal understanding because Parsons was concerned to comprehend the antecedent causes of modern political life. However, Parsons, following Durkheim, was also concerned to analyze the functional significance of religion for the integration of American society. Goudsblom's critique of Parsons is focused on the functional analysis of system needs, but Parsons also undertook causal analyses of historical change and this form of explanation in Parsonian sociology is neglected by his critics.

This comment, however, still leaves open to question the relationship (if any) between causal and functional analysis. The response of neo-functionalists has been to argue that there is nothing logically incompatible between causal analysis (for example in terms of historical change being brought about by conflicts between social groups) and functional analysis of the conditions of social stability (in terms of the system prerequisite of social stability on the basis of shared values). It is in fact possible to specify this relationship even more precisely. Functional analysis specifies the conditions for the reproduction of social system requirements (Y) by social structures (X). A causal/historical analysis merely tells us how by antecedent causes the relationship Y–X came into existence as a consequence of a cause (Z). The "functional circle" between Y–X is explained by the causal sequence Z. For example, the functional relationship between possessive individualism and capitalism is explained by both the functional requirements of the capitalist society (private property) and by a causal analysis of the peculiar developments of English Protestantism, which gave a special emphasis to the authority of the individual in relation to the interpretation of the Bible. The fact that this hypothetical example is historically dubious does not influence the formal claim as to the nature of the relationship between causal mechanisms and functional requirements (Abercrombie, Hill, and Turner, 1986). It follows that the logical grounds for the critique of Parsonian functionalism in relation to historical accounts of social reality are not warranted.

The intention here is not to attempt a critique of Elias's figurational sociology in order to mount a defense of Parsons's functionalism. However, it is important to identify a crucial difference between Elias and Parsons in order to clarify an important dimension of Parsons's approach to the sociological analysis of institutions. While Elias has given special emphasis to military conflicts and social violence in his study of the civilizing process, he has almost completely neglected the historical and comparative nature of religious culture, the sacred, the priesthood, and the Church in the history of western society. This analytical silence with respect to the regulative function of religious norms in the historical process of civilizing military violence, the court, and the bourgeois household is a remarkable absence in Elias's treatment of the institutional matrix of western nation-states. By contrast, religion as a basic component of the social as such dominated Parsons's view of social relations (1962) and processes from his translation of Weber's *The Protestant Ethic and the Spirit of Capitalism* (1930) to his final reflections on the classics in sociology (Parsons, 1981; Robertson, 1982).

By contrast, Elias has written about medieval court society (1982) and western civilization with hardly any reference to Roman Catholicism in particular or to Christianity in general. It is interesting in this respect to compare Elias's historical analysis of this period with, for example, the work of George Duby, whose analysis of marriage, alliances, the knighthood, and chivalry depends on an extensive inquiry into the social role of Catholic doctrine (Duby, 1978, 1983). It is also interesting to compare Elias with an older tradition of historical scholarship from Germany, in particular Ernst Troeltsch's magisterial analysis of western Christendom (Troeltsch, 1931).

Elias's failure to discuss the role of religion in relation to the civilizing process, or more specifically to consider the place of Roman Catholicism in the history of the court, has been defended by a number of scholars. For example, Steven Russell (1996), in his excellent application of Elias's notion of figurational or process sociology to Jewish identity, argues that Elias ignores organized Christianity because his focus was on the secular court. This defense fails to address the more fundamental question: can one develop a general sociology of the civilizing process without reference to how western Christianity shaped, for example, conscience? It is difficult to see how a theory which owes so much to Freudian philosophy regarding the tensions between instinctual gratification and religious asceticism could ignore the role of religious norms in shaping behavior and normative constraint. In this respect, it would be valuable to carry out a thorough comparison of Elias on civilizing processes and the work of Benjamin Nelson on conscience, confession, and constraint (Huff, 1981).

There remains one final issue in Goudsblom's account of Elias and Parsons. If Parsons's sociology was defective and deficient for the reasons outlined by Goudsblom, how can one explain the differential success and failure (in academic terms) of these two men? While Parsons enjoyed considerable institutional success (becoming, for example, President of the American Sociological Association), Elias was not recognized until late in his career. The answer offered by Goudsblom is relatively simple. Parsons at Harvard was at the core of the American academic establishment, whereas at Leicester in England Elias "attained only a modest position at a new university" (Goudsblom, 1987: 327).

Clearly Parsons enjoyed considerable intellectual and institutional advantages, but it is absurd to refer to Leicester as a "modest" or "new university," implying thereby that it was relatively marginal. In fact, sociology in Britain was primarily carried out in "provincial" centres at Hull, Leeds, Manchester, and Leicester. Under the headship of Ilya Neustadt, the department at Leicester has produced many of the leading sociologists in England in the contemporary period, including Joe Banks, John Goldthorpe, Bryan Wilson, and Anthony Giddens. Of course, while the United Kingdom provided a haven for many European intellectuals in the Nazi period, there were many obstacles to their academic promotion. Some migrant intellectuals failed to achieve even "modest" positions, such as the marxist sociologist of science Alfred Sohn-Rethel (1978). The institutional location of Elias and Parsons cannot by itself explain the differences in their academic careers. In any case, Parsons's professional influence in American sociology declined rapidly after 1960.

Goudsblom's criticism of Parsons is based, as we have seen, on the assumption that these two sociologists represent entirely different intellectual traditions and embraced incompatible projects. In this section of my reply to Goudsblom, I argue that one can detect a convergence between Elias and Parsons – a convergence which provides the pretext for sketching out a different interpretation of Parsons's sociology.

The core motif of Elias's process sociology (1978a) is a study of the long-term processes by which the untutored and vulgar interpersonal behavior of feudal times was eventually replaced by codes of good manners and courtesy, and finally by a culture of bourgeois education into a formal system of personal control. His historical inquiry is superficially into the emergence of "manners," but this project is also connected with the emergence of the modern state which regulates public violence in a situation where the individual has to exercise increasing self-control. The emotions of self-attention play an important role or function in securing an appropriate level of social conformity (Barbalet, 1998: 80). We can see part of Elias's argument as a combination of a Freudian theory of instinctual regulation and a Weberian analysis of the state as that institution which has a legitimate monopoly of violence. In this respect one may interpret Elias's sociology as in fact a social psychology of the historical transformation of systems of restraint. The history of manners is an account of how "natural passions" are managed and regulated by "culture"; more simply, it is an account of how "biology" is coerced into socially useful activities. Behind Elias's account of civilization is the theory of social contract as the basis of social life, whereby individuals (who are by "nature" violent brutes) submit to the state (as a third-party authority) and to the civilizing process of culture. It would not be inappropriate to suggest that Elias has provided us with a brilliant historical analysis of the classical problem of political theory, namely the Hobbesian problem of order.

It is now very easy to see an initial point of contact between Parsons's *The Structure of Social Action* which was published in 1937 and Elias's *The Civilizing Process* which was originally published in Basel in 1939. Whereas Elias gave a historical analysis of the Hobbesian question ("How is society possible?"), Parsons in 1937 proceeded to criticize rationalist and reductionist views of action (especially in the economic theories of Alfred Marshall and Vilfredo Pareto). Parsons's answer was in this sense a theoretical response to the social contract problem by arguing that action (as opposed to behavior) was only intelligible if we take notice of the role of choice with reference to the ends of action which are structured by values. It is only because there are values behind actions that agreements over social order can be maintained. Social order becomes possible (but not inevitable) because there are shared values; in short, there is a non-contractual or cultural element of contract.

It is well known that this (largely implicit) general theory in *The Structure of Social Action* was then elaborated at great length by Parsons in his "middle" phase in *The Social System* (1951), *Economy and Society* (Parsons and Smelser, 1956), and in collections such as *Social Structure and Personality* (1964). It was in this period that Parsons developed a more elaborate account of structural functionalism in which he argued that there is an interpenetration between society and personality whereby individuals experience psychological rewards for social conformity. The linkage between the cultural system and the social system is provided by internalization and socialization, whereby social order is grounded in a common value system. This development is also a major aspect of successful system adaptation, because social differentiation is accompanied by a higher level of integration. It was this version of structural functionalism which explained system equilibrium and which became the central target of criticism of Parsons, namely that he had produced an "oversocialized theory of man" which had excluded the tensions and contradictions addressed by Freud (Wrong, 1961). Elias's sociology of civilizational processes can be read as a historical account of the tensions between instinctual gratification and the necessities and requirements of civilized life.

While one can agree with those commentators who suggest that "*The Social System* represented a departure from the action theory of *The Structure of Social Action*" (Scott, 1963), there is also a strong sense of continuity in Parsons's work connecting the early interest in action theory, the middle-career focus on the sick role, and the final focus on "the human condition." There is no significant rupture of interest. In short, the linking theme in Parsons's sociology is action theory as a version of life-philosophy. While Parsons's interest in culture and value integration was shaped by the Durkheimian tradition, his action theory was the product of his encounter with the sociology of Weber. Although Parsons was especially influenced by Weber's analysis of capitalism, there was a broader impact through Weber's sociology of "character" and social orders.

There are good reasons (Hennis, 1988) for seeing Weber as part of the German *Lebensphilosophie* tradition, which was important in the German intellectual tradition between 1880 and 1930 (Schnabelbach, 1984). In turn this *Lebensphilosophie* tradition had some common roots in the earlier Romantic philosophy which in Germany was associated with the idea of life as a work of art (Engelhardt, 1988). Following the philosophical critique of Nietzsche and Bergson, the search for an "authentic" life became a dominant theme in the youth movement, in neo-romanticism, and in aesthetics (for example, the *Jugendstil*). This notion of "life" was opposed to Hegelian rationalism and to empiricism. This life-philosophy tradition established the basis for a romantic critique of technology, science, and capitalism in the philosophy of writers such as Stefan George and Ludwig Klages (Stauth and Turner, 1988).

There are some connections between this German tradition of life-philosophy (which grounded human action in life processes against the state and urban civilization) and the action theory of Parsons and his followers (Turner, 1994a). One can speculate that this influence in Parsons's work emerged out of Parsons's encounter with the work of Karl Jaspers at Heidelberg. Although the early action theory had been overshadowed by systems theory in the 1950s and 1960s, the themes of life-philosophy as action theory re-emerged in Parsons's work in the 1970s. We might with plausibility therefore call Parsons's primary project the establishment of a "life-sociology" organized around the idea of the situation of action in which social actors in a structured life-context select ends by reference to personality needs, interactional requirements, and shared values. In short, the notion of "institutionalized individualism" could describe some dimensions of the German tradition of *Lebensphilosophie*.

Although Parsons never really solved the relationship between the biological and the social, it remained a constant theme in his sociology of action. In *The Structure of Social Action*, Parsons was interested in the biological conditions of action. In *Toward a General Theory of Action* (Parsons and Shils, 1951) and *The Social System* (1951), the "biological" was translated into an interest in affect, affectual action, and emotional questions relating to cathexis. In this period, Parsons explored the interaction of the biological processes and social interaction in the sick role. Parsons also developed the basis for a sociology of aging as a bio-social process in various essays on youth, activism, and social structure. Finally, towards the end of his career, issues relating to the gift of life, blood, religion, and death became prominent in *Action Theory and the Human Condition* (1978). The *Lebensphilosophie* focus on the patterns of the life process became in Parsons's action theory a general framework for the sociological analysis of the complex interaction between human nature (being-in-the-world of the agent), the regulative world of civilization, and the solidarities which are enduring consequences of endless, but fleeting, human exchange.

Parsons and Elias converge, therefore, around a number of common empirical concerns – the moral problem of death (Elias, 1985a), the social regulation of emotions (Elias, 1987a), and the relations between the sexes (Elias, 1987b). Of course, there is much that divides Elias's and Parsons's versions of sociology in terms of epistemology, approaches to theory, and underlying presuppositions. However, what signals their common or overlapping concerns was a profound ethical interest in the "human conditio" (Elias, 1985b) or the "human condition" (Parsons, 1978) as the ultimate focus of sociology.

Parsons and Economic Sociology

I have sought to defend Parsons against a number of common criticisms, partly by comparing his analysis of the origins of modernity with Elias's analysis of the civilizing process. There are, however, other dimensions to the intellectual coherence of Parsons's work which are best appreciated through a commentary on his economic sociology. The issue of intellectual coherence and continuity in the academic life of major social theorists is a topic much debated in the history of sociological thought. In the case of Parsons, it has often been thought that there was a major division between his work before 1951 and the subsequent growth of functionalism with the publication of *The Social System*. Whereas the work of the early Parsons was seen to be concerned with the development of a voluntaristic theory of action, the publications of the later Parsons were believed to be focused on structural functionalism as a model for the analysis of social systems in terms, for example, of their subsystem properties.

If one wanted to identify a thematic continuity in the work of Parsons from the early essays on economic theory, to *The Structure of Social Action*, and beyond into his collaborative work with Neil Smelser, then it would be his interest in the intellectual and academic relationship between economics and sociology. Parsons's persistent attention to economic theory had been relatively neglected by critics of Parsons who, in attacking the alleged functionalism of Parsonian sociology, concentrated on the issues of value consensus and normative integration, believing that Parsons had relatively little interest in the "economic base" of society. This neglect of Parsons's economic sociology was probably intensified by the marxist undercurrent of much so-called conflict theory. In recent years, there has fortunately been considerable interest shown in Parsons's analysis of economic theory and more specifically in his economic sociology (Gansmann, 1988; Holton, 1991; Holton and Turner, 1986; Robertson and Turner, 1991). Following the work of Charles Camic (1991) and Bruce Wearne (1989), we have a much better understanding and appreciation of Parsons's early immersion in debates about the nature of economic theory. It was this engagement with institutional economics in his early career that marked Parsons's departure from biology into the social sciences.

At one level economics presented Parsons with a model of a successful social science, in particular as a model of a general theory of action. Economics as a discipline was successful in two separate ways. First, it was an established and prestigious discipline within the university system, and second, it offered the opportunity to create an analytically coherent but parsimonious account of rational behavior. Economics promises to explain social reality by reference to an elementary list of propositions which are to do with rational behavior in a context of scarcity. The principle of marginal utility lies at the core of this elementary account of human behavior. By contrast, sociology lacks parsimony and precision, giving rise instead to a welter of imprecise, competing observations and propositions about social actions and social relations. In this context, sociology was also subject to competition from the biological sciences and biologically based psychology which attempted to explain human behavior by a process of reductionism. Parsons's general theory of action was an attempt to reconcile these conflicting sociological approaches and perspectives. Parsons's sociology grappled with: the relationship between economics and sociology as competing explanations of rational action; the problem of biological reductionism with respect to human values and culture; the question of so-called "misplaced concreteness" in the philosophy of the social sciences; and the nature and role of analytical schema in the development of sciences. Parsons sought to solve these issues via a voluntaristic theory of action, in order not only to resolve a set of intellectual puzzles but to contribute to the professional establishment of sociology as an autonomous and recognized discipline within the pantheon of the academic social sciences.

If the social sciences are in general concerned with action systems, then Parsons saw the relationship between sociology and economics in terms of a continuum in the means–end schema, whereby sociology was concerned with the value end of the action chain and economics with the specific means by which scarcity is resolved. In practice, sociology has evolved more as a commentary on the marginal problems of economic theory, that is the nature of nonrational and irrational behavior in a context of scarcity of means for the satisfaction of needs.

In *The Structure of Social Action*, Parsons approached this problem of the relationship between sociology and economics by reference to what he called "residual categories," namely the hidden and taken for granted set of assumptions within economic theory whereby such phenomena as social stability and contracts are explained. The problem facing economics was the explanation of social order in rational terms, in a context where fraud and force are rational solutions to conditions of scarcity. Economics has traditionally solved this Hobbesian problem of order by reference to such notions as sentiment and the hidden hand of history. Sociology as an academic discipline has by contrast been concerned with such issues as culture, values, and morality as foundations of social relations.

If we compare economics, politics, and sociology as social sciences of action, then economics is the discipline concerned with the reduction of scarcity by the application of means to ends, politics is a science concerned with the distribution of power in relation to scarce resources, and finally sociology is that discipline concerned with the conditions and maintenance of social solidarity (namely value integration) in a world of risk, scarcity, and uncertainty. The term "sociology" is itself derived from the Latin for friendship (*socius*), that is, sociology is a science or discipline concerned with the explanation of companionship via such phenomena as rituals, values, and culture. Parsons addressed this issue primarily by drawing on Durkheim's sociology of religion, namely *The Elementary Forms of the Religious Life* (1954), as a model of the religious sources of social integration through the collective possession of authoritative norms and values.

In his early discussion of culture, we see Parsons beginning the process of establishing an alternative approach to institutional economics and to psychological reductionism by understanding the framework within which, for example, economic contracts work in terms of culture and values. This perspective is Parsons's substantive answer to the economic analysis of scarcity, namely that collective behavior and social agreements depend upon a bedrock of shared cultural assumptions which are handed down to new generations by the processes of socialization and internalization of values, for example, within the domestic or familial context. This substantive understanding of the relationship between scarcity and solidarity occupied Parsons's sociology throughout his mature academic and intellectual life, and we see this contrast emerging once more in the famous AGIL subsystem analysis within his approach to systems theory (Parsons, 1951). The AGIL paradigm depends upon a fundamental distinction or contrast between the allocative problems of society (which are primarily to do with economics and politics) in a context of scarcity and the integrative and motivational problems of social systems (which are to do with the creation of solidarity and commitment through values and mores). The allocative problem is the essence of political economy, while the integration and commitment issues are fundamental to sociology.

In trying to develop an analytical framework for sociology, Parsons sought to avoid the traditional dichotomy between idealism and positivism. In general terms, the natural and social sciences in the nineteenth century, particularly in the Anglo-Saxon world, had emerged on the basis of a positivistic science of reality. Within this paradigm, biological accounts of human behavior were significant in the positivist reduction of values to nature. Parsons, by contrast, wanted to assert the autonomy and emergence of culture and values as independent phenomena in the explanation and understanding of action. This principle of emergence was not fully developed until *The Structure of Social Action*, and in his later work he absorbed the idea of the "super organic" from the work of anthropologists such as A. L. Kroeber. In attempting to grapple with issues about biology and environment in the Amherst papers, we find in the early work the intellectual seed of what Parsons came to call the "external conditions of the action schema" in the unit act concept of *The Structure of Social Action*. Parsons came to conceive of the action schema in terms of a means–end chain in which ends are selected by reference to values and means by reference to norms, but the orientation of the actor toward his or her social situation is always conducted in the context of what Parsons called the conditions of action, which were basically the physical or environmental conditions of action and choice.

Parsons did not substantially depart from this framework, although he came to conceptualize the embodiment of the social actor in more complicated terms in his later work partly as a consequence of his engagement with the psychoanalytic theories of Freud and a more sophisticated understanding of cybernetics and teleology. Whether or not Parsons came to an appropriate understanding of the "embodiment of the human actor" (Turner, 1992) is an issue beyond the confines of this introduction.

Conclusion

While wanting to defend Parsons from false or irrelevant criticism, one has to acknowledge and confront the characteristically abstract and formalistic character of much of Parsons's work – an issue which has been addressed by Alexander in his *Theoretical Logic in Sociology* (1984). There is a tendency to over-use and over-extend, for example, the heuristic validity of the AGIL model, which produces a formalism devoid of any content. Although I have attempted also to defend Parsons from the criticism that he lacked any sense of historical change, there is a valid criticism that Parsons rarely engaged in debates about the historical specificity of his examples or cases. Furthermore, although Parsons attempted to present his sociology as a component within a broader understanding of the social sciences (including economics, politics, and psychoanalysis), there is little sustained evidence of any sensitivity to the place of anthropology, history, and geography in the scheme of "social relations."

Despite these and other difficulties, I remain confident with the argument that an understanding of Parsons's sociology is essential for those who wish to understand modern social science with any depth or sophistication. In summary, Parsons provides us with the most robust and unashamed account of modernity (from within a liberal perspective). His sociology is the perfect foil by which to understand both the strength and the weakness of postmodernism. Parsons's sociology is the most coherent exposition of the grand narrative of modernity. Second, although his work is a defense of modernization, it is also a powerful criticism of utilitarian rationalism, the underlying foundation of so-called economic rationalism. Third, Parsons's criticisms of rationalism and his account of modernity are grounded in a comparative study of culture. Differences between societies are primarily differences between cultural systems. This focus on culture is a strikingly contemporary emphasis in sociology. These reasons can be taken as powerful justifications for a collection of essential readings.

References

Abercrombie, N., S. Hill, and B. S. Turner (1986) *Sovereign Individuals of Capitalism*, London: Allen & Unwin.

Adriaansens, H. (1980) *Talcott Parsons and the Conceptual Dilemma*, London: Routledge & Kegan Paul.

Alexander, J. (1984) *Theoretical Logic in Sociology, vol. 4, Talcott Parsons*, London: Routledge & Kegan Paul.

Alexander, J. (ed.) (1985) *Neofunctionalism*, Beverly Hills: Sage.

Alexander, J. (1987) *Twenty Lectures: Sociological Theory Since World War II*, New York: Columbia University Press.

Alexander, J. (1988a) *Neofunctionalism and After*, Oxford: Basil Blackwell.

Alexander, J. (1988b) *Action and Its Environments: Toward a New Synthesis*. New York: Columbia University Press.

Barbalet, J. (1998) *Emotion, Social Theory and Social Structure*, Cambridge: Cambridge University Press.

Bogner, A. (1986) *Zivilisation und Rationalisierung ein Vergleich, der Zivilisation Theorien Max Webers, Norbert Elias', Max Horkheimers und Theodor W. Adornos*, dissertation, Universitat Bielefeld.

Bogner, A. (1987) Elias and the Frankfurt school, *Theory, Culture & Society*, 4 (2–3), 249–86.

Bourricaud, F. (1981) *The Sociology of Talcott Parsons*, Chicago and London: University of Chicago Press.

Buxton, W. (1985) *Talcott Parsons and the Capitalist Nation-State*, Toronto: University of Toronto Press.

Camic, C. C. (ed.) (1991) *Talcott Parsons: The Early Essays*. Chicago: University of Chicago Press.

Cancian, F. (1960) Functional analysis of change, *American Sociological Review*, 25, 118–27.

Dahrendorf, R. (1968) *Essays in the Theory of Society*, London: Routledge & Kegan Paul.

Duby, G. (1978) *Medieval Marriage: Two Models from Tweflth-Century France*, Baltimore and London: Johns Hopkins University Press.

Duby, G. (1983) *The Knight, the Lady and the Priest*, New York: Pantheon Books.

Durkheim, E. (1954) *The Elementary Forms of the Religious Life*, London: Allen & Unwin.

Durkheim, E. (1958) *The Rules of Sociological Method*, Glencoe, IL: Free Press.

Durkheim, E. (1992) *Professional Ethics and Civic Morals*, London: Routledge.

Elias, N. (1956) Some problems of involvement and detachment, *British Journal of Sociology*, 7 (3), 226–52.

Elias, N. (1978a) *What is Sociology?*, London: Hutchinson.

Elias, N. (1978b) *The Civilizing Process*, Vol. 1, *The History of Manners*, Oxford: Basil Blackwell.

Elias, N. (1982) *The Civilizing Process*, Vol. 2, *State Formation and Civilization*, Oxford: Basil Blackwell.

Elias, N. (1985a) *The Loneliness of the Dying*, Oxford: Basil Blackwell.

Elias, N. (1985b) *Humana Conditio Beobachtungen zur Entwicklung der Menschheit am 40. Jahrestag eines Kriegsendes*, Frankfurt: Suhrkamp.

Elias, N. (1987a) On human beings and their emotions: a process-sociological essay, *Theory, Culture & Society*, 4 (2–3), 339–65.

Elias, N. (1987b) The changing balance of power between the sexes – a process-sociological study: the example of the ancient Roman state, *Theory, Culture & Society*, 4 (2–3), 287–316.

Engelhardt, D. V. (1988) Romanticism in Germany. In A. R. Porter and M. Teich (eds), *Romanticism in National Context*, Cambridge: Cambridge University Press, pp. 109–33.

Ferry, L. and A. Renaut (1990) *Heidegger and Modernity*, Chicago and London: University of Chicago Press.

Gansmann, H. (1988) Money – a symbolically generalised medium of communication, *Economy and Society*, 17 (3), 285–316.

Gerhardt, U. (ed.) (1993) *Talcott Parsons on National Socialism*, New York: Aldine de Gruyter.

Goldman, H. (1992) *Politics, Death and the Devil. Self and Power in Max Weber and Thomas Mann*, Berkeley: University of California Press.

Goudsblom, J. (1987) The sociology of Norbert Elias – its resonance and significance, *Theory, Culture & Society*, 4 (2–3), 323–38.

Gouldner, A. W. (1970) *The Coming Crisis of Western Sociology*, New York: Basic Books.

Heidegger, M. (1977) *The Question Concerning Technology and Other Essays*, New York: Harper.

Hennis, W. (1988) *Max Weber: Essays in Reconstruction*, London: Allen & Unwin.

Holton, R. J. (1991) Talcott Parsons and the integration of economic and sociological theory, *Sociological Inquiry*, 61 (1), 102–14.

Holton, R. J. and B. S. Turner (1986) *Talcott Parsons on Economy and Society*, London: Routledge.

Huff, T. H. (ed.) (1981) *On the Roads to Modernity: Conscience, Science and Civilizations*, Totowa: Rowman & Littlefield.

Lidz, C. W. and V. M. Lidz (1976) Piaget's psychology of intelligence and the theory of action. In J. J. Loubser, R. C. Baum, A. Effrat, and V. M. Lidz (eds), *Explorations in General Theory in Social Science. Essays in Honor of Talcott Parsons*, New York: Free Press, vol. 1, chapter 8.

Lockwood, D. (1992) *Solidarity and Schism: "The Problem of Order" in Durkheimian and Marxist Sociology*, Oxford: Clarendon Press.

MacIntyre, A. (1981) *After Virtue*, South Bend, In: University of Notre Dame Press.

Marshall, T. H. (1964) *Class, Citizenship and Social Development*, Chicago: University of Chicago Press.

Mills, C. W. (1959) *The Sociological Imagination*, New York: Oxford University Press.

Munch, R. (1981) Talcott Parsons and the theory of action, *American Journal of Sociology*, 86, 709–40.

Nagel, E. (1956) A formalization of functionalism. In *Logic Without Metaphysics*, New York: Free Press, pp. 247–83.

Parsons, T. (1937) *The Structure of Social Action*, New York: McGraw-Hill.

Parsons, T. (1942) Democracy and the social structure in pre-Nazi Germany, *Journal of Legal and Political Sociology*, 1, 96–114.

Parsons, T. (1950) The prospects of sociological theory, *American Sociological Review*, 15, 3–16.

Parsons, T. (1951) *The Social System*, London: Routledge & Kegan Paul.

Parsons, T. (1959) An approach to psychological theory in terms of the theory of action. In S. Koch (ed.), *Psychology: A Study of a Science*, New York: McGraw-Hill, vol. 3, pp. 612–711.

Parsons, T. (1960) *Structure and Process in Modern Societies*, New York: Free Press.

Parsons, T. (1962) Christianity and modern industrial society. In E. A. Tiryakian (ed.), *Sociological Theory, Values and Sociocultural Change: Essays in Honor of Pitrim A. Sorokin*, New York: Free Press, pp. 33–70.

Parsons, T. (1964) *Social Structure and Personality*, New York: Free Press.

Parsons, T. (1967) *Sociological Theory and Modern Society*, New York: Free Press.

Parsons, T. (1971) *The System of Modern Societies*, Englewood Cliffs, NJ: Prentice-Hall.

Parsons, T. (1975) The sick role and the role of the physician reconsidered, *Millbank Memorial Fund Quarterly*, 53 (3), 257–78.

Parsons, T. (1978) *Action Theory and the Human Condition*, New York: Free Press.

Parsons, T. (1981) Revisiting the classics throughout a long career. In Buford Rhea (ed.), *The Future of the Sociological Classics*, London: Allen & Unwin, pp. 183–94.

Parsons, T. and K. Clark (eds) (1966) *The Negro American*, Boston: Houghton Mifflin.

Parsons, T. and R. C. Fox (1953) Illness, therapy and the modern urban American family, *Journal of Social Issues*, 8, 31–44.

Parsons, T. and E. A. Shils (eds) (1951) *Toward a General Theory of Action*, New York and Evanston: Harper & Row.

Parsons, T. and N. Smelser (1956) *Economy and Society*, London: Routledge & Kegan Paul.

Renaut, A. (1997) *The Era of the Individual. A Contribution to a History of Subjectivity*, Princeton, NJ: Princeton University Press.

Robertson, R. (1982) Parsons and the evolutionary significance of American religion, *Sociological Analysis*, 43 (4), 307–25.

Robertson, R. and B. S. Turner (eds) (1991) *Talcott Parsons: Theorist of Modernity*, London: Sage.

Rojek, C. and B. S. Turner (eds) (1998) *The Politics of Jean-François Lyotard. Justice and Political Theory*, London and New York: Routledge.

Russell, S. (1996) *Jewish Identity and Civilizing Processes*, London: Macmillan.

Schnabelbach, H. (1984) *Philosophie in Deutschland, 1831–1933*, Frankfurt: Suhrkamp.

Sciulli, D. (1992) *Theory of Societal Constitutionalism. Foundations of a Non-Marxist Critical Theory*, Cambridge: Cambridge University Press.

Scott, J. F. (1963) The changing foundation of the Parsonian action scheme, *American Sociological Review*, 29, 716–35.

Sohn-Rethel, A. (1978) *Intellectual and Manual Labour. A Critique of Epistemology*, London: Macmillan.

Stauth, G. and B. S. Turner (1988) *Nietzsche's Dance. Resentment, Reciprocity and Resistance in Social Life*, Oxford: Basil Blackwell.

Troeltsch, E. (1931) *The Social Teachings of the Christian Churches*, New York: Macmillan.

Turner, B. S. (1987) A note on nostalgia, *Theory, Culture & Society*, 4 (1), 147–56.

Turner, B. S. (1992) *Regulating Bodies: Essays in Medical Sociology*, London: Routledge.

Turner, B. S. (1994a) Lebensphilosophie und Handlungstheorie. Die Beziehungen zwischen Talcott Parsons und Max Weber innerhalb der Entwicklung der Soziologie. In G. Wagner and H. Ziprian (eds), *Max Webers Wissenschaftslehre. Interpretation und Kritik*, Frankfurt: Suhrkamp, pp. 310–31.

Turner, B. S. (1994b) *Orientalism, Postmodernism and Globalism*, London: Routledge.

Turner, B. S. (1995) *Medical Power and Social Knowledge*, London: Sage, 2nd edn.

Wearne, B. (1989) *The Theory and Scholarship of Talcott Parsons to 1951. A Critical Commentary*, Cambridge: Cambridge University Press.

Weber, M. (1930) *The Protestant Ethic and the Spirit of Capitalism*, London: Allen & Unwin.

Wrong, D. (1961) The oversocialized conception of man in modern sociology, *American Sociological Review*, 26, 183–93.

Part I

Religion and Modern Society

1

Christianity and Modern Industrial Society

The volume [for which this chapter was originally written was] conceived as a tribute to Professor Pitrim Sorokin as a distinguished elder statesman of sociology, not only in the United States but also throughout the world. One of the highest achievements, particularly in a rapidly developing discipline in its early phases of development, is to serve as a generator and focus of creatively important differences of opinion. Such differences pose problems which, though not solved or in any immediate sense soluble in the generation in question, still serve to orient the thinking of professional groups. For such differences to be fruitful there must be a delicate balance of commonly accepted premises, which make a fruitful meeting of minds possible, and difference of interpretation in more particularized questions which are open to some sort of empirical test.

In the sociological profession today Professor Sorokin and the present author are probably defined predominantly as antagonists who have taken widely different views on a variety of subjects.[1] The objective of this chapter is to take explicit cognizance of one, to me crucial, field of such difference of opinion, but to attempt to place it within a framework of common problems in the hope that consideration of the difference may help others toward a fruitful solution of these problems.

In the highly empirical atmosphere of American sociology in recent times there has been a tendency to neglect the importance of the great problems of the trends of development of Western society and culture in a large sense, of its place relative to the great civilizations of the Orient, and similar problems. Within this field the problem of the role of religion and its relation to social values stands in a particularly central position. In my opinion it is one of Sorokin's great services to have held these problems consistently in the forefront of concern, and to have refused to be satisfied with a sociology which did not have anything significant to say about them. In this fundamental respect Sorokin stands in the great tradition of Western sociological thought. This emphasis coincides with my own strong predilections, shaped as they were by European experience under the influences in particular of Max Weber and Durkheim.

It can, I think, safely be said that we share the convictions, first, of the enormous importance of the general evolutionary and comparative perspective in the interpretation of social phenomena and, second, of the crucial role of religion and its relation to values in this large perspective. When, however, we turn to more particular problems of spelling out this context, differences of opinion emerge. A particularly important test case is that of the interpretation of the relations of religious orientation, values, and social structure in the course of that development in the modern Western world which has eventuated in modern industrialism. I propose to set over against a very schematic but I hope accurate outline of Sorokin's view, my own, which I think may be the kind of alternative which, though differing sharply from his view, may pose fruitful empirical questions on which future research may be expected to throw light. Only in this broadest contrast will I attempt to take account of the Sorokin position. My objective is not to present either a full statement or a critique of his conceptions as such, but to state my own as clearly as possible.

The heart of the Sorokin position which is relevant here I take to be his classification and use of three fundamental types of cultural orientation – the "ideational," "idealistic," and "sensate."[2] What may be called orientations in terms of the grounds of meaning on the one hand and values for social and personal conduct on the other, are treated as by and large varying together.

The ideational pattern is one which gives unquestionable primacy to transcendental and other-worldly interests in the religious sense. Reality itself is defined as ultimately beyond the reach of the senses, as transcendental. The goal of life must be to reach the closest possible accord with the nature of transcendent reality, and the path to this must involve renunciation of all worldly interests. Broadly speaking, other-worldly asceticism and mysticism are the paths to it. The ethical component which is so prominent in Christianity generally is not missing from Sorokin's conception. It takes, however, the form on which his later work has placed increasing stress: that of altruistic love, of pure personal selfless acts of love by individuals. In this discussion I would like to differentiate this form of altruism from the *institutionalization* of Christian ethics to become part of the structure of the society itself. It is the latter with which my analysis will be concerned.

The opposite extreme to the ideational pattern is the sensate. Here the empirical, in the last analysis the "material," aspect of reality is taken as ultimately real or predominant. In practical conduct the implication of a sensate view of the world is to make the most of the opportunities of the here and now, to be concerned with world success, power, and – in the last analysis – to put hedonistic gratifications first of all.

The idealistic pattern is conceived as intermediate between the two, not in the sense of a simple "compromise," but rather of a synthesis which can achieve a harmonious balance between the two principal components.

This basic classification is then used as the framework for outlining a developmental pattern leading, in the history of a civilization, from ideational to idealistic predominance and in turn from idealistic to sensate. Though very generally applied, the two most important cases dealt with in Sorokin's works are the civilization of classical antiquity and that of the Christian West. In both cases there was an early ideational phase which gradually gave way to an idealistic synthesis: in the classical that of fifth-century Greece, in the Western that of the high Middle Ages. The idealistic synthesis has then proceeded to break down into an increasingly sensate phase – in the classical case the late

Hellenistic and Roman periods, in the Western the modern "capitalistic" or industrial period. Sorokin tends to regard the contemporary period, exemplified particularly in the United States, but also in the Soviet Union, as close to the peak of the sensate phase of development and destined for a general breakdown comparable to that of Greco-Roman civilization before a new ideational pattern can become established.

From one point of view the general developmental trend Sorokin outlines may be described as a progressive decline in the "religiousness" of the society and culture until a radical reversal is forced by a general societal breakdown. In the Western case the phase of early Christianity was the most religious, characterized by a primarily ascetic disregard for virtually all worldly interests, and the practice of brotherly love within the Christian community itself. Correspondingly, however, Christianity in this phase had little power to organize social relationships beyond the church. With the development of the idealistic phase, however, for a time it was possible to permeate secular life with at least an approximation of Christian ethics, but the balance was precarious and broke down relatively soon.

There may well be a considerable measure of agreement up to this point. Sorokin, however, clearly regards Protestantism, compared with medieval Catholicism, as primarily a step in the general decline of religiousness, and the secularism which has been prominent since the Age of the Enlightenment as the natural further step in the same direction. It is hence on the interpretation of Protestantism in the general process of Western social development and its sequel after the Reformation period that I would like to focus my own view. It will be necessary, however, to say a few things about more general theoretical orientation, and about the earlier historical phases as background for this analysis.

An Alternative Interpretation

There are two interrelated theoretical issues which need to be discussed briefly before entering into a historical analysis. These concern factors in the structure of a religious orientation itself on the one hand and the senses in which religious orientations and their institutionalization in the social system can undergo processes of structural differentiation on the other.

In the former respect Professor Sorokin seems to think primarily in terms of a single variable which might be called "degree of religiousness." This in turn tends to be identified with transcendental orientation in the sense of *other-worldliness* as defining the acceptable field of interest and activity. This is to say that, so far as religious interests are in any sense paramount in a motivational system, the religious person will tend to renounce the world and engage so far as possible in ascetic or devotional practices or mystical contemplation and purely spontaneous acts of love, reducing his involvement in "practical" affairs which involve institutionalized obligations to a minimum. He will therefore tend to be oriented to the reduction of all desires to participate positively and actively in worldly activities like political or economic functions. By the same token, positive commitment to such worldly interests and responsibilities is taken as an index of relative lack of religious interest.

Relative to the degree of religiousness we suggest the relevance of a second variable which we think is independent. This is the one which Max Weber formulated as the variation between other-worldly and inner-worldly orientation. Combined with a high degree of religiousness, the choice of one alternative leads to religious rejection of the world, the choice of the other to an orientation to mastery over the world in the name of religious values. There are further complications in the problem of a general typology of religious orientations, but suffice it to say for the present that I propose to explore the possibilities implicit in the hypothesis that Western Christianity belongs in the category of orientation which is high in degree of religiousness, with a predominantly inner-worldly orientation so far as the field of expected action of the individual is concerned. In ways I shall try to explain, this applies even to early and medieval Christianity, but becomes most clearly evident in "ascetic Protestantism." I feel that this hypothesis is excluded by Sorokin's assumption that religiousness *ipso facto* implies other-worldliness, supplemented only by spontaneous altruism.

The second main theoretical point concerns the question of differentiation. I think of religion as an aspect of human action. Like all other aspects, in the course of social, cultural, and personality development it undergoes processes of differentiation in a double sense. The first of these concerns differentiation within religious systems themselves, the second the differentiation of the religious element from nonreligious elements in the more general system of action. In the latter context the general developmental trend may be said to be from fusions of religious and nonreligious components in the same action structures, to increasingly clear differentiation between multiple spheres of action.

A special problem arises when we deal with a system over a sufficiently long period of time to include two or more stages in a process of differentiation. Structural parts of the system have to be named. It is in the nature of the process of differentiation that what was one part at an earlier stage becomes two or more distinct parts at a later. The simple logical question then is whether the name applied at the earlier stage is still used to designate any one of the parts surviving at the later. If the process is one of differentiation, clearly the surviving entity which carries the same name will be narrower in scope and more "specialized" in the later than it was in the earlier stage. It will then, by mere logic, have lost function and become less important than in the earlier phase. The problem then becomes one of analyzing the continuities, not only of the component called by the same name in the different stages, e.g., *religion*, but also of the senses in which the patterns of orientation given in the earlier stages have or have not been fundamentally altered in their significance for the system as a whole, considering the exigencies of the situations in which action takes place and the complex relations of this part to the other parts of the more differentiated system, e.g., the nonreligious or secular.

It is my impression that Professor Sorokin has not given sufficient weight to these considerations and has tended to measure the influence of religion, from earlier to later stages, as if it were reasonable to expect maintenance of the same "degree of inclusiveness" in the direct "definition of the situation" for action which it enjoyed in the early stage of reference. Judged by this standard the degree of religiousness of Christian society has clearly suffered a progressive decline by the mere fact that the society has become functionally a more highly differentiated system of action than was the early "primitive" church.

The Setting of the Problem: Christianity–Society

As a first step it is necessary to outline a few essentials of the nature of the early Christian church and its relations to the secular society of the time. Its structure comprised, as is well known, a very distinctive synthesis of elements derived from Judaism, Greek philosophy, the Greek conception of social organization, and of course distinctive contributions of its own.

The Hebrew and the Greek patterns had in common the conception of a solidary, religiously sanctioned social unit, the organization of which was based on values fully transcending the loyalties of kinship. In the Hebrew case it was the confederation of "tribes" bound to Jahweh and to each other by the Covenant. These units became fused into a "people" whose main orientation to life was defined in terms of the Law given to them by Jahweh, a firm collectivity structure defining its role as the fulfillment of God's commandments. In the historical course, by what precise stages need not concern us here, two crucial developments occurred. First Jahweh became a completely universal transcendental God who governed the activities not only of the people of Israel but of all mankind. Second, the people of Israel became, through the exile, depoliticized. Their religion was the essential bond of solidarity. Since this was no longer expressed in an independent political community, it was not exposed to the "secularizing" influences so importantly involved in political responsibility.

On the Greek side the *polis* was a comparable solidary confederation, in the first instance of kinship lineages. It was the "political" society almost par excellence, but one which eventually came to be based on the principle of the universalistic equality of citizens. Religiously it was oriented not to a transcendental God but to an immanent polytheism. The conception of the ultimate unity of divinity emerged in Greek civilization, but essentially as a philosophical principle the necessity of which was demonstrated by reason.

Seen against the background of Judaism and in certain respects also of the Greek component, the most important distinctive feature of Christianity of importance here was its religious individualism. In Judaism the primary religious concern was with the fate of the Jewish community as God's chosen people. In Christianity it became the fate of the individual soul; God was concerned with the salvation of individuals, not simply with the extent to which a social community as such adhered to His commandments.

This new conception of the relation of the individual soul to God might seem, given the fundamental transcendental character of the God of Judaism, to imply the virtual abandonment of concern with life in the world, to make the life of the Christian center primarily in devotional interests in preparing for the life to come. Indeed this strain in Christianity has always been a crucially important one and marks it off sharply from the main trend of Judaism. In this respect Christianity, however different its theological orientation, was closely analogous to Indian religion. But there was another aspect to Christian individualism: the fact that its adherents came to constitute a very special type of social collectivity on earth, the Christian church. The theological significance of the Christ figure as the mediator between God and man is central as defining the nature of man's relation to God, in and through the Church of Christ. It was the conception of the church which underlay the nature of the ethical conception of Christianity and was the basis from which the moral influence of Christianity could operate on secular society.

In theoretical terms this may be expressed by saying that the conception of the church, which implied the fundamental break with the Jewish law which Paul made final, constituted the *differentiation* of Christianity as a religious system (a cultural system) from the conception of a "people" as a social system. Given the Roman ascendancy in the secular society of the time, this differentiation was expressed in the famous formula "Render unto Caesar the things that are Caesar's" – i.e., the church did not claim jurisdiction over secular society as such.

At the same time this church was a solidary collectivity. The keynote here was the conception of "brothers in Christ." Its members were by no means concerned only with their respective personal salvations, but with the mission of Christ on behalf of mankind. This had the dual meaning of an obligation to extend the Christian community by proselytizing and, within it, to organize its internal relations on the basis in the first instance of mutual brotherly love.

Though, religiously speaking, this was a radically individualistic doctrine, it was not an anarchistic, but what we have come to call an "institutionalized" individualism. The Christian doctrine of the Trinity, compared with Jewish unitarianism, is intimately connected with this development. Instead of a single "line" of relationship between an ultimately transcendental God and man, God became related to man *through* the Christ figure who was both God and Man, and Christ became the head of the Church, the "essence" of which was formulated as the third person of the Trinity, the Holy Spirit.

As I interpret it, this implied, correlative with the differentiation of the church from secular society, a differentiation *within* the religious system itself, in the broadest respect between the aspect of devotion and worship on the one hand, and the aspect of the Christian's relation to his fellow men on the other. The Christian community was constituted by the fact of common faith and common worship, but the contexts in which worship was paramount were differentiated from the context of love and charity which bound the community together in bonds of human mutuality.

From the present point of view this differentiation was just as important as the first, and intimately connected with it. The Jewish law had held the individual to highly detailed prescriptions of conduct which were "rationalized" for the most part only in the sense that they were declared to be Divine commandments. Now, as a member of the church he was held to a set of principles of conduct – the obligation to act in accord with the Holy Spirit. And though obviously directly connected with his commitment to God through faith, conduct in this world could be made to a degree independent of this, above all, in the sense that detailed prescriptions of behavior were not taken as religiously given but only the general principles of ethical action. Thus action decisions in particular cases had to be left to the conscience of believers and could not be prescribed by a comprehensive religious law. The context of worship was an independent context which generated motivation to act in accord with the spirit, but was not exactly the same thing as this action.

This differentiation occurred, however, within a genuine unity. The key theological problem here was the doctrine of the Creation and whether it implied an ontological dualism. In the great formative period this came to a head in the struggle with Manichaeism, and Augustine's fundamental decision against the latter broadly settled the issue. The sphere of the church as that part of man's life on earth directly dominated by the Holy Spirit was then a point of mediation between the direct expression of Divine will through Christ and the rest of the Creation. But the implication was that this remainder of the Creation could not be governed by an ontologically independent principle of evil and was hence inherently subject to Christianization.

Thus religious individualism, in the sense in which it became institutionalized in the Christian church, represented, relative to Judaism, a new autonomy of the individual on two fronts. In his own relation to God as an object of worship, the individual was released from his ascriptive embeddedness in the Jewish community. Whatever the relation of dependence on God implied in this, it was as an individual in the religious relation that he could be saved. There was also a new autonomy in his relation to the field of human action, in the first instance as a member of the church and in his relations to his fellow members in brotherly love. The church was an association of believers, manifesting their attachment to God in their conduct in this world. The church was thus independent, not an ascribed aspect of a total society. There was hence, through these channels, a basic legitimation of the importance of life in this world, but in a situation where the church could reserve a basic independence from those aspects of secular society not felt to be permeated with the Holy Spirit.

Life in this world clearly includes human society. Indeed the church itself is clearly a social entity. But the early Christians judged the secular society of their time, that of the Roman Empire, to be ethically unacceptable, so the Christian life had to be led essentially within the church. This was connected with the Chiliastic expectation of an imminent Last Judgment. But gradually this expectation faded and the church faced the problem of continuing to live *in* the world and of attempting to come to some sort of long-run terms with the rest of the society outside itself.

I have stressed both the social character of the church and its radical break from the Jewish community because the pattern I have sketched formed a basic set of conditions under which Christian orientations could exert a kind of influence on secular society different from that which was possible to religion in the Jewish pattern. First, proselytizing on a grand scale was possible without carrying along the whole society immediately. While conversion to Judaism meant accepting full membership in the total Jewish community, a converted Christian could remain a Roman, a Corinthian, or whatever; his new social participation was confined to the church itself. There were important points at which the church potentially and actually conflicted with the societies of the time, but most of them could be solved by relative nonparticipation in "public affairs."

If in this respect the church limited its claims on its members, it also maintained a position of independence from which further influence could be exerted. It established a "place to stand" from which to exert leverage, and it developed a firm organization to safeguard that place. But the process was not to be one of absorption of the secular society into the religious community itself; it was rather one of acceptance of the fundamental *differentiation* between church and state, but the attempt to define the latter as subject to Christian principles.

There were certainly tendencies to a radical rejection of secular society in principle, but at least for the Western branch of Christianity by the time of St. Augustine the door was opened to the possibility that a Christian society as a whole could be attained. The most important vehicle for this trend was the building into Christian thought of the Greco-Roman conception of natural law. This implied a differentiation of life between spiritual and temporal spheres and a *relative* legitimation of the temporal, provided it was ordered in accordance with natural law. From this point of view, Roman society could be defined as evil, not because it was a secular society as such, but because as a society it failed to live up to norms present in its own culture.

The other principal focus of the process of Christianizing of society lay in the implications of the attempt to universalize Christian adherence within the society. Christianity was gradually transformed from a sect that remained aloof and in principle expected a Christian life only for the segregated special group of its own members into *the* church which was the trustee of the religious interests of the whole population. In proportion as this happened, persons in positions of responsibility in secular society automatically became Christians, and the question could not but arise of the relation between their church membership and their secular responsibilities. The focus of the emerging conception was that of the Christian monarch. The great symbolic event in this whole connection was the coronation of Charlemagne by the Pope. The symbolism of this event was dual. It was an act by the head of the church of legitimation of secular authority, which could be interpreted as the definitive ending of the conception of aloofness on the part of the church, of the position that it could take no moral responsibility in relation to the secular sphere. It also symbolized the acceptance by the monarch of the obligation to act, in his capacity as chief of government, as a Christian. Church and state then symbolically *shared* their commitment to Christian values.

It is not, in my opinion, correct to interpret this as the subordination of secular authority to the church. It was definitely a putting of the seal of religious legitimacy on the differentiation of the two spheres and their fundamental independence from each other as organized collectivities. But a true differentiation always involves at the same time an allegiance to common values and norms. In terms of the ultimate trusteeship of these values, the church is the higher authority. Perhaps a good analogy is the administration of the oath of office to an incoming American President by the Chief Justice of the Supreme Court. This clearly does not mean that the Chief Justice is the "real" chief of government and the President his organizational subordinate. What it means is rather that the Supreme Court is the ultimate interpreter of the Constitution, and the legitimation of presidential office by the Chief Justice is a symbolization of the subordination of the Presidency to constitutional law, which is equally binding on the Court.

In very broad outline this seems to be the way the stage was set for the development of a process of the "Christianizing" of secular society, not, be it repeated, through absorption of secular spheres into the "religious life" in the sense of the life of the church or its religious orders, but by exerting influence on a life which remained by the church's own definition secular, hence, in the Catholic phase, religiously inferior to the highest, but still potentially at least quite definitely Christian.[3]

The first main phase was the medieval synthesis, which produced a great society and culture. But from the present point of view it must also be considered a stage in a process of development. The dynamic forces which led beyond the medieval pattern were in the present view inherent on both the religious and the secular sides. Brief consideration of some of the essential constituents which both went into the medieval synthesis and led beyond it will help to lay a foundation for understanding a little of the mechanisms by which a religious influence could be exerted on secular society.

First let us take the church itself. Differentiation of the church from secular society represented in one sense a renunciation of influence on secular life. There was no longer a detailed, divinely sanctioned law to prescribe all secular conduct. This may, however, be looked on as a kind of renunciation similar to that involved in a process of investment, a step toward a higher order of "productive" results in the future by a more roundabout process. Here resources are not simply mobilized to maximize short-run production. Some current resources are diverted into temporarily "unproductive" channels in uses which prepare a later production effort. To do this, however, this set of resources must be protected against pressures for their immediate consumption. In the religious case the church was such a base of operations which was kept secure from absorption in the secular life of the time. Such pressures to absorption were indeed very prominent in the period after Constantine, in the West perhaps above all through the tendency of bishops to become heavily involved in secular political and economic interests.

The most important single fortress for the maintenance of the purity of religious orientation through this period was certainly the religious orders where segregated communities were devoted to a special religious life. Even this, however, had its this-worldly aspect, notably through the place taken by useful work in the Benedictine rule, which in many cases expanded into a generally high level of economic rationality. Furthermore the orders served as a highly important direct ground for the development of social organization itself; there were highly organized communities, administered in much more universalistic and less traditionalized ways than was most of the secular society of the time.

Secondly, however, that part of the church which served the laity through the secular clergy in the early medieval period underwent a major reform, significantly under monastic impetus. This of course is particularly associated with the Cluniac order and the name of Pope Gregory VII, himself a Cluniac monk. In one major aspect at least, it consisted of an extension of the monastic conception of purity of religious orientation to the roles of the secular clergy. There were two particularly important and closely related points here. One was the final defeat of the Donatist heresy and the firm establishment of the principle that priesthood was an office with powers and authority clearly separable from the person of the individual incumbent, or any particularistic network of relationships in which he might be involved. The second was the doctrine of clerical celibacy, which not only had not previously been enforced but also had not even been firmly established as a policy, and never was in the Eastern church.

These crucial reforms had two orders of significance. First, they served to consolidate and extend the independence of the church from secular influences. The particularly important extension was of course to the region of most direct and continuing contact with the laity through the secular clergy. Second, however, the structure of the medieval church came to serve, well beyond the Orders, as a model of social organization which could be extended into secular society. As Lea made so clear, in a society very largely dominated by the hereditary principle, clerical celibacy had a special significance.[4] Put in sociological terms, we may say that it made possible a social island which institutionalized a universalistic basis of role-allocation manifested in careers open to talent. The clergy was of course very far from being immune to class influence and at various times bishoprics and cardinalates were virtually monopolized by narrow circles of noble lineages. But this is not to say that the institution of celibacy and with it the barrier to inheritance of clerical office was unimportant.

There also was an intimate connection between the conception of clerical office which became crystallized in the Middle Ages and the building of much of Roman law into the structure of the church itself through canon law. In place of the relatively unrationalized and historically particularized Jewish law, the Christian church developed for its own internal use a highly rationalized and codified body of norms which underlay the legal structure of the whole subsequent development of Western society. Certainly the reception of secular Roman law in the late Middle Ages could not have happened without this.

Closely related to the church's use of Roman law was the place it made for the secular intellectual culture of antiquity. There is a sense in which this was already implicit in the place taken by Greek philosophy in theology itself. It was greatly reinforced by adoption of the conception of natural law as governing the secular sphere. Its medieval phase culminated in the very central place accorded to the work of Aristotle by Thomas Aquinas.

There was, however, also a structural aspect of the place of intellectual culture. Though in the earlier period it was only in the monasteries that the culture of antiquity was preserved and cultivated at all, as the medieval universities began to develop, the role of scholar and teacher assumed an important degree of independence both from the orders and from the hierarchy of the church. Though most of the schoolmen were monks, as scholars and teachers their activity was not directly controlled by their orders or chapters, nor by the bishops of the territories where they worked and taught. In terms of the crucial role of intellectual culture in later social development, notably through the rise of science, the structural basis of its independence is of an importance hardly to be exaggerated. This is perhaps the most critical single point of difference between the development of Western Christianity and of Islam, since in the latter case the influence of orthodoxy was able to suppress the independence of the scholarly class who had made such brilliant beginnings in the reception and extension of classical culture. The church's censure of Galileo should not be allowed to obscure the fact that, compared to other religious systems, Catholic Christianity made a place for an independent intellectual culture which is unique among all the great religions in their medieval phase.

There is one further important focus of the synthesis between medieval Christianity and the classical heritage. The universalism of Christianity held up a conception of a moral order for Christendom as a whole, with Christendom ideally expected eventually to comprise all mankind. This matched and was without doubt greatly influenced by the Roman conception of a universal socio-political order governed by a single universal system of law, a natural law coming to be institutionalized as the law of a politically organized society.

In basic Christian thinking, the Roman Empire as the secular order of the world had never ceased to exist. But since Charlemagne it could be defined as the *Holy* Roman Empire, as the normative framework of a universal Christian society. The empirical course of political development in Europe was to be such as to make this dream of unity under law in some respects progressively less realistic, at least for a very considerable period. Nevertheless the importance of the conception of a universal order should not be underestimated.

I have argued above that Christianity originally involved a cultural "marriage" between Judaic and Greco-Roman components. Though the early church repudiated the secular society of the contemporary Roman Empire, the above considerations make it quite clear that the normative aspect of classical culture was not repudiated; essentially a fundamental trusteeship of this heritage was built into the basic structure of the Christian church itself. It became the primary source from which this heritage was rediffused into the secular world and became the basis for further developments which somehow had failed to materialize in the ancient world. It is essential to my general argument here that this was a genuine integration.

Perhaps particularly from a Protestant point of view it is common to think of medieval Catholicism as mainly a pattern of compromise between a set of religious ideals and the exigencies of life in the world. It is quite true that, as Troeltsch so clearly brings out, the conception was that of a series of levels of closeness to and distance from full contact with the Divine, with the monastic life at the top. But this is not to say that positive religious sanction was withheld from everything except devotional self-sacrifice, that for example natural law was thought of merely as a concession to human weakness. Very much on the contrary, a secular world governed by natural law was thought of as ordained by God, as the part of His Creation which was to serve as the field for man's activity. Secular society was, to be sure, a field of temptation, but also of opportunity to lead a Christian life. And an essential part of the Christian life came to be the control, if not the shaping, of secular society in the interest of Christian ideals.

Professor Sorokin is quite right, I feel, in regarding this as a synthesis rather than merely a compromise. But, as noted, it is my view that this was not the end of the road, the point from which the process of religious decline started, but rather an essential station on a road which has led much farther. A few more general things about the nature of the process need to be said. The point of view I am taking here is meant to be very far indeed from any idealistic "emanationist" conception of the process of social development.

A crucial initial point is the one stressed throughout, that the church was from the beginning *itself* a special type of social organization. We do not have to think of the cultural aspect of Christianity as socially "disembodied" and suddenly, by a kind of sociological miracle, taking over the control of a society. On the contrary, it developed, survived, and exerted its influence through the same kinds of processes of interaction between cultural and social systems which operate in other connections. First, we have noted, it maintained and consolidated its independence, and developed its own internal structure. Second, it became diffused so that, within the society in which it operated, it could assume that the whole population was, in the religious sphere, subject to its jurisdiction; it successfully eliminated all organized internal religious competition – by "propaganda" and various types of more or less political process.

It had in its own social structure institutionalized a set of values. Through the universality of membership in it, it had the opportunity to play a critical part in the socialization process for all members of the society. Though not directly controlling secular social organization, at certain levels of personality its "definition of the situation" and the importance of its special sanctions could, however imperfectly, be universalized. There was much revolt and much "backsliding," but relatively little indifference to the Christian point of view was possible. The long-run influence of such a set of forces should not be underestimated.

The church was not only an agency of reward for approved behavior and punishment of what it disapproved. It was a crucial focus of psychological support over a very wide range of human concerns – its role in administration of the *rites de passage* is a good index of this position. Finally it was a source of direct models, not only for values at the most general level, but for modes of organizing social relationship patterns at a relatively general normative level, in such fields as law, and careers open to talent.

This phase of the "Christianization" of secular society can, like others, be summed up in terms of a formula which has proved useful in other connections for the analysis of the progressive type of change in a social system.[5] Given a base in an institutionalized value system (in this case in the church) there have been three main aspects of the process. First there has been *extension* of the range of institutionalization of the values, above all through the influence on the laity through the secular clergy. Secondly, there has been a process of further *differentiation*. The church itself has become further differentiated internally in that its sacramental system has been more clearly marked off from its administrative system, and its system of prescriptions for the ethical life of Christians through the canon law more clearly differentiated from both the others. At the same time the differentiation of the church *from* secular society has become more clearly marked. There has been a process of disengagement of the church from secular society through much more stringent control of the political and economic interests of bishops and clergy, and through sacerdotal celibacy. The beginnings of a revived Roman civil law have greatly aided in this process by more clearly defining the normative order of secular society.

Finally, third, there was a process of *upgrading* in terms of fulfillment of the requirements of the value system. Internally to the church itself this is the primary meaning of its internal reform, the strengthening of its administration, the elevation of standards in the orders and among the secular clergy. Externally, it was the gradual pressure toward a higher ethical standard among the lay population. The immense lay participation in enterprises like the building of the cathedrals is the most conspicuously manifest aspect of the general wave of "religious enthusiasm" in the Middle Ages.

The Reformation Phase

Perhaps the most important principle of the relation between religion and society which was institutionalized in the Middle Ages was that of the *autonomy* of secular society, of the "state" in the medieval sense, relative to the church, but within a Christian framework. The Christianity of secular society was guaranteed, not by the subjection of secular life to a religious law, but by the *common* commitment of ecclesiastical and temporal personnel to Christian faith. The Reformation may be seen, from one point of view, as a process of the extension of this principle of autonomy[6] to the internal structure of religious organization itself, with profound consequences both for the structure of the churches and for their relation to secular society. It may be regarded as a further major step in the same line as the original Christian break with Judaism.

The essential point may be stated as the religious "enfranchisement" of the individual, often put as his coming to stand in a direct relation to God. The Catholic Church had emancipated the individual, as part of its own corporate entity, from the Jewish law and its special social community, and had given him a notable autonomy within the secular sphere. But within its own definition of the religious sphere it had kept him under a strict tutelage by a set of mechanisms of which the sacraments were the core. By Catholic doctrine the only access to Divine grace was through the sacraments administered by a duly ordained priest. Luther broke through this tutelage to make the individual a *religiously* autonomous entity, responsible for his own religious concerns, not only in the sense of accepting the ministrations and discipline of the church but also through making his own fundamental religious commitments.

This brought faith into an even more central position than before. It was no longer the commitment to accept the particularized obligations and sacraments administered by the Church, but to act on the more general level in accordance with God's will. Like all reciprocal relationships, this one could be "tipped" one way or the other. In the Lutheran case it was tipped far in what in certain senses may be called the "authoritarian" direction; grace was interpreted to come only from the completely "undetermined" Divine action and in no sense to be dependent on the performances of the faithful, but only on their "receptivity." In this sense Lutheranism might be felt to deprive the individual of autonomy rather than enhancing it. But this would be an incorrect interpretation. The essential point is that the individual's dependence on the *human* mediation of the church and its priesthood through the sacraments was eliminated and *as a human being* he had, under God, to rely on his own independent responsibility; he could not "buy" grace or absolution from a human agency empowered to dispense it. In this situation the very uncertainties of the individual's relation to God, an uncertainty driven to its extreme by the Calvinistic doctrine of pre-destination, could, through its definition of the situation for religious interests, produce a powerful impetus to the acceptance of individual responsibility. The more deeply felt his religious need, the sharper his sense of unworthiness, the more he had to realize that no human agency could relieve him of his respons-ibility; "mother" church was no longer available to protect and comfort him.

An immediate consequence was the elimination of the fundamental distinc-tion in moral-religious quality between the religious life in the Catholic sense and life in secular "callings." It was the individual's direct relation to God which counted from the human side, his faith. This faith was not a function of any particular set of ritual or semi-magical practices, or indeed even of "discipline" except in the most general sense of living according to Christian principles. The core of the special meaning of the religious life had been the sacramental conception of the earning of "merit" and this was fundamentally dependent on the Catholic conception of the power of the sacraments.

From one point of view, that of the special powers of the *church* as a social organization, this could be regarded as a crucial loss of function, and the Lutheran conception of the fundamental religious equivalence of all callings as secularization. My interpretation, however, is in accord with Max Weber's; the more important change was not the removal of religious legitimation from the special monastic life, but rather, the endowment of secular life with a new order of religious legitimation as a field of "Christian opportunity." If the ordinary man, assumed of course to be a church member, stood in direct relation to God, and could be justified by his faith, the *whole person* could be justified, including the life he led in everyday affairs. The counterpart of eliminating the sacramental mediation of the secular priesthood was eliminating also the special virtues of the religious. It was a case of further *differentiation* within the Christian framework.

Protestantism in its Lutheran phase underwent a process, analogous to that of the early church, of relative withdrawal from direct involvement in the affairs of secular society. With the overwhelming Lutheran emphasis on faith and the importance of the individual's *subjective* sense of justification, there was, as Weber pointed out, a strong tendency to interpret the concept of the calling in a passive, traditionalist, almost Pauline sense. It was the individual's relation to his God that mattered; only in a sense of nondiscrimination was his secular calling sanctified, in that it was just as good, religiously speaking, as that of the monk.

We have, however, maintained that the conception of the generalization of a Christian pattern of life was an inherent possibility in the Christian orientation from the beginning and it came early to the fore in the Reformation period in the Calvinistic, or more broadly the ascetic, branch of the movement. Here we may say that the religious status of secular callings was extended from that of a principle of basic nondiscrimination to one of their endowment with positive instrumental significance. The key conception was that of the divine ordination of the establishment of the Kingdom of God on Earth. This went beyond the negative legitimation of secular callings to the assignment of a positive *function* to them in the divine plan.

In terms of its possibility of exerting leverage over secular society this was by far the most powerful version of the conception of the possibility of a "Christian society" which had yet appeared. First the stepwise hierarchy of levels of religious merit, so central to the Thomistic view, was eliminated by Luther. Then the individual became the focus not only of secular but also of religious responsibility emancipated from tutelary control by a sacramental church. Finally, precisely in his secular calling the individual was given a positive assignment to work in the building of the Kingdom.

The consequence of this combination was that, with one important exception, every major factor in the situation converged upon the dynamic exploitation of opportunity to change social life in the direction of conformity with religiously grounded ideals.

The basic assumption is that for Protestants the Christian commitment was no less rigorous than it had been for Catholics; if anything it was more so. In both Lutheran and Calvinistic versions the conception was one of the most rigorous submission of the individual's life to divine will. But in defining the situation for implementing this role of "creature," the Protestant position differed from the Catholic broadly as the definition of the preschool child's role relative to his parents differs from that of the school-age child's relation to his teacher. Within the family, important as the element of discipline and expectations of learning to perform are, the primary focus is on responsibility of the parents for the welfare and security of their children; the permeation of Catholic thought with familial symbolism along these lines is striking indeed.

In the school, on the other hand, the emphasis shifts. The teacher is primarily an agent of instruction, responsible for welfare, yes, but this is not the primary function; it is rather to help to equip the child for a responsible role in society when his education has been completed. To a much higher degree the question of how far he takes advantage of his opportunities becomes his own responsibility. Thus the function of the Protestant ministry became mainly a teaching function, continually holding up the Christian doctrine as a model of life to their congregations. But they no longer held a parental type of tutelary power to confer or deny the fundamentals of personal religious security.

If the analogy may be continued, the Lutheran position encouraged a more passive orientation in this situation, a leaving of the more ultimate responsibility to God, an attitude primarily of receptivity to Grace. (This is the exception referred to above – one of relatively short-run significance.) Such an attitude would tend to be generalized to worldly superiors and authorities, including both ministers and secular teachers. Ascetic Protestanism, on the other hand, though at least equally insistent on the divine origins of norms and values for life, tended to cut off this reliance on authority and place a sharper emphasis on the individual's responsibility for positive action, not just by his faith to be receptive to God's grace, but to get out and *work* in the building of the Kingdom. This precisely excluded any special valuation of devotional exercises and put the primary moral emphasis on secular activities.

Next, this constituted a liberation in one fundamental respect from the social conservatism of the Catholic position, in that it was no longer necessary to attempt to maintain the superiority of the religious life over the secular. Hence one essential bulwark of a hierarchical ordering of society was removed. The Christian conscience rather than the doctrines and structural position of the visible Church became the focus for standards of social evaluation. This should not, however, be interpreted as the establishment of "democracy" by the Reformation. Perhaps the most important single root of modern democracy is Christian individualism. But the Reformation, in liberating the individual conscience from the tutelage of the church, took only one step toward political democracy. The Lutheran branch indeed was long particularly identified with "legitimism," and Calvinism was in its early days primarily a doctrine of a relatively rigid collective "dictatorship" of the elect in both church and state.

Third, far from weakening the elements in secular society which pointed in a direction of "modernism," the Reformation, especially in its ascetic branch, strengthened and extended them. A particularly important component was clearly law. We have emphasized the essential continuity in this respect between classical antiquity and modern Europe through the medieval church. Broadly, the revival of Roman secular law in Europe was shared between Catholic and Protestant jurisdictions; in no sense did the Reformation reverse the trend in Continental Europe to institutionalize a secular legal system. In England, however, as Pound has emphasized, Puritanism was one of the major influences on the crystallization of the common law in the most decisive period. This is very much in line with the general trends of Protestant orientation, the favoring of a system of order within which responsible individual action can function effectively. The protection of rights is only one aspect of this order; the sanctioning of responsibilities is just as important.

Perhaps most important of all is the fact that the change in the character of the church meant that, insofar as the patterns of social structure which had characterized it by contrast with the feudal elements in the medieval heritage were to be preserved, they had to become much more generalized in secular society. This is true, as noted, of a generalized and codified system of law. It is true of more bureaucratic types of organization, which developed first in the governmental field but later in economic enterprise. It is by no means least true in the field of intellectual culture. The Renaissance was initially an outgrowth of the predominantly Catholic culture of Italy, but the general revival and development of learning of the post-medieval period was certainly shared by Catholic and Protestant Europe. It is a significant fact that John Calvin was trained as a lawyer. And of course, particularly in science, ascetic Protestantism was a major force in cultural development.

It is particularly important to emphasize the breadth of the front over which the leverage of Protestantism extended because of the common misinterpretation of Max Weber's thesis on the special relation between ascetic Protestantism and capitalism. This has often been seen as though the point were that Protestantism provided a special moral justification of profit-making as such, and of that alone. In view of the deep Western ambivalence over the conception of profit, the role of ascetic Protestantism in this context could easily be interpreted as mainly a "rationalization" of the common human propensity to seek "self-interest," which is the very antithesis of religious motivation.

First, it will be recalled that Weber was quite explicit that he was not talking about profit-making in general, but only about its harnessing to systematic methodical work in worldly callings in the interest of economic production through free enterprise. Weber was also well aware of a number of other facets of the same basic orientation to work in a calling, such as its basic hostility to various forms of traditionalism, including all traditional ascription of status independent of the individual, and its relation to science, a relation much further worked out by Merton.

Even Weber did not, however, in my opinion, fully appreciate the importance of the relation to the professions as a developing structural component of modern society, a component which in certain respects stands in sharp contrast to the classical orientation of economic self-interest.

The essential point is that private enterprise in business was one special case of secular callings within a much wider context. But it was a particularly strategic case in Western development, because of the very great difficulty of emancipating economic production over a truly broad front – on the one hand from the ascriptive ties which go with such institutions as peasant agriculture and guild-type handicraft, on the other hand from the irrationalities which, from an economic point of view, are inherent in political organization, because of its inherent connection with the short-run pressures of social urgency such as defense, and because of its integration with aristocratic elements in the system of stratification which were dominated by a very different type of orientation.

There is very good reason to believe that development of the industrial revolution *for the first time* could have come about only through the primary agency of free enterprise, however dependent this was in turn on prior conditions, among the most important of which were the availability of a legal framework within which a system of contractual relations could have an orderly development. Once there has been a major breakthrough on the economic front, however, the diffusion of the patterns of social organization involved need not continue to be dependent on the same conditions.[7]

Weber's main point about the Protestant ethic and capitalism was the importance of the subordination of self-interest in the usual ideological sense to the conception of a religiously meaningful calling; only with the establishment of this component was sufficient drive mobilized to break through the many barriers which were inherent not only in the European society of the time but more generally to a more differentiated development of economic production. Basically this involves the reversal of the commonsense point of view. The latter has contended, implicitly or explicitly, that the main source of impetus to capitalistic development was the *removal* of ethical restrictions such as, for instance, the prohibition of usury. This is true within certain limits, but by far the more important point is that what is needed is a powerful motivation to innovate, to break through the barriers of traditionalism and of vested interest. It is this impetus which is the center of Weber's concern, and it is his thesis that it cannot be accounted for by any simple removal of restrictions.

However deep the ambivalence about the morality of profit-making may go, there can be little doubt that the main outcome has been a shift in social conditions more in accord with the general pattern of Christian ethics than was medieval society, provided we grant that life in this world has a positive value in itself. Not least of these is the breaking through of the population circle of high death rates and high birth rates with the attendant lengthening of the average span of life. Another crucial point is the vast extension of the sphere of order in human relationships, the lessening of the exposure of the individual to violence, to fraud and to arbitrary pressures of authority.

So-called material well-being has certainly never been treated as an absolute value in the Christian or any other major religious tradition, but any acceptance of life in this world as of value entails acceptance of the value of the means necessary to do approved things effectively. Particularly at the lower end of the social scale, grinding poverty with its accompaniments of illness, premature death, and unnecessary suffering is certainly not to be taken as an inherently desirable state of affairs from a Christian point of view.

Another major theme of developments in this era which is in basic accord with Christian values is a certain strain to egalitarianism, associated with the conception of the dignity of the individual human being and the need to justify discriminations either for or against individuals and classes of them in terms of some general concept of merit or demerit. Certainly by contrast with the role of ascriptive discriminations in the medieval situation, modern society is not in this respect ethically inferior.

Also important has been the general field of learning and science. Perhaps the educational revolution of the nineteenth century was even more important in its long-run implications than was the industrial revolution of the late eighteenth century. It represents the first attempt in history to give large populations as a whole a substantial level of formal education, starting with literacy but going well beyond. Associated with this is the general cultivation of things intellectual and particularly the sciences through research. It is the marriage of the educational and industrial revolutions which provides the primary basis for the quite new level of mass well-being which is one major characteristic of the modern Western world. In both developments cultures with primarily Protestant orientations have acted as the spearheads.

The Reformation phase of Western development may be said to have culminated in the great seventeenth century, which saw the foundations of modern law and political organization so greatly advanced, the culmination of the first major phase of modern science, the main orientations of modern philosophy, and much development on the economic front. However important the Renaissance was, the great civilizational achievements of the seventeenth century as a whole are unthinkable without Protestantism. It coincided with a new level of leadership centering in predominantly Protestant northern Europe, notably England and Holland, and also with much ferment in Germany.

In spite of the very great structural differences, the essential principles governing the process by which society has become more Christianized than before were essentially the same in the Reformation period as in the earlier one. Let us recall that the Christian church from the beginning renounced the strategy of incorporation of secular society within itself, or the direct control of secular society through a religious law. It relied on the common values which bound church and secular society together, each in its own sphere, but making the Christian aspect of secular society an autonomous responsibility of Christians in their secular roles. My basic argument has been that the same fundamental principle was carried even farther in the Reformation phase. The sphere of autonomy was greatly enlarged through release of the Christian individual from the tutelage of the church. This was essentially a process of further differentiation both within the religious sphere and between it and the secular.

In all such cases there is increased objective opportunity for disregarding the values of the religious tradition and succumbing to worldly temptations. But the other side of the coin is the enhancement of motivation to religiously valued achievement by the very fact of being given more unequivocal responsibility. This process was not mainly one of secularization but one of the institutionalization of the religious responsibility of the individual through the relinquishment of tutelary authority by a "parental" church.

For purposes of this discussion the Reformation period is the most decisive one, for here it is most frequently argued, by Professor Sorokin among many others, that there was a decisive turn in the direction of secularization in the sense of abandonment of the values inherent in the Christian tradition in favor of concern with the "things of this world." As already noted, we feel that underlying this argument is a basic ambiguity about the relation of "the world" to religious orientations and that the Christian orientation is not, in the Oriental sense, an orientation of "rejection of the world" but rather in this respect mainly a source for the setting of ethical standards *for* life in this world. In line with this interpretation, the Reformation transition was not primarily one of "giving in" to the temptations of worldly interest, but rather one of extending the range of applicability and indeed in certain respects the rigor of the ethical standards applied to life in the world. It was expecting more rather than less of larger numbers of Christians in their worldly lives. It goes without saying that the content of the expectations also changed. But these changes indicated much more a change in the definition of the situation of life through changes in the structure of society than they did in the main underlying values.

Let us try to apply the same formula used in summing up the medieval phase to that of the Reformation. The most conspicuous aspect of extension was the diffusion of religious responsibility and participation in certain respects beyond the sacramentally organized church to the laity on their own responsibility. The central symbol of this was the translation of the Bible into the vernacular languages of Europe and the pressure on broad lay groups to familiarize themselves with it. The shift in the functions of the church from the sacramental emphasis to that of teaching is directly connected with this. This extension included both the elements of worship and that of responsibility for ethical conduct.

With respect to the church itself as a social system, the Reformation clearly did not involve further internal differentiation but the contrary. But it involved a major step in the differentiation of the religious organization *from* secular society. The Reformation churches, as distinguished from the sects, retained their symbiosis of interpenetration with secular political authority through the principle of Establishment. But the counterpart of what I have called the religious enfranchisement of the individual was his being freed from detailed moral tutelage by the clergy. The dropping of the sacrament of penance, the very core of Luther's revolt against the Catholic church, was central in this respect. Repentance became a matter of the individual's direct relation to God, specifically exempted from any sacramental mediation. This was essentially to say that the individual was, in matters of conscience, in principle accountable to no human agency, but only to God; in this sense he was *humanly* autonomous. This development tended to restrict the church to the functions of an agency for the generation of faith, through teaching and through providing a communal setting for the ritual expression of common anxiety and common faith.

There were two principal settings in which this differentiation of lay responsibility from ecclesiastical tutelage worked out. One was the direct relation to God in terms of repentance and faith. This was paramount in the Lutheran branch of the Reformation movement. The other was the primacy of moral action in the world as an instrument of the divine will, the pattern which was primary in ascetic Protestantism. In a sense in which this was impossible within the fold of Catholic unity on the level of church organization, both these movements become differentiated not only from the "parent" Catholic church but also from each other. Hence the ascetic Protestant branch, which institutionalized elements present from the beginning in Western Christian tradition, notably through Augustine, was freed from the kind of ties with other components which hindered its ascendancy as the major trend of one main branch of general Christian tradition. Clearly this is the branch which had the most direct positive influence on the complex of orientations of value which later proved to be of importance to modern industrialism.

The third point of upgrading is most conspicuous in the placing of secular callings on a plane of moral equality with the religious life itself. In crucial respects this shift increased the tension between Christian ideal and worldly reality. This increase of tension underlay much of the Lutheran trend to withdrawal from positive secular interests and the corresponding sectarian and mystical phenomena of the time. But once the new tension was turned into the channel of exerting leverage for the change of conduct in the secular world, above all through the imperative to work in the building of the Kingdom, it was a powerful force to moral upgrading precisely in the direction of changing social behavior in the direction of Christian ideals, not of adjustment to the given necessities of a non-Christian world.

The Denominational Phase

A common view would agree with the above argument that the Reformation itself was not basically a movement of secularization but that, in that it played a part in unleashing the forces of political nationalism and economic development – to say nothing of recent hedonism – it was the last genuinely Christian phase of Western development and that from the eighteenth century on in particular the trend had truly been one of religious decline in relation to the values of secular society. Certain trends in Weber's thinking with respect to the disenchantment of the world would seem to argue in this direction, as would Troeltsch's view that there have been only three authentic versions of the conception of a Christian society in Western history – the medieval Catholic, the Lutheran, and the Calvinistic.

Against this view I should like to present an argument for a basic continuity leading to a further phase which has come to maturity in the nineteenth and twentieth centuries, most conspicuously in the United States and coincident with the industrial and educational revolutions already referred to. From this point of view, the present system of "denominational pluralism" may be regarded as a further extension of the same basic line of institutionalization of Christian ethics which was produced both by the medieval synthesis and by the Reformation.

It is perhaps best to start with the conception of religious organization itself. Weber and Troeltsch organized their thinking on these matters within the Christian framework around the distinction between church and sect as organizational types. The church was the religious organization of the whole society which could claim and enforce the same order of jurisdiction over a total population as did the state in the secular sphere. The sect, on the other hand, was a voluntary religious association of those committed to a specifically religious life. The church type was inherently committed to the conception of an Establishment, since only through this type of integration with political authority could universal jurisdiction be upheld. The sect, on the other hand, could not establish any stable relation to secular society since its members were committed to give unequivocal primacy to their religious interests and could not admit the legitimacy of the claims of secular society, politically or otherwise, which a stable relation would entail.

This dichotomy fails to take account of an important third possibility, the denomination. As I conceive it, this shares with the church type the *differentiation* between religious and secular spheres of interest. In the same basic sense which we outlined for the medieval church, both may be conceived to be subject to Christian values, but to constitute independent foci of responsibility for their implementation. On the other hand, the denomination shares with the sect type its character as a voluntary association where the individual member is bound only by a responsible personal commitment, not by *any* factor of ascription. In the American case it is, logically I think, associated with the constitutional separation of church and state.

The denomination can thus accept secular society as a legitimate field of action for the Christian individual in which he acts on his own responsibility without organizational control by religious authority. But precisely because he is a Christian he will not simply accept everything he finds there; he will attempt to shape the situation in the direction of better conformity with Christian values. This general pattern it shares with all three of the church types, but not with the sect in Troeltsch's sense.

Two further factors are involved, however, which go beyond anything to be found in the church tradition. One of these is implicit in the voluntary principle – the acceptance of denominational pluralism – and, with it, toleration. However much there may historically have been, and still is, deep ambivalence about this problem, the genuine institutionalization of the constitutional protection of religious freedom cannot be confined to the secular side; it must be accepted as *religiously* legitimate as well. With certain qualifications this can be said to be the case in the United States today and, in somewhat more limited forms, in various other countries. From a religious point of view, this means the discrimination of two layers of religious commitment. One of these is the layer which defines the bases of denominational membership and which differentiates one denomination from another. The other is a common matrix of value-commitment which is broadly shared between denominations, and which forms the basis of the sense in which the society as a whole forms a religiously based moral community. This has, in the American case, been extended to cover a very wide range. Its core certainly lies in the institutionalized Protestant denominations, but with certain strains and only partial institutionalization, it extends to three other groups of the first importance; the Catholic church, the various branches of Judaism, and, not least important, those who prefer to remain aloof from *any* formal denominational affiliation. To deny that this underlying consensus exists would be to claim that American society stood in a state of latent religious war. Of the fact that there are considerable tensions every responsible student of the situation is aware. Institutionalization is incomplete, but the consensus is very much of a reality.

The second difference from the church tradition is a major further step in the emancipation of the individual from tutelary control by *organized* religious collectivities beyond that reached by the Reformation churches. This is the other side of the coin of pluralism, and essentially says that the rite of baptism does not commit the individual to a particular set of dogmas or a particular religious collectivity. The individual is responsible not only for managing his own relation to God through faith *within* the ascribed framework of an established church, which is the Reformation position, but for choosing that framework itself, for deciding as a mature individual *what* to believe, and *with whom* to associate himself in the organizational expression and reinforcement of his commitments. This is essentially the removal of the last vestige of coercive control over the individual in the religious sphere; he is endowed with full responsible autonomy.

That there should be a development in this direction from the position of the Reformation church seems to me to have been inherent in the Protestant position in general, in very much the same sense in which a trend to Protestantism was inherent in the medieval Catholic situation. Just as Catholics tend to regard Protestantism in general as the abandonment of true religious commitment either because the extension of the voluntary principle to such lengths is held to be incompatible with a sufficiently serious commitment on the part of the church (if you are not willing to coerce people to your point of view are you yourself *really* committed to it?) or because of its legitimation of secular society so that church membership becomes only one role among many, not the primary axis of life as a whole. But against such views it is hard to see how the implicit individualism of all Christianity could be stopped, short of this doctrine of full responsible autonomy. The doctrine seems to me implicit in the very conception of faith. Asking the individual to have faith is essentially to ask him to *trust* in God. But, whatever the situation in the relation of the human to the divine, in *human* relations trust seems to have to rest on mutuality. Essentially the voluntary principle in denominationalism is extending mutuality of trust so that no *human* agency is permitted to take upon itself the authority to control the conditions under which faith is to be legitimately expected. Clearly this, like the Reformation step, involves a risk that the individual will succumb to worldly temptations. But the essential principle is not different from that involved in releasing him from sacramental control.

This is of course very far from contending that the system of denominational pluralism is equally congenial to all theological positions or that all religious groups within the tradition can fit equally well into it. There are important strains particularly in relation to the Catholic church, to Fundamentalist Protestant sects, to a lesser degree to very conservative Protestant church groups (especially Lutheran), and to the vestiges of really Orthodox Judaism. My essential contention is not that this pattern has been or can be fully universalized within Judaeo-Christianity, but that it is a genuinely Christian development, not by definition a falling away from religion. But it could not have developed without a very substantial modification of earlier positions within Protestantism. In particular it is incompatible with either strict traditional Lutheranism or strict Calvinism.

It was remarked above that the Reformation period did not usher in political democracy, but was in a sense a step toward it. There is a much closer affiliation between denominational pluralism and political democracy. But before discussing that, a comparison between the two may help illuminate the nature of the problem of how such a system of religious organization works. Legitimists for a long period have viewed with alarm the dangers of democracy since, if public policy can be determined by the majority of the irresponsible and the uninformed, how can any stability of political organization be guaranteed? There is a sense in which the classical theory of political liberalism may be said to play into the hands of this legitimist argument, since it has tended to assume that under democracy each individual made up his mind totally independently without reference to the institutionalized wisdom of any tradition.

This is not realistically the case. Careful study of voting behavior has shown that voting preferences are deeply anchored in the established involvement of the individual in the social structure. Generally speaking, most voters follow the patterns of the groups with which they are most strongly affiliated. Only when there are structural changes in the society which alter its structure of solidary groupings and expose many people to cross-pressures are major shifts likely to take place. There are, furthermore, mechanisms by which these shifts tend, in a well-institutionalized democratic system, to be orderly.[8]

I would like to suggest that similar considerations apply to a system of denominational pluralism. The importance of the family is such that it is to be taken for granted that the overwhelming majority will accept the religious affiliations of their parents – of course with varying degrees of commitment. Unless the whole society is drastically disorganized there will not be notable instability in its religious organization. But there will be an important element of flexibility and opportunity for new adjustments within an orderly system which the older church organizations, like the older political legitimacy, did not allow for.

If it is once granted that this system of religious organization is not by definition a "falling away" from true religion, then its institutionalization of the elements of trust of the individual has, it seems to me, an important implication. On the religious side it is implicit in the pattern of toleration. Members of particular churches on the whole trust each other to be loyal to the particular collectivity. But if some should shift to another denomination it is not to be taken too tragically since the new affiliation will in most cases be included in the deeper moral community.

But such a situation could not prevail were the secular part of the system regarded as radically evil. The individual is not only trusted with reference to his religious participation, but also to lead a "decent" life in his secular concerns. Indeed I should argue, therefore, that for such a religious constitution to function, on the institutional level the society must present not a less but a more favorable field for the Christian life than did the society of earlier periods of Western history; its moral standards must in fact be higher.

There is a tendency in much religiously oriented discussion to assume that the test of the aliveness of Christian values is the extent to which "heroic" defiance of temptation or renunciation of worldly interests is empirically prevalent. This ignores one side of the equation of Christian conduct, the extent to which the "world" does or does not stand opposed to the values in question. If one argues that there has been a relative institutionalization of these values, and hence in certain respects a diminution of tension between religious ideal and actuality, he risks accusation of a Pharisaic complacency. In face of this risk, however, I suggest that in a whole variety of respects modern society is more in accord with Christian values than its forebears have been – this is, let it be noted, a *relative* difference; the millennium definitely has not arrived.

I do not see how the extension of intra- and interdenominational trust into a somewhat greater trust in the moral quality of secular conduct would be possible were this not so. The internalization of religious values certainly strengthens character. But this is not to say that even the *average* early Christian was completely proof against worldly temptation, *independent of any support from the mutual commitments of many Christians in and through the church.* Without the assumption that this mutual support in a genuine social collectivity was of the first importance, I do not see how the general process of institutionalization of these values could have been possible at all except on the unacceptable assumption of a process of emanation of the spirit without involvement in the realistic religious interests of real persons.

However heroic a few individuals may be, no process of mass institutionalization occurs without the mediation of social solidarities and the mutual support of many individuals in commitment to a value system. The corollary of relinquishment of the organizational control of certain areas of behavior, leaving them to the responsibility of the autonomous individual, is the institutionalization of the basic conditions of carrying out this responsibility with not the elimination, but a relative minimization of, the hazard that this exposure will lead to total collapse of the relevant standards.

Let us try to sum up this fourth – denominational – phase of the line of development we have traced in terms of our threefold formula. First I would suggest that the principle of religious toleration, inherent in the system of denominational pluralism, implies a great further extension of the institutionalization of Christian values, both inside and outside the sphere of religious organization. At least it seems to me that this question poses a sharp alternative. Either there is a sharp falling away so that, in tolerating each other, the different denominations have become fellow condoners of an essentially evil situation or, as suggested above, they do in fact stand on a relatively high ethical plane so that whatever their dogmatic differences, there is no basis for drawing a drastic moral line of distinction which essentially says that the adherents of the other camp are in a moral sense not good people in a sense in which the members of our own camp are. Then the essential extension of the same principle of mutual trust into the realm of secular conduct is another part of the complex which I would like to treat as one of extension of the institutionalization of Christian values.

So far as differentiation is concerned, there are two conspicuous features of this recent situation. First, of course, the religious associations have become differentiated from each other so that, unlike in the Reformation phase (to say nothing of the Middle Ages), when there was for a politically organized society in principle only one acceptable church, adherence to which was the test of the moral quality treated as a minimum for good standing in the society, this is no longer true. The religious organization becomes a purely voluntary association, and there is an indefinite plurality of morally acceptable denominations.

This does not, however, mean that Christian ethics have become a matter of indifference in the society. It means rather that the differentiation between religious and secular spheres has gone farther than before and with it the extension of the individualistic principle inherent in Christianity to the point of the "privatizing" of formal, external religious commitment, as the Reformation made internal religious faith a matter for the individual alone. This general trend has of course coincided with an enormously proliferated process of differentiation in the structure of the society itself.

In this respect the religious group may be likened (up to a point) to the family. The family has lost many traditional functions and has become increasingly a sphere of private sentiments. There is, however, reason to believe that it is as important as ever to the maintenance of the main patterns of the society, though operating with a minimum of direct outside control. Similarly religion has become largely a private matter in which the individual associates with the group of his own choice, and in this respect has lost many functions of previous religious organizational types.

There seem to be two primary respects in which an upgrading process may be spoken of. Approaching the question from the sociological side, we may note that the development of the society has been such that it should not be operated without an upgrading of general levels of responsibility and competence, the acquisition and exercise of the latter of course implying a high sense of responsibility. This trend is a function of increase in the size of organization and the delicacy of relations of interdependence, of freedom from ascriptive bonds in many different ways, of the sheer power for destruction and evil of many of the instrumentalities of action.

Responsibility has a double aspect. The first is responsibility *of* the individual in that he cannot rely on a dependent relation to others, or to some authority, to absolve him of responsibility – this is the aspect we have been referring to as his *autonomy* in the specific sense in which the term has been used in this discussion. The other aspect is responsibility *for* and *to*, responsibility for results and to other persons and to collectivities. Here the element of mutuality inherent in Christian ethics, subject to a commonly binding set of norms and values, is the central concern.

That the general trend has been to higher orders of autonomous responsibility is, in my opinion, sociologically demonstrable.[9] The central problem then becomes that of whether the kinds of responsibility involved do or do not accord with the prescriptions of Christian ethics. This is essentially the question of whether the general trend stemming from ascetic Protestantism is basically un-Christian or not. Granting that this trend is not un-Christian, the critical *moral* problems of our day derive mainly from the fact that, since we are living in a more complicated world than ever before, which is more complicated because human initiative has been more daring and has ventured into more new realms than ever before, greater demands are being put on the human individual. He has more difficult problems, both technical and moral; he takes greater risks. Hence the possibility of failure and of the failure being his fault is at least as great as, if not greater than, it ever was.

There is a widespread view, particularly prevalent in religious circles, that our time, particularly some say in the United States, is one of unprecedented moral collapse. In these circles it is alleged that modern social development has entailed a progressive decline of moral standards which is general throughout the population. This view is clearly incompatible with the general trend of the analysis we have been making. Its most plausible grain of truth is the one just indicated, that as new and more difficult problems emerge, such as those involved in the possibility of far more destructive war than ever before, we do not feel morally adequate to the challenge. But to say that because we face graver problems than our forefathers faced we are doubtful of our capacity to handle them responsibly is quite a different thing from saying that, on the same levels of responsibility as those of our forefathers, we are in fact handling our problems on a much lower moral level.

Our time by and large, however, is not one of religious complacency but, particularly in the most sensitive groups in these matters, one of substantial anxiety and concern. Does not the existence of this concern stand in direct contradiction to the general line of argument I have put forward?

I think not. One element in its explanation is probably that new moral problems of great gravity have emerged in our time and that we are, for very realistic reasons, deeply concerned about them. My inclination, however, is to think that this is not the principal basis of the widespread concern.

The present discussion has, by virtue of its chosen subject, been primarily interested in the problems of the institutionalization of the values originating in Christianity as a religious movement, which have been carried forward at various stages of its development. But values – i.e., moral orientations toward the problems of life in this world – are never the whole of religion, if indeed its most central aspect. My suggestion is that the principal roots of the present religious concern do not lie in *relative* moral decline or inadequacy (relative, that is, to other periods in our society's history) but rather in problems in the other areas of religion, problems of the bases of faith and the definitions of the ultimate problems of meaning.

The very fact that the process of the integration of earlier religious values with the structure of society has gone so far as it has gone raises such problems. The element of universalism in Christian ethics inherently favors the development of a society where the different branches of Christianity cannot maintain their earlier insulation from each other. The problem of the status of Judaism has had to be raised on a new level within the structure of Western society, one which came to a very critical stage in the case of German Nazism. It is a society in which all the parochialisms of earlier religious commitments are necessarily brought into flux.

But beyond this, for the first time in history something approaching a world society is in process of emerging. For the first time in its history Christianity is now involved in a deep confrontation with the major religious traditions of the Orient, as well as with the modern political religion of Communism. ← → whe? weWdo.

It seems probable that a certain basic tension in relation to the "things of this world" is inherent in Christianity generally. Hence any relative success in the institutionalization of Christian values cannot be taken as final, but rather as a point of departure for new religious stock-taking. But in addition to this broad internal consideration, the confrontation on such a new basis with the non-Christian world presents a new and special situation. We are deeply committed to our own great traditions. These have tended to emphasize the exclusive possession of the truth. Yet we have also institutionalized the values of tolerance and equality of rights for all. How can we define a meaningful orientation in such a world when, in addition, the more familiar and conventional problems of suffering and evil are, if not more prevalent than ever before, at least as brought to attention through mass communications, inescapable as facts of our world?

It is the inherent tension and dynamism of Christianity and the unprecedented character of the situation we face which, to my mind, account for the intensive searching and questioning, and indeed much of the spiritual negativism, of our time. The explanation in terms of an alleged moral collapse would be far too simple, even if there were more truth in it than the evidence seems to indicate. For this would imply that we did not need new conceptions of meaning; all we would need would be to live up more fully to the standards familiar to us all. In no period of major ferment in cultural history has such a solution been adequate.

Notes

1   Cf. Pitrim Sorokin, *Fads and Foibles in Modern Sociology and Related Sciences* (Chicago: Henry Regnery, 1956).

2   The most important general statements of his position are in *Social and Cultural Dynamics* (New York: American Book Company, 1937), Vol. I, Part 1, and *Society, Culture, and Personality* (New York: Harper, 1947), Part 7.

3   In this general interpretation I follow in particular Ernst Troeltsch, *Social Teachings of the Christian Churches* (New York: Macmillan, 1931).

4   H. C. Lea, *The History of Sacerdotal Celibacy* (New York: Russell and Russell, 1957).

5   Perhaps the fullest statement of this scheme is contained in T. Parsons and W. White, "The Link between Character and Society," in S. M. Lipset and L. Loewenthal (eds), *Culture and Social Character* (New York: The Free Press of Glencoe, 1961).

6   By autonomy I mean here *independence* of direct authoritarian control combined with *responsibility* defined in moral-religious terms. It is close to "theonomy" as that concept is used by Tillich.

7   This thesis is further developed in my two essays published as Chapters III and IV of *Structure and Process in Modern Societies* (New York: The Free Press of Glencoe, 1960).

8   Basing myself on the studies of voting behavior by Berelson, Lazarsfeld, et al., I have analyzed this situation in " 'Voting' and the Equilibrium of the American Political System," in Eugene Burdick and Arthur J. Brodbeck (eds), *American Voting Behavior* (New York: The Free Press of Glencoe, 1959).

9   Cf. Parsons and White, *op. cit.*, for a brief statement of the case for this view.

2

Belief, Unbelief, and Disbelief

As a general commentator on the Symposium on the Culture of Unbelief, there are two aspects of my position which should be made explicit at the outset. First, I am not a Roman Catholic, but a somewhat backsliding Protestant of Congregationalist background. Second, I am not a theologian, but a sociologist by profession. My commentary will not attempt a summary of the discussions – though the Agnelli Foundation has kindly made a copy of the transcript available to me – but rather will be critical in the sense of ranging about some of the principal issues which figured in the papers and discussions in my own terms, hoping in the process to help to define the situation for future stages of discussion and research in this field.

Belief, Disbelief, and Unbelief

The relevant context of the use of the terms "belief" and "unbelief" was of course religious. It does not seem useful here to attempt discussion of "What is religion?" in general terms. At certain points aspects of that question will arise and can be dealt with on those occasions. Since, however, the concept belief is so central, a brief commentary on it does seem to be in order. First a point of logic. In Western culture at least there has been a strong tendency to think in terms of dichotomies, often accentuated in their mutual exclusiveness by such expressions as "versus." Thus we have rational versus irrational, heredity versus environment, *Gemeinschaft* versus *Gesellschaft*.

If members of such dichotomous pairs are to be treated as types, however, they have frequently turned out, not only to admit of intermediate or mixed types, but to be resultants of a plurality of variables, so that study of the possible combinations of the component variables might at the typological level, yield, not a single dichotomous pair, but a larger "family" of possible types, which differ from each other, not on one, but on several dimensions.

I think – or "I believe" – that this is true of the concept of belief itself, at religious and at other levels. I might suggest that stating the problem in terms of belief-unbelief is already a start in this pluralistic direction in that the alternative to belief need not be simply disbelief but might be some way of avoiding being placed in the category either of believer or of disbeliever. The logic here is similar to that involved in the history of the concept of rationality and its antonyms. Namely, it was a major advance when rationality was contrasted not with irrationality but with nonrationality; there could be types which, though nonrational, were not irrational.

Certainly in the Western tradition, the concept of belief has a cognitive component. This is to say that however difficult this may be in practice, beliefs are capable of being stated in propositional form and then tested by standards of "truth" or cognitive validity. It is true that most propositions of religious belief are not subject to what we generally call empirical verification. But they still must, ideally, be tested by standards of conceptual clarity and precision, and logically correctness of inference.[1] The equivalent of the empirical component in science is the authenticity of the nonlogical components of religious belief, for example, revelation, or some kind of religious experience.

Another aspect of the problem, however, is brought out by the distinction which was discussed early in the conference, namely between what is meant by "belief *that*..." and "belief *in*..." In my view, it would not be appropriate to use the term belief in the latter context if there were *no* cognitive content involved, that is, if the action referred to were completely nonrational expression of emotions. The little word "in," however, suggests a noncognitive component which is not included in "that," which may be called commitment. The "believer in..." of course must, explicitly or implicitly, subscribe to cognitively formulable and in some sense testable propositions, but in addition to that, he commits himself to act (including experiencing) in ways which are, to put it in the mildest form, congruent with the cognitive components of his belief.

An important, perhaps the premier, example here is the Protestant doctrine, especially associated with Luther himself, of "salvation by faith alone." This is faith *in* the Christian God. The formula as such contains no reference to the cognitive set of beliefs, but it clearly implies them in the sense that faith is faith *in God*; with no cognitive conception of God the commitment would be meaningless. The alternative, for Luther, to salvation by faith, was clearly that by works through the Catholic sacraments. The definition of these alternatives did not challenge the general strictly *theo*logical conceptions of God and his relations to man.

From the point of view of the Catholic Church of his time, Luther was a heretic. But his disbelief in the mission of the historical church and in the sacraments was only one form of unbelief. Surely in many ways he was not only a believer in some vaguely general sense, but he was a believer in Christ and the Christian God. This is to say, he accepted much of the cognitive framework of the inherited tradition.

Professor Bellah has spoken of a strong cognitive bias in Christian religious tradition. That the emphasis on the cognitive component has been strong does not seem to be seriously open to doubt. That it has been a bias in the sense that over the long run it has distorted Western religious development is a question on which I prefer to withhold judgment. Prior to rendering a necessary basis for arriving at such a judgment, it seems to me more urgent to attempt to clarify the nature of the components, both cognitive and noncognitive, rational and nonrational, of religious orientation, and certain aspects of their relations to each other.

That there must be a major set of noncognitive components is a view which has been accepted in the introductory statements of this commentary and is indeed very widely accepted. This noncognitive component is, to my mind, what distinguishes religion both from philosophy on the one hand, and science on the other, both of which are intellectual disciplines. While theology may well be considered to be such a discipline, clearly religion is not. Durkheim's famous dictum about religion, *c'est de la vie serieuse*, is one way of stating that difference and seems to be more or less adequately expressed in the term commitment which I have used above.

The Rational and Nonrational Components of Action

Bellah, in a paper presumably written almost immediately after the conference,[2] discusses explicitly the prominent role of the noncognitive and nonrational components of action in the work of the three great transformers of thinking about man and society in the generation of the turn of the century, namely Freud, Durkheim, and Max Weber. All three were prominently unbelievers in our sense though not unequivocally disbelievers, and all three were deeply concerned with religion. Bellah suggests that they were "symbolic reductionists" in that they granted a certain "reality" to religion, but held that the content of explicit beliefs must be taken to be the symbolic expression of something else.

It is in the realm of that "something else" that, according to Bellah, all three formulated the decisive noncognitive categories, namely in Freud's case the *unconscious*, in that of Durkheim, *society*, in a sense which in this context of usage clearly requires much interpretation, and in that of Weber, *charisma*, which also requires interpretation. Though these three formulations are by no means directly congruent with each other, they all constitute in some sense "residual categories" which are defined mainly by contrast with their antonyms, rather than positively.

In order to formulate a more adequate conceptual scheme it seems necessary to introduce at least two further distinctions in addition to that between the cognitive and the noncognitive. One touches the interpretation of the status of the noncognitive categories introduced by Freud and Weber, whereas the other concerns the interpretation of Durkheim's usage of society as a referent of such symbolism.

In the intellectual setting in which he introduced the concept of charisma, Weber had worked out what seems to the author a major clarification of certain aspects of the structure of the cognitive world. This occurred mainly in his famous essays on *Wissenschaftslehre* and eventuated in a special version of what is usually considered to be a "neo-Kantian" position. One aspect of it was the full extension of the cognitive paradigms, which had basically come to be established in the natural sciences, to what Weber called the *Kulturwissenschaften*, a category which included both the social sciences and the humanities. The second, however, was the introduction or clarification, in the area which Kant had left cognitively unstructured under the rubric of "practical reason," of a category of cognitive knowledge concerning values, and the underlying "problems of meaning" in reference to the human condition. Here Weber's contribution is the establishment of this category – of course he by no means stood alone – as a category of rational knowledge.[3]

This was the basis on which, in his classification of "types of action," Weber was able to introduce two rather than one rational type. Since the context was action rather than knowledge as such he called them *Zweckrationalität* (which I have translated as "instrumental") and *Wertrationalität* ("value") respectively. From the beginning Weber's classification assumed that the rational types would be complemented by nonrational – not irrational – types. The duality on the rational side, however, strongly suggested the usefulness of a corresponding duality on the nonrational. In his actual classification Weber did indeed introduce two such categories, namely "affectual" and "traditional" action.

The line of distinction between the two rationalities of Weber's classification clearly concerns the direction of orientation, on the one hand downward to the empirically given conditions of human action, physical, biological and on certain levels even social and cultural and, on the other hand, upward toward the "grounds of meaning" of action and their modes of symbolization. In the paradigm we are outlining, this line of distinction should be extended onto the nonrational side. The nonrational category corresponding to instrumental rationality is that of the motivational components which are rooted in the biological nature of man, his needs and their affective modes of expression, modified as these have been from pure biologically inherited propensities, by various features of the processes of learning and socialization. Though the references of the term are highly complex and raise difficult theoretical problems, Weber's term "affectual," though perhaps not quite in the sense in which he defines it, is probably as good as any.[4]

The other category of the nonrational, like value-rationality, is a mode of orientation to the grounds and problems – in this sense interpreted in a largely noncognitive sense – of meaning. Here, curiously, Weber utilized the logic of the residual category in a special way, and placed here the concept "traditional," which was clearly nonrational, but oriented wholly to stability. He then introduced that of charisma as specifically a nonrational orientational force of innovation, but did not explicitly relate it to the types of action. Once, however, that it is seen that a typology of the components of action at the most general level should include their contribution to both stability and change and the balance between them, including the fact that Weber himself used the concept charisma outside the context of change,[5] charisma emerges as the appropriate concept in Weber's terms for the meaning-oriented category of the nonrational side.[6]

Seen in these terms, Freud's concept of the unconscious was definitely a residual category, originally formulated by contrast with the naïver versions of the conception of rationality of action, at both cognitive and behavioral levels. This is not the place to follow through the complex developments of Freud's theoretical thinking. Originally, however, the content of the unconscious was overwhelmingly interpreted to be focused on instinct. This, however, proved to be unstable and Freud himself eventually placed the superego mainly in the unconscious and distinguished it from the id. The extent to which the superego was exhausted by its unconscious components and how it articulated with internalized culture more generally remained problematical, but in a rough sense it can clearly be said that Freud's distinction between id and superego paralleled that of Weber between affectual and charismatic components of action. Hence we may say that in both Weber and Freud the analytical basis for studying a nonrational aspect of religious orientation had been laid down in the great tradition of emerging social science.

Durkheim and the Moral Component of Society

For both Weber and Freud, the primary direct referent of their symbolic reductionism, as Bellah calls it, was values; references to the reality by virtue of which values were rendered meaningful, remained in different ways problematical for both. There is a major overlap in this focus with Durkheim's position, but the difference is of great significance for the problems of the symposium. Durkheim made a great deal of the thesis that sacred things were symbols, the referents of which should be sought out by research.

The basis on which he established the connection with society was the common attitude of moral respect. In his earlier work in areas quite other than the study of religion he had gradually come to give a special place to what we can now call the internalized and above all institutionalized structure of norms and values carrying what he called "moral authority." Indeed, when Durkheim presented his famous definition of religion in the *Elementary Forms of the Religious Life*,[7] he featured the crucial phrase "moral community." The normative regulation of secular life, for Durkheim, was interpretable in terms of Weber's value-rationality. The set of beliefs and practices which he called religious, constituted symbolic expressions of the same moral community.

Weber would emphasize the consensus on values which at least in considerable part derived from the belief system, including both the cognitive component and that of commitment. Durkheim, on the other hand, did not really go beyond the existence, as institutionalized, of this moral community; Weber's was thus the deeper analysis. In stopping where he did, however, Durkheim brought to light – or to explicit attention – a most important concept which has flowered in Bellah's conception of the civil religion.[8] For Durkheim, the society was never only the community in which its members participated but was also, precisely to them, as well as to an outside observer, an object. As such the moral, and as another aspect the sacred, quality of it constituted one of its major constitutive properties.

In the French situation of his time Durkheim was a "laicist"; though of Jewish origin he was not a religiously practicing Jew and he belonged to the anticlerical left. These circumstances help to explain his views about the Church as that concept was included in his definition of religion. From his own normative point of view he repudiated two primary institutional developments of the Christian world. The one was that of the established Church, especially in the Roman Catholic form, but with differences in some Protestant cases, where the church, though established, was differentiated from the secular social order, with both the laity and the secular priesthood participating in both – members of religious orders were, however, minimally in the secular world. The second is the institutional form which was first clearly developed in the United States but has increasingly become the dominant institutional form for the noncommunist Western world, namely denominational pluralism with religious freedom and toleration, and in the more logically developed cases, separation of church and state.

Such processes of differentiation, however, have been deeply grounded in the structure of predominantly Christian societies, with either Establishment constitutions or pluralistic ones, and doubtless further steps of differentiation are likely to occur, some of which will be suggested below. Hence we cannot accept Durkheim's identification of the societal moral community with a church. Bellah, however, has still been able to show, most clearly for the American case, that these differentiations are by no means incompatible with the societal community at the same time being secular and yet having a religious aspect. In that sense, of course, Durkheim was right. [...]

The Concept of Secularization

The main Durkheimian position, however, sharply raises the question of the meaning of the concept of secularization about which something needs to be said before returning to the problems of belief, unbelief, and disbelief in the current socio-cultural situation.

In this commentary and for many years, the general view which I have been espousing is that, in the socio-cultural sphere, and indeed also the psychological, what has come generally to be called "religion" stands at the highest level in the cybernetic hierarchy of the forces which, in the sense of defining the general directionality of human action among the possible alternatives permitted in the human condition, controls the processes of human action.[9] This is a view obviously shared with Max Weber, but also I think by Durkheim and Freud, though Freud has been widely interpreted to hold directly contrary views.

The question of secularization should be approached on this background. The term clearly refers, even etymologically, to concern with the world by contrast with the transcendent. It is clearly its claim to some kind of contact with the transcendent which is the hallmark of religion, whether the contact be conceived or felt as "knowledge of," as some noncognitive "experience of" or as being instrumental to the "will of" some transcendent entity. One suspects that all of these components, and probably others, are involved in an authentic religion, though in different combinations in different religions. It is in the nature of the case that there should, if the concept of transcendence is meaningful at all, be a sense of tension between the transcendent referent and the worldly. But just as there are various ways of experiencing or having contact with the transcendent, it is also true that the world is not to be conceived as a constant given entity, the properties of which are in no sense a function of human action and history.

If there is a generic meaning of the concept secularization it is probably a change, in this area of inherent tension, in the direction of a closer relation of the one to the other. The concept has, in the Western world and especially in religious circles, been widely interpreted to mean a one-way change, namely the sacrifice of religious claims, obligations and commitments, in favor of secular interests. The other possibility, however, should not be forgotten, namely that the secular order may change in the direction of closer approximation of the normative models provided by a religion, or by religion more generally. The tension seems to have been particularly pronounced in the Judeo-Christian religious tradition, or at least has been defined in ways familiar to most of us there. On the one hand, we have the conception of man as irrevocably sunk in "sin and death," whereas on the other hand we have the conception of man as created "in the image of God" and hence as the "lord of the Creation." Indeed the very center of the constitutive symbolism of Christianity would be meaningless without this duality – to put it in one way, if man were totally "lost" why should God make his "only begotten son" a *man* of flesh and blood in order to make human salvation possible?[10]

It was Weber, perhaps more than any other recent Western mind, who seriously began to explore the possibility that the second alternative should be taken seriously, namely of change in the world in the direction of institutionalization of religious values, though of course Troeltsch, in his conception of Christian Society, also moved in that direction about the same time, and they both had many antecedents. Put in sociological terminology, there is the possibility that religious values should come to be institutionalized, by which we mean that such values come to be the focus of the definition of the situation for the conduct of members of secular societies, precisely in their secular roles. The processes by which this occurs are highly complex and would require an elaborate treatise to analyze at all fully. That it has in fact happened, however, seems to be indisputable. When it happens, however, tensions do not disappear, but come to be restructured; the world as such is in its very nature *never* the transcendently defined ideal.[11]

The Institutionalization of Religious Values

It is by this path that a society – and in different ways its various subsectors – comes to be a moral community in Durkheim's sense, and hence acquires religious significance so that at least some of its institutions are, within certain limits of course, sacred things in the quite literal sense. If this is the case, then the totally concrete dichotomy between sacred and profane entities, transcendentally meaningful and worldly, becomes untenable. A particular human society, in different aspects, is both sacred and profane, both an embodiment (to use a specifically Christian image) of the transcendent and part of the secular world.

There is another of Durkheim's fundamental contributions the understanding of which is essential to our analysis. This lies in the implication of his decision to devote his basic analysis of religion and society to the case of the most primitive religion, as well as society, about which he thought there was adequate record, namely that of the Australian Aborigines. The fundamental contention is that there is no human society without religion. The two are concretely, though not analytically, indivisible. It follows that both the religious and the secular parts of the complex are involved in a process of evolution and that this process always involves interdependence between them – and human personality as well.[12]

It is, I think, fully established that one major aspect of any process which can be called evolutionary is differentiation. In the course of such processes it is to be expected that both the religious and the secular aspects of both cultural and social systems should undergo differentiation within themselves and that there should be processes of differentiation between them. It is in this frame of reference that I should like to see the two-way aspects of what is frequently called the "process of secularization."

Where we of the Judeo-Christian tradition now stand on these matters is perhaps best made clear in terms of an exceedingly schematic sketch of the main historical stages by which we have arrived where we are.[13] First, the early Christian Church became differentiated, not only from the people of Israel, but from the society of the Roman Empire. The latter was defined as pagan, the former perhaps as sacred, but in a kind of a "quasi" sense. The great structural innovation, however, was the establishment of the Church as a religious association of individuals. In the early period, of course, in part buoyed by eschatological expectations, the church remained as aloof from both the Jewish community and Roman society as possible.

With the process of proselytization, however, this aloofness became decreasingly feasible. The process of growth ended with a dual change, namely first the acceptance of Christianity as the official religion of the Roman Empire and, within the Church itself, the differentiation between the religious orders and the laity (see Paolo Tufari, forthcoming Ph.D. dissertation, Harvard University). This development set the stage for the Catholic pattern which culminated in the Middle Ages. Another major development was the split between Eastern and Western churches, connected with the decline of the Western Empire. Our concern will be with the development of the West under the jurisdiction of the Roman papacy.

The medieval system, theologically defined above all by St. Thomas, interlarded, in ideal conception, a stratified church-state system – an internally stratified secular society (state in the medieval sense) and an internally stratified Church. In terms of the religious values the Church was clearly higher than the state. It was the field for the implementation of spiritual as distinguished from temporal commitments. But the significant new element, by contrast with the early Church, was the inclusion of the secular society, the state, as temporal arm in a Christian collective system. The layman then inherently came to play a dual role. He was a member of the church conceived as the "Body of Christ" but at the same time he was a member of the secular social order. To mediate between them there developed the secular priesthood, precisely as distinguished from the religious orders. The former were implementing the Mission of Christ at one level down, as it were, in that they were both consecrated and members of the secular community, indeed its spiritual leaders.

This meant the basic moral and spiritual upgrading of secular society, on a basis which justified Troeltsch in calling it a "Christian Society," a designation which no Christian would have applied to the Roman Empire in the time before it became "Holy." At the same time the hierarchy relative to spiritual values was preserved in institutional structure at three levels. First, the priority, not in power but in legitimacy, of church over state. Second, within the church, in the priority of the still aloof religious orders over, not only the laity, but the mediating secular clergy. Third was the priority of the aristocracy, to which the medieval system certainly gave a fundamental moral sanction, over the common people. This sanction was predicated on the presumption of higher levels of spiritual and moral commitment on the part of aristocracies as compared with the populace.

This inclusion of secular society in the religiously legitimated system could not occur without profound theological changes from the early Fathers. It was Thomas who brought these to a culmination with the conception of a stratified Christian Order, in which spiritual and temporal, divine and human, Church and state were interlarded. The crucial point, however, was the religious legitimation of the secular order in a sense which could not be asserted of the early Christian view of pagan society. It was on this basis that medieval society could, in Durkheim's sense, be considered to constitute for Christians a "moral community" by virtue of its institutionalization of the sacred order.

From the Reformation to Ecumenicism

Grandly architectonic as it was, the medieval system proved not to be stable. The great crisis at the level of constitutive symbolism, and hence of belief, came with the Reformation. Whatever the causal factors leading up to it, Luther and other Reformers launched a fundamental attack on the Thomistic system. The crux of it of course concerned the status of the Church, especially through the sacramental system, as the machinery of salvation, and with it the status of the priesthood. The sacraments came to be by-passed by the direct relation of the individual believer to God through faith. The true church then became the invisible church of the faithful in communion with God, with no spiritual necessity for intermediary structures. The clergy then became spiritual guides and teachers but were deprived of the "power of the keys."

The reaction of the Church of course was to outlaw the Reformers as heretics and to assert the integrity of the "catholic" system more militantly than ever in what is usually called the counter-Reformation. The full reestablishment of the older system was widely considered to be the sole condition on which Western Christendom could be viable. On the other side, the more radical Reformers maintained that the total destruction of Catholicism was equally essential from their point of view (some of my ancestors were in this category). Neither position, however, prevailed, but rather a quite different one. Many will still call it a dishonorable compromise, but I suggest another interpretation.

The first stage, signalized by the Peace of Westphalia, seemed to be one of resignation dictated by sheer exhaustion from the terrible costs of the Wars of Religion. But the formula *cuius regio, eius religio*, proved not only to be a formula of truce but also the beginning of consolidation and extension of a new process of differentiation and attendant related changes in the Western socio-religious system. First the coexistence within the same system of both Protestant and Catholic Principalities meant that there were common interests, for example, in maintaining peace or in promoting political alliances, which cut across the religious line. In the longer run, the effect of this was to confirm the differentiation between religious and secular collectivities by dissociating secular political interests from religious affiliation – as, for example, in the eighteenth-century political alliance between the France of Richelieu and the Prussia of Frederick the Great. It was not a terribly long step from there to the conception of the legitimacy of a pluralistic religious constitution internal to the principality, a step first taken in Holland and England after the Reformation. This of course is the origin of the system of denominational pluralism within the politically organized society, and hence of the differentiation between churches as primarily religious bodies and the moral community in Durkheim's sense, which is also in the civic sense a religious entity.

Eventually, through many conflicts and struggles, Protestantism and Catholicism have come to constitute differentiated sectors of the same ecumenical religious community. The inclusion of Jews in such a community was, again, not a very long step. There is a parallel with the growing tolerance, in democratic polities, of differing political parties, where choice among alternative party affiliations does not jeopardize the individual's status as a loyal citizen.

With this change in the underlying structure, gradually the definition of each of the plural denominational groups began to attenuate their initial tendency to define each other's members radically as disbelievers and often as heretics. Only in our own time, however, has the ecumenical movement reached the point where a new position is being widely institutionalized or approaching that status, namely where the individual is held to have a right to the religious adherence, including beliefs, of his own choice and, whatever the element of stratification in the religious system, that right includes recognition of the religious legitimacy of the adherents of other faiths. The great steps of our time have, of course, been those taken by the Roman Church with the Papacy of John XXIII and Vatican Council II, which he called into being.[14]

It is not, I think, too much to say that ecumenicism, however incomplete and, indeed, in certain respects precarious its institutionalization still is, represents a stage where belief can clearly no longer be assessed in terms of cognitive or nonrational (or both) commitment to one religious collectivity at the Church level. The contemporary Catholic, Protestant, or Jew may, with variations within his own broader faith, even for Catholics, be a believer in the wider societal moral community. This level he does not share in regard to specifics with those of other faiths. He has, however, as I have put it, come to respect the religious legitimacy of these other faiths. The test of this legitimacy is that he and the adherents of these other faiths recognize that they can belong in the same moral community – which may be a predominantly secular, politically organized society – and that this common belongingness means sharing a religious orientation at the level of civil religion. Hence we must speak of at least three references of the concept of believer, namely (1) full adherent of an established denominational religious body, usually though not always called a church; (2) the status of an adherent of another such denominational body (from the point of view of believers in (1) those in category (2) are clearly disbelievers, or at least unbelievers); (3) common membership in a moral community which is characterized by a civil religion. In this context members of both categories (1) and (2) can in common be believers.

The Enlightenment and Radical Secularism

Clearly, however, the complications do not stop here. As early as the seventeenth century, thought about man and society began to appear which purported to be wholly secular, repudiating the entire religious tradition. Perhaps the earliest representative of the highest intellectual stature was Thomas Hobbes, who was an especially thoroughgoing materialist. This movement of secular thought gathered force and came to play a highly salient role in the Enlightenment of the eighteenth century, then underwent still further developments in the Positivism, especially of the nineteenth century, which are still reverberating.

This movement tended to repudiate traditional religion, Catholic, Protestant, or Jewish, specifically from the point of view of the status of the cognitive component of religious belief systems. Over part of the world of cultural sensitivity in the West, this movement led to a genuine polarization, perhaps most prominent in the secular anticlericalism which has been so prevalent in many predominantly Catholic countries.[15]

Positivism, of course, purported to make of empirical science the only valid mode of cognition accessible to man at all. Starting as early as Rousseau and certainly conspicuously with Comte and somewhat later Marx, though the belief component in the cognitive sense was purportedly held to the level of science, the commitments to action which were so prominent in these movements certainly came to include noncognitive components, as perhaps most vividly obvious in the connection of these rationalisms with the Romantic movement.

It is perhaps safe to say that a purely secular, positivistic counter-system to traditional Western religion reached a kind of apogee in the nineteenth century and then began to break down in a sense parallel to that in which the Protestant counter-system to Catholicism has broken down into ecumenicism, a process which of course required major modifications in the earlier Catholic system itself.[16]

Within the positivistic system, clearly the major modification is the abandonment of the closed materialistic determinism which was so prominent in intellectual circles over a long period, perhaps culminating in the later nineteenth century. The alternative could not, however, be philosophical idealism of the Hegelian variety, nor an idealism too closely Kantian. Many other participants in the conference are far more competent than I to assess the significance of a wide variety of these philosophical movements. Let me only say that for me personally, from the philosophical side, a particularly important figure was A. N. Whitehead.

The positivistic systems, to an important degree in the very process of trans-cending their scientism, reintroduced, in modified form, both nonempirical cognitive components and nonrational components into the picture. On the cognitive-rational side what was important was the reintroduction of compon-ents which are, to say the least, exceedingly difficult to treat as purely empirical. Perhaps the most conspicuous example is the dialectic of history of the Marxian system, which is a kind of restatement in secular-rationalistic terms of the Christian eschatological myth that, after the expulsion from Paradise (primitive communism), there have been many agonies of subjection to the sinful powers – both feudalism and capitalism – but that finally the, this time, *collective* savior, the proletariat, is born in the humblest of circumstances and mediates between the contemporary man and his sinful past, history, and is destined to bring about the imminent "second coming," the state of communism.

This intellectual (or symbolic) construction has occasioned problems of validation and indeed interpretation which are in important respects parallel to those confronted by the theologians of the Christian Church. It was suggested above that the early Church was confronted with not only one but two foils, namely, the historic, and clearly to it, sacred socio-religious community of the people of Israel, and the world of the gentiles, namely the rest of the population of the Roman Empire. Perhaps it is not too fantastic to suggest that the secular religion movement, culminating in Marxism, has faced, on the one hand, the partly "sacred" religio-moral community of capitalism, from which it has felt a special urgency to differentiate itself, but beyond that a much diffuser "pagan" world, namely that of the underdeveloped societies. Perhaps Moscow has become the "Rome" of one part of the new system, very clearly differentiated from the "Palestine" which might include the Rhineland, Paris, London, and New York.

In this context, however, events seem to have moved much faster than in the earlier developments. If the socialist movement was a kind of functional equival-ent of the Reformation, in certain respects sanctifying the secular social world, then the ecumenical phase seems to have begun to develop with surprising rapidity. These conflicts and tensions are much farther from being resolved than are those having to do with Catholic-Protestant relations, or those of both Judaism and Jewry – though in the latter connection it should not be forgotten how recent the demise of Nazism is. Nevertheless the current differ-ence in the Catholic case, especially since John XXIII, from the many pro-nouncements especially of Pius XII about "atheistic Communism," parallels in secular society the attentuation on the part of American political spokesmen of the not-so-distant past, of the virulent "cold war" ideological confrontation, the accusation, from the capitalist side that there is a communist conspiracy to conquer the world.

It may seem farfetched to set up the Communist movement, as the most politically effective outgrowth of Marxian theory and the socialist political movement, as a kind of culmination of the conception of the ideal of the totally secular socio-cultural order. I think, however, that this view is defensible. Mak-ing allowances for the relevant differences in the stage of evolution of the Western system, the Communist societies are very closely comparable to those dominated by strict Calvinism, especially Calvin's own Geneva, John Knox' Scotland for a brief period, the apogee of Cromwell's ascendancy in England, and very early New England. The difference has not lain in the basic pattern, but in the level of secularity of the system idealized and subjected to drastic controls.

The new religio-secular ecumenicism is not, however, grounded only, or even mainly, in the intellectual confrontation between Christian theology, and Marxism, or other secularist, theory, but also in the emergence of emphasis on essentially noncognitive components. Perhaps because of my special intellectual standard, it seems to me – and I am happily in agreement with Bellah on this – that the especially important intellectual mediators have been Freud, Durkheim, and in somewhat different ways, Marx Weber.

As I have already noted, the decisive factor was the emergence of the conception of the moral component, both in the structure of societies and in the personality and motivation of the individual. For Weber, it was exemplified above all by the internalization and institutionalization of the concept of the calling in ascetic Protestantism, and with it the new level of sanctification of secular callings. For Freud it centered on the concept of the superego and its intimate involvement with the unconscious. It was Durkheim, however, who most clearly and definitely saw and characterized the moral aspect of society, both as seen by its members as object, and as defining their orientations as participants. This, combined with Durkheim's conception of religious evolution, opened the door, as we have seen, to Bellah's fruitful conception of civil religion.[17]

This seems to me to be the main path by which what are often called "secular humanists" have been brought into the moral community of modern society, including the religious implications of its existence as such a community. Both the separation of church and state in the American tradition, and the inclusion of a lay component in full citizenship in continental Europe, seem to me to imply this. Many of these secularists never had any connection with Marxism; I have concentrated on Marxism because it is the most salient grand-scale anti-religious (in the traditional sense) movement.

In terms of the paradigm of contexts of belief and unbelief outlined above for the ecumenical process of inclusion, one can say that secular humanists in this sense are not even believers in the "faith of their own choice." At the level of the moral community and civic religion, however, they must be accorded the status of believers. At this level it may be suggested that disbelievers are the revolutionaries who basically challenge the moral legitimacy of modern societal communities, and commit themselves to their overthrow, and unbelievers those who, though not actively combating such communities, are alienated from them and seek to minimize participation.

From the point of view of the traditional Western religions, the most important epithet aimed in this direction has been "atheism." It is now relatively commonplace that preoccupation with this issue is at least partly an expression of Judeo-Christian religious parochialism since other advanced religions, notably Buddhism, have been said to be atheistic, but of course nonetheless religions for that reason. This, however, seems to be too simple an argument in the present context. A much more important point is the emergence, as defined explicitly as such, of the "civil religions" – the American is clearly one variant in a wider complex.

This is the result of a process of inclusion directly parallel to that sketched above in relation to ecumenism. Durkheim's equation is here, as we have noted, decisive. Those who recognize and participate in a moral community may or may not, according to matters of definition, constitute a church, but they must share in what in some sense is a common religion. Conversely, those who share what can properly be called a religion must to some extent and in some respects, constitute a moral community.

 The crucial point is that, in the development of modern societies and cultures, memberships have come to be pluralistic. There is not one moral community which is an undifferentiated unity after the manner of Rousseau, nor is there one true religion outside of which nonparticipants, or disbelievers, are cast into the "outer darkness." In its secular version Rousseauism led to exclusive nationalism and the Terror; in the religious versions, counter-Reformation Catholicism to the Inquisition, Calvinism to the execution of Servetus, and Communism to the great purges of Stalin's time.

Of course in this process it is highly significant that the great mediators, the three we have named (Freud, Durkheim, and Weber) and doubtless others, were neither believers in the traditional denominational senses, nor "principled atheists." Their roles have been more closely analogous to those of an Erasmus, a John Locke, a Thomas Jefferson, a Tocqueville, and indeed, if we stretch a point, a John XXIII.

The mediation process by which old dichotomous polarities have come to be mitigated, and new inclusions facilitated, in general has not only promoted new integrations, but has also opened new possibilities, which from many points of view have constituted versions of Pandora's box. From the medieval point of view, the Reformation did this, and from that of even relatively ecumenical Christianity, the Enlightenment did it again.

The New Resurgence of the Nonrational

With all the salience in these previous phases of problems of the nonrational, notably in the case of faith in the Lutheran sense, and of both personality needs and collective urgencies in such fields as nationalism and other forms of community, the main line of Western religio-social restructuring has centered on the cognitive component of religious commitment or "belief in...."

The new phenomenon in the present generation [...] seems to me to be the emergence, perhaps for the first time in a comparable way since the early Christians before the Alexandrian Fathers, of the nature and significance of the nonrational components of religious systems and all their complex relations to the secular world.

There have, of course, been many outbreaks of the nonrational in Western religious history, such as perhaps the Children's Crusade, the Waldensian disturbances, and the Anabaptist outbreak in the early Reformation. There is, however, a sense in which the extension of the differentiation and inclusion process which we have been outlining, to the "sanctification" of a whole series of levels and aspects of secular society, starting with that of "worldly callings" in Weber's sense, has now reached something approximating an end of the line. There is indeed now a sense in which church religion has come to be largely privatized, but concomitantly religious or quasi-religious significance generalized to an immense range of what previously were defined as more or less purely secular concerns, such for example as racial equality and the elimination of poverty.

A particularly good indication of this end-of-the-line situation from the religious point of view is the fact that what, in its terms, has for nearly two centuries been defined as the most subversive cultural movement, namely materialistic rationalism, now seems to be in course of being brought "into the fold." Furthermore, from the societal point of view, perhaps it can be said that we are witnessing the last throes of the disappearing institutional legitimacy of aristocracy; the demand for inclusion of all human classes on a basis of some kind of fundamental equality has become irresistible.

From the point of view of the conventional criteria of progress, in spite of the turbulent vicissitudes of recent times, and the very present threats of engulfment by the Nazis, of victory of the Communist conspiracy or of mutual destruction in nuclear war, the story has been on the whole still one of progress, namely higher levels of welfare, of education, of health and longevity, of access, for the previously disadvantaged classes, to the good things previously monopolized by the privileged.

For partisans of the new movements of dissent and revolt, the refusal to be impressed by these achievements of modern society and the tendency to declare the latter to be basically corrupt indicates that the tensions underlying the current cleavages have taken a qualitatively new turn.[18] Far deeper than this, however, lies the problem of what in some sense is legitimacy. The questions are becoming such as "If now we have unprecedented facilities for attaining whatever goals are desired, how will the relevant goals be defined?" and second, "Among the goals professed in a liberal society, by what processes and criteria will priorities among them be set?"

The conflict over legitimacy, however, does not rage most fiercely over the failures of modern society with respect to these more or less classic problems of social justice – with perhaps the critical exception of commitment to the elimination of war, which I think has progressed considerably in recent decades. They come to focus, rather, on the legitimacy of areas of expressiveness in behavior, one major aspect of which, on the historic background, is a new permissiveness, in areas where highly restrictive codes have been institutionalized for many centuries.

In attempting to designate this focus we immediately run into terminological difficulties of the kind noted above. Probably the most widely acceptable term for the main thrust of the new striving for liberation is for affective concerns. These run all the way from the grossest levels of eroticism, and indeed aggression, to the most highly sublimated levels of love. Here, however, the critical thing is to remember that on the nonrational as well as the rational side of the action paradigm we have set forth, there is a dual, not a unitary reference. Only in one respect is everything expressive the same, namely by contrast with the nonexpressive.

We can then presume that, within the expressive rubric which is contrasted with the rationalism of the modern establishment, there is involved a charismatic component in Weber's sense, as well as permissiveness for the expression of nonrational motivational components. In Freud's terms, there may be superego as well as id components.

The New Religion of Secular Love

The current new movements, of the "Christening" of which Bellah so eloquently spoke, seem to have one very important kind of relation to early Christianity, namely their immense concern with the theme of love. So far as I can see, however, there are two especially prominent differences from the early Christian case, directly in this connection, and certain others on its boundaries.

First, the source of inspiration of reorientation is not seen in the same kind of theistic terms which linked Christianity with Judaism. In this connection probably another phenomenon of ecumenicism is important, namely, the increasing interest in and acceptance of the legitimacy of non-Western religions, notably those of the Hindu–Buddhist complex. It is of course well known that these have had a particularly strong appeal, often in seriously garbled form, in socially and culturally radical circles.[19]

Probably, however, the most important motivation for an avoidance of theism concerns the desire to emphasize the this-wordly location of the valued objects and interests. From one point of view, then, the new movement may be a kind of culmination of the trend of secularization we have traced which has sanctified, by inclusion, and moral upgrading component after component of what originally was conceived to be the world by contrast with the spiritual order.[20] If, as Weber stressed, the order of secular work could be so sanctified, why not the order of human love? The immediacy of this orientation pattern, however, is too oblivious to the need for a transcendent anchorage which must somehow include both affectively adequate symbolizations and some elements of cognitive belief. So far the dominant tone seems to be the repudiation of the inherited symbols and beliefs, but that may well prove to be temporary.

The second central feature which is different from early Christianity is closely related. It is that the community of love is not felt to be properly defined as a separated entity concerned primarily with the afterworld (a *Heilsanstalt*, as Weber called it) but as an integral part of human society in the here and now. It is set apart only by the conflict between such movements, vague and relatively unorganized as they have been, and those elements of society which resist them and are unsympathetic to them. There is no clear equivalent of the Christian church's self-definition as separate and apart by virtue of its transcendental mission.

Though, as suggested, even expressive symbolization, to say nothing of belief systems, is still incipient, probably the master symbol has become that of community, that is, of secular collectivities in the organization and solidarity of which the dominant theme is the mutual love of the members. In the more radical versions, the ideal is that not only the national level of societies, but world society should become one vast concrete community of love. It seems to follow, to what Pareto called the "logic of the sentiments," that any other motivations and mechanisms of social control are inherently immoral and should not be accepted on any terms. This obviously is a Utopian ideal, certainly in Mannheim's sense, with a vengeance. It can, however, be said to be a legitimate socio-cultural descendant of Christianity.

Objectively, so far, the trial institutionalization of the new religious orientation is confined to small, more or less self-isolated groups, which in some respects resemble the conventicles of early Protestantism. Whether or when it will crystallize into an organized mass movement depends on many factors, not the least of which is leadership. In the sense in which Luther and Calvin were the major prophets of the Reformation, Rousseau of the Enlightenment, and Marx of socialism, it does not seem that a major prophet of the new religion of love has yet appeared. Perhaps, in retrospect, Gandhi will appear as a kind of John the Baptist.

Moral Absolutism, Eroticism, and Aggression

The above two characteristics of the new, presumptively religious ferment help to explain, if their designation is correct, three aspects of the fermenting mix which are disturbing to those who are not themselves caught up in the ferment, but who are more disposed to be sympathetic with it than to condemn it out of hand. These are its tendency to moral absolutism, to forthright, indeed flamboyant eroticism, and to a seemingly new attitude of permissiveness toward or even legitimation of aggression and violence which seems difficult to reconcile with the stress on love.

The key to understanding these disturbing phenomena seems to me to lie in the phenomenon of regression and the understanding of it which has been attained in the last generation and more of the development of social science. The essential framework lies in the great principle of evolutionary biology, that "ontogeny repeats phylogeny," however complicated the empirical application of that principle may be. In terms closer to our own, the process of differentiation and its related processes are critical to the evolution of human action systems, including their cultural, social, and personality and organic subsystems.

Regression then means that under pressure, a system will revert to patterns which have been dominant and appropriate in earlier stages of its development. Perhaps the most graphic demonstrations of the phenomenon have been provided in the field of psychopathology, especially through the insights of Freud. Fixation on and at particular levels of regression is the primary hallmark of psychopathological states, but the recognition and understanding of such fixations is the starting point of successful therapy. Therapy in turn is the first cousin of creativity. New creative developments in the personality or the cultural or social system are overwhelmingly associated with phases of regression.[21]

Throughout this paper I have stressed the importance of the moral aspect of the interface between the transcendental and the worldly references of the human condition, between religious commitments and coping with the given situation of action. What I here call moral absolutism is the product of dedifferentiation of the inherently pluralistic moral complexity of evolutionarily advanced social and cultural systems, to the point of fixation on what seems, under stress, to be the one essential moral commitment which not only must outrank others in a priority scale, but to which all others must unequivocally be subordinated, as presumptively the only way in which the treasured central value can be asserted and protected against abandonment.

The phenomenon itself is of course by no means new. It in fact, characterizes charismatic movements rather generally, including early Christianity itself, the Reformation, Jacobinism, and Communist socialism. It is clear, however, that it generates severe conflicts in the course of developmental processes of the sort we have been analyzing, because of its incompatibility with the moral bases of structural pluralism. It challenges the legitimacy of the moral commitments of all elements in the system which will not give the demanded priority to the one absolutized value and hence escalates the conflict to the level of a value-conflict, which can be much more serious than the usual conflict of interests. Proverbially, religious wars are particularly bitterly fought.

This circumstance, combined with the centrality of the valuation of love in the new movement, helps to make understandable the complex set of relations among love and the erotic on the one hand, aggression and violence on the other. The involvement of religion with erotic themes is of course as old as the history of religion itself. Modern psychology and sociology, however, have made it possible to gain better analytic insight into the reasons for this interrelation than have previously been available. One such insight concerns the continuities between the erotic component in child care and its functions for socialization of the child, with the nature and function of genital eroticism for the adults.

In one sense the primordial solidarity is that between mother and child – as beautifully symbolized in the Renaissance Madonna theme. This is at the same time ideally a relation of mutual erotic gratification and of love. This critical feature is repeated at the adult level. There are many variants as a function of variations of kinship systems. The modern isolated nuclear family, however, precisely because in this case the family is highly differentiated from components of social structure with other functions, presents a particularly concentrated case of the relationship. Here, especially as analyzed by the social anthropologist David M. Schneider,[22] it becomes clear that sexual intercourse between spouses has become the primary cultural symbol of what Schneider calls their "diffuse enduring solidarity," which may well be translated as love, and not only as between themselves, but in their sharing of mutual responsibility for their children since they constitute the senior component in the family.

The incest taboo has an important bearing here, in that it draws a sharp line between the erotic relations of the married couple and, after early childhood, the prohibition of such relations between parents and children and between siblings.

I should postulate that love in a nonerotic sense must be the core concern of a religious movement in the sense suggested above. There is, however, at the same time the deeply rooted relation between eroticism and love, which in an important sense is a major bridge from organism to personality. Under the kinds of pressure which have been discussed, I should argue that there is a strong tendency to regression, in precisely the above sense, from the level of sublimated love, as Freud would have put it, to that of erotic attachment, and indeed a tendency to absolutize the significance of erotic experience. Especially as it occurs between two persons – autoeroticism is something else – it can seem to be almost the ultimate in genuine solidarity.

There are, however, two problems about a primarily erotic basis of the wider solidarities which, if we are to believe Durkheim, religions must involve. One concerns the regressive relations of the erotic complex in its significance for individual personality development. To give too great primacy to erotic relations in this sense is to skate on the edge of acting as a child and treating partners as children. The binding-in of the erotic component of motivation to adult capabilities and responsibilities is clearly a major function of the incest taboo.

The second problem derives from the fact that mutual erotic solidarity is bound to intimate bodily contact, by far most fully expressible in the diadic relation. Though group sex has certain attractions, its serving as a primary symbolization, even, of wider solidarities seems to be severely limited. Putting it simply, the wider the circle of erotic relations and the more casual that to any particular partner, the less is it possible for erotic experience to symbolize diffuse enduring solidarity. A full, culturally generalized language of love must be couched in terms of other media. Such languages have, by and large, been predominantly religious rather than carnal.

It seems to me that early Christianity solved the problem by drawing a very sharp line between religiously significant love and carnal appetites. The Pauline dictum "it is better to marry than to burn" was not exactly a glorification of conjugal love. The religious orders then, on their emergence, adopted full celibacy as a matter of principle and this was later extended to the secular priesthood.

Luther's marriage, however, in violation of his monastic vows and, significantly, to a former nun, was a symbolic act of new legitimation of the erotic complex and could not very well be interpreted, in the morally rigorous climate of early Protestantism, as simply "surrendering to the flesh." The fact that the institution of a married clergy was universalized in all branches of Protestantism is of course critical.

Various of the movements which led to the institutionalization of new sectors of religiously legitimate secular society have been accompanied by movements toward sexual liberation. This was true of the French revolution and also of the socialist movement. But where political freedoms and release from economic exploitation are felt to be the main stakes, neither love nor eroticism is likely to be central. In the current situation, however, I suggest that the institutionalization of love at some level of community has become central, and that regressive pressures operate strongly toward the erotic emphasis. These emphases, however, I also suggest, lead to unstable states because unsublimated erotic motivations do not form a sufficiently firm and generalized basis for solid attachments to ground a religiously legitimate and viable network of units and of moral community – remembering always that modern community must be pluralistic.

The early Christian pattern of radical segregation between love and the erotic component thus seems not to be viable nor, I should venture to say, even legitimate in the modern situation. At the very least the erotic relation of husband and wife, independently of the procreative function, must be legitimized, or it cannot function, in Schneider's phrase, as a primary symbol of diffuse enduring solidarity. What extensions beyond the conjugal relation may come to be legitimized I may perhaps be pardoned for not entering into here, not only because of the delicacy of the issues, but because this is already perhaps an overly long concluding paper. I do, however, think that there will be others.

The deepest reason why the early Christian pattern is not acceptable now, I hope has been made clear. This is that the new religious movement, which I feel will almost certainly prove to be largely Christian, cannot define itself as a separated collectivity outside of what has been called secular society, but must be defined as an integral part of the latter which hopes to permeate its moral and spiritual qualities. Not only the love component – which is not the same as the moral – of solidarities, but the erotic component, is too deeply intertwined in the texture of society, especially at the level of the interpersonal intimate relations which are coming to be so highly valued, for it to be extirpated. If, indeed, this extirpation were possible, which I doubt short of major convulsions, the price would be the postponement of any new community of love, probably for many centuries.

Finally, perhaps these considerations throw at least a little light on what to many of us seems to be the most irrational aspect of the new movements, namely the resurgence of aggression and violence. Important as these may be, a very large part of it seems to go beyond natural resentment or anger at being unjustly discriminated against, exploited, subordinated to dubiously legitimate authority, blocked in pursuing legitimate goals, or simply not listened to. In making any such judgment of overdetermination it is of course essential to bear in mind that when we speak of the aggression and violence of the proponents of the new presumptively religious groups, they do not stand alone. There is also aggression and violence in other quarters, and there is little hope of disentangling who is guilty of aggression and who is understandably reacting aggressively.

Psychodynamically by now the interconnections between love and hate have become familiar. In one aspect they are the positive and negative sides, respectively, of the bonds of emotional significance of objects, in Freud's term of cathexis. As Freud put it, cathexis means an investment in relation to other persons – or groups as such – in social interaction, and failure of positive reciprocity can readily flip over into negativity, that is, hostility, hate, and aggression. The bitterness of family quarrels attests to this – far from it proving that the members do not in some sense love one another it is evidence that they do.

From this it seems to follow that he who makes a special commitment to love, by that very fact becomes especially vulnerable to hatred, where his expectations of reciprocation are frustrated. It takes an especially elevated level of love to transcend this dilemma, one which Christianity did in fact attain, but never succeeded in fully institutionalizing – it was most poignantly put in the injunction "love thine enemies."

Again, there is an enormous difference from early Christianity deriving from the fact that the current movements are so integrally involved with the affairs of secular society. When combined with moral absolutism, as it very generally is, the love-orientation disposes its proponents to aspire to political effectiveness, that is to power, which necessarily means coping with opposition at many levels. Where resort to violence, or confrontation, seems effective, the temptation is enormous. But in addition to the temptation of tactical effectiveness there is the emotional seduction. If you can convincingly think of your opponent as really wicked he must deserve to be hated, not loved – and isn't the mere fact of his opposition almost sufficient proof of his wickedness?

In a situation where political stakes were very high, Gandhi's nonviolent resistance movement achieved remarkable discipline in maintaining nonviolence, but when the British finally left India, there were disastrously violent clashes between Hindus and Muslims with many thousands killed. Perhaps one can suggest that in nonviolent movements aggression in the motivational sense is by no means generally absent. If the discipline of nonviolence is impaired, the aggressive component may easily break through into violent action and, short of that, of course verbal abuse and humiliation of opponents and the like may figure very prominently.

If, as many of us feel, there is enormous creative potential in the emerging religion of love, the danger of lapsing into aggression and violence, along with that of moral absolutism, which are of course related to each other, seem to me more serious than the danger of regression into eroticism – or the related retreat into dependence on drugs. The point about the former two is the extent to which they serve as triggers to mobilize, not only legitimate opposition, in the sense of adherence to values somewhat different from those absolutized, or of defense of rights against violence or insult, but they release the irrational affective factors which lie back of the tensions inherent in such conflict situations, factors which in general in relation to creative movements operate repressively.

I may perhaps end this discussion on a Durkheimian note. The affective-charismatic components of a religiously innovative movement are likely to be self-defeating and to lapse into some sort of antinomian anarchy if they are not somehow combined with the factors of the discipline which goes with moral order. I even venture to think that a substantial component of cognitive belief is an essential ingredient of the stabilization of religious innovation.

Conclusion

The basic structure of the belief-disbelief-unbelief problem in the contemporary phase just sketched is the same as in the earlier phases. Two differences, however, complicate the too literal reference to precedents. The first is the overwhelmingly this-worldly orientation of the new religion of love, if I may consolidate a little the use of that term. The other is the salience, indeed primacy, in the movement of the nonrational components. Here there is a temptation, on the side of the proponents, to declare that problems of belief are totally irrelevant, and of opponents, that the movement is a simple case of disbelief in a sense which implies an obligation to combat it with the utmost vigor.

Deeply rooted cultural precedents predispose many in the West to the feeling that the only truly religious love is profoundly other-worldly and must be sharply contrasted with any basis of worldly love, even though it is love of "thy neighbor." In the other context, far more than in the past, the reaction is against the rationality complex in very general terms. There is a crucial sense in which the most immediate antagonist is not the traditional organized religions, but the most secularized rationality systems, notably though perhaps ambiva-lently, Marxian socialism, but ramifying much more broadly into nonsocialist aspects of rationality, both in cultural systems and in social institutions, in the latter context, notably bureaucracy, but also clearly academic professionalism.

We have, however, argued that belief systems prominently involving cognitive components are essential ingredients in all religious systems which have a prospect of stabilization. For the principled antirationalist the construction of a viable cognitive belief system presents peculiar difficulties, which are not altogether unprecedented, but which becomes especially acute in these circum-stances. I venture to suggest, however, that certain resources essential for this task are available, at least incipiently, in some of the social science sources which have been reviewed.[23] It is interesting to note that, from the point of view of the incipient religion, these sources are predominantly secular in a sense parallel to that in which the Greek intellectual tradition was secular from the point of view of the early Christian church. Clearly Freud, Durkheim, and Weber were not prophets of the religion of love any more than the Neoplatonists were prophets of Christianity, but what they, various of their successors, and others not associated with their names have done may well prove essential to the new movement. The fact that, in a profound sense, especially the latter two understood but rejected Marxian socialism, seems to me critical in this connection.

There has been much discussion of the role of youth, especially student youth, in this movement. This is, in my opinion, indeed crucial as a kind of spearhead, but this is not the place to go into the reasons why such appeals are so attractive to the contemporary student generation on a nearly world-wide basis. Social science, in my opinion, has progressed toward making such under-standing possible.[24] It should, however, be clear that a student base is not a sufficient anchorage in the structure of societies for the institutionalization of a major religious pattern. Students remain students for only a few years, and they must face the dilemma of either relinquishing their legitimacy with relinquish-ment of student status, or extending the basis of legitimacy from the student phase to later phases in the life cycle. The slogan "Never trust anyone over thirty" is a typical "chiliastic" aphorism which manifests a sentiment but cannot be stably institutionalized.

Each additional step in secularization, in the sense of the institutionalization of Christian patterns in the secular world, which we have traced adds a new set of complications to the belief-disbelief-unbelief problem. A most important point then needs to be emphasized. When the institutional resolution, inclusion, and upgrading has in fact occurred, the older patterns do not disappear, but continue to function, though in modified form, which often means in more restricted circumstances than before. Thus to go way back, Christianity did not extirpate Judaism, but the latter is now persisting ecumenically together with a wide variety of Christian churches and sects. Protestantism did not extirpate Catholicism, nor vice versa, and they not only coexist peacefully but have become integrated into a more general religious structure. Then, very recently, I suggest, rationalistic secularism has not only failed to extirpate church religion, but has gone far toward becoming included with it as a still broader religious framework, in which all the older religious groups – with some qualifications – survive.[25]

I see no reason why the general pattern of emergence of a movement, starting in acute conflict with its most immediate predecessor in the role of institutional establishment, moving to truce in that conflict on the pattern of *cuius regio, eius religio*, then eventually to the process of resolution by inclusion and upgrading, should not be repeated in the present case, as well as those which have gone before. I am sure that we are barely entering upon the phase of acute conflict, which we can only hope will not eventuate, for the next century, in a new cycle of wars of religion which might indeed be fatal to civilization, but most particularly to the religion of love, because, however partially justified their accusation of hypocrisy against their opponents may be, they simply cannot afford to let hatred and antagonism prevail over their central orientation. This factor and, among other things its cognitive understanding, plus of course the antiaggressive components of the whole great religious tradition of the Western world, give considerable hope that the sense of conflict will not be escalated to the point of the most serious threats of mutual destruction.

I have been so bold as to suggest that the contemporary situation, in which the problem of the meaning of unbelief has become so salient, may constitute both an end, and a turning point leading into a beginning, of a major cycle of human religious development. The key connecting symbol, which may, in Bellah's sense, be interpreted realistically as well as in the framework of symbolic reductionism, is clearly love. This was certainly the keynote of the Gospels, and has become so again today. The cycle, however, is not a simple return to the beginning, but a spiral, in the course of which much has happened, which, schematically, may be called the Christianization of the world.

Though in the current turbulent stage, it must be expected that conflict, confrontation, aggression, and hatred will be exceedingly prominent on both sides, the orientational content points to a pattern of resolution, which is inherently precarious in its initial stages, but which, if it materializes, may well usher in, not paradise, for this is not given to human societies, but a new phase of religious and social progress.

However important, on the one hand, insistence by the proponents of the new on their claims, at the risk of over-reliance on moral absolutism and aggression, on the other hand by the defenders of the, after all not totally bankrupt, older values on their legitimacy – again at the risk of refusals to concede and insistence on discipline which will be interpreted as intolerably punitive – there is a basically solid foundation in Christian tradition for the resolution of these conflicts.

This frame of reference will necessarily, I think, apply on both sides of the conflict. There are, it seems to me, three main components of the essential orientation. The first is humility, in the historic Christian sense, which is inherently incompatible with moral absolutism, as the arrogation of the right to punish because the other has sinned and you are pure.[26] Note that I apply this on both sides – the proponents of love have no better moral right to punish their opponents than do those of the establishment. The second orientation may be called the sense of tragedy. Moral dichotomization into the "good guys" and the "bad guys" is proverbially unproductive. The nonrational sense, as well as the cognitive understanding, that the good are always engaged in a struggle with the evil elements within them, and that conversely the bad are always in some sense trying to overcome their evil motives, is an essential ingredient of resolution. Human history is not a morality play in which the good are rewarded and the evil punished, but a struggle for salvation, enlightenment, progress, or community in which many, indeed most, of the participants have been and are caught up in tragic conflicts and dilemmas. The third component, compassion, seems almost to follow from the importance of the first two. If we love a person – or a group or a symbol – we must at the same time understand and empathize with his difficulties and his conflicts, including those which from our point of view are destructive of our values, and still love him, not only in the sense of particularized affection, but of giving him support for the implementation of the value of universalized love.

It seems to me that this was the basic message of Pope John XXIII. It was that Christian humility, a sense of tragedy, and compassion form the essential basis for a much greater extension of the regime of love than we have ever known before.

Notes

1   The aphorism of Tertullian, "*Credo quia absurdum est,*" could not prevail in Western religion.

2   Robert Bellah, "Between Religion and Social Science," chapter 14 of R. Caporale and A. Grumelli (eds), *The Culture of Unbelief* (Berkeley: University of California Press, 1971).

3   Talcott Parsons, "The Sociology of Knowledge and the History of Ideas," in the *Dictionary of the History of Ideas* (New York: Charles Scribner's Sons, forthcoming).

4   It will be noted that Durkheim also used this term. See the introduction in Émile Durkheim, *Elementary Forms of the Religious Life*, trans. Joseph Ward Swain (New York: The Free Press, 1965; first published in French in 1912).

5   Cf. Talcott Parsons, *The Structure of Social Action* (New York: The Free Press, 1949). The distinction between the rational and nonrational components of *action* does not in any direct way concern the problem of "irrationality." Put slightly differently, the

problem of irrationality does not reside in the nature of any of the components of action, but in their combination. Rationality is in one aspect a normative category. There are rational components of action because knowledge is so essentially involved with it. But rational action or deviation from its norms is always a function of the combination of all the components, including both rational and nonrational. Irrational action, then, is the outcome of tensions and conflicts within the organization of action, in which, it is essential to note, what at the more analytical level here have been called rational and nonrational components are involved on both sides (or several) of the tensions and conflicts. The exigencies of combination will of course vary according to the types of action, and their organization in systems, which are involved.

6   For Durkheim perhaps the nearest equivalent was sentiment which appeared in his original definition of the collective conscience. See Émile Durkheim, *Division of Labor in Society,* trans. George Simpson (New York: The Free Press, 1964; first published in French in 1893, second edition with additional preface, 1902).

7   In my translation into English it reads that, a religion is "an integrated (*solidaire*) system of beliefs and practices relative to sacred things, that is separate and taboo, which unite in one moral community called a church all those who adhere to it." Talcott Parsons, *The Structure of Social Action,* p. 412.

8   Robert Bellah, "Civil Rights in America," reprinted in William McLaughlin and Robert Bellah, eds, *Religion in America* (Boston: Houghton Mifflin, 1969).

9   It should be made clear that exercise of authority or power constitutes only *one* mode of control in the present sense, and in the context of this discussion, by no means the most important mode. There is an unfortunate tendency, which is by no means justified, to equate control with dominance and coercion.

10   On the general relations of moral order and original sin see Kenneth Burke, "The First Three Chapters of Genesis," in *The Rhetoric of Religion* (Boston: Beacon Press, 1961).

11   In writing in the present context for what is, sociologically speaking, mainly, though by no means wholly, a nontechnical readership, it is difficult to know how far to go in the exposition of underlying sociological frames of reference and paradigms. In part I am being deliberately paradoxical in attributing to the concept secularization what has often been held to be its opposite, namely not the loss of commitment to religious values and the like, but the institutionalization of such values, and other components of religious orientation in evolving cultural and social systems. This latter process, with which the remainder of the present paper is primarily concerned, has often, especially perhaps in religious circles, been held to constitute secularization in the former sense, though when seen in the larger perspective this turns out to be a misinterpretation. Such misinterpretations have, however, been extremely prevalent and have appeared repeatedly at various stages of the larger process.

Secularization in the second sense constitutes a dual process, on the one hand, of the differentiation of religious components from the secular – as in certain respects was the case for the differentiation of the Christian Church from both the Jewish ethnic community and the society of the Roman Empire. Such differentiation clearly involves a diminution of the religious value of the social and cultural components from which the newly emergent religious one becomes differentiated. Thus, while Roman society was in a certain sense quasi-sacred, for Christians it came to be, for the time being, entirely deprived of this quality.

Once this process has occurred, however, the questions which are crucial to us are not resolved by the process of differentiation alone, but concern a complex sequence of sequels which are, at various stages, contingent on inherently variable factors. In a very schematic way, the following seems to be the central one: The initial process of differentiation is very generally associated with sharp antagonisms between the newly emerging complex and that from which it is coming to be differentiated – thus early Christians versus both Jews and Romans, later, Protestants versus Catholics. If, however, the conditions for a successful process of institutionalization are present – which is by no means to be taken for granted – then three further modes of change must occur, in roughly the following temporal sequence, though clearly this is by no means rigid.

1. What will later be referred to as *inclusion*. By this I mean that the older order from which the new religious movement has come to be differentiated, will regain positive religious significance and be included within a broader sacred order. The medieval synthesis is a major case – secular society, the state in the medieval sense, came to be part of the same order as that of the Christian Church and incorporated many components of both Jewish and Roman institutions, e.g., both the Old Testament and Roman Law. The modern civil religions are cases of this phenomenon.

2. *Adaptive upgrading*, by which, in this context, I mean the reevaluation of the older, previously downgraded components to constitute assets from the point of view of the broader system. In the above case, the accord of a new positive religious value to secular life, as distinguished from the view that members of the segregated orders were the only groups which were in any real sense Christian, constitutes a massive phenomenon of upgrading.

3. *Value-generalization*. If both inclusion and upgrading, as outlined, are to be legitimized, this cannot take place literally in terms of the value-orientations of the religious movement which previously declared the excluded elements to be in principle illegitimate. There must be a restructuring of the valuational base at a more general level, according to which, in our example, both religious and laity are in some sense really Christian.

12 See Robert Bellah, "Religious Evolution," reprinted in his *Beyond Belief* (New York: Harper & Row, 1970) and also my own *Societies: Evolutionary and Comparative Perspectives* (Englewood Cliffs, NJ: Prentice Hall, 1966), chapter 3, on "Primitive Societies."

13 See my article "Christianity," in David Sills, ed., *The International Encyclopedia of Social Sciences* (New York: Macmillan and the Free Press, 1968).

14 In the United States, which has played a rather special part in these developments, the new ecumenicism was very sharply symbolized by the funeral of the assassinated President John F. Kennedy in November, 1963. This was particularly significant because Kennedy was the first Roman Catholic to be elected president of the United States. Since he was a faithful Catholic, the services were conducted in the Catholic Cathedral of Washington by the "parish priest" of the Kennedy family, Cardinal Cushing of Boston. The attendants at the funeral mass, however, were persons of all faiths, starting with the new president, Lyndon Johnson, very much a Protestant. Burial, finally, was in what Bellah calls the most sacred place of the American civil religion, the Arlington National Cemetery.

An almost equally symbolic event, which I personally attended, occurred in Boston, Kennedy's home city, two months later. This was a memorial Requiem Mass, held in the Cathedral of the Holy Cross in Boston with Cardinal Cushing officiating. What was new, however, was the fact that, as part of the service itself, the Mozart Requiem was played by the Boston Symphony Orchestra, a citadel of Boston Protestant "Brahmanism." It was the first time that the Boston Symphony has, as an orchestra, ever participated in a religious service. The ecumenical character of the occasion was further emphasized by the fact that the clergy of all faiths marched in the procession and sat in the sanctuary.

15 In this connection Weber spoke, with a certain awe, of the forms of "extreme rationalistic fanaticism" which appeared in the course of the French Revolution and in various connections during the nineteenth century. He clearly felt that such fanaticism was not a simple matter of cognitive beliefs alone.

16 I am quite ready to acknowledge that the pattern of sequences outlined here closely resembles that of the Hegelian-Marxian dialectic.

17 In this respect, it has long seemed to me, Marxian theory has been notably ambivalent and vacillating. On the one hand materialism seemed to dictate a conception of the real forces of history as totally independent of any normative component. On the other hand the collective voluntarism of the social movement went far beyond extending opportunities for its members to satisfy their interests. On the contrary, it allegedly generated genuine solidarity and thereby imposed moral obligations on participants. In a sense, in between lay what Marx called the "relations of production" as distinguished from the "forces of production." The key component here was the system of legal norms, to which we may say Marxians have attributed a kind of semi- or pseudolegitimacy, as part, no doubt, of the more general semilegitimacy of capitalism as referred to above.

18 The above negative evaluation of contemporary industrial society and its dangers for community were most fully expressed in the symposium by Bryan Wilson. As the transcript shows, I took rather sharp issue with his diagnosis of the situation, and I could have said a good deal more. There is, however, no doubt about the prevalence among intellectuals of these views, and probably of their strategic importance, whatever their status by standards of sociological correctness. In terms of the argument of this paper it might be said that they have the function of defining aspects of the world which can be religiously and morally condemned, thereby facilitating the acceptance and eventually the sanctification of other worldly elements, some of which are now present, others in process of emergence, and others which will necessitate directed attempts to bring them about.

19 An interesting and important index of this new trans-Western ecumenicism is the rapid decline of interest in Christian missions, both Catholic and Protestant. In the nineteenth century and the earlier part of the present one we quite literally believed in the urgency of converting the "Heathen Chinese," as the only half satirical phrase went. Now there is probably a disposition toward romantic overevaluation of exotic religions.

A related point is that we have had a strong modern tendency toward a cynical interpretation of the past, e.g., to the effect that the Europeans involved in the exploration and exploitation of the extra-European world were motivated only by concerns for money, profit and power, especially through slavery. That there were genuine religious concerns involved is, however, clear, not only in the American mythology about the settlement of New England, but also of Virginia – cf. Perry Miller, *Errand into the Wilderness* (Cambridge: Harvard University Press, 1956). Clearly very similar things were true of Catholic, Spanish, and French settlements; they were, in substantial part, missionary enterprises.

20 With all due allowance for the basic differences, when a very central Christian aphorism is "For God so loved the world that He gave His only begotten Son...," it is perhaps understandable that mere humans should "love the world."

21 An already classical explication of this phenomenon is presented in Erik Erikson's *Young Man Luther* (New York: W. W. Norton, 1962). See also his paper, "Reflections on the Dissent of Contemporary Youth," *Daedalus*, Winter 1970.

22   David Schneider, *American Kinship: A Cultural Account* (Englewood Cliffs, NJ: Prentice Hall, 1968).

23   Robert Bellah, "Between Religion and Social Science."

24   Talcott Parsons and Gerald Platt, "Higher Education, Changing Socialization and Contemporary Student Dissent," in Matilda White Riley, et al., eds, *A Sociology of Stratification*, VIII of *Aging and Society* (New York: Russell Sage, 1972) and Erik Erikson, *Young Man Luther.*

25   Indeed, I look forward to the day when, in a Jewish, Catholic, or Protestant high ceremony like the Kennedy Memorial Mass, the Director of the Institute of Philosophy of the Soviet Academy of Sciences – a post which I interpret to be the equivalent of "Dean of the theological faculty of the religion of Marxism-Leninism" – will march in the procession and sit in the sacristy as one of the assemblage of the clergy of all faiths.

26   There are, of course, other bases of the legitimation of punishment. The arrogation referred to is a version of the Donatist heresy.

3

Religious Symbolization and Death

In this paper I attempt to describe the framework of constitutive symbolism within which death is defined in cultures with a Judeo-Christian background. One might consider such a framework to be specifically related to the concept of *definition of the situation* as this has been used in recent theorizing at the level of the general system of action. My principal reference points will be the Old Testament, especially the Book of Genesis; the Christian development in its Roman Catholic version, especially as symbolized in Renaissance art; and some further changes from that position associated first with Protestantism and then with what some authors might call a "post-Protestant" phase.

My thesis is that the primary symbolism of death is part of a larger complex of constitutive symbolism – the complex which sociologists and anthropologists have come to call that of "age and sex." It concerns meanings of the human life cycle from conception and birth through the phases of earthly "living" to death and the problem of orientation to the possibility of any meaningful "after death."

The life cycle of the individual, however, is inseparable from the problems of reproduction and the succession of generations. No human individual is isolated in this respect. Cooperation of persons of opposite sex is an essential condition of reproduction, and one aspect of the meaningfulness of death is to "make room" for the succeeding generation and those yet to follow it.

The myth of the Garden of Eden, as stated in Genesis, portrays Adam as "the Lord of the creation" who has been created by God "in His own image," where the immortality of Adam is clearly presumed. The Tree of Life standing in the center of the Garden seems to be the symbol of this immortality. It is not clear whether immortality was to be extended to other living species. I presume not, because it is said of animals, before the creation of Adam, that "male and female created He them." The necessity for both sexes at the creation itself suggests reproduction and, of course, with it the mortality of the preceding generations.

However this may be, the myth says in an extremely interesting phrase that it was "not good for Adam to be alone"; so God created Eve. Her function in the Garden was presumably that of companionship rather than reproduction.

The existence of Adam and Eve in the Garden was not only free of the limitations of mortality, but was free of all responsibility – their every want was automatically and, one presumes, instantaneously satisfied. This literal "condition of paradise" was subject, however, to one prohibitory condition – the famous commandment, "Thou shalt not eat of the fruit of the tree of the knowledge of good and evil," with its accompanying warning that, if the commandment was disobeyed, "Thou shalt surely die." Eve, so the story goes, allowed herself to be seduced by the wily serpent, and she in turn seduced Adam. The divine reaction was to expel Adam and Eve from the Garden and to impose on them not only mortality as punishment but also the two extraordinary curses – on Eve that woman should bring forth in pain and travail, and on Adam that man should subsist "by the sweat of his brow," interesting in their dual reference to childbirth and to work. The French word *travail*, usually rendered in English by "labor," has an interesting connotation, because in English the word "travail" suggests suffering in a rather strong way, even as contrasted with "labor." In other words, the "human condition" after expulsion from the garden was conceived as a condemnation to suffering and death with strongly negative valences attached to "this life."

If, however, human life was to be conceived as continuing from generation to generation, the reproductive function became essential, and the roles of Adam and Eve were no longer simply those of companions but of partners in bringing about reproduction. It seems quite clear that the sin of Adam and Eve was a dual one. In the first instance it was that of disobedience. In the Garden they were subjected to one and only one prohibition: "eating the fruit." This is what Kenneth Burke refers to as the capacity for the negative on the part of man as a symbol-using animal, but there is a further connotation beyond mere disobedience as such. In presuming immortality and "knowledge" together – knowledge of the meaning of good and evil – Adam was presuming to act as if he were God. This, I feel, is the most fundamental meaning of original sin. The imposition of death is conceived as God's crucial assertion that man may not presume to be God but must accept his mortality and all the costs of living the life of a mortal. Another common Christian phrasing is that the fundamental sin was "idolatry of the flesh."

In the continuation of the myth, the divine anger seems to have been virtually unappeased, and culminated after a long time in God's decision to destroy his own creation of living beings on the earth, including humanity. God relented, however, in the case of Noah, Noah's wife, their sons, and the sons' families, and he instructed Noah to build the Ark to save his own extended family and the famous "animals two-by-two." In this connection Noah, who from the divine perspective was the only "good man" of his generation, became the recipient of the first covenant with Yahweh. On condition of giving faith and obedience to the divine commandments, Noah and his issue not only were permitted to exist after the recession of the great flood, but became the nucleus of Yahweh's chosen people, the vicissitudes of which are well known through the stages of Abraham and the new covenant with him, the exile, Moses, and the entry after Moses' death into the Promised Land.

The fate of the individual was, in classical ancient Judaism, in a sense absorbed in that of the people of Israel. The primary religious focus was on the people, including not only its existence and vicissitudes as a corporate entity but, above all, the Law, observance of which was the divine condition of continuance in divine favor. The people of Israel constituted a kin-based ethnic group, to which the members' descent from Noah was a primary symbol of belonging. This may be one main point of entry of the symbol blood into the Judeo-Christian story. Another particularly interesting feature of the myth with regard to the Promised Land, is that it was the land of "milk and honey." Milk surely is a fundamental symbol of feminine nurturance which leads beyond the purely biological reproductive function assumed by Eve and her successors to one of nurturant solicitude for the welfare of offspring and – since all members of the people of Israel were "offspring" in this symbolic sense – for the people generally. Honey has another symbolic connotation: it is a prototype of an unproduced food substance found in nature. The availability of honey, then, is associated with the plenitude of life in the Garden of Eden; it is something good, not a human product, to be found in the natural environment. Indeed, the combination of milk and honey may be considered to be a kind of prototype symbol of material well-being in a human situation.

It is a big jump to the symbolism of the much later Christian development, but our concern is not primarily with cultural history, but with the meaning structure of a symbolic complex. There is a crucial difference between the relation of God to Adam on the one hand, to Jesus on the other. God *created* Adam, but Jesus was "his only *begotten* son." We may perhaps infer that, by the virtue of the series of covenants, God has committed himself to the continuance of the human species – particularly, but presumably not exclusively, to that of his chosen people. His intervention in the human condition, therefore, could not, as in the case of the flood and Noah, be for the purpose of continuing or destroying his creation, but it had to be intervention in the affairs of humanity as "a going concern." Mary and the myth of the Annunciation is the symbolic focus of the divine recognition that "cooperation" with humanity is essential in order to carry out the grand plan. It is in this context that the very critical symbol blood becomes central as referring to the continuity of the succession of human generation, which, of course, assumes the death of each individual person but the continuity of the population through sexual reproduction – "begetting," to use the Old Testament term. The "blood" of Jesus had therefore both a divine and a human component, the latter being the blood of Mary.

Another crucial symbolic note is sounded in the Christ story. In Judaism on the whole, though Yahweh treated the people of Israel as his chosen people, and protected them and favored them in many ways, his primary concern with respect to them was their obedience, that is, their observance of the Law he had imposed upon them. In the Christian story the new note is that of love. Perhaps the primary mythic statement is, "For God so loved the world that He gave His only begotten Son." It is noteworthy, of course, that God is said to have loved not only the people of Israel, but "the world." This surely is a fundamental anchor point for the universalistic features of Christianity.

There was a new conception of the relation between the "eternal" and temporal orders, the divine and the human, in the New Testament. Through Mary's "Immaculate Conception," the divine became human. Jesus was conceived to be both God and man at the same time. This definition of the situation fundamentally altered the Judaic conception by its potential for upgrading the status of humanity. Again, in spite of certain tendencies within Hellenistic Judaism, I think we can correctly say that Judaism was not a religion of the salvation of the individual in the sense that Christianity has been. Burke has pointed out that the idea of a redeemer is implicit in the Genesis myth, but how the role of the redeemer should be conceived, and, in particular, what the relation of this role to the fate of the people of Israel should be, remained an open question.

The redemptive event, which was the founding event of Christianity, was mythologically, we may presume, the sacrificial death of Jesus by crucifixion. It has been basic to the Christian tradition that this was a real death; it was not, as would be common in Greek mythology, the disappearance of a divine personage who had chosen to spend a certain time on earth disguised as a mortal. Jesus, that is, really died on the cross and had to be "resurrected" in order to reenter the divine sphere of eternal life.

It is of course central that the meaning of Jesus' death was symbolized as *giving* his *blood*. Blood, it seems to me, symbolizes a special combination of two things. The first is what in another connection we may speak of as the *gift* of life, which is expressed in maternity. In the Christian myth Mary was the giver of life to Jesus, a specially symbolic case of the more general conception of a woman *giving* birth to her child. In ordinary usage the word "give" has not been stressed in this expression, but I think it is symbolically crucial. The human component of the blood of Christ, therefore, was a gift from Mary, who only in more extravagant phases of Catholic symbolization has herself been considered divine. This human component, however, was combined with the divine component originating from the begetting of Jesus by his divine father. In these circumstances Jesus' own death was relativized. The concept death applied only to the human component, not to the divine. The symbol blood is the primary focus of the unity of the divine and the human. And this unity is the focus of the Christian conception of the transcending of death.

In the act of dying – which was in a very important sense voluntary on Jesus' part, since Jesus might be said to have provoked the Roman authorities into crucifying him – there was another component which has Hebrew antecedents but was profoundly modified in the Christian phase. In the symbolism of the Last Supper, which was built into the basic sacramental ritual of Christianity – the Eucharist – not only the blood of Christ but also the "body" of Christ is symbolized by the bread of the Eucharist. The body of Christ, meaning of course the risen Christ, came to be the symbol for the church conceived as a supernatural entity, which came to have the "power of the keys," the capacity to elevate the fate of the individual human being from the limitations of mortality and the other "Adamic" features of the human condition.

I do not think it is too far-fetched to suggest that the church was symbolically meant to "identify," in a sense not very different from the psychoanalytic-sociological use of the word, the ordinary human being with Christ. As a member of the church, man became part of the "body of Christ." In dying he thus became capable of *giving* his life, symbolized by blood, in a sense parallel to that in which Jesus gave his blood in the crucifixion. There seems to be a deep duality of meaning here. Death is conceived, on the one hand, to be deeply traumatic, as symbolized by the suffering on the cross – a kind of a "supreme sacrifice." At the same time, the death of the human individual is conceived not merely as paving the way for his own entrance into "heaven" but as a sacrifice for the redemptive benefit of humanity in general. Quite apart from the metaphysical problems of what can possibly be meant by "survival" of the individual after death, I think that this second view of death is a kind of a sublimation, in the positive sense, of the grimly tragic view of the human condition as defined by the consequences of Adam's original sin. By the acceptance of the divine commandments and by the acceptance of Christ as the redeemer, man is not in principle totally expelled from the Garden, to be dominated by "sin and death," but has the opportunity to participate in the divine order and not to be in the Adamic sense only human. We can say that this represents a major upgrading of the religio-metaphysical status of man.

A theme in Western religious history which I have several times emphasized is that the biblical conception of God's making man in his own image and making him Lord of the creation was later transformed into the conception of a "kingdom of God on earth." This in turn implied that human society and personality could be permeated with a divine spirit and thus in some sense narrowed the gap between the divine order of things and "the things of this world." What I have called the relativizing of the meaning of death seems to me to be a central part of this development. Every human individual's death may thus be seen as a sacrifice on the one hand, a *gift* on the other.

The human individual's capacity to die in the role of giver of gifts – most explicit in the case of a soldier or martyr who "gives his life for his country" or "for a cause" – is dependent on three other crucial gifts having preceded his. The first of these was the gift on the part of God the Father of what sometimes religiously is called the "living Christ" to humanity – given, it should be noted, through the process of "begetting." Christ, after all, was God's only begotten son. And this was a gift to humanity *from* God, not a sacrifice *to* God on the part of some human group or individual. It was, moreover, a gift said to have been motivated by "love" of the world. The second was Mary's gift of life as a man, as a human being, to Jesus – a gift symbolized in the person of Mary. Thus, the Christian conception of the human feminine role focuses upon "Mary, Mother of God," who has given the human component of the blood which could be sacrificed for the redemption of humanity. The third gift was the sacrificial death of Jesus, which has frequently been symbolized as the *giving of his blood* for our redemption. Within this framework, then, the death of the human individual can be conceived as a sacrifice for others but also as a gift to others for the future of humanity.

The question now arises of what modifications of this predominantly Catholic definition of the situation should be introduced to take account of the Protestant development and more recent phases which are no longer predominantly Protestant.

Before discussing the Protestant phase and what has followed it, let me sum up what seem to me the four principal steps in the development from the Book of Genesis to full-fledged medieval Catholicism.

1.   It is clear that the original meaning of death was as punishment for the disobedience of Adam and Eve in the Garden. The sin, however, was not merely disobedience but the pretention to the status of divinity, and mortality is the *primary* symbol of nondivinity. The imposition of death and the expulsion from the Garden were linked with the conception that this life should be burdened with travail.

2.   With the development of the covenant relationship between Yahweh and his chosen people, death took on a new meaning. The biblical phrase is reception into "the bosom of Abraham," which may be interpreted to mean that the dead achieve the honorific status of ancestors (as in traditional Chinese religion) in the transgenerational collectivity of the people. Mortality is accepted as part of the generalized human condition with all its limitations but with a note of special value emphasis on the concept of chosenness. The symbol blood emerges in the first instance as a symbol of ethnic belongingness, not only in one generation, but in the continuity of successive generations. This continuity in turn is linked with the special significance of the Law, which was divinely ordained through Moses.

3.   In the original Christian syndrome, a major shift took place. There was a relative disassociation from an ethnic community, and both the spiritual and temporal fates of the individual acquired a new salience. Human life, with its continuities, is in a new sense conceived as given. The primary symbol here is the portrayal of Jesus as the only *begotten* son of God the Father. God's begetting of Jesus is quite different from his creation of Adam. It presumes the continuity of humanity and the human reproductive process. Mary gives Jesus the gift of life at the human level, and it is the synthesis of the divine element and the human as symbolized in the Annunciation which qualifies Jesus to be the redeemer of mankind. In his role as redeemer, by his sacrificial death, "He gave His blood" for the redemption of mankind. It must be remembered that blood in this sense was neither wholly divine nor wholly human but a special synthesis of the two, which transcended the stark dichotomy of divine and human in the Book of Genesis.

4.   It seems to be clear then that the primary symbolic effect of Jesus' sacrifice was the endowment of ordinary humans with the capacity to translate their lives into gifts which simultaneously express the love of other human beings and the love of God, reciprocating God's love for "the world." The sacrifice of Jesus by dying on the cross was therefore conceived in a generalized manner so that all human deaths could be conceived in sacrifices. The element of sacrifice, however, emphasizes the negative side, the cost side, of dying, which was so salient for the crucifixion because of its excruciating suffering. The positive side is the *gift*, not Mary's gift of the particular human life of Jesus, but the gift of his own life by the living, human Jesus. This seems to me to be the primary symbolic meaning of the Christian conception of death transcended. Death acquires a transbiological meaning because the paramount component of its meaning is the giving of a life, at the end of a particular life, to God. It is conceived as a perpetuated solidarity between the bio-human level, symbolized by the blood of Mary, and the divine level, symbolized by the blood of Christ. In the ideal Christian death, one came to participate in the blood of Christ at a new level.

In the Catholic system, the mutuality of giving as the expression of love was mediated by the sacramental system of the church and fragmented by particularized absolutions from time to time. In the Protestant version, however, the sacramental system no longer had this capacity. The "power of the keys" was eliminated, and the clergy became essentially spiritual leaders and teachers. Most important, the life of perfection – the life conceived to be both sacrifice and gift to God, namely, that of members of religious orders – lost its special status, and every human being, layman and clergyman alike, was placed on the same level. I think it legitimate, as Weber did, to see this as basically an upgrading of the status of the laity rather than a downgrading of that of the religious. As Weber put it, "Every man was to become a monk."

In one sense, the accent on life in this world was strengthened rather than otherwise. The Calvinist thought that it was the mission of man to build the kingdom of God on earth. In this context the whole life of the human individual was considered a unity, and its basic meaning was that of contribution to the building of the kingdom, that is, insofar as the individual lived up to religious expectations. His death then was seen as consummatory, as signaling the completion of the task for which he was placed in this world. The consummatory aspect, of course, requires divine legitimation, but it also means that dying becomes in a sense a voluntary act, as it was for Jesus. It is, for example, striking that a sharp distinction is made between dying a natural death and being killed. Dying as consummation is beautifully symbolized in the phrase in the Episcopal funeral service, "His work is done" (also in "Well done, good and faithful servant"). The individual human being is brought into a special kind of partnership with God in the implementation of the divine plan for the world. One might say that the Genesis conception of the life of travail and its bitter ending by death following expulsion from the Garden has been transformed into the conception of life in this world as a great opportunity to serve as an instrument of the divine will in the great task of building the kingdom. One of the marks of Protestantism is acceptance of worldly life as basically good and of death as the natural and divinely ordained consummation.

There is, however, an underlying conflict. This positive and, one might say, optimistic view of life and death is essentially conditional on fulfillment of the divine mandate, on actually *doing* God's will. Fulfillment, however, cannot be guaranteed. What Burke calls the element of the negative, the capacity to disobey, is just as characteristic of modern man as it was of Adam. Hence, the problem of what is to happen to the inveterate sinner cannot be avoided, because it cannot be guaranteed that sinners will cease to exist. The note of death as punishment and its symbolic aftermath is always a counterpoint note to the positive Protestant conception.

It seems to me that the same basic view of life and death has survived the often suggested abandonment of the traditional Judeo-Christian conceptions of the transcendental God. It has survived most conspicuously in Marxian socialism, which, at least in its Communist version, bears striking resemblances to early Calvinism. Here, clearly, the basic human assignment is the building of socialism. The fate of the individual "soul" after death is clearly thought of differently than in theistic Protestantism. But I think that the basic pattern is very similar, that is, mortality and the other fundamental features of the human condition are accepted and, therefore, the completion of a total life in the ideal case gives death a consummatory meaning.

Recent movements suggest a shift from the Protestant Ethic emphasis on "work" to a communally organized regime of love, which, of course, links with the Christian traditions of love at both the divine and the human levels. It is not clear just how these movements are going to crystallize, if at all; but one thing is almost certain: that they will share with Puritan Protestantism and Marxian socialism the conception of the religious sanctification of life in this world.

We must not forget, however, that the early Christians were eschatologically oriented: they looked forward to a second coming of Christ and, with it, the day of judgment and the end of the world as it had existed and been known. Those who were saved would then enter into a state of eternal life in a new paradise, in some respects resembling the Garden of Eden, yet different from it. The belief in some kind of preexistent paradise in which man participated has reverberated through the centuries, especially during the Enlightenment, in Rousseau's idea of the state of nature. A preexistent state of nature has been dynamically linked with the conception of a terminal state where all the problems of the tragic human condition are believed to have been solved. This kind of a utopia, of course, has been exceedingly prominent in the socialist movement, most notably in the idea of communism as the end state of socialist societies, guided by the communist vision of Marxism-Leninism.

Very similar orientations seem to be characteristic of the movement that I have elsewhere (1971) called the new "religion of love." Indeed, in its extreme versions it is suggested that the regime of total love can be set up in the immediate future. It will, however, have to be a terrestrial regime which cannot conceive "the end of the world" in the sense in which early Christians used that phrase. It would mean only the end of the evil parts of the world. A clear conception of the meaning of death has not yet emerged in these circles. But there is a fantasy of immortality – a feeling that death, as it has been known since the abandonment of Christian eschatological hopes, is somehow unreal – that is attributable to new understandings of the centralness of human life. It will be interesting to follow developments in this area.

Note

This paper is a slightly different draft version of the first part of the article "The 'Gift of Life' and its Reciprocation," of which the coauthors were Renée C. Fox and Victor M. Lidz and which was published in *Social Research*, Fall 1972.

Reference

Parsons, Talcott (1971) "Belief, Unbelief, and Disbelief," pp. 207–45 in R. Caporale and A. Grumelli (eds), *The Culture of Unbelief*. Berkeley: University of California Press.

4

The Symbolic Environment of Modern Economies

This article constitutes an attempt to characterize a phase of the reactions, especially of intellectuals, toward the modern industrial economy. It attempts to go a step beyond the analysis of the economy's place in the society as a whole to consider the broader cultural framework as also of major importance. Instead of its being mainly an analysis of the social structure, it concentrates on the symbolic meaning of the kind of concern for "things economic" which the modern, especially Western world has shown and certain ways in which this meaning has come to be symbolized. The thesis is that, following the notable book of Louis Dumont,[1] the antithesis between the socialist and the "capitalist" versions of what Dumont calls the economic ideology conceals a common ideological selectivity which exalts the relative importance of the economic realm over others to an unacceptable degree.

The Institutional and Dynamic Environments

In my previous work in this field, there have been two principal phases, each of which may be briefly characterized. The first was concerned, I think it may be said now, with the *institutional* environment of a modern industrial economy. I developed this kind of theme in relation to analysis of the relations between economic theory and theory appropriate to the study of the larger society as a system, but in substantive terms this led me into problems of the role of institutional structure. Certain of the themes along that line came to a head in evaluating the nature of Émile Durkheim's contribution to these problems, with special reference to his famous book, *The Division of Labor in Society*. Here a central conception was that of the nature and importance of the institution of contract and its relation to the structure and regulation of market relationships. In two directions, then, there were important ramifications into the field of the institution of property and the forms it had taken in modern economic conditions, and secondly to the institutional structure of occupational systems. The latter started with concern not only with the labor role in the traditional sense in which economic theory has treated it, but also with that of the business entrepreneur. From this starting point, however, I embarked in that same period, after completion of *The Structure of Social Action* (1937), on a study of the institutional character of the modern professions, with special reference at that period to medical practice.

A number of years later, stimulated by the invitation to deliver the Marshall Lectures at Cambridge University, I embarked on another phase of treatment of this problem area, which may be called analysis of the dynamic environment of the economy in the larger society. This phase was above all documented in the book in which I collaborated with Neil J. Smelser, entitled *Economy and Society* (1956).

The essential strategy of this development was in terms of the then recently developed four-function paradigm to treat the economy as one of four primary functional subsystems of the total society, namely, that the function of which was adaptive. This fitted the long-standing economic conception of the economy as a primary focus of agencies of the generation of generalized allocable resources for an indefinite variety of uses.

Then the attempt was made to deal with outputs from the economy to the other subsystems of the society and correlative inputs to the economy from the other subsystems. A very striking numerical correspondence governed this analysis. This was that in a paradigm which described four primary functional subsystems there were input–output relations between any one and the other three. There seemed to be a clear relation between this conception and that of the shares of income of traditional economic theory, conceived as outputs from the economy to others, and the factors of production, conceived as inputs to the economy from the others.

Since Marshall and Schumpeter, however, the tendency had been to deal with four factors of production and shares of income, rather than the three employed by the classical economists. The factors of production were land, labor, capital *and organization* in Marshall's version. Three categories in each set could be fitted into the input-output conception, whereas the fourth had to be treated as a special case which did not enter into this order of transactions. Clearly land, from the beginning of modern economic theory, has been treated as a special factor of production and the corresponding share of income, namely rent, as equally special.

We were then faced with the problem of locating the three "negotiable" factors of production and shares of income in the set of interchanges between functional subsystems. Our primary clue to location was the well-known Keynesian interchange between producing firms and consuming households. The output to households from the economy was categorized as consumers' goods, which were paid for in money terms by consumers' income. The second interchange was that of labor as an output of the household, paid for by wages in the technical economic meaning of the concept. The consuming and labor-producing household we conceived to be part of what, in our technical terms, we called the pattern-maintenance subsystem of the society. Then, to make a long story short, for technical reasons we located the source of the input of capital to the economy in the "political system" and the payment of interest to it as a share of income there as well. The other interchange had to do with the command of political organization, conceived in an analytical sense and not simply as units of government, on the control of economic resources.

Finally, the third "negotiable" set of interchanges concerned what Marshall meant by organization as a factor of production and its relation to claims to the allocation of fluid resources, notably as between entrepreneurship as a function of commitment to economic expansion and the great variety of consumption uses. We then held that land was not involved in a comparable interchange, the economic justification for this judgment being the economic dictum that the quantity of land in the aggregate is not a function of its price.

All of these developments involved us heavily in the problem of the nature and functions of money as a generalized medium regulating the types of interchanges we have been discussing. We came to the conclusion that the functions of money must depend on its symbolic character, rather than it being in any sense closely comparable with any class of commodities. We relied heavily on the doctrine of the classical economists that money has value in exchange but not value in use.

The Symbolic or Ideological Environment

The main body of the present article will be devoted to a third conceptualization of what I consider to be an important environment of the modern economy. In the title of the article I have referred to it as the *symbolic* environment. An alternative characterization might refer to it as the "ideological" environment. This concerns a set of symbols which have figured prominently in discussions, controversies, and conflicts about the nature of the present or primary economic system in the industrialized world, and of the various alternatives to it. Probably the most important single reference point for analyzing these symbolizations has been the concept *capitalism.*

The concept capitalism seems at least to have been popularized first by the socialist movement, which grew up, of course, in opposition to the new modes of economic organization which had developed in the course of what we ordinarily call the Industrial Revolution. It thus early acquired, especially as used by intellectuals, a pejorative tone. As we shall attempt to spell out, the sources of this pejorative character are many and complex. The most immediate focus, however, was on the concept of alleged "exploitation" of the newly emerging industrial working class.

By and large, however, the proponents and opponents of the new economic order have both for a long period tended to make use of the concept capitalism. Under the impact of the moral attack, however, an important line of thought centering on Alfred Marshall has attempted to substitute the concept "free enterprise," in important part, of course, because the word "free" has positive connotations in modern ideological settings. As an ideological term, the concept capitalism of course crystallized above all in the theory put forward by Karl Marx and Friedrich Engels, which has now powerfully reverberated not only in Western societies but on a worldwide basis for substantially more than a century.

Thus the immediate reference points to the realities of the human condition were categories taken from the economic sphere. These categories have been the concept of a capitalistic order and of socialism as an organizational alternative to capitalism. In a striking way, however, both proponents and opponents have concentrated attention on the status of the category they call "labor," the definition of which is by no means a simple matter. More broadly, the symbolic environment with which I am concerned may be interpreted, however, as attempting to build symbolic bridges between the emerging economic order on the one hand and some of the historic, deeper-lying aspects of the human situation on the other. My particular interest is in calling attention to some of the themes of religious orientation which have figured very prominently in the history, in particular, of Western society.

First, there is a notable resemblance of pattern between what some might call the "scenario" of Marxism and the basic pattern of Christianity. The Marxist scenario portrays modern man in industrial societies as faced with a basically evil social order, although in the background this status as evil is mitigated by the fact that it has advanced what Marxian theory calls the "forces of production." There is, however, in spite of this mitigation, a crying need for radical change, which may even be likened to "salvation." This change is to be brought about by a collective act, that of the new working class created by capitalism, the *proletariat*. The act of reorganization or regeneration is thus to come about through revolution, the result of which will be to introduce an ideal state of affairs, in Marxian theory called the state of *communism*. Though this state is not very circumstantially defined in the theory, it is made clear that it will be free of all the fundamental sources of human frustration which have characterized capitalistic societies. Above all, it will be free of exploitation and, one is given to believe, any form of coercion or alienation. The state as the symbol of coercive authority, it is said, will "wither away." Indeed, it will be a millenarian utopian society which presumptively will endure indefinitely without any of the problems of previous society.

Perhaps this is a sufficient sketch to point up the structural parallel. In Christianity, the state of man is said to be lost in sin. This allegedly intolerable state can be overcome only by a dramatic transformative event, by the advent of a savior. The savior is a God-man, the Son of God who became human. The dramatic transformative events are, of course, his birth, his activity in the human world, and his sacrificial death on the cross. For a very long time, the belief existed in the Christian world that there would be a second coming of Christ after his ascension, and on that occasion all the moral and spiritual accounts of participating humanity would be finally settled. Such humanity as survived in the state of salvation would be, in perpetuity, free of all the ills, sufferings, and sins which had plagued the human condition since its conception (i.e., the sin of Adam and Eve) and, of course, death. The most conspicuous difference between the Marxian "myth," if I may use that term, and the Christian myth (I do not mean anything pejorative by this usage) is that the Marxian is confined in substantive references entirely to this world. The transcendental references of the Christian myth have been dropped out and replaced by concepts derived in particular from economic theory but in part from the philosophical context in which nineteenth-century economic theory was embedded. Granted that, however, we may make the following comparisons. First, the contemporary status of the human condition is one in both cases which is defined as so radically evil that a drastically far-reaching transformation is necessary for its cure. In the Christian sense, the evil was focussed on the concept of sin.[2] In the Marxian case, it may be said to be the state of alienation of capitalistic men, which may be said to cover both the capitalistic classes and that part of the proletariat which has not yet been awakened to class consciousness. In the Christian sense, the transformative process is conceived as the mission of Christ. In connection with the second coming, the human condition as permeated by sin is conceived to be destined for permanent abolition. What will replace it? In the Marxian case, the state of communism. In that of Christianity, total salvation is in principle incommensurable with the human condition as it has previously been known. It will not be faced with any of the "social and economic" – or one may say, for the Christian case, "moral and existential" – problems which existed beforehand.

A particularly interesting and important parallel is between the Christian mission and that of the proletariat. Both missions are conceived to be possible and meaningful by virtue of a very special duality of nature or status. In the Christian case, the Christ figure is both God and man, is God become human, and in the ascension the full status of divinity is resumed, the human status relinquished by death through the crucifixion. In the Marxian myth, proletarians, like other members of capitalistic society, are afflicted by alienation, and so long as this persists, will share the deplorable fate of capitalistic society in general. Only the vanguard of the proletariat, which has achieved the state of class consciousness, escapes the state of alienation, and it becomes the primary agent of the introduction of the new and totally ideal society.[3]

In both cases there is a sharp dichotomy postulated. In that of Christianity, it is that between the saved and the damned. Those anchored in the existing society are, in the nature of the case, not saved, since they have either not been exposed to or have not acted upon the mission of Christ. In the Marxian case, the analog of heaven is clearly the state of communism, and only those who have made the transition from the bourgeois or capitalistic society to the state of communism by way of socialism can be said, in this sense, to be saved. It is left somewhat equivocal whether previous bourgeois are eligible for this benefit. Certainly proletarians will be the overwhelming proportion, and of course their descendants, who have never been tainted by the evils of capitalism, will inherit their happy state. One might suggest that bourgeois such as Marx and Engels themselves and other socialist leaders have acquired the status of "honorary proletarians." They have been proletarians in spirit if not in personal class status.

I think it is important to point out that there has been, in spite of the doctrine of radical evil, a certain ambiguity in the conception of the nature of unregenerated man in both cases. In the Christian case, it has taken the form of the doctrine that, way back in the creation of Adam and Eve, God "made man in His own image." It is this which "explains" human capacity for salvation. On the other hand, man in ordinary society is sunk in sin and is incapable of lifting himself out of that situation without the help of divine grace. Similarly, in the Marxian view modern capitalistic society is not devoid of fundamental virtues, above all in the field of productivity. Capitalism, as noted above, is said greatly to have enhanced the level of productivity. This society, therefore, is, as it were, redeemable, although its redemption must await the proletarian revolution. It is

therefore both evil and good, good in that it carries the potentiality of transcending the evil components.

Ascetic Protestantism and the Marxist Paradigm

In assessing this parallel, it is essential now to take note of a very fundamental
transformation which occurred in the relatively recent history of Christianity, in
particular, Western Christianity. By this I mean the Protestant Reformation,
which gathered force in the sixteenth century, and particularly that branch of it
which Max Weber called ascetic Protestantism, of which the great proponent
was John Calvin.

The most important thing about this movement, from the present point of
view, was that it collapsed the duality of previous forms of Christianity as
between the empirical world of this life and the transcendental world. The
most important symbolic expression of this was the conception of the duty of
the Protestant Christian to contribute to the building of the Kingdom of God on
Earth. Ascetic Protestantism, that is to say, established the conceivability that a
secular society could be in principle, from a Christian point of view, a morally
and spiritually "good" society. This change opened a very important door, but
also created a very fundamental dilemma for post-Reformation societies, in that
the question could not be avoided how far they had in fact succeeded in fulfilling
the mission of building the Kingdom of God on Earth, that is, in their own
contemporary, secular societies.

From the present point of view, it is very obvious that the ascetic Protestant
position brought the problem of the moral quality of the social order very
much closer to hand than previous versions of Christianity had done. It seems
to me particularly important that the main conceptual framework of modern
economics developed particularly in England in the aftermath of this movement. Perhaps its most important single protofounder was John Locke, who
above all contributed the conception that the value of the products of economic
production derive from labor, thereby adding human agency to the "gifts of
nature."

Locke's discussion of labor was built by the technical economic theorists,
notably David Ricardo, into what came to be called the "labor theory of value,"
which treated labor as the one crucially important factor of production. It was
Ricardo's version of the labor theory of value which Karl Marx took over and
put into a quite different setting from that of Ricardo and his fellow economists
– the drama of secular eschatology, namely, the development and demise, with
replacement by communism, of the capitalistic economy.

I have been taught, notably by the late Joseph Schumpeter, that the primary
reason why Ricardo promulgated the labor theory of value was that, as a
technical theorist, he did not see any way to reach a determinate conception
of the contributions of plural factors of production to the value of economic
output. Subsequent not only to Ricardo but also to Marx, a way was indeed
found, through the concept of marginal utility and its related analysis of
marginal productivity. This eventuated in, as noted, a four-factor theory

of production in the hands of Marshall, who was one of the inventors of marginal utility, and of Schumpeter. The four-factor theory of economic productivity was in turn related to a very different conception of society from that of earlier times, about which I shall comment in a few moments.

Before that, however, it should be noted that, for Marx, labor became something far more than a factor of production in the economic sense. It became the central symbol of the drama of man's emancipation from the alienation of the capitalistic order. It goes without saying that labor had enormous moral significance in this context, but its significance transcended even the moral. The labor of the working class was the primary agent of the enormous enhancement of the forces of production which had occurred within capitalism. Beyond that, it was also the agent of the transformation of the capitalistic order into the morally flawless order of communism. The question then arises, in what way did the role Marxism imputed to labor have symbolic resonance with any elements in the Christian drama?

It seems to me clear that the connection is most importantly established by the relation of labor to the conception of suffering. It was through his suffering that Jesus was conceived to be the agent of the divine mission. This suffering took various forms according to the biblical stories, starting with obscurity and lack of recognition, for example in the incident of the boy Jesus confounding the scribes and Pharisees in the temple, the general state of contempt and derision in which Jesus was held once he embarked upon his mission, and culminating in the crucifixion, which was not only the imposition of compulsory death, but death involving both a maximum of derision and a maximum of suffering in the process.

One cannot but compare these themes with the conception which developed among the early economists of the "disutility of labor." In fact, not only in socialist circles but more generally, there has been the idea that people would not engage in labor without the prodding of necessity, and that the ideal life would be the life without labor of any sort. It does not seem, therefore, too far-fetched to suggest labor in the Marxian myth has a symbolic significance which is parallel to that of suffering in the Christian myth. There is, after all, biblical justification for this equation. We should not forget that in expelling Adam and Eve from the Garden of Eden, God in the Book of Genesis is said to have condemned Adam to live by his labor, by "the sweat of his brow," and to have condemned Eve to "bring forth in pain and suffering." There certainly must be continuity, since Marxism arose in a culturally Christian milieu, between the famous "curse of Adam" and the parallel curse visited upon Eve and the whole complex having to do with the status of labor in the newly developing modern economy.[4]

I have suggested above that the Marxian line of development from Locke's beginnings in formulating a framework of economic theory did not stand alone in the field. This observation, of course, had to do with the fact that the Marxian conception of capitalism and the process of change which was leading from it has not monopolized the field all by itself. What most Western scholars would consider to be the main line of economic theorizing has been pluralistic, starting with the pluralistic concept of eventually four factors of production instead of the single factor of labor. This pluralism, however, has gone well beyond the sphere of economic theory and has been associated with pluralistic conceptions in a variety of contexts, notably, of course, the political context. The conception of a population both regulated by a single system of law in the pursuit of a highly variegated set of interests, and enjoying constitutionally guaranteed rights in a variety of spheres of freedom, is part of this conception. It is difficult to find master symbols which adequately express this alternative, but I think "liberalism," with its variants, is the best single one.

We have not touched on the many complex vicissitudes of Marxian theory since it first crystallized and gained a major foothold in the latter part of the nineteenth century. There are also comparable vicissitudes in the history of what may be called the liberal alternative to socialistic theory, notably of the Marxian variety. Going back, however, also to Locke as the most prominent figure of what might be called a secularized Puritanism in the transition from the Puritan movement to the Enlightenment, we may briefly mention the Utilitarian movement. This, of course, has been particularly important as the larger quasi-philosophical framework within which modern economic theory, up to a point including the Marxian theory, developed.

The focal problem of this whole intellectual tradition has been that of the integration of the interests of plural actors interacting with each other in the system. The Marxian assertion has been that this process of what has often been called the "rational pursuit of self-interest" inevitably led to drastic structural conflict. Indeed, the Marxian version was preceded by that of Hobbes, whose picture of the "war of all against all" was far more unpleasant even than Marx's picture of capitalism. Marx, however, strongly emphasized that his version of class conflict offered a possibility of transcendence of that conflict through the revolution and introduction of the state of communism.

The version of the theory of the pursuit of discrete, if not individual, interests within a utilitarian framework tended to erase or at least weaken the lines which the Marxian movement drew between the classes, notably between bourgeois and proletariat. The justification of such erasure, for example, includes the special role of the professions in modern industrial societies, which cannot be neatly fitted into the categories of capitalists on the one hand and proletariat on the other.

Essentially what I am suggesting is that the parallel between the religious myth and the "economic" or "socioeconomic" myth can be extended from that between the basic Christian pattern and the basic Marxian one to a more general parallel. On each side of the distinction, this is to say, there is both a highly simplified and dramatized dual structure and postulated conflict in the one set of cases, and the conception of a pluralistic, more individualistic pattern of religiosocial organization on the other. I may suggest that early ascetic Protestantism, what is called often the old Calvinism, was closest to the Marxist paradigm when it dealt with expectation that the kingdom of God would be established on earth. Later Puritanism, however, was associated with a major change of orientation which erased the earlier sharp Calvinistic distinction between the elect and the damned and which underlay the development of modern liberal democracy in the political sphere and of the modern free-enterprise economy in the economic sphere, with democratic-socialist movements figuring prominently in these developments.

Parallel to that in a certain respect was the religious development which started from the sharp emphasis on orthodoxy in early Calvinism and underwent a gradual process of liberalization, one of the important effects of which was essentially to erase the line between elect and nonelect and to establish the equality of presumptive religious status of all believers. In its later stages, this pattern of religious development transcended the limits of the Protestant movement and within the setting of denominational pluralism entered into an ecumenical phase. Now most modern liberal-democratic countries in the Western world have institutionalized complete or partial separation of church and state, religious tolerance and religious freedom of the individual and the expectation that religious bodies, though still enjoying certain privileges such as tax exemption, are essentially private associations which do not enjoy the sanctions of the state.

Just as this pluralization process in certain modern societies cannot be narrowly conceived in strictly economic terms, so, I think, its normative frame of reference and value system cannot be adequately formulated in terms of the utilitarian frame of reference. Adequate conceptual analysis of the conditions under which such a system is possible requires something more than a utilitarian theory of the rational pursuit of self-interest and related political ideas. It requires the idea that such societies are characterized by systems of common values, which include the common value basis of commitment to individualism in a variety of ways. Essentially following Durkheim, they are understandable only in terms of an *institutionalized* individualism, which must be distinguished from utilitarian individualism with its overwhelming emphasis on *self*-interest.

The Suffering Bourgeois

In order to complete the picture of this intricate parallelism between the Christian myths and the economic myths of Marxism and the ideology of liberal economies, perhaps a word about Max Weber's relevance to it may be in order. There is a sense in which Weber, more than any other writer, perceived the nature of the bridge between them. His famous essay, *The Protestant Ethic and the Spirit of Capitalism*, was of course clearly post-Marxian, having been written in the early years of the present century. It was, however, clearly oriented to the interpretation of the significance of Marxian thought, and most obviously to the conception of there being, as its title indicates, such a thing as a capitalist system.

What Weber did was to take as his example the attitudes which were prevalent in one important phase of the more recent development of Christianity, that is, the Puritan movement, with special reference to its role in the England of the seventeenth century. I think a brief discussion of Weber's idea may be illuminating, since it rounds out the analysis which has just been presented.

In the Marxian analysis, the capitalist or the bourgeois class are curious, robot-like human beings. They seem to be conceived as actuated purely by the rational pursuit of self-interest defined in terms of the profit motive. But anything so human as "labor," especially with its presumption of suffering, is denied to this capitalistic robot. What Weber did was, through his concept of the calling and its imputation to the Puritan doctrine, radically to change this situation. Precisely the capitalist was actuated by the motive to work, and to work *not* for profit *but* for disinterested achievement, in the background of which lay the obligation to contribute to the building of the Kingdom of God on Earth. Since Marx had lent the members of his working class a monopoly of not merely the necessity to work but the ethical virtues of the attendant suffering, Weber threw a kind of bombshell into the Marxian camp by depriving the proletariat of their monopoly of this all-important virtue. From his point of view, proletarians and bourgeois were "all in the same boat." Exploitation, instead of being the act of the impersonally mechanistic operation of profit-oriented self-interest through the market, would have to be dealt with in a much more complicated and "human" setting as a function of more complicated social variables than the highly simple Marxian formulate could deal with. In this connection, it did not follow that the ethical valence of labor was greatly changed. It will be remembered that Weber did not view the capitalist commitment to work with too great favor. In fact, the necessity as opposed to the desirability of doing so was the keynote of his famous statement about the Iron Cage. One might even go so far as to suggest that, for Weber, whoever lived in the capitalist society, in *whatever* class status, was to be condemned to suffering, that is, the kind of suffering entailed in the commitment to work. However that may be, work as a human fate was no longer the monopoly of the exploited proletariat but was general to all members of society.[5]

The above is, within the limits of the present occasion, a very sketchy account of a subject which would justify much more extended treatment. As I said in my introductory statement, I hope it will be seen in the context of its relation to at least two other ways in which the modern tendency to treat the economy as very nearly theoretically self-sufficient needs to be qualified. As I said, the first of these sets of qualifications is the one on which I concentrated in my discussion of these matters in my early career, particularly in the book *The Structure of Social Action,* and called the *institutional* framework of the economy. A second set of qualifications had to do with the interdependence of the economy, through mediated interchanges, with at least three other primary noneconomic sectors of the structure of highly differentiated modern societies. Beyond the society itself, it also ramified into the cultural system and the personalities of individuals.

The present article has been designed above all to call attention to still another aspect of the way in which the modern economy is not an altogether isolated and independent entity. Even in the human theoretical thinking, which is most directly oriented to attempting to understand the structure and processes of the economy, I hope I have at least induced some readers to take seriously the idea that there are types of symbolization involved which historically and comparatively have been closely related to religion. Understanding the modern economy has not been a simple matter of developing technical conceptual schemes for use in its analysis, which have no other connotations than their relevance to the technical tasks of economic science. They ramify in the whole cultural system of our type of society in complex and, I think, sometimes very surprising ways. I hope this discussion will at least be suggestive of further development of some of these themes as distinguished from those more familar to students of economics.

Notes

1   Louis Dumont, *From Mandeville to Marx: The Genesis and Triumph of Economic Ideology* (Chicago: University of Chicago Press, 1977).
2   Thus, in Marxism, the concept of alienation is the equivalent of the Christian sin. It is the name for the drastically undesirable state in which all members of the capitalist societies, except the minority of Marxian "saints," find themselves. Like sin, it cannot be attributed only to personal fault, but has been imposed by the workings of "history," the Marxian equivalent of God. Also like sin, it can only be escaped from through a great redemptive act transcending any individual, in this case the Proletarian Revolution.
3   The possibility of at least *some* proletarians leading the redemptive Revolution is clearly derived from their status of presumptive purity. Having given their labor in economic production, they have gained merit by the attendant suffering. At the same time, as members of the exploited class, they cannot, like capitalists, be held directly responsible for the evils of the capitalistic system. This moral purity of the proletarian class is its most important qualification for playing the role of savior. In this respect it resembles the "disinherited of the earth" in Christian tradition.
4   It may seem relatively far-fetched, so I do not put the following consideration in the text of the article. As between Adam and Eve, however, the element of suffering was in biblical tradition imposed even more upon Eve than upon Adam. It seems to me, therefore, to be at least plausible to suggest that there are respects in which labor, in not merely socialist but in other respects of modern thinking, is connected particularly with femininity. The most obvious context of such connection, of course, would be the mother role, that is, the fact that the daughters of Eve have been condemned to bring forth in pain and suffering. Indeed, a woman in the process of childbirth is said to be "in labor."

The above line of thought might be carried one step further to suggest that there are Oedipal themes in the background of this symbolic complex. The argument would be to the effect that the capitalist has certain resemblances to the Oedipal father as a forbidding, hostile, exploitative figure, in particular one who is thought unfairly to abuse the beloved mother, "labor." The mother, on the other hand, is thought of as tender and loving and desirable. From this point of view, then, the Marxian version of the class conflict might at least have overtones of the Freudian version of the Oedipal conflict. The purity theme noted above is given conspicuous feminine symbolization in Catholic Christianity in the figure of the Virgin.
5   Indeed, I should hold that it is desirable to go a step beyond Weber to treat labor and suffering or even the milder "disutility" as essentially independently variable. Much that is classified as labor – that is, work in occupational roles – is clearly enjoyable to the performer, though of course much is not.

Part II

Life, Sex, and Death

5

Illness and the Role of the Physician:
A Sociological Perspective

The present paper will attempt to discuss certain features of the phenomena of illness, and of the processes of therapy and the role of the therapist, as aspects of the general social equilibrium of modern Western society. This is what is meant by the use of the term "a sociological perspective" in the title. It is naturally a somewhat different perspective from that usually taken for granted by physicians and others, like clinical psychologists and social workers, who are directly concerned with the care of sick people. They are naturally more likely to think in terms of the simple application of technical knowledge of the etiological factors in ill health and of their own manipulation of the situation in the attempt to control these factors. What the present paper can do is to add something with reference to the social setting in which this more "technological" point of view fits.

Undoubtedly the biological processes of the organism constitute one crucial aspect of the determinants of ill health, and their manipulation one primary focus of the therapeutic process. With this aspect of "organic medicine" we are here only indirectly concerned. However, as the development of psychosomatic medicine has so clearly shown, even where most of the symptomatology is organic, very frequently a critically important psychogenic component is involved. In addition, there are the neuroses and psychoses where the condition itself is defined primarily in "psychological" terms, that is, in terms of the motivated adjustment of the individual in terms of his own personality, and of his relations to others in the social world. It is with this motivated aspect of illness, whether its symptoms be organic or behavioral, that we are concerned. Our fundamental thesis will be that illness to this degree must be considered to be an integral part of what may be called the "motivational economy" of the social system and that, correspondingly, the therapeutic process must also be treated as part of that same motivational balance.

Seen in this perspective illness is to be treated as a special type of what sociologists call "deviant" behavior. By this is meant behavior which is defined in sociological terms as failing in some way to fulfill the institutionally defined expectations of one or more of the roles in which the individual is implicated in the society. Whatever the complexities of the motivational factors which may be involved, the dimension of conformity with versus deviance or alienation from the fulfillment of role expectations is always one crucial dimension of the process. The sick person is, by definition, in some respect disabled from fulfilling normal social obligations, and the motivation of the sick person in being or staying sick has some reference to this fact. Conversely, since being a normally satisfactory member of social groups is always one aspect of health, mental or physical, the therapeutic process must always have as one dimension the restoration of capacity to play social roles in a normal way.

We will deal with these problems under four headings. First something will have to be said about the processes of genesis of illness insofar as it is motivated and thus can be classed as deviant behavior. Secondly, we will say something about the role of the sick person precisely as a social role, and not only a "condition"; third, we will analyze briefly certain aspects of the role of the physician and show their relation to the therapeutic process and finally, fourth, we will say something about the way in which both roles fit into the general equilibrium of the social system.

Insofar as illness is a motivated phenomenon, the sociologist is particularly concerned with the ways in which certain features of the individual's relations to others have played a part in the process of its genesis. These factors are never isolated; there are, of course, the constitutional and organically significant environmental factors (e.g., bacterial agents), and undoubtedly also psychological factors internal to the individual personality. But evidence is overwhelming as to the enormous importance of relations to others in the development and functioning of personality. The sociologist's emphasis, then, is on the factors responsible for "something's going wrong" in a person's relationships to others during the processes of social interaction. Probably the most significant of these processes are those of childhood, and centering in relations to family members, especially, of course, the parents. But the essential phenomena are involved throughout the life cycle.

Something going wrong in this sense may be said in general to consist in the imposition of a strain on the individual, a strain with which, given his resources, he is unable successfully to cope. A combination of contributions from psychopathology, learning theory and sociology makes it possible for us to say a good deal, both about what kinds of circumstances in interpersonal relations are most likely to impose potentially pathogenic strains, and about what the nature of the reactions to such strains is likely to be.

Very briefly we may say that the pathogenic strains center at two main points. The first concerns what psychiatrists often call the "support" a person receives from those surrounding him. Essentially this may be defined as his acceptance as a full-fledged member of the group, in the appropriate role. For the child this means, first of all, acceptance by the family. The individual is emotionally "wanted" and within considerable limits this attitude is not conditional on the details of his behavior. The second aspect concerns the upholding of the value patterns which are constitutive of the group, which may be only a dyadic relationship of two persons, but is usually a more extensive group. Thus rejection, the seducibility of the other, particularly the more responsible, members of the group in contravention of the group norms, the evasion by these members of responsibility for enforcement of norms, and, finally, the compulsive "legalistic" enforcement of them are the primary sources of strain in social relationships. It is unfortunately not possible to take space here to elaborate further on these very important problems.

Reactions to such strains are, in their main outline, relatively familiar to students of mental pathology. The most important may be enumerated as anxiety, production of fantasies, hostile impulses and the resort to special mechanisms of defense. In general we may say that the most serious problem with reference to social relationships concerns the handling of hostile impulses. If the strain is not adequately coped with in such ways as to reduce anxiety to manageable levels, the result will, we believe, be the generating of ambivalent motivational structures. Here, because intrinsically incompatible motivations are involved, there must be resort to special mechanisms of defense and adjustment. Attitudes toward others thereby acquire the special property of compulsiveness because of the need to defend against the repressed element of the motivational structure. The ambivalent structure may work out in either of two main directions: first, by the repression of the hostile side, there develops a compulsive need to conform with expectations and retain the favorable attitudes of the object; second, by dominance of the hostile side, compulsive alienation from expectations of conformity and from the object results.

The presence of such compulsive motivation inevitably distorts the attitudes of an individual in his social relationships. This means that it imposes strains upon those with whom he interacts. In general it may be suggested that most pathological motivation arises out of vicious circles of deepening ambivalence. An individual, say a child, is subjected to such strain by the compulsive motivation of adults. As a defense against this he himself develops a complementary pattern of compulsive motivation, and the two continue, unless the process is checked, to "work on each other." In this connection it may be especially noted that some patterns of what has been called compulsive conformity are not readily defined as deviant in the larger social group. Such people may in a sense be often regarded as "carriers" of mental pathology in that, though themselves not explicitly deviant, either in the form of illness or otherwise, by their effects on others they contribute to the genesis of the kinds of personality structure which are likely to break down into illness or other forms of deviance.

Two important conclusions seem to be justified from these considerations. The first is that the types of strain on persons which we have discussed are disorganizing both to personalities and to social relationships. Personal disorganization and social disorganization are, in a considerable part, two sides of the same concrete process. This obviously has very important implications both for psychiatry and for social science. Secondly, illness as a form of deviant behavior is not a unique phenomenon, but one type in a wider category. It is one of a set of alternatives which are open to the individual. There are, of course, reasons why some persons will have a psychological make-up which is more predisposed toward illness, and others toward one or another of the alternatives; but there is a considerable element of fluidity, and the selection among such alternatives may be a function of a number of variables. This fact is of the greatest importance when it is seen that the role of the sick person is a socially structured and in a sense institutionalized role.

The alternatives to illness may be such as to be open only to the isolated individual, as in the case of the individual criminal or the hobo. They may also involve the formation of deviant groups as in the case of the delinquent gang.

Or, finally, they may involve a group formation which includes asserting a claim to legitimacy in terms of the value system of the society, as in joining an exotic religious sect. Thus to be a criminal is in general to be a social outcast, but in general we define religious devoutness as "a good thing" so that the same order of conflict with society that is involved in the criminal case may not be involved in the religious case. There are many complex and important problems concerning the genesis and significance of these various deviant patterns, and their relations to each other, which cannot be gone into here. The most essential point is to see that illness is one pattern among a family of such alternatives, and that the fundamental motivational ingredients of illness are not peculiar to it, but are of more general significance.

We may now turn to our second main topic, that of the sense in which illness is not merely a "condition" but also a social role. The essential criteria of a social role concern the attitudes both of the incumbent and of others with whom he interacts, in relation to a set of social norms defining expectations of appropriate or proper behavior for persons in that role. In this respect we may distinguish four main features of the "sick role" in our society.

The first of these is the exemption of the sick person from the performance of certain of his normal social obligations. Thus, to take a very simple case, "Johnny has a fever, he ought not to go to school today." This exemption and the decision as to when it does and does not apply should not be taken for granted. Psychiatrists are sufficiently familiar with the motivational significance of the "secondary gain" of the mentally ill to realize that conscious malingering is not the only problem of the abuse of the privileges of being sick. In short, the sick person's claim to exemption must be socially defined and validated. Not every case of "just not feeling like working" can be accepted as such a valid claim.

Secondly, the sick person is, in a very specific sense, also exempted from a certain type of responsibility for his own state. This is what is ordinarily meant by saying that he is in a "condition." He will either have to get well spontaneously or to "be cured" by having something done to him. He cannot reasonably be expected to "pull himself together" by a mere act of will, and thus to decide to be all right. He may have been responsible for getting himself into such a state, as by careless exposure to accident or infection, but even then he is not responsible for the process of getting well, except in a peripheral sense.

This exemption from obligations and from a certain kind of responsibility, however, is given at a price. The third aspect of the sick role is the partial character of its legitimation, hence the deprivation of a claim to full legitimacy. To be sick, that is, is to be in a state which is socially defined as undesirable, to be gotten out of as expeditiously as possible. No one is given the privileges of being sick any longer than necessary but only so long as he "can't help it." The sick person is thereby isolated and by his deviant pattern is deprived of a claim to appeal to others.

Finally, fourth, being sick is also defined, except for the mildest cases, as being "in need of help." Moreover, the type of help which is needed is presumptively defined; it is that of persons specially qualified to care for illness, above all, of physicians. Thus from being defined as the incumbent of a role relative to people who are not sick, the sick person makes the transition to the additional role of patient. He thereby, as in all social roles, incurs certain obligations, especially that of "cooperating" with his physician – or other therapist – in the process of trying to get well. This obviously constitutes an affirmation of the admission of being sick, and therefore in an undesirable state, and also exposes the individual to specific reintegrative influences.

It is important to realize that in all these four respects, the phenomena of mental pathology have been assimilated to a role pattern which was already well established in our society before the development of modern psychopathology. In some respects it is peculiar to modern Western society, particularly perhaps with respect to the kinds of help which a patient is felt to need; in many societies magical manipulations have been the most prominent elements in treatment.

In our society, with reference to the severer cases at any rate, the definition of the mental "case" as sick has had to compete with a somewhat different role definition, namely, that as "insane." The primary difference would seem to center on the concept of responsibility and the mode and extent of its application. The insane person is, we may say, defined as being in a state where not only can he not be held responsible for getting out of his condition by an act of will, but where he is held not to be responsible in his usual dealings with others and therefore not responsible for recognition of his own condition, its disabilities and his need for help. This conception of lack of responsibility leads to the justification of coercion of the insane, as by commitment to a hospital. The relations between the two role definitions raise important problems which cannot be gone into here.

It may be worth while just to mention another complication which is of special interest to members of the Orthopsychiatric Association, namely, the situation involved when the sick person is a child. Here, because of the role of child, certain features of the role of sick adult must be altered, particularly with respect to the levels of responsibility which can be imputed to the child. This brings the role of the mentally sick child in certain respects closer to that of the insane than, particularly, of the neurotic adult. Above all it means that third parties, notably parents, must play a particularly important part in the situation. It is common for pediatricians, when they refer to "my patient," often to mean the mother rather than the sick child. There is a very real sense in which the child psychiatrist must actively treat the parents and not merely the child himself.

We may now turn to our third major problem area, that of the social role of the therapist and its relation to the motivational processes involved in reversing the pathogenic processes. These processes are, it is widely recognized, in a certain sense definable as the obverse of those involved in pathogenesis, with due allowance for certain complicating factors. There seem to be four main conditions of successful psychotherapy which can be briefly discussed.

The first of these is what psychiatrists generally refer to as "support." By this is here meant essentially that acceptance as a member of a social group the lack of which we argued above played a crucial part in pathogenesis. In this instance it is, above all, the solidary group formed by the therapist and his patient, in which the therapist assumes the obligation to do everything he can within reason to "help" his patient. The strong emphasis in the "ideology" of the medical profession on the "welfare of the patient" as the first obligation of the physician is closely related to this factor. The insistence that the professional role must be immune from "commercialism," with its suggestion that maximizing profits is a legitimate goal, symbolizes the attitude. Support in this sense is, so long as the relationship subsists, to be interpreted as essentially unconditional, in that within wide limits it will not be shaken by what the patient does. As we shall see, this does not, however, mean that it is unlimited, in the sense that the therapist is obligated to "do anything the patient wants."

The second element is a special permissiveness to express wishes and fantasies which would ordinarily not be permitted expression in normal social relationships, as within the family. This permissiveness must mean that the normal sanctions for such expression in the form of disapproval and the like are suspended. There are of course definite limits on "acting out." In general the permissiveness is confined to verbal and gestural levels, but this is nonetheless an essential feature of the therapeutic process.

The obverse of permissiveness, however, is a very important restriction on the therapist's reaction to it. In general, that is, the therapist does not reciprocate the expectations which are expressed, explicitly or implicitly, in the patient's deviant wishes and fantasies. The most fundamental wishes, we may presume, involve reciprocal interaction between the individual and others. The expression of a wish is in fact an invitation to the other to reciprocate in the complementary role, if it is a deviant wish, an attempt to "seduce" him into reciprocation. This is true of negative as well as positive attitudes. The expression of hostility to the therapist in transference is only a partial gratification of the wish; full gratification would require reciprocation by the therapist's becoming angry in return. Sometimes this occurs; it is what is called "countertransference"; but it is quite clear that the therapist is expected to control his countertransference impulses and that such control is in general a condition of successful therapy. By showing the patient the projective character of this transference reaction, this refusal to reciprocate plays an essential part in facilitating the attainment of insight by the patient.

Finally, fourth, over against the unconditional element of support, there is the conditional manipulation of sanctions by the therapist. The therapist's giving and withholding of approval is of critical importance to the patient. This seems to be an essential condition of the effectiveness of interpretations. The acceptance of an interpretation by the patient demonstrates his capacity, to the relevant extent, to discuss matters on a mature plane with the therapist, who shows his approval of this performance. It is probably significant that overt disapproval is seldom used in therapy, but certainly the withholding of positive approval is very significant.

The above four conditions of successful psychotherapy, it is important to observe, are all to some degree "built into" the role which the therapist in our society typically assumes, that of the physician, and all to some degree are aspects of behavior in that role which are at least partially dependent of any conscious or explicit theory or technique of psychotherapy.

The relation of support to the definition of the physician's role as primarily oriented to the welfare of the patient has already been noted. The element of permissiveness has its roots in the general social acceptance that "allowances" should be made for sick people, not only in that they may have physical disabilities, but that they are in various ways "emotionally" disturbed. The physician, by virtue of his special responsibility for the care of the sick, has a special obligation to make such allowances. Third, however, the physician is, by the definition of his role, positively enjoined not to enter into certain reciprocities with his patients, or he is protected against the pressures which they exert upon him. Thus giving of confidential information is, in ordinary relationships, a symbol of reciprocal intimacy, but the physician does not tell about his own private affairs. Many features of the physician-patient relationship, such as the physician's access to the body, might arouse erotic reactions, but the role is defined so as to inhibit such developments even if they are initiated by the patient. In general the definition of the physician's role as specifically limited to concern with matters of health, and the injunction to observe an "impersonal," matter-of-fact attitude without personal emotional involvement, serve to justify and legitimize his refusal to reciprocate his patient's deviant expectations. Finally, the prestige of the physician's scientific training, his reputation for technical competence, gives authority to his approval, a basis for the acceptance of his interpretations.

All of these fundamental features of the role of the physician are given independently of the technical operations of psychotherapy; indeed they were institutionalized long before the days of Freud or of psychiatry as an important branch of the medical profession. This fact is of the very first importance.

First, it strongly suggests that in fact deliberate, conscious psychotherapy is only part of the process. Indeed, the effective utilization of these aspects of the physician's role is a prominent part of what has long been called the "art of medicine." It is highly probable that, whether or not the physician knows it or wishes it, in practicing medicine skillfully he is always in fact exerting a psycho-therapeutic effect on his patients. Furthermore, there is every reason to believe that, even though the cases are not explicitly "mental" cases, this is necessary. This is, first, because a "psychic factor" is present in a very large proportion of ostensibly somatic cases and, secondly, apart from any psychic factor in the etiology, because illness is always to some degree a situation of strain to the patient, and mechanisms for coping with his reactions to that strain are hence necessary, if the strain is not to have psychopathological consequences. The essential continuity between the art of medicine and deliberate psychotherapy is, therefore, deeply rooted in the nature of the physician's function generally. Modern psychotherapy has been built upon the role of the physician as this was already established in the social structure of Western society. It has utilized the existing role pattern, and extended and refined certain of its features, but the roles of the physician and of the sick person were not created as an application of the theories of psychiatrists.

The second major implication is that, if these features of the role of the physician and of illness are built into the structure of society independent of the application of theories of psychopathology, it would be very strange indeed if they turned out to be isolated phenomena, confined in their significance to this one context. This is particularly true if, as we have given reason to believe, illness is not an isolated phenomenon, but one of a set of alternative modes of expression for a common fund of motivational reaction to strain in the social system. But with proper allowances for very important differences we can show that certain of these same features can also be found in other roles in the social system. Thus to take an example of special interest to orthopsychiatrists, there are many resemblances between the psychotherapeutic process and that of the normal socialization of the child. The differences are, however, great. They are partly related to the fact that a child apparently needs two parents while a neurotic person can get along with only one psychiatrist. But also in the institutions of leadership, of the settlement of conflicts in society and of many others, many of the same factors are operative.

We therefore suggest that the processes which are visible in the actual technical work of psychotherapy resemble, in their relation to the total balance of forces operating within and upon the individual, the part of the iceberg which protrudes above the surface of the water; what is below the surface is the larger and, in certain respects, probably still the more important part.

It also shows that the phenomena of physical and mental illness and their counteraction are more intimately connected with the general equilibrium of the social system than is generally supposed. We may close with one rather general inference from this generalization. It is rather generally supposed that there has been a considerable increase in the incidence of mental illness within the last generation or so. This is difficult to prove since statistics are notably fragmentary and fashions of diagnosis and treatment have greatly changed. But granting the fact, what would be its meaning? It could be that it was simply an index of generally increasing social disorganization. But this is not necessarily the case. There are certain positive functions in the role of illness from the social point of view. The sick person is isolated from influence upon others. His condition is declared to be undesirable and he is placed in the way of reequilibrating influences. It is altogether possible that an increase in mental illness may constitute a diversion of tendencies to deviance from other channels of expression into the role of illness, with consequences less dangerous to the stability of society than certain alternatives might be. In any case the physician is not merely the person responsible for the care of a special class of "problem cases." He stands at a strategic point in the general balance of forces in the society of which he is a part.

6

Toward a Healthy Maturity

The problem of health and illness generally lies at a major cross-roads between the biological and the social reference points for the study of human affairs, with the psychological aspect strategically situated somewhere in the middle. If this be true generally, perhaps it is even more so where the older age groups are concerned. In this connection, the biological reference must be extended from the consideration of the relatively short-run state of the individual organism to that of the life cycle as a whole.

On the biological side, then, it seems to be an essential basic assumption that the life cycle as a whole must be considered to be a base-line of "normality." Death itself is clearly among the biologically normal phenomena, and the changes which are inseparably connected with the passage of time are equally so. Only premature death and the disabilities of later life which, relative to the main pattern of the cycle are "adventitious," can be considered to be pathological, and, hence, appropriately categorized in the domain of illness. Thus, a person clearly approaching death "from old age" is, properly speaking, no more "sick" than is a pregnant woman approaching the end of her term, however much both may have special requirements of care and however much the proper care may be defined, in part at least, as "medical." However vague this criterion of distinction between the normal and the abnormal may be, it will be taken as a base-line for this discussion; its filling in must be a problem for the biological sciences and the health professions, not for the sociologist.

Certain more specific facts, however, are so important that they must be made explicit. First, it is well known that, though the average length of human life has greatly increased, for example, during the present century, its maximum span has increased very little, if at all, within the period for which reliable information has been available; and much the largest decreases of death rates have been in infancy and childhood. Nevertheless, once past these early critical periods, there is a greatly enhanced probability that the individual will survive until a "normal old age." As a result of factors such as these, the proportion of our population in the older age groups, taking for instance the conventional cutting point of 65, has been steadily increasing for a considerable period, and can be expected to do so further for a considerable period of time. In 1900, only 4.1 per cent were 65 and older. In 1955, the proportion had grown to 8.5 per cent. If anticipated trends hold, in 1975 it will be 9.7 per cent, or nearly one-tenth. Hence, by sheer weight of numbers, if nothing else, the older groups are becoming increasingly important in our society, as in all others where the demographic revolution is taking place.

The Older Age Groups in Two Contexts

In discussing the implications of these facts for our society, and for the health problem in particular, it is important to emphasize two main contexts. The first of these is the American value system in its implications for our fundamental attitudes in this field, while the second is the trend of change in our society, with special reference to the process of structural differentiation which it is undergoing.

The American value system

In spite of the complexity of our contemporary society and the heterogeneity of its population by ethnic origin, region, class, religion and other variables, it can be said that there is a relatively coherent, unified and, on the whole, stable set of values institutionalized in America. By the values of the society is meant conceptions of the desirable *type of society*, not of other things the valuations of which may or may not be shared by its members.

The American value system may be characterized as one of the *instrumental activism. Instrumental*, in this connection, means that neither the society as a whole nor any aspect of it, like the state, is elevated into an "end in itself," but it is considered to be an instrumentality for "worth while" things, with a very widely open range of conceptions of what things in particular may be considered to be worth while. The element of activism, however, narrows this range. For the unit of the society, whether it be a collectivity or an individual, it means the *achievement* of something important. So far, in turn, as these achievements are contributions to the society, they must consist in maintenance or, still better, improvement of the society as a base and environment for achievement.

The spelling out of this abstract formula brings up a number of familiar themes. Valuing achievement, we must value the conditions which are essential to it. From the point of view of the achieving unit, we may speak of freedom and opportunity as the essential parts of the environment. Freedom here implies absence of unnecessarily hampering restraints, while opportunity is a structuring of positive possibilities. Indeed, we may go a step further and suggest the importance of positive rewards for achievement which are in some respects involved in the somewhat maligned "success" complex. This essentially is to say that, if achievement is valued, not only should people be given freedom and opportunity, but if they in fact achieve admirably, this achievement should be recognized in some way.

A strong emphasis on achievement, however, raises inevitably the problem of equality; because an inherent unevenness of achievement and its rewards creates positions of differential power and privilege. Hence, we not only value achievement as such and the freedoms, opportunities and rewards that go with it, but also *access* to these good things. The basic formula in this respect is equality of opportunity. Opportunity in turn is, however, a relative concept. What is an opportunity for one trained, or financially able, to take advantage of it may not be an opportunity at all for others. What is realistically an opportunity in particular depends on the capacity of the individual to do what the opportunity in turn makes possible. Capacity is the potentiality for achievement which, in turn, is partly a matter of innate ability, but probably even more of the "advantages," or their reverse, which the individual has experienced in his earlier life history.

The activism of our values makes clear that we do not value a static, unchanging society. Rather, we value one which is continually changing in a "progressive" direction, which is to say in accord with the central values. Above all, it may be said that this direction is defined as a progressive increase in capacities and opportunities for achievement, not only on the same, but on progressively higher levels, and in the freedoms necessary to use them. The maintenance of certain equalities – or improvement of them – goes without saying. We value stability, but a stability *in* change, not a stagnant total absence of change.

The importance of the value-complex

What is the bearing of this value-complex on our problem? One would very readily associate this value-complex with the much discussed "accent on youth" of American society. The most important resources of a society are the capacities and commitments to achievement of its people and, in the nature of the case, the longer the prospective time available to an individual, the greater his potential contribution. Hence, the capacities of the young above all, through the two fundamental channels of health and education, have formed a major focus of concern in our society, as has the level of opportunity open to young people in the educational system and in what it leads to. It is therefore not surprising that we have had a very grave concern for the young, particularly in the period of our very rapid territorial, population and economic expansion of the last century. What many European observers have seen as the "child-centered" character of American society is perhaps less to be interpreted as "indulgence" of children than as the centering of concern on them and the investment of resources, economic and other, in their futures.

This tendency is reinforced by another important structural fact, namely that the succession of the generations tends to focus responsibility for the young on the parental generation. The younger generation then eventually achieves its independence; but it is not so obviously a problem what is to happen to the elders after their main responsibilities for their children have been discharged. As the formerly self-sufficient ones from whom independence had to be gained, it is perhaps not surprising that it should be assumed they should "take care of themselves."

Pursuing this line of thought, it seems logical that the first major basis of concern with the older groups should be a manifestation of the more humanitarian aspect of our values – our concern with the more elementary bases of need, namely, the fundamentals of economic subsistence and health. Indeed, concern with the older groups as a resource could very well be inhibited by a certain prodigality of a young and expanding society which has coincided with certain types of structural change.

These changes include the immense process of urbanization and industrialization which we have been through. In the simpler rural society of our past, where most productive activity was carried on in household units, the problem of retirement, as it has developed with the growth of large employing organizations, was not nearly so acute. Much more generally, as is true of such conditions today, a person's capacities were more likely to be utilized as long as he was physically able to be useful.

Provision for the elderly in a situation where their relative numbers were increasing and where, for a variety of reasons other than sheer economic capacity, it was becoming progressively more difficult to integrate them in the households of their children, tended to leave increasing proportions more or less stranded and created an emergency situation the first major reaction to which was the social security legislation of the 1930s.

With increasing maturity of the society, however, it is natural that attention should turn to the fuller utilization of its less obvious resources; just as after a somewhat prodigal exploitation of natural resources a major conservationist movement developed in the early part of this century, so in the far more important field of human resources we are moving into an era of major concern with those resources we have not been adequately utilizing.[1] This concern and the directions it can take will be the principal subject of the remainder of this discussion.

By way of transition, however, from the subject of general American values to that of the special problem of the older groups, it is apropos to discuss briefly the problem of biological "decline" and our attitudes toward it, including first of all the implications of American values for the problem of death.

American values and the denial of death

It has sometimes been said that we Americans do our best to deny the reality of death. We dislike to think or talk about it, or to face up to its inevitability; and, when it does occur, we try to get the necessary observances over as quickly as possible and go back to living as nearly as possible as if nothing had happened. In other cultures there is something like this picture, but it is not so extreme as this, except in certain deviant manifestations.

The most important point seems to be that we (as Americans) cannot glorify death simply because we value achievement in this life, and death necessarily puts an end to that achievement. Its acceptance within the context of our values rests, in part, on the general realistic recognition of the "facts of life" which is one major cultural imperative and, in part, on a sense of the self-limiting features of the individual's "task in life" – the sense that the time comes when *his* job is done – though for the society the job is in principle never done. Whatever the philosophical and religious views involved, death may be thought of as a natural marking of the completion of an inherently self-limited – and increasingly self-assigned – task. In certain respects, the metaphor of the well-earned rest, with its release from pressing responsibilities, is an appropriate one. Though there is a "projection" beyond earthly limits, there certainly tends to be no trend in the predominant Protestant tradition to glorify an after-life, if the latter term is used to mean primarily a "release" from the "bondage" of the flesh. The very religious sanction of conscientious living in this world precludes a certain order of evaluative contrast which, in the great cultures of the world, is perhaps most marked in India. Indeed, Indian society seems to involve almost a glorification of death as that for which life is really lived.

Broadly this interpretation seems to be confirmed by medical and other experience – for example, from the New England Age Center.[2] This is to the effect that the primary anxieties of older people do not tend to center on the expectation of death as such; persons who are knowingly approaching death, in general, do so relatively without fear. Anxiety focuses rather on the definition of the individual's role for the remainder of his life, on his own capacities to do the things he thinks worth while or obligatory to do, the welfare of those he loves, and the fulfillment of what he feels to be his obligations. The same basic interlocking of considerations of task or obligation with those of self-interest which applies at other age-levels seems also to be present here. Of course, people's needs have to be met; but, given a reasonably adequate situation in this respect, they will continue to do what they can that they feel to be "worth while" until called to leave the field. The essential question is: *what* things are to be considered most worth while?

Changing culture and capacity for what?

This brings up the question of the relations between capacity and disability with respect both to health and to other aspects of the problem. Here, it is well known that the content of the concept *health* includes certain elements of relativity. This point has been most thoroughly explored with reference to cross-cultural perspectives, but here it is relevant in two other contexts, namely within the population of one society, our own, as a function of age, and in terms of the changing definition and relative importance of its different components over time.

The most important consideration, here, is the relativity of "capacity," the maintenance of which is focused in our meanings of health. The central question is, then, capacity for what? In the more pioneering phases of the development of a country there tends to be a high premium on physical prowess, on sheer strength, agility and endurance. Quite clearly the high points of these capacities are reached quite early in life, perhaps in the early twenties; and, while maintenance of good levels is possible for many years after that, the process is still one of "decline." The symbolic importance of this complex in our culture is clearly shown in the virtual cult of athletics and its relation to the whole complex of the valuation of youth.

With increasing differentiation of the society and higher cultural levels, however, a different set of capacities comes to be increasingly salient – accumulated and organized knowledge, technical competence and sophisticated skills, capacity to plan and carry sustained responsibilities, and balanced judgment. Though much is unknown in these areas, the major trend is unmistakable, namely, that the age-peak of such capacities comes very much later than is the case with physical prowess. Furthermore, it seems probable that the course of medical development leads in this direction, rather than in simply allowing more people to live longer and without the grosser disabilities. The ground for this suggestion is that such capacities seem to be dependent on the maintenance of relatively good states of the most important organ systems and not on the highest peaks, in particular, of the perceptual and motor systems. The main organic base seems to lie in the central nervous system which does not seem, except probably for vascular conditions, to be subject to an early physiological "decline" that leads to an impairment of "mental capacity" which closely resembles the much advertised impairment of capacity for physical prowess after the early twenties.

There is naturally a limit, the ultimate one being death. But the basic emphasis is on the point that, the more sophisticated the culture, the higher the levels of intellectually defined technical competence, of responsibility and the like, the more it seems likely that people past their physical "prime" will have capacities of the first importance for the society.

In sociological terms, the importance of these capacities may be related to the *upgrading* aspect of the development of the society. With its general process of social growth and differentiation, bigger and more difficult things are continually being undertaken which, for increasing numbers of individuals, call into play their higher capacities along the lines which have been indicated. The problem is that of the basis of these capacities in the biological equipment of the individual and in his personality structure. The very broad hypothesis is that, with some exceptions, the higher the capacity, the later is its maturing, and perhaps, though not as certainly, the less is it subject to the kind of decline of which the decline of physical prowess has become the prototype.

This problem of the different types of capacity in relation to social role performance, and their relations to the stages of the life cycle, certainly should be a major object of research interest, one in which the disciplines converging on the health problem need to cooperate very closely with those associated with education and the analysis of social problems generally. It is now time to take up the second main theme of the relation of these questions to the process of differentiation in the society.

The Implications of the Process of Structural Differentiation

It is characteristic of a society, which is involved in a major process of growth, that its internal structure will be continually differentiating. There are many complex features of such a process, but the ones which concern us here are those that impinge directly on the individual through the structure of his roles. The most obvious of these is the development of mutually independent *multiple* participations for increasing proportions of the population. We have jobs and family memberships which, though articulated, are not ascriptively bound to each other. We have memberships in the families into which we were born and those we establish by our marriages, which again are importantly independent. We have religious group memberships, roles as citizens at the various community levels, and we are likely to participate in a number of more specialized associational groups. All of this, of course, occurs simultaneously at any given point in the life of a particular person.

The aspect of immediate concern, however, is differentiation with respect to the life cycle. The same person, that is to say, not only participates in more different kinds of relational contexts at the same time, he does more different kinds of things at different periods of his life. We may follow this theme through in a broad way.

Implications for education

It goes without saying that all human beings must start as helpless infants and go through the combined process of biological maturation and psychosocial training which leads to adulthood. But we can see that a particularly important reference point in this connection is given by formal education which, as including the whole population, is barely over a century old. Its more elementary phases may be interpreted as mainly different ways of treating the "immature" who, in any case, are not yet ready for adult responsibilities. The history of education has, however, been not only one of extension to increasingly larger proportions of the age cohort, but, also, its prolongation to later periods of the life cycle.

If we take the eighth grade as the termination of "elementary" education and the average age of its completion as fourteen, those who have completed it, in the more routine work-contribution senses, very generally have been ready for assumption of adult roles, though, in most of the Western world, marriage as early as that has been rare. Hence, even secondary education may be taken to be a case of an "investment" in the future through the "segregation" of an age group, on grounds other than their biological capacity, to perform the simpler sorts of adult functions, in the sense that, if this age group is withheld from functional performance and subjected to training, its future contributions will be far greater than they otherwise would have been. American society now has reached the point where completion of secondary education has become the nearly universal norm for satisfactory preparation for adult role-performance.

On top of this, there has emerged a vastly extended resort to still further formal education. Now about one-third of the total age-cohort go on to some college education. This proportion is steadily growing, and can be expected to do so for the foreseeable future. Finally, at the educational top, postgraduate training in the professional fields still takes only a small proportion. But it has become appreciable and is by far the most rapidly growing sector of the educational system.[3]

This is to say that, today, an increasing proportion of every age cohort is spending an increasing proportion of the period of what, from the older point of view, is that of adult capacity in pursuits which are clearly differentiated from their principal adult "contributions." Moreover, the stages of formal education have become clearly differentiated from each other. After the elementary grades, and certainly after the secondary, it seems improbable that biological maturation is the primary factor in the differentiation. Its main basis is rather that of the stages in which a cumulative development of *learned* capacity has to take place.

[margin note: endet bw. →]

Let us now turn to the occupational side. A kind of base-line may be said to be the performance of the ancient work-jobs of maintaining households, the more elementary types of cultivation of the soil, and the traditional handicrafts – rough carpentry and the like. The necessary skills could be adequately learned by a child in the early teens. A peak of competence could be reached within a short time, and nothing left to change or "advance" until physical disabilities set in in advanced old age. The whole structure of the educational system just sketched introduces a different set of dimensions. It is preparation for functions which must be elaborately prepared for, with respect to which anything like peak proficiency can be attained only much later and after longer preparation.

The structure of careers is another example of the same basic principle. The simplest "worker" role is almost undifferentiated over time. But the higher the level of performance the more likely it is that the peak will have to be attained by way of a series of stages of "gaining experience" through the performance of easier and less demanding tasks. It will be only after a considerable period of years that a person, even after he is "trained," will be performing at the very highest level of which he is capable. This seems to be particularly true of the functions in which responsibility and judgment play a central part.

Quite obviously, "capacity" is only one factor in the structuring of careers. Opportunity, or the "demand" factor, is equally essential. Thus, a man is not likely to be called upon to carry the highest responsibilities until he has established a reputation on the basis of which others have a high level of "confidence" in him. He may be capable of carrying the responsibility long before this confidence is established. Nevertheless, with due allowance for these factors, the central proposition certainly holds, namely that the differentiation of appropriate kinds of things to do through the stages of the career line continues on bases which are independent of formal "preparation." The pattern is not that one is "prepared" and, then, functions on a fixed "plateau" until decline sets in.

The central question, then, is how the limits of this process of differentiation in relation to upgrading are to be defined. It should be noted, in approaching the question, that upgrading is accompanied with differentiation of *kinds* of performance and function. The student is doing a different kind of work from the man on the job; even professional training is only very partially apprenticeship, important as this component is. Similarly, the junior executive, even though he is likely to become the "top boss" in time, is as a junior executive doing something very different from his top superior.

The thesis is that we are only beginning to explore the possibilities of extension of this pattern of differentiation beyond what has come to be institutionalized as the peaks of careers. Above all, we may question the ready assumption that the appropriate conception for everything beyond that institutionalized peak is "decline" and that the problem is one of accepting the limitations imposed by "disability" and <u>learning to live within these limitations, rather than one of having an opportunity for new and different kinds of achievement and contribution.</u>

Implications for the feminine role

One very important aspect of the problem concerns the family rather than the occupational sphere, and its special relation to the feminine role. Perhaps some attention to it will help clarify the problem for the occupational sphere. The family and the feminine role in American society have, in the past half century or so, been undergoing a notable process of differentiation. First, the family itself has become a far more specialized agency and, by virtue of that fact, has lost many of its previous functions, notably in the field of economic production. Above all, the household, as a place to "live" and a group with whom one shares this living, has become structurally segregated from the organizations in which occupational work is carried on, and has turned over many of its previous functions to such organizations. In connection with this development, however, the place of woman has come to be decreasingly confined to "the home." One major development is the enormously increased participation of women in formal education at the higher levels as well as the lower. Another is involvement in many kinds of community interests outside the home, while not least is the increased participation of women in the labor force. The proportion of healthy single women under 65 not employed (except widows) has come to be minimal, but the most striking recent development is that of the employment of married women living with their husbands.

<u>Overwhelmingly, the central specifically feminine function is the rearing of children.</u> There has been an important resurgence of devotion to this function in our generation through the famous "baby boom," which is all the more significant because it has occurred in a population where knowledge of contraceptive measures is certainly more widely spread than ever before. But another interesting thing has happened. This is the concentration of childbearing within a substantially shorter time period than before. As of the most recent information,[4] women are on the average likely to bear their *last* child at the age of 26 or 27; and so parents, by the time their youngest child has left home, are likely to be under fifty, with, on the average, about a third of their married life still ahead of them.

This phenomenon is associated with the very rapid recent increase in the employment of married women who are in their forties, fifties, or older. This has, indeed, been the largest single factor in the recent growth of the labor force relative to the total population of working age. It thus appears that special devotion to child-rearing, notably of course of younger children, is becoming a more differentiated role in the life cycle of the mother as well as in other respects. Thus, she is freed for other functions, partly by living longer in a better state of health and partly by concentrating her primary attention to motherhood within a shorter time-span.

This seems to be associated, in turn, with another set of phenomena. We do not have to go back farther than the early years of this century to find a time when the average woman in her mid-forties was, by current standards, definitely "old." It was as if her child-rearing function had virtually exhausted her capacities and she had relatively little left to do. The preservation of feminine "attractiveness" into much more advanced ages is an important symptom of a major change in this respect.

One aspect of this problem concerns the continuity of kinship relations and responsibilities. The older type woman, as grandmother, exercised more responsibility and authority for the families of her children than does her current opposite number. It is, however, perhaps not illegitimate to suggest that the lessened responsibility of the older woman in this respect has been balanced by the upgrading of the role of mother; the younger woman takes a larger share of the total responsibility for her children than did her forebears. This frees *her* mother, and, later, herself, for other functions. With all the strains and difficulties symbolized by the famous Helen Hokinson cartoons, it can be said fairly that an enormous upgrading in the utilization of feminine capacities has resulted from this general process of differentiation. Furthermore, a particularly conspicuous part of it has been better utilization of the capacities of the woman past the child-bearing ages. The menopause is no longer, in any comparable sense, the sign of a termination of important usefulness and status.

The principle involved here can be generalized. If child-rearing has been the primary center of the feminine role, occupational achievement has been that of the masculine. There are very important reasons why the "job" should have come to be such an important focus in the role-organization of our type of society, and within this more general category, why the career and its peak should be so important. These are, above all, the central symbols of the masculine "contribution" to social welfare; they have, above all, provided the standards by which the utilization of masculine capacity has been judged. If, given the overwhelming importance of this category of contribution, the individual is no longer wanted or needed, or if his capacity declines, the obvious conclusion seems to be that he should be placed in a lower category of social worth.

Implications for patterns of retirement

Seen in this context, the development of the age 65 as the canonical age of retirement is an interesting social phenomenon. Obviously, the changes of relevant capacity, whatever the part played by biological-genetic and by experiential factors, are in the nature of the case gradual, except for suddenly drastic changes which do not often conveniently fall on the 65th birthday. There is enormous individual variation as to whether there will or will not be a social loss from dispensing with the services of the particular individual in his particular job at this point of time. Clearly, a system based on evaluation of particular capacities would, in an abstract sense, be far more rational.

Very generally, however, the main lines of differentiation in social structure cannot be so neatly tailored to the needs and capacities of the individual as this would require. Clearly, the emergence of this pattern was a product of the rise in employment by large-scale organizations and the necessity to establish general policies in their conduct. Furthermore, it is understandable that, in its first phase, the negative uses of such a policy should be stressed, namely the relieving of the organization from being burdened with responsibility for workers so old that often their capacities were not up to the demands of the job, and with this, the hastening of the opening of opportunities for younger people.

The retirement pattern may, however, be looked upon as not simply a protection of standards of efficiency and of openness of opportunity, but a focus for a process of differentiation, by drawing a clearer line than had obtained and otherwise would obtain between phases of the life cycle. We are entering now the process of redefining the content of the later phase; as this process meets with success, it is likely to turn out that the earlier rigidity of the retirement line will be substantially mitigated.

There is still, however, a good deal of pressure for earlier retirement, so long as financial security is reasonably assured; there is also a good deal of anticipation of the finally compulsory retirement age. Furthermore, it has been pointed out that there are, from the point of view of the person retiring, as well as the employer, certain advantages in the general rule. This, above all, has to do with protection of the autonomous dignity of the individual. If permission to stay on the job beyond the regular age limit is dependent on the judgment of the "boss" from month to month or whatever, then the security of expectation, which we have come to regard as normal even without formal tenure, is undermined and the individual may often come to feel that his fate is in the hands of the arbitrary judgment or whim of another. The impersonal rule at least avoids any such invidious implications.[5]

Summary of Forces Making for a Redefinition of the Role of the Older Person

In the nature of our society at the present phase of its development, there is a powerful set of forces leading to a positive redefinition of the role-expectation of the older person who has passed the normal occupational career peak, as that has been defined. The first factor to mention again is that of the direction of pressure exerted by the value system. As previously contended, it seems that this direction will have to be compatible with the idea of instrumental activism; it will have to define opportunities and expectations to *do* things that in these terms are worth while. This need not be in the least incompatible, however, with withdrawal from many of the activities and involvements which are considered normal for younger groups.

The second major factor is the increase in numbers and in proportion of the total population of people in these categories; and the third is the actual, and still more, the prospective improvement in their average levels of capacity. Health is one major component of this capacity; but other capacities are certainly equally important. A very central complex of these is that associated with education; and it is another cardinal fact that, as a result of the general educational upgrading of the population, after the requisite time-lag, this older group will, on the average, be far more highly educated than any of their predecessors. This may be expected to make them more, rather than less, demanding of a satisfactory place in the society.

There is a most intimate connection between this educational trend and the direction in which the solution of our problem is to be sought. The general tendency of the upgrading process, at one pole, leads to the downgrading of physical prowess; at the other, it leads toward increasing emphasis on cultural concerns. This, in turn, is associated with capacity to think abstractly and generally and to take the long view. For a long time there has been something like general agreement that certain types of functions could be particularly well performed by older persons. One of the most conspicuous of these is that of judge. Informally, judicial type functions are often performed by people with a kind of "elder statesman" status. Certainly, in many fields of scholarship, distinguished contributions are made in later years. That eminently successful organization, the Roman Catholic church, has for centuries been governed mainly by old men, a fact which is associated with its trusteeship of very long-run interests.

It has often been suggested that influence in the hands of the old, almost by definition, leads to a bias toward conservatism in an undesirable sense. That this sometimes happens is undoubtedly true, but it seems to be far from inevitable. Above all, the issue here is not so much about the exercise of power over current organizational decision-making; the trend is, and rightly so, away from putting more of that power in the hands of the old. It is rather concern for the highest institutional interests of the society and the culture in the longest perspective. The very fact that the older person no longer has a career to make, that his basic position in the society has already been decided, and that his time is running out, means that under favorable conditions he can afford to be more "disinterested," to see things not in terms of what he personally can gain or lose, but from a larger point of view.[6]

A research group engaged in study of aging has put forward the interesting formula of "disengagement" as a pattern for describing the main tendency of older people.[7] Relative to the concerns of middle life, the main theme may legitimately be included under this formula. It should, however, be interpreted not only in terms of disengagement *from* previous obligations, but also a disengagement *for* new tasks. It may be thought of as one more case of the freeing of the individual from ascriptive ties, which is such a central theme in the general development of advanced societies. It involves, as the authors say, a relative freeing from the more intensely affective attachments to persons and causes.[8]

Finally, a set of reasons why the problem of health occupies such a central place in the whole range of problems may be presented. In spite of the conception of the normality of aging and death here put forward, it is obvious what a very close connection there is, realistically and symbolically, between illness, disability and aging. The significance of this needs to be seen on the background of the more general significance of the problems of health and illness in American society.[9] Illness, that is to say, is to a very high degree a pattern of *deviant behavior*. Health is valued as capacity for achievement. The enormous American effort to improve health is legitimized above all in terms of our achievement values and of the equalizing of opportunity for achievement.

At the same time, however, since it is conditionally legitimized, sickness provides for the individual, perhaps, the most important single escape hatch from the pressure of obligations to achieve; pressures which, because of the upgrading process which has been stressed here, are becoming, for the average individual, more rather than less intense. Seen in this light, illness is far from being an exclusive and unmitigated evil; it is also an important "safety valve" for the society.

The most obvious field in which such considerations operate is that of so-called mental illness. The evidence, however, is overwhelming that it is not possible to draw a rigid line, that the "psychosomatic" area is of cardinal importance to most of the problems of health and illness. However efficacious our methods of somatic control may be, it is very doubtful if a stable situation can be achieved independently of the social and cultural structuring of the group whose health is the object of concern.

This seems to be preeminently true of the aging groups. It seems almost obvious that illness is a *particularly* important form of deviant behavior for them. Its basic meaning in this connection is very clear. If it is the broad societal verdict upon older people that they are "useless," then the obvious way to legitimize their status is to *be* useless through the incapacitation of illness. The channels through which such influences operate are still understood only in the most fragmentary fashion, but *that* they operate in this direction seems to be beyond doubt.

The most fundamental task in our society in "caring for" (itself a pejorative expression) the aged, therefore, seems to be that of giving positive *meaning* to their place in the society. To be an *authentic meaning*, it must be in accord with our general value system. It not only need not, but by and large should not, however, mean pretending that there is no important difference between capacities and, above all potential contributions, at different age levels. Our greatest deficiency has been in this area of defining positive opportunity for the persons of advanced age. That there should have been a lag in this respect is understandable, but this does not lessen the urgency of the task. The medical and public health aspects of the care of illness and disability, in this even more than other connections, depends on providing such opportunity as its most fundamental precondition. For why should a person recover from an illness or take good care of his health, if there is nothing worth while for him to live for? He cannot be "forced to be free" unless freedom is the condition of something beyond it, which *both* he and the others whom he respects, really want, and value.

Notes

1   In the field of race relations which is so acute just now, for understandable reasons the primary accent at this stage is on the simple matter of social justice in terms of the values embodied in constitutional rights. Underlying this, however, in a society with

our type of values, is the fundamental fact that the attempt to hold the Negro to a menial status is also a fundamental waste of human resources. For the type of value system sketched above, justice and equality are inseparable from capacity and opportunity to achieve.

2   A study being completed, under the direction of Hugh Cabot, on "Prejudices and Older People" at the Age Center of New England, Inc., 160 Commonwealth Avenue, Boston 16, Massachusetts.

3   To take one atypical example, in the 1920s about 20 per cent of a graduating class of Harvard College went on to any type of postgraduate formal education. In the 1950s, it had become about 75 per cent.

4   Paul C. Glick, *American Families* (New York: John Wiley & Sons, 1957), p. 66.

5   This point was underlined in particular by Mr. Hugh Cabot of the Age Center of New England (in a personal discussion).

6   The most obvious examples are from high social statuses, but the point is meant to apply to all levels. Who among us cannot cite examples of the special disinterestedness of old people in all walks of life?

7   Cf. "Disengagement, A Tentative Theory of Aging" (Elaine Cumming, et al., mimeographed, from the Kansas City Study of a panel of 108 individuals equally distributed as to age and sex and comprising three age groups; conducted by The Committee on Human Development, the University of Chicago, 5835 Kimbark Avenue, Chicago, Illinois).

8   Certainly, one major feature of the experience of aging is that of the deaths of a considerable proportion of other individuals who have been the most important "significant others" in the individual's life experience. If the traumatic effects of these experiences are to be surmounted, we can say on psychological grounds that it must be through the internalization of the "lost objects;" and perhaps it can be said that the process of disengagement in this sense goes back to the first emancipation from infantile dependency on the mother.

9   Cf. Talcott Parsons, "The Definitions of Health and Illness in the Light of American Values," in E. Gartly Jaco, ed., *Patients, Physicians, and Illness* (Glencoe: The Free Press, 1958), pp. 165–87.

7

The "Gift of Life" and Its Reciprocation

TALCOTT PARSONS, RENÉE C. FOX, AND VICTOR M. LIDZ

Introduction

A few years ago, two of us (Parsons and Lidz) ventured to write a rather general article under the title "Death in American Society."[1] For the present venture we have been joined by Renée Fox, and the three of us have decided both to extend the analysis of the earlier article and to narrow the focus. The "extension" consists in going considerably deeper into the background of current American orientations toward death and its meaning in the Judeo-Christian religious tradition than was attempted in the earlier paper. The "narrowing" consists in trying to focus on the institutionalization in America of the promotion of health and the care of illness, with special reference to the medical profession and its ethical orientations.

This focus seems particularly appropriate since the most important empirical argument of the earlier paper concerned the distinction between the inevitability of the death of every person, marking the completion of a full "life course," and the "adventitious" components of the death complex. The latter includes two types of premature death: that brought about by "impersonal" causes – for the most part disease, but also accident – and that imposed by what is in some sense willful human action, such as "violence." It is often difficult to draw a line between accidental and violent death, but the analytical distinction is crucial.

The most dramatic consequence of recent developments in health care has been – and within somewhat more than a century in the "advanced" societies – the doubling, if not slightly more, of life expectancy at birth. To a degree never before true, it has become customary for the aware individual to expect that he will live to complete a "normal" span of life and for parents, that their children, if born alive and healthy, will also do so. The differentiation of the inevitable from the adventitious aspects of death has focused a more powerful light than before on the component of inevitability. If so much is controllable by human action, one must ask, what does it mean that there is nevertheless an absolute limit to our control? This problem of meaning, of course, bears with special cogency on members of the medical profession because they are *par excellence* the institutionalized trustees of society's interest in the preservation of life.

We will note that there has been in recent years a significant increase in both medical and popular concern with the "existential" aspects of death and also suffering. Indeed, the volume which Dr. Shneidman edited – part of a rapidly growing literature – attests to this fact, as does the greatly enhanced concern of medical students and physicians themselves.

The earlier Parsons–Lidz article used as a foil a paper by Peter Berger in which he claimed that the "denial" of death was a basic aspect of the American outlook.[2] We still think we were right in refusing that interpretation. We now believe, however, that it is not necessary to make an either/or choice between "acceptance" and "denial"; we believe that, as in many cases involving underlying conflicts, what is often interpreted as denial is in reality a kind of "apathy" – i.e., being in a situation of not knowing quite what to say or do and thus minimizing overt expression or action. This may also be reinforced by the "stoical" component of the Puritan tradition. We shall attempt to show how certain features of the medical situation and medical ethics have involved this kind of conflict with this kind of result.

On the positive side, we wish to re-emphasize what we consider the fully established view – that it is biologically normal for all individual organisms to die. Death is now understood to be an important mechanism enhancing the adaptive flexibility of the species through the sacrifice of individuals; i.e., it makes certain that the bearers of newly emergent genetic patterns will rapidly succeed the bearers of older ones. Death may be even more critically important in contributing to cultural growth and flexibility than in supporting genetic change. Thus, we may regard death as a major contributor to the evolutionary enhancement of life, and thereby it becomes a significant part of the aggregate "gift of life" that all particular lives should end in death. That is why it cannot be a rational pursuit of modern medicine to try to end or even minimize the "inevitable" aspect of death.

Our approach will emphasize theoretical continuity between the organic and the human socio-cultural levels, through the premise that the mortality of individuals has a positive functional significance for both human societies and the organic species. Beyond that, yet intimately related to it, is the fundamental distinction between, on the one hand, the "phenotypical" incorporation of genetic patterns in the lives of individual organisms and populations, and the genetic components themselves, and on the other hand, the modes and conditions of their preservation, implementation and development in the evolutionary sense. It is in this spirit that we devote our first substantive discussion to the field of *cultural* symbolization which in America bears on the problem of the meaning of death and, of course, its opposite, life. We think that the most important themes are found in the "constitutive symbolization" of the religious heritage.[3] To be sure, a substantial part of our contemporary population purports to "take no stock in religion." We feel, however, that the patterns of symbolization which we shall review have come to be constitutive of the *whole* culture by which we live, and that their relevance is by no means confined to the lives of self-consciously "religious" people. As social scientists we do not think that "science" in the usual sense has provided "functionally equivalent" symbolic patterns of orientation, though we think that the evidence just cited of the positive biological function of death and the recent enhancement of life expectancies is highly pertinent to our problem.

We shall be dealing with religious symbolism predominantly in the context of what has come to be called *myth*, in the sense used by Lévi-Strauss and Leach, and in another, related field, by Kenneth Burke and Northrop Frye.[4] We are not concerned with the problem of the historical veracity of the Books of Genesis and Exodus, or of the Four Gospels, but with clarifying the "structure," as Lévi-Strauss would put it, of certain of the themes expressed in such documents insofar as they bear on the problem of orientation to the death–life aspects of the human condition. Neither will we be concerned with the metaphysical question of the "existence of God." For us this belief is simply a basic element of the myth.

In addition, a principal theoretical emphasis has become much more salient than it was in the Parson–Lidz paper, and has been especially emphasized by Fox in connection with her work with Judith Swazey on the "existential" problems involved in organ transplants, which will be discussed below.[5] This is the theme of the importance of the *gift* and of gift-exchange, as it was classically introduced into social science literature – though not without antecedents – a generation ago by Marcel Mauss.[6] It will be remembered that Mauss stressed not only the ubiquity, in human cultures, of the theme of the *giving* of gifts, but also how this *giving* creates, for the recipients of gifts, an *obligation to reciprocate*, which on occasion can be onerous indeed.

In the following section of the paper it will be our principal thesis that in the Judeo-Christian tradition – and especially in the Christian phase – life, for the individual, is defined in the first instance as a *gift*, directly or indirectly, from God. It may be a niggardly gift, as with those born only to misery, want and suffering, or a munificent gift, as with those born with great talent and good fortune. Yet in both cases the gift of life creates an obligation to reciprocate. Our second main thesis will then be that the trend of religio-cultural development within this tradition has been toward defining the death of the individual, especially in the fullness of a complete life, as itself the gift which constitutes a full reciprocation of the original gift of life.

Not only may the obligation to reciprocate gifts be onerous, but the tragic view of the human condition has been in many vital respects structured about this onerousness. First, recipients must somehow be motivated to *try* to reciprocate: religiously, this commitment has, in our tradition, often been formulated as "faith." But the gifts, as we have noted, are by no means of equal value, and the sheer difficulties of reciprocation, except by "giving up," may be insurmountable. Particularly potent as a focus of tragedy is the fact that the fates of individuals are never neatly ordered in relation to those of the social collectivities in which they hold deeply meaningful membership. God is concerned not only with individuals but with "peoples" in the Old Testament sense. The problems of the beneficence or malevolence of God and of the shortcomings of individual human beings, religiously formulated as sin, are not to be neatly shoved aside by an equation of the reciprocity of gifts alone.

The Judeo-Christian Symbolization of Life and Death

To the social scientist, the sequence "life-death" strongly suggests the "life-cycle" or "life-course" of the individual, sometimes formulated as "age"-grading or structure. But in alluding to this category, which includes both life and death, the social scientist almost automatically adds to the stimulus word "age," the words "and sex." With regard to individuals rather than species, these categories provide a frame of reference for analyzing the interface between the organic aspects of the human and the social, with the necessary relation to the cultural. "Age" connotes the passage through time of the individual, within the human-social matrix, from a beginning to an end. Since, however, individuals are mortal, the continuation of the socio-cultural system beyond the individual life-span depends on the mechanism of continuing replacement, through reproduction, of the passing generation. For man, as for almost all of the "higher" animal species, this mechanism is that of *bisexual* reproduction, with rather clearly differentiated biological roles for the two sexes in the reproductive process and, more problematically, differing roles at the social and cultural levels. "Age and sex" seem clearly to belong together in their biological and socio-cultural references. Sex is of course clearly dichotomously structured, while at first glance "age" may seem a linear continuum; but if one focusses on the terminal points of a clearly limited process, birth and death can also be treated as a dichotomous reference-base. Putting the two together we derive the familiar four-fold table of two dichotomous variables.

The myth of Genesis clearly embodies both variables, though in ways which are at one level somewhat contradictory. It is clear that God created man "as the Lord of the Creation" and "in His own image" to enjoy a very special status relative to the rest of the creation. In the first version, man is included with the animals in the formula "male and female created He them"; in the second, however, Adam was the sole human Creature, and when God saw that it "was not good for Adam to be alone," He created Eve out of Adam's rib so that they were of "one flesh and blood."

As Kenneth Burke[7] says, man, as the symbol-using animal, has the unique capacity of the "negative," i.e., he may not only assent, but also may say "no." There was one and only one prohibition imposed on Adam, and later Eve, in the Garden – namely that against "eating of the fruit of the tree of the knowledge of good and evil." Man, being even at that point what he was and is, defied that prohibition and, tempted by the serpent via Eve, "ate of the fruit." This was the mythical origin both of death – by divine decree at the point of expulsion from the Garden – and of sexual reproduction for humans, since in the Garden Eve was only companion to Adam, not sexual partner.

The symbolic implication of the Fall seems to have been a double one. On the one hand, the Fall was the simple result of disobedience to a divine command. On the other hand, having been told that if man disobeyed he would "surely die," it can be argued that Adam and Eve thought they could evade this consequence and presume to immortality, symbolized in the Garden by the "Tree of Life." It seems clear that "original sin" had this dual character –

disobedience and the claim to an immortality which, since it was a divine prerogative, meant the claim to Godhead. The imposition of mortality on expulsion from the Garden indicates an emphatic divine insistence that man, as creature, was *not* divine.

At this stage the "gift" theme seems to be subordinate. To be sure, God gave life to Adam and Eve and enabled them to reproduce, through (in a sense) "compensating" them for their disobedience by giving them the "knowledge of good and evil." This knowledge has been interpreted by Leach[8] as comprising both knowledge of the inevitability of individual death, and knowledge of the "difference of the sexes," which can be further interpreted to mean the possibility of species survival beyond individual death through bisexual reproduction. Both must, in our view, be interpreted as at once good *and* evil. The evil side, besides death itself, is embodied in the famous curses by God during the expulsion from the Garden – for Eve, condemnation to childbearing in pain, for Adam, the need to subsist "by the sweat of his brow." Indeed, a major biblical interpretation has held that the whole of human life since the expulsion could be summed up in the formula "sin and death."

Another theme, however, appears in early Genesis, that of a *mediator*. As Leach suggests, even the serpent may be interpreted in this light. Just possibly, God "wanted" Adam and Eve to sin, or at least was not too angry that the serpent seduced them. Further along, Eve, as the symbolically prototypical woman, becomes a kind of mediator, a theme which much later becomes central in the figure of Mary, Mother of God.

Meanwhile, the great theme of most of the Old Testament is not the spiritual fate of individuals, but the fate of a religiously-sacred social community, the People of Israel. Symbolically, they end as Yahweh's *chosen* people – but not without many vicissitudes. In the first major phase, God was basically displeased with His highest creature and contemplated destroying His entire creation, but relented to save Noah and his extended family. In a way, He purified mankind by the flood, leaving only the descendants of Noah to inherit – this was the first "Covenant." Following this came a series of further decisions, the most notable of which were the Covenants with Abraham asserting that his descendants should become the chosen people, and later with Moses, in a sense the main mythical founder of Israel. Leach has circumstantially analyzed the many vicissitudes of this selection process by which the People of Israel are said to have become established as a religiously-grounded socio-political community.[9]

Moses, however, not only led the Exodus from Egypt and renewed the Covenant of Abraham, but also introduced the Law as a major innovation. This came to be constitutive of Judaism and, in a sense, of all its cultural derivatives. Throughout, little was heard of the "cure" of individual "souls," though such themes began to emerge in Hellenistic Judaism.

It should nevertheless be kept in mind that, not only by originally creating the human species but also by "choosing" Abraham and his "seed" and maintaining the Covenant with them, God gave his people the gift of corporate existence under divine sanction. This theme reappears later, in the conception of the Church of Christ and of a whole society as the "Kingdom of God on Earth." In the Old Testament, for the most part, both birth and death are treated within the framework of the sacred community, with the conception of death seen as "reception into the bosom of Abraham." The dead become honored ancestors of the living, with both incorporated in a time-extended, multi-generational community. As a background to the Christian phase, it is essential that the *permanence* of this community be assumed. There was no further divine threat to destroy it, as in the story of Noah; any further divine intervention would have to be different in character.

Early Christianity

It is a big jump to the symbolism of the much later Christian development, but our primary concern is not with cultural history but with a symbolic complex. There is a crucial difference between the relation of God to Adam on the one hand and to Jesus on the other. God *created* Adam in His own image, but Jesus was "His only *begotten* son." As just noted, we may infer that, by virtue of the series of covenants, God had committed Himself to the continuance of the human species, particularly but presumably not exclusively of His chosen people. His intervention in the human condition, therefore, had to be intervention in the affairs of humanity as "a going concern." Mary and the myth of the Annunciation is the symbolic focus of the divine recognition that "cooperation" with humanity is essential in order to carry out the grand plan. It is in this context that the very critical symbol, blood, becomes central, referring to the continuity of human generations which, of course, assumes the death of each individual together with the continuity of the population through sexual reproduction, what the Old Testament calls "begetting." The "blood" of Jesus had therefore both a divine and a human component, the latter being the blood of Mary.

Within the framework of the People of Israel, continuity was established in another way, through the role of Joseph as, in Leach's term, Jesus' "sociological father." Whatever the theological subtleties of the problem of the Virgin Birth may be, Jesus is forthrightly declared to be descended from Abraham through Isaac, and most especially to be of the "House of David." This genealogy is *through Joseph* (Matthew, Ch. 1), and the emphasis on continuity in the sequence of generations is clearly another reference to "blood" as an essential symbol of Christianity.

Another crucial symbolic note is sounded in the Christ story. In Judaism, though Yahweh treated the people of Israel as His chosen people, protecting them and favoring them in many ways, His primary concern was with their obedience – that is, their observance of the Law He had imposed upon them. God was continually testing them, perhaps half expecting them to "betray" Him. The severity of the testing may be said to have culminated in the command to Abraham that he sacrifice his one fully "legitimate" son, Isaac. In Christianity, the new note is that of love, with its evident relations to the theme of giving. The crucial Gospel statement should perhaps be quoted in full: "For God so loved the world that he gave his only begotten son, that whosoever believeth in him should not perish, but have everlasting life. For God sent not his Son into the world to condemn the world, but that the world might be saved" (John, 3: 16, 17).

It will be noted that God is said to have loved not only his chosen people but "the world" as a whole. This universalistic note could of course have a double cultural derivation, from the Prophetic movement in Israel and from Hellenism. It is, in any case, fundamental to Christianity. Salvation was still basically contingent on faith – it was not to be open to "unbelievers," though the punitive tone of much of the Old Testament, as in the phrase "The Lord thy God is a Jealous God," is very much played down. Perhaps, above all, salvation was conceived as a gift *from* God, whereas earlier most of the giving had been the other way around, as "sacrifices" *to* God and obedience to His commandments.

In the New Testament there was a new conception of the relation between the "eternal" and temporal orders, the divine and the human. Through Mary's "Motherhood of God," the divine became human (John, Ch. 1). Jesus was taken to be both God and man at the same time. This view fundamentally altered the Judaic conception by making possible the upgrading of the status of humanity – "the world might be saved."[10] Again, in spite of certain tendencies within Hellenistic Judaism, I think we can correctly say that Judaism was not a religion of individual salvation in the sense that Christianity is. Burke has pointed out that the idea of a redeemer is implicit in the Genesis myth, and Leach has also emphasized the role of "mediators," but how the role of the redeemer should be conceived and in particular what the relation of this role to the fate of the People of Israel should be was still very much an open question.

Here it is crucial to note that the founding event of Christianity was mythologically the sacrificial *death* of Jesus by crucifixion. Christianity has traditionally held this to be a real death, and not, as was common in Greek mythology, the mere disappearance of a divine personage who had chosen to spend a certain amount of time on earth disguised as a mortal. Jesus really died on the cross and had to be "resurrected" in order to re-enter the divine sphere of eternal life. It is of course central that the meaning of Jesus' death was symbolized as *giving* His *blood*. Blood is what we may speak of as that *gift* of life which is above all centered in the conception of maternity. In the Christian myth Mary was the giver of life to Jesus, a specially symbolic case of the more general conception of a woman *giving* birth to her child. In ordinary usage the word "give" is not stressed in this expression, but we think it symbolically crucial. The human component of the blood of Christ, therefore, was a *gift* from Mary, who only in the more extravagant phases of Catholic symbolization has herself been considered divine. This human component, however, was combined with the divine component originating from the begetting of Jesus by His divine Father. In these circumstances Jesus' own death was relativized. The concept of death applied only to the human component, not to the divine. The symbol of blood is the primary focus of the unity of the divine and the human, the focus of the Christian conception of the transcending of death. Another meaning of the symbol, blood, which has Hebrew antecedents but was profoundly modified in the Christian phase, is reflected in the act of dying, which again was in an important sense voluntary on Jesus' part – that is, Jesus in a certain sense provoked the Roman authorities into crucifying Him. In the symbolism of the

Last Supper, built into the basic sacramental ritual of Christianity, the Eucharist, there is not only the blood of Christ, symbolized by the wine, but also the "body" of Christ, symbolized by the bread. The body of Christ, meaning of course the risen Christ, came to be the symbol for the Church conceived as a supernatural entity embodying the Holy Spirit, which came to have the "power of the keys," the capacity to elevate the individual above the limitations of mortality and the other "Adamic" features of the human condition.

We do not think it too far-fetched to suggest that the Church was symbolically meant to "identify," in a sense not very different from the psychoanalytic-sociological sense, the ordinary human being with Christ. As a member of the Church, he became part of the "body of Christ" and thereby, *in dying* he became capable of *giving* his life, symbolized by blood, in a sense parallel to that in which Jesus gave His blood in the crucifixion. There seems to be a deep duality of meaning here: on the one hand, death is conceived to be deeply traumatic, symbolized by the suffering on the cross, and as such, a kind of "supreme sacrifice." On the other hand, the death of the individual can be conceived as not merely paving the way for his entrance into "heaven" but also as a sacrifice for the redemptive benefit of humanity in general. Quite apart from the metaphysical problems of what can possibly be meant by "survival" of the individual after death, this is a kind of positive sublimation of the grimly tragic view of the human condition as defined by the consequences of Adam's original sin. By the acceptance of the divine commandments and of Christ as the redeemer, man is not in principle totally expelled from the Garden to be dominated henceforth by "sin and death," but has the opportunity to participate in the divine order. He is thereby not in the Adamic sense *only* human. This represents a major upgrading of the religio-metaphysical status of man.

The collective reference has not been simply omitted here. It is through symbolic identification as part of the "body of Christ," i.e., the Church, that the individual can, even before death, participate in the "spiritual" as distinct from the "temporal" order. In a certain sense the old collectivity of the "people" became the model for a spiritual collectivity, membership in which was not by kinship but by faith, that is, acceptance of Christ. Yet Jesus was conceived not only as the "Son of God," but as "born of woman." His "body," though "mystical," was a means of mediating between divine and human.

Furthermore, this pattern seems to underlie a theme in Western religious history which has been emphasized repeatedly in the literature: this theme is that the biblical conception that God made man in His own image and Lord of the creation eventually materialized as the conception of a "Kingdom of God on Earth." This is turn implied that human society and personality could be permeated with a divine spirit, and thus the gap between the divine order of things and "the things of this world" was narrowed. What we have called the relativizing of the meaning of death seems to be a central part of this pattern. This is a relativizing that centers on the conception that every individual's death is both a *sacrifice*, and a *gift*.

The individual's capacity to die in the role of a giver of gifts[11] is dependent on three earlier and crucially important gifts. The first is the gift given by God the Father of what is sometimes religiously called the "living Christ" to humanity –

given, it should be noted, through the process of "begetting" (Christ, after all, was God's only begotten son). It is of great importance that the giving of this gift was motivated by "love" of the world. Again, this was a gift to humanity *from* God, not a sacrifice *to* God. The second gift was the gift of life as a human being given to Jesus by Mary. The crucial symbolic focus of the Christian conception of the feminine role is that of "Mary, Mother of God," who has given the human component of the blood that is to be sacrificed for the redemption of humanity. The third basic gift is the sacrificial death of Jesus which has frequently been symbolized – for example, in the final chorus of Handel's *Messiah* – as the *giving of His blood* for our redemption. Within this framework, then, the death of the human individual can be conceived not only as a sacrifice *for* others, but also as a gift *to* others for the future of humanity.

The question now arises, what modifications of this predominantly Catholic vision should be introduced to take into account both Protestantism and more recent developments that are no longer predominantly Protestant? Before discussing the Protestant phase and what has followed it, let us sum up what seem to be the four principal steps in the development from the Book of Genesis to full-fledged medieval Catholicism.

1. It is clear that the original meaning of death was as punishment for the disobedience by Adam and Eve of the one prohibition imposed upon them in the Garden. Their sin, however, was not merely disobedience, but pretention to the status of divinity. Mortality being the *primary* evidence of non-divinity, the imposition of death and expulsion from the Garden was linked with the conception that this life should be burdened with travail.

2. With the development of the covenant relationship between Yahweh and His chosen people, death took on a new meaning. The biblical phrase is reception into "the bosom of Abraham," which we have interpreted to mean, in a sense parallel to the Chinese tradition, that the dead achieve the honorific status of ancestors in the transgenerational collectivity of "the people." This is an acceptance of mortality as part of the acceptance of the generalized human condition with all of its limitations but with a note of special valence in the concept of chosenness. The symbol of blood then emerges as a symbol of ethnic belongingness, not only in one generation, but in the continuity of successive generations. This in turn is linked with the special significance of the Law as divinely ordained through Moses.

3. In the original Christian system, a major step in differentiation took place. There was a relative dissociation from an ethnic community, with both the spiritual and temporal fates of the individual acquiring a new salience. Human life, however, is conceived as *given*. The primary symbol here is that of Jesus portrayed as the only *begotten* son of God the Father. God's begetting is quite different from the creation of Adam. It presumes the continuity of humanity and the human reproductive process. Mary gives Jesus the gift of life at the human level, and it is the synthesis of the divine and human elements, symbolized in the Annunciation, which qualifies Jesus to be the redeemer of mankind. Blood in this sense was neither wholly divine nor wholly human, but a special synthesis of the two which transcended the stark dichotomy of divine and human of the Book of Genesis.

4. It seems clear, then, that the primary symbolic effect of Jesus' sacrifice was the endowment of ordinary humans with the capacity to translate their lives into gifts that simultaneously express love for other human beings (as "neighbors") and a love for God reciprocating God's love for "the world." These are the two fundamental commandments of the Gospel.

There is, therefore, a profound sense in which the sacrifice of Jesus on the cross becomes generalized so that all human deaths can be conceived as sacrifices. The element of sacrifice, however, emphasizes the negative, the cost side, of dying, which was so salient in the crucifixion because of Jesus' excruciating suffering. The positive side is the *gift* not by Mary of the particular human life of Jesus but to any living human person of *his* life. This seems to us to be the primary symbolic meaning of the Christian conception of the transcending of death. Death acquires a transbiological meaning because the paramount component of its meaning is the giving of life, at the end of a particular life, to God as an expression of love of God. This seems to symbolize the conception of a perpetuated solidarity between the bio-human level, symbolized by the blood of Mary, and the divine level, symbolized by the blood of Christ. In the ideal Christian death, one came to participate in the blood of Christ at a new level. This is the reciprocation of God's gift to mankind through Mary.

Protestantism

In the Catholic system this mutuality of giving as an expression of love was mediated by the sacramental system of the Church and from time to time fragmented by particularized absolutions. In the Protestant version, however, the sacramental system no longer had this power. The "power of the keys" was eliminated and the clergy became essentially spiritual leaders and teachers. Most important is that the life of perfection, the life which as a whole could be conceived to be both sacrifice and gift to God – namely, that of members of the religious orders – lost its special status, and every human being, layman and clergyman alike, was placed on the same level. We think, as Weber did, that this was basically an upgrading of the status of the laity rather than a downgrading of the status of the clergy. As Weber put it, "Every man was to become a monk."[12]

In one sense, the accent on life in this world was strengthened. This is seen in the Calvinist concept that it was man's mission to build the kingdom of God on earth. In this context the whole life of the individual was conceived as a unity. Its basic meaning was that of contribution to the building of the kingdom – that is, insofar as the individual lived up to religious expectations. His death then was *consummatory*, signalling the completion of the task for which he was placed in this world. This consummation, of course, required divine legitimation – i.e., through "faith" – but it also meant that in a curious sense dying became a voluntary act. A sharp distinction was made between dying in the ordinary sense and being killed. This conception is beautifully symbolized in a phrase in the Episcopal funeral service, "His work is done." (Also: "Well done, thou good and faithful servant.")

The implementation of the divine plan for the world brings the individual into a special kind of partnership with God. One might say that it completes the transformation from the Genesis conception of a life of travail following expulsion from the Garden and its bitter ending in death to the conception of life in this world as an opportunity to serve as an instrument of the divine will in the great task of building the kingdom. It is in this sense that Protestantism has been permeated with an acceptance of wordly life as basically good, and acceptance of death as the natural and divinely ordained consummation for the individual, but not the society.

There is, however, an underlying conflict. This positive and, in a sense, optimistic conception of life and death is conditional on fulfillment of the divine mandate – actually *doing* God's will. And this cannot be guaranteed. What Burke calls the element of the negative, the capacity to disobey, is just as characteristic of modern man as it was of Adam. The problem of what is to happen to the inveterate sinner cannot be avoided, because it cannot be guaranteed that sinners will cease to exist. Hence the note of death as punishment and its symbolic aftermath is always counterposed to this positive Protestant conception. Furthermore, no *given* state of society can be considered to be *the* "good society." Individuals must combat not only their own sinfulness, but the collective phenomena blocking fulfillment of the "Kingdom."

Another negative aspect is the consequence of the psychological connections between love and hate and the parallel conflicts at the social level. What psychologists call aggression toward others generally involves a desire to injure them or see them suffer injury, and in more extreme forms to see them die, even to kill them. Such wishes are also often directed against the self and figure prominently in the urge to suicide. All this is clearly contrary to the interpretation of the death of an individual as consummatory. Furthermore, conflict, accompanied by hostile wishes, between social classes, ethnic groups and nations is not easily compatible with the conception of a society as approximating a "Kingdom of God on Earth." Considerations such as these seem to have something to do with the extent to which populations with a culture close to the Protestant model are prone to rather violent fluctuations between moods of optimism and benevolence, and pessimism, hostility, and guilt.

It seems to us that the same basic pattern has survived the secularization which has led to the abandonment of the traditional Judeo-Christian conceptions of the role of the transcendental God in relation to humanity. The most conspicuous, though by no means only case, has been Marxian socialism, which – at least in its communist version – bears a great many resemblances to early Calvinism. Here the basic human assignment is to contribute to the building of socialism. The view of the fate of the individual "soul" after death is clearly different from that of a theistic Protestantism; indeed, in some respects it is similar to Judaism.[13] But the basic pattern seems very similar – that is, acceptance of mortality and the other fundamental features of the human condition, and, therefore, a conception of the completion of life, in the ideal case giving death a consummatory meaning.

Recent movements suggest a shift from the emphasis on "work" in the "Protestant Ethic" sense to a communally-organized regime of love which, of course, links with the earlier Christian traditions of love at both the divine and the human levels. It is not clear just how these movements are going to crystallize, if at all, but one thing is almost certain, that they will share with Puritan Protestantism and Marxian socialism a religious sanctification of life in this world.

One other important point should not be neglected. The early Christians were eschatologically oriented to the idea of a second coming of Christ and with it the day of judgment and the end of the world as it had been known to people of their time. The saved would then enter a state of eternal life in a new paradise resembling in some respects the Garden of Eden, yet different from it. The idea of some kind of pre-existent paradise in which man once lived has reverberated through the centuries, perhaps most conspicuously in the idea of the state of nature that was so prevalent during the Enlightenment. Rousseau seems to be its most prominent single exponent. A pre-existent state of nature, however, has been dynamically linked with the conception of a terminal state where all the problems of the tragic human condition are conceived to have been resolved. This kind of utopia has been exceedingly prominent in the socialist movement, most notably in the vision of communism as the end state of the task of building socialist societies.

There seems to be evidence that very similar orientations characterize the movement that one of us has elsewhere[14] called the new "religion of love." Indeed, in its more extreme versions the suggestion is made that a regime of total love can be set up in the immediate future. It will, however, have to be a terrestrial regime which cannot conceive "the end of the world" as that phrase was meant by the early Christians. It could mean only the end of the evil parts of the world. We have the impression that a clear conception of the meaning of death has not yet emerged in these circles, but almost certainly there is a fantasy of immortality. Death, as it has been known since the abandonment of specifically Christian eschatological hopes, is somehow felt to be unreal and this conception may be attributed to the new versions of the centrality of previous human life.[15]

The Moral Basis of Modern Medical Ethics

The physician's involvement with problems of life and death

If modern man has experienced the religious dimension of his life in the world as a gift from God, he turns in secular contexts to medical practitioners in order to gain expert assistance in preserving and enhancing his personal giftedness. In contemporary circumstances, the physician routinely takes part in the "giving" of birth, makes the first survey of the newborn's "gifts," including announcement of sex, and begins to prescribe for the preservation of its life. In the early years, when life is deemed fragile, the doctor is consulted frequently by responsible parents. Throughout mature life, the individual has the positive responsibility as well as freedom to seek a physician's aid whenever his gifts are endangered by disease or severe stress. Perhaps this obligation becomes especially strong when aging begins to enfeeble at least certain capacities. Unless death arrives suddenly and unexpectedly, medical treatment will ordinarily be involved, and in any case a physician will "pronounce" the death. Within the course of the individual's life-cycle, the services of a physician are now often involved in many crucial transitions of life-stage and social status. Thus, medical examinations, discussion, and prescriptive advice commonly accompany first entrance to school, the attainment of sexual maturity, enrollment in college, marriage, pregnancy and the birth of children, menopause, etc. Proper completion of such transitions in life status seems to require that a verification or determination of the giftedness of the individual be made by competent medical authority. Moreover, it is not unusual for relationships with a doctor to involve a diffuseness of concern for the welfare of the patient's life that is quite unusual outside the sphere of intimate primary ties – otherwise approximated only perhaps by religious-confessional and some educational relationships.

Modern, scientifically rationalized medicine may thus be regarded as a special set of instrumentalities and procedures for protecting the "gift of life." Not only does it penetrate very deeply into the routine social processes by which normal lives are constructed, but it is believed to act upon divinely given materials in circumstances of fragility, transformation, and danger. If the role of the physician involves not simply high status and honor but also a potential and frequently activated charisma of office, it derives these qualities from a fiduciary responsibility for maximizing those basic human gifts which individuals actually receive. In this respect the role of physician is closely related to that of teacher. In the context of the value patterns of instrumental activism that are institutionalized in modern society,[16] this specific type of responsibility constitutes a major normative structure in the articulations between religious premises and the secular social order.

The protection of the gifts of life involves practical efforts to control the causes of unnecessary and premature death. Despite this, the conditions under which particular deaths often occur represent the frustration of individuals' efforts to fulfill their personal roles in life. In a society that emphasizes occupational achievement as strongly as ours, this attitude toward death is perhaps especially poignantly felt when a promising individual dies in mid-career. The suffering and the disruption of the lives of others, generally family members, friends, and sometimes occupational associates, which usually accompany such a death must also be regarded as phenomena that hinder or reduce the realization of life potentials.[17] For many, the very prospect of death – especially in ways that symbolically touch upon powerful negative images in our culture, such as the degeneracy and loss of bodily control involved in cancer – produces horror that can substantially inhibit abilities to engage in many areas of social life. It is upon these reducible aspects or modalities of death that the life-enhancing efforts of modern medicine have tended to focus most sharply.[18]

Modern medicine can be distinguished from the practices with which most pre-modern societies have attempted to control the human impact of death by the strong specialization of its instrumentalities about the meliorable modalities of death. Modern medicine has tended to differentiate itself very sharply from religious, magical, and expressive means of orientation to the problems posed by death. It has tended not to deal directly with the existential issues of meaning raised by death. It does not claim to help patients deal with the "ultimate" problems associated with the eventual and sometimes imminent inevitability of their deaths. Rather, it has attempted to set such matters aside in order to develop specialized means of "treating" specific syndromes which are believed on scientific and empirical grounds to be "treatable."

Historically, this instrumental focus of modern medicine has been a difficult achievement. In many respects – for example, the continued competition of Christian Science, widespread fears in society of medical violations of the body, common suspicions about efforts to "treat" mental disturbances – it remains a partial achievement. Perhaps substantial tension resulting from forces within religious, moral, and expressive culture, which even now tend to place some limitations upon the scope of practice and treatment, remains intrinsic even to specialized, modern medicine.

Indeed, there appear to be some very strong factors operating within the cultural and social organization of medicine that are profoundly interdependent with the limiting cultural forces. Perhaps we have explicated enough of the interrelations between religious orientations and the patterning of medical practice to make it a conveniently paradigmatic case. It should be clear that religious orientations toward the meanings of life and death have comprised an important historical source of the instrumental activism embodied in modern medical institutions. Synchronically, the instrumental activism of the general religious culture contributes both crucial legitimation and patterning of commitments toward sustaining the pragmatically activistic institutional forms that modern medicine has developed. Here, the religiously-grounded commitments provide important foundations for the role performances of both medical personnel and the patients and their families who must cooperate with the special types of treatment that can be legitimated within modern medicine. Thus the special legitimation and value-commitments required by modern medicine seem to depend on the existence of congruent religious orientations in the broader society.

Religious patterns condition the practice of medicine in at least one other principal respect. Physicians, nurses, and other medical personnel, as well as patients who are severely ill, are confronted by the phenomena of death in massive ways. People in these roles must often carry grave responsibilities and make extremely difficult decisions, while acting under the stresses generated by impending or probable death. In this difficult situation, and perhaps especially for those who must routinely confront it, a strong religious or philosophical faith seems essential to sustaining legitimate commitments to role performance. The very specificity and instrumentality of the proper performances, which do not permit the primary emphasis on treatment to be compromised by direct involvement of religious concerns – to say nothing of "spontaneous" emotional reactions – add to the extent to which certain *underlying* commitments must be profoundly *serious*, in the sense of Durkheim's definition of religion as belonging to "the serious life."[19] They must be serious enough to maintain their integrity even when denied direct expression.

"Scientific" medicine and the "existential" problem

A theoretical interpretation of the position of modern medicine must emphasize, then, both its comparative independence from direct or particularistic limitation by religion and its underlying dependence upon and penetration by religious culture.

What we now wish to examine is the comparable balance between independence and interdependence that characterizes the relations of medical orientations toward death with the general system of ethical beliefs in American culture. On the one hand, modern, scientific medical practice must operate independently of the diffuse processes of moral judgment in society. The physician's treatment of the patient is structured in terms of a professional exercise of applied science, not directly as a moral process of social control. The cooperative relation of physician and patient is often constricted, damaged, or undermined when the intrusion of diffusely moral judgment displaces instrumental calculation as the focus of treatment. Here, the modern physician's role contrasts sharply with that of the primitive witch-doctor or the archaic curer. There can be no presumption that the practitioner's efficacy is intrinsically bound up with the ways in which he exercises moral sanctions over the patient. Treatment is intrinsically technical and not dependent on moral judgment of the patient. On the other hand, the life-and-death responsibilities of the medical relationship impose strong moral exigencies upon all concerned just as inexorably as they raise religious problems. Hence, the treatment relationship must itself be controlled in terms of an autonomous ethical complex that is rationalized with respect to medical treatment that gives primacy to instrumental-technical calculation. Commitment to a specialized ethical system by physician, patient, and auxiliaries (e.g., the patient's family as well as nurses, aides, and hospital administrators) creates a crucial condition for stabilizing treatment relationships so as to offset the often severe and baffling stresses of uncertain diagnosis, treatment, and prognosis. Medical ethics have come to be rationalized so as to provide a set of categories of responsibility which can give general assurance that due care has been taken to protect the "gifts of life," whatever undesirable outcomes may ensue.

Although medical ethics require autonomy in adapting to the special moral problems of medical practice, they also require legitimation. And this can be gained only through integration with the general moral-evaluative system of the encompassing culture. In order to convey moral authority to specific medical practices and institutions, medical ethics must themselves be relatively congruent with the principles of the surrounding moral culture.[20] Moreover, the responsibilities and limits allocated to different actors – e.g., doctors and patients – must not conflict too overtly with the expectations structured in other specialized sectors of the moral system.

Our frame of reference is here specifically cultural. Broadly, we conceive a moral-ethical system as transforming religiously grounded premises or "themes" into more specific moral prescriptions that provide authoritative bases for the organization of institutions and the planning of sequences of action.[21] Obversely, the same processes of transformation must come to terms with the moral problems generated by the various institutional operations affected by specific prescriptions. Moral-ethical functioning may be seen as simultaneously involving the "spelling out" of the complex practical implications of general religio-ethical principles and the reduction of these implications to certain consistent grounds of solution.[22] But problems of meaning are continually raised by the impact of specific principles on a variety of institutional situations and by the uncertainties which specific institutional situations bring to bear on a variety of ethical principles. Particular prescriptions generally draw upon a number of independent principles and have implications for a considerable range of interactive situations. Any equilibrium of consistency concerning specific ethical issues is apt to be short-lived, and problems of meaning are apt to reassert themselves with changes in institutional conditions or even in other specialized complexes of the moral system. Hence, despite the stability of many major structures of moral-evaluative culture over considerable periods of history, ethical order at the practical level must be a continually renewed achievement. Moreover, it must be achieved specifically at the cultural level, that is, through the abstract and generalized rationalization of interrelations among symbols, references, premises, principles, hypotheses, etc.

We interpret the religiously established theme of the great value of the divine "gift of life" as comprising a principal premise for medical ethics. Yet, it is important to recognize that it also comprises a premise for many other ethical complexes in our culture: police activity protects the "gift of life," educational activity serves to enhance the "gifts" of individuals, and automobile traffic is regulated with a view to restricting the loss of life – to cite only a few examples. However, as a general construct within the moral culture as a whole – although not necessarily in its bearing on medical ethics – the "gift of life" theme has not generally established an absolute principle of ethics. Thus, the general prescription of "give me liberty or give me death" has also been honored in American culture, and may even be said to have provided moral legitimation for conscription which has obligated men to risk their lives when the national freedom was believed to be in danger. Yet the moral authority of the "gift of life" theme is not simply overridden in this case. Ideals associated with the "freedom" of society have exerted powerful symbolic meaning and moral authority in part because of the willingness of many individuals to die for them.[23] Moreover, particular freedoms which can be viewed as more costly in lives than beneficial to society – for example, the freedom of private citizens to carry handguns – are apt to lose much of their moral authority. We may expect that leadership in efforts to redefine the scope of such freedoms will often be exercised by individuals whose special moral responsibilities to protect lives have been stimulated by social conditions. For example, physicians who repair many gunshot wounds in emergency rooms of large city hospitals are apt to be proponents of stricter gun control laws. The theme of the dignity of life not only enters a variety of areas of moral discourse but does so in a complex array of combinations with other evaluative premises, such as that of freedom. We must now ask whether similar conditions apply to the functioning of the "gift of life" theme within the realm of medical ethics.

We may suggest that the major burden of the articulation of medical ethics within the broader moral-evaluative culture is carried by the principle of the dignity and importance of *divinely*[24] given human life. Within the broad manifold of human activities, medicine takes on its special moral authority and somewhat charismatic status – qualities apparently essential for effective treatment in many difficult situations – from its commitment to, and ability to implement, this crucial value. Medicine is continually engaged in an effort to increase the level of rationalization of its instrumental techniques for protecting health and life against a very broad range of threatening conditions and sentiments. Similarly, there are constantly on-going efforts to rationalize medical ethics as means for assuring the implementation of the basic commitment to preservation of the "gifts" of life, especially through the allocation of firm responsibilities for the care of individuals. The functional viability of modern medicine, then, may be seen to rest upon a crucial constraint on the system of medical ethics, namely, that a position of strong predominance must be given to the principle of the dignity of life. Other principles must be firmly relegated to secondary positions of importance.

The maintenance of this structural arrangement appears to be quite problematic in two respects. First, the institutional ordering of treatment relationships requires that attention be paid to other principles of value in medical ethics. For example, there must be considerable emphasis laid on mutual respect between patient and physician, on honesty and fairness in communication, on limiting the costs of treatment to "reasonable" levels, etc. In many situations, and perhaps especially when illness is severe and/or treatment technically difficult, attention to these themes may conflict with the maintenance of a superordinate orientation to the value of sustaining life. Secondly, there is a latent or potential conflict between medical ethics and other sectors of the moral-evaluative system in which the principle of preserving life is not directly given the same priority. Medical institutions, therefore, require ethical means of assuring that actors involved in medical situations, including patients and their families as well as medical personnel, will in fact act upon the normative priorities given in medical ethics rather than upon some others. This exigency exerts strong pressure toward giving medical ethics an autonomous and clearly bounded form vis-à-vis other complexes in the moral-evaluative system.

If we may speak in somewhat ideal-typical terms of a classical form of modern medical ethics, its principal structural features appear to be understandable as adaptations to the functional exigencies we have just highlighted. The structural core has been an absolutizing of the value of preserving life. Both the life of the individual patient and the physician's obligation to protect or save the patient's life have been taken as *divinely given*. The physician could then take the obligation to attempt to stave off the patient's death as an absolute prescription – a "Commandment" – having no explicit limitations. Only the insufficiencies of the physician's instrumental resources would limit his effort to combat the patient's death. There thus has been very strong ethical motivation to increase the technical capacities of the physician in order to better implement his obligation to save lives under ever more difficult circumstances. Indeed, it would seem that the extraordinary growth in technical capacity achieved by modern medicine should be explained by reference not only to the general prominence of the value pattern of "instrumental activism" in modern culture, but also to the way in which instrumental improvement has served to ease severe tensions within the system of medical ethics.

Orientation to the nearly absolute "commandment" to combat the death of his patient provided a very strong and clear definition of the situation[25] for the physician in several respects. It assured the physician that he could act in direct relation to a value of great importance without having to embroil himself in a broad range of difficult problems of meaning. It permitted, indeed required, that he pursue the "saving" of life at almost any cost, that is, by subordinating almost all other value considerations. This nearly absolute commitment to preserve life strongly insulated medical ethics from any ethical system or complex that did not place a commensurate emphasis upon the value of preserving life, and thereby firmly grounded the autonomy of medical ethics. Finally, it offered a clear basis for disparaging any other ethical position, for it could reasonably be argued that no other position *really* respected the divine gift of life when hard choices had to be made.

Despite these impressive strengths, the classical ethics of modern medicine has contained some serious strains and weaknesses. One principal source of difficulty is that this ethical pattern allows little room for positive definitions of the significance and meaning of death. The primary meaning of death is structured to be seen as a medical defeat,[26] either for the physician personally or for the "state of the art" with which he is strongly identified. Especially when the circumstances are such that the physician is bound to "lose" many patients, he is placed under great personal strain. Empirical studies in hospitals have shown that there is a consequent tendency for physicians to be unable to give high levels of attention, emotional support, and careful treatment to their dying patients.[27] Often the attitude of the physician becomes extremely defensive just at the time when the dying patient and his family need assistance in managing the problems of adjustment to the impending death.[28] When the physician feels that he may have "caused" his patient to die by making a "mistake" in diagnosis or treatment, his burden of guilt (and perhaps fear of a legal suit or loss of professional standing) often severely restricts his capacity to treat and relate honestly to his patient.[29] Indeed, it seems that rather devious communication with the patient, often supported by other hospital personnel, is at least not infrequent under such circumstances. It also seems that many dying patients are better able than their physicians to orient themselves to the positive "consummatory" meanings of their impending deaths.[30] The physician may engage the patient in highly moralistic discourse, attempting to mobilize his "will to live" or his "fighting spirit" against death, even when death in the near future appears to be inevitable and the patient is more or less ready to accept his situation.[31] The physician may even make his continued close attention to the patient conditional upon a display of "fighting spirit" while the patient might prefer franker discussion of his prognosis. Treatment may be given more as a ritual commitment to the value of fighting death than out of rational expectation that it will help the patient. The patient's family – or indeed, the hospital – may be encouraged to make ill-afforded expenditures on such ritualistic treatment, while being discouraged from adapting their life circumstances – and especially their relationships with the patient – to the inevitable death.[32]

Exacerbation of strain by technical advances

Some additional strains have been created by modern medicine's very high level of technical mastery, but these have become problematic for medical ethics only in relatively recent years. Despite the physician's "absolute" obligation to save lives and the givenness of the patient's life, the moral authority of the ethic is reinforced when the life being saved still holds much unrealized promise. Thus, medical treatment is generally undertaken with the greatest energy when at stake are the lives of children or adults "in the prime of life" or endowed with special talents or social responsibilities.[33] The physician's contribution to the patient's future fulfillment of promise or a calling comes to seem essential to the meaning of treatment. Under present conditions, however, it is not unusual that some of the most intensive and sophisticated treatment goes to aged patients dying from degenerative diseases. Often such patients can be kept alive only through massive artificial support, and have prognoses that do not permit realistic hopes of future fulfillment of a calling.[34] Sometimes treatment seems to contribute more to unwanted suffering than to preservation of the "gifts" of life. Under such conditions, severe problems of meaning are bound to arise within the classical framework of medical ethics, for the benefits of treatment are not obvious and the efforts to preserve life face comparatively rapid defeat.

The ethical focus on the obligation to defeat death through the mobilization of intense commitments and great quantities of medical resources has perhaps had some irrational effects on the development and allocation of medical resources. American medicine has become most clearly pre-eminent in providing the most intensive, most technically elaborate and "modern," and least cost-conscious treatments for patients who are already engaged in well-defined struggles with death or debilitating diseases. In this situation, there is a strong tendency to demonstrate – again in a fashion having a strong ritual and religious quality – that "everything possible" is being done to aid the patient. Notably, this is the situation in which doctors speak of themselves as engaging in "heroics." Such medical activity clearly makes a potent statement about the valuation of individual lives, both within medicine and in the society at large. Nevertheless, the stress on such medical heroics has diverted attention and resources from public health measures that, in other societies, have preserved more lives at less cost – although leaving the physician with fewer "heroic" measures for the patient already struggling with death.

Emergence of new definitions of the situation

The strains we have just noted have been complemented by certain developments in medicine that tend to undermine the conception of the absolute givenness of human lives. One crucial area of change has concerned the understanding and definition of death as the "end" of life. Much attention has been given to the recent trend toward redefining death, so that brain function rather than breathing or heart function serves as the criterion of life. How this redefinition facilitates the transplantation of cadaver organs has gained much public notice. The broader background of this change is that a variety of recently perfected resuscitative and life-supporting techniques have confronted physicians with the routine experience of having large numbers of patients on the very border between life and death. Even early in their training, physicians now engage not merely in "saving" lives, but actually in bringing people back to life.[35] Large proportions of hospital patients lack, at least temporarily, the capacity to live but are "kept alive" artificially. Sometimes the decision to "allow" a patient to die by removing the artificial supports of life seems to be the most reasonable recourse, although it is a decision which physicians generally try to avoid. There are patients of whom it can reasonably be claimed that they have died more than once. Some transplant patients live only by virtue of the functioning of organs which were originally the "gifts" of another person.[36] Although these circumstances have been the result of gradual, incremental improvements in medical technique, they clearly raise some new and difficult questions about the meaning and medical significance of life and death.

The problematic nature of the boundary between life and death has also come to involve the origins of life in conception and birth. Both contraception and abortion have, of course, very long histories. Yet, recent improvements in technique, if complemented by mass campaigns for "birth control," will make possible an entirely new level of mastery not simply of numbers but also of inherited traits of those born into society. Indeed, if abortion becomes widespread, already foreseen developments in genetic counselling will permit very considerable control over the inborn "gifts" of babies, and perhaps even their distribution in society.[37] The ethical issues posed by birth control, and especially by the abortion of viable fetuses, however, are very difficult to resolve. Most attention has been given to the question of when, in the development from conception to birth, the fetus obtains the "gift of life" which makes it an autonomous being entitled to legal and moral protection. Perhaps more interesting in our present perspective is the disjunction between, on the one hand, the pro-abortion arguments that fetal life may be terminated in the interest of furthering the parents' mastery of their own life circumstances or the environment in which they will rear children and, on the other hand, the absolute valuation of life within classical medical ethics.

Two other developments seem also to bear stressfully on the absolute conception of the givenness of life. One is the emergence in recent years of surgical procedures, usually employed in conjunction with careful psychiatric analysis and treatment, for altering the sex of individuals.[38] Here, medical treatment is used to change the most diffuse and general of stable social identities that is ordinarily given with birth. The second concerns the treatment of individuals handicapped by markedly "subnormal" intelligence due to genetic causes. Together with increasing use of genetic counselling to minimize the number of births of such individuals, there has been a growing disinclination to place them in special institutions from birth or early childhood. Removing them from the general community may be interpreted as setting a certain boundary to the level of "giftedness" minimally characteristic of members of society. The tendency to reintegrate "subnormals" into the society, then, has the effect of somewhat blurring this boundary. Perhaps it is significant that persuasion of parents to keep their mentally handicapped children with the family has emphasized not only the benefits for the mental development of such children, but also the human pleasures and moral satisfaction to be gained by other members of the family.

That the increasing flux in definition of the boundaries of a human life has occurred at *both* ends of the "age" span seems to us to be particularly significant, as does the new possibility of deliberately changing biological sex identity. This seems to justify our focus, articulated at the beginning of this essay, on the "age and sex" frame of reference. Furthermore, the fact that there is a trend to include the mentally retarded in more normal social relationships is also very much related to the problem of the treatment of illegitimate children, especially by the institution of adoption.[39] Both of these developments relate to another of the main themes of our discussion of the religious background of the life–death complex, namely, that of the status of persons and groups gained through "inclusion" in significant collective entities, both temporal and spiritual; one may also add the current intensive preoccupation with the status of the "poor" and of various kinds of "minorities."

The restructuring of medical ethics

The pressures on the classical form of modern medical ethics have by now become so powerful that there is a quite widespread feeling that the profession must undertake a very general re-examination of its morals. In some quarters, there is exasperation – almost despair – over the difficulty of the problems that must now be confronted. Yet, we think the process of re-examination is already underway and that the outline of a new ethic is becoming visible.

The emerging medical ethic may be termed "a relativized ethic" or, in Weber's sense, an ethic of responsibility.[40] While this newer ethic has major continuity with the absolute ethic in making the principle of protecting life its highest value-premise, it no longer treats this priority as an absolute. Instead, the physician is given positive responsibility for calculating rational articulations between this principle and other evaluative principles recognized in the ethical system, so that normative prescriptions can be flexibly adapted to ethically difficult situations. The physician is no longer under an absolute commandment to preserve life, but may make a relatively free judgment – generally after consultation with colleagues, the patient, and the patient's family – about the extent to which treatment should be directed toward the preservation of life and the extent to which other ends should be given priority.

This form of ethics is more rational in that, by recognizing more explicitly the conditions under which direct struggle with death must be fruitless and even counter-productive in terms of other values, it permits fuller implementation of a broad range of ethical principles. At the same time, it allows firmer action to be taken with respect to a broad range of the modalities in which death is socially disruptive. A further impetus to adopting the ethic of responsibility is that it provides a stronger basis for dealing with the problems of meaning which recent medical developments have been generating. However, this ethic imposes some very serious responsibilities upon the physician. He no longer has the emotional support of an absolute which gives him clear prescriptive guidelines. He can no longer externalize the ethical grounds of his action through comparatively simple logical operations. Rather, he must bear personal responsibility for the specific ethical grounds of actions. He must subject issues of the practical valuation of life, suffering, death, departure from social ties, the fulfillment of "promise," etc., to personal examination. In order to act honestly, he must often engage patients and their families in dialogues on these disturbing issues at times when they are apt to be profoundly troubled themselves.[41] These obligations do not make for an easy calling.

Change in ethical orientation to death seems roughly to index the extent to which the ethic of responsibility has come to prevail. The relativized ethic provides a greatly enhanced basis for recognizing the consummatory meanings of death. The impending, inevitable death of a patient need not be taken as a defeat of treatment. The efforts of the physician may then – in a certain sense – facilitate the patient's death, supporting his sense of dignity and his ability to put his affairs in order,[42] encouraging a readjustment in his relations with his family, and meliorating the trying conditions of a death. These activities also aid the patient to employ his "gifts of life," but involve the mastery of death as social and psychological rather than physiological processes.

The relativized ethic also renders the boundaries of medical ethics more flexible in relation to other components of moral-evaluative culture. The physician must take more responsibility for admitting the medical significance of ethical considerations structured in other sectors of the moral system. The recognition of the consummatory significance of death is one example of the new penetration of medical ethics by a religio-moral perspective having essentially non-medical origins.

Perhaps the most massive recent penetration of extra-medical considerations into medical ethics has been the acknowledgement, partly under political compulsion, that the distribution of medical care in our society must be rationalized to a greater extent in terms of "health rights" which citizens hold simply by virtue of membership in society.[43] Here, medicine is adapting its ethical system to moral considerations of a predominantly political and legal character. However, it is clear that the long-run effect should be a substantial upgrading in the quality of medical care available to the citizenry at large, especially to those in the lower economic classes. In terms of medical ethics, this change must be adjudged a great victory. One concomitant of this victory – in certain respects a cost and in others a benefit – will be the further projection of medical responsibilities into the realm of public discourse. When massive social planning for new systems of health care is undertaken, medical advice takes on a new importance in public affairs. The fiduciary responsibilities of the medical profession then come to include the task of providing expert leadership for the public's deliberation on health policy.

It would be a mistake, however, to regard this extension of the medical role in any simple sense as only political. At issue are many questions of value with moral and even religious dimensions. Reformulations of quite fundamental aspects of our societal value system are underway which constitute its generalization and upgrading, not abandonment. The meanings of life and death are so centrally at issue that the medical contribution to the discussion seems bound to be substantial. If the ethical reorientation we have discussed becomes consolidated in the medical profession and is projected into the realm of public deliberations, perhaps medicine will provide the leadership in some very interesting developments in modern normative culture.

Most important for the theme of this paper is the fact that the direction of this change opens new areas of freedom for defining a meaningful consummatory death as the reciprocation of the gift of life which the person received at his birth. In addition to the enormous contribution of the medical complex in differentiating the inevitable from the adventitious components of death, and to the very great diminution in the incidence of the latter, this change may not only help to enable the dying person to leave in the spirit of a giver of gifts, but also may enable members of the medical profession to facilitate this definition of impending death instead of blocking it. The ideal outcome would be a coincidence of the meaning of the words we have already quoted – "His work is done" – for the roles of both dying patient and physician. The patient is hopefully "ready to go," whereas the physician has not only done his best to "save" his patient's life, but has complemented these efforts by facilitating a dignified and meaningful death.

The "Existential" Problem of Death in Medical Perspective

For social scientists who conceive "society" in a restricted way, the foregoing discussion of the relation of life and death to medical ethics might seem to "stand on its own feet" without reference to the considerations of the earlier part of the paper. We believe, however, that the trends of change in medical ethics outlined above are inherently intertwined with the problems of the meaning of life and death. Furthermore, we believe that the structure of mythic themes which we selected from the Judeo-Christian religious tradition constitutes the best available framework for understanding these phenomena.

Over the course of the past ten to fifteen years, what might be called the religious dimension of modern American medicine – its relationship to the gifts of life and death and their consummatory meaning – has begun to be more overtly expressed. Although this existential aspect of medicine is an irreducible part of its deeper significance in a modern society, as in all others, until recently the strong instrumental focus of twentieth-century American medicine exerted a repressive influence on its outward manifestation. Various social control mechanisms existed in the medical profession that actively discouraged involvement with so-called philosophical issues. In the medical school climate of the 1950s,[44] for example, faculty virtually never raised questions with students like "what is death?" "why death?" or "in what deeper senses, if any, does death differ from life?" Even in situations conducive to such querying – notably, the anatomy laboratory, the autopsy, or in the face of students' early confrontation with terminally ill patients – instructors rarely initiated such discussions. And if a student made a timorous effort to do so, he was likely to be silenced by classmates and faculty alike with the quip, "that's too philosophical." Decoded, this meant "the matters of which you speak are not sufficiently rational, object-ive, scientific, or pragmatic to fall within the proper domain of medicine, or of truly professional behavior." It was also characteristic of this decade that profes-sionals were more inclined to speak euphemistically about the death of a patient – "he (she) expired," "passed on," or "was transferred to Ward X," – than straightforwardly to state that death had occurred.

In sharp contrast to such medical attitudes in the 1950s (at least in academic milieux where new physicians were being trained and scientific research em-phasized), the late 1960s and early 1970s appear very "philosophical," indeed. Currently, along with an increased social concern about the inadequacies and inequities in our system of delivering care, American medicine is publicly pondering more existential matters: problems of uncertainty, meaning, life and death, solidarity, and of intervention in the human condition. In fact, one might almost say that a certain amount of "radical chic" now accrues to engaging these topics, most particularly that of "death and dying."

There are those who contend that this discernible shift in the orientation of modern medicine is due to recent biomedical advances – actual and anticipated developments in genetics and genetic engineering, life support systems, birth technology, including asexual reproduction, the implantation of human, animal and artificial organs, behavior and thought control – and to the problems of decision-making and longer range consequences ensuing from them. Although we would not deny the important role that these scientific and technological events have played in making the moral and metaphysical concerns of modern medicine both more visible and legitimate, we would maintain that the greater interest in such issues is part of a broader and deeper process of cultural change in our society. It is not only in medicine, for example, that concern about the "quality of life," equity, human solidarity and societal community is manifesting itself. From an evolutionary perspective, both the scope and intensity of these preoccupations in American society at the present time suggest that we may be entering a new stage of advanced modernity.

As fundamental as any changes in the meta-ethics of contemporary medicine is the process by which conceptions of life and death, in relation to the physi-cian's role responsibilities, are being reformulated. Reverence for the gift of life, and dedication both to its protection and prolongation are still basic value commitments of modern medicine. If anything, in recent years physicians have been more vocal than ever about their disinclination to "play God," as they themselves put it: that is, to arrogate to themselves the right to determine "who shall live and who shall die," by making more vigorous and continuing efforts to prevent the deaths and perpetuate the lives of some categories of patients over others. References to the Nazi medical war crimes as the ultimate sacrilege to which medicine can be brought are often made in such discussions.

What is implied is that, because the role of physician centers on knowledge that pertains to life and death, unless great moral vigilance is continually exercised, the equivalent of original sin will again and again be committed. And in the collective extreme, this can become holocaust. There are evident relations between these medical concerns and the persistence of adventitious death in war and by other forms of violence as these concern a more general public.

Nevertheless, the profession of medicine has been steadily moving towards a less absolute position on what constitutes sanctity of life and the value of preserving it. Serious attempts are being made to distinguish vital processes which maintain the individual sheerly as a low-grade biological organism, from those which are essential to "humanness" and "person-hood." The new operational definition of death now in the process of being institutionalized in the medical profession and the larger society crystallizes this distinction. For, in defining death as the irreversible cessation of higher brain activity, it codifies the position that although the heart may beat and respiration continue (either naturally or by artificial means), without neocortical function and the cerebration that it makes possible, essentially *human* life does not exist. Thus, in the face of irreversible coma, the medical profession now seeks and is progressively obtaining justification for declaring a person dead, and for suspending life-sustaining efforts on his behalf. It is the opinion of the ethical scholar, Joseph Fletcher, that this redefinition of death represents a cardinal step in what he considers an at once needed and desirable evolution of medicine from an ethic based on the unconditional "sanctity of life" to one premised on the "quality of life."[45]

These changes seem to us, in general theoretical terms, to be interpretable as part of a more general process of "progressive social change."[46] As noted above, they constitute processes of differentiation, e.g., from the "absoluteness" of the physician's obligation to prolong life, to the opening up of several degrees of freedom in this area, with the consequence of imposing new burdens of decision on both physician and patient. There has been a process of upgrading, not only of the technical levels of medical service, but also of the opportunities to participate in a new "quality of life" for sick people and others, as well as a process of "value-generalization" by which the older formulae of the meaning of life and death are coming to be redefined.

Perhaps as a harbinger of these changes, more than thirty years ago one of us (Talcott Parsons) was startled, again at the Massachusetts General Hospital, by the sudden statement of an eminent senior surgeon, "no, human life is not sacred." At first blush this statement was wholly "meaningless." Fortunately, however, it was possible – knowing the background of the remark – to interpret its meaning. The speaker referred to a case which he had been discussing with his clinical clerkship group of medical students: it concerned an older woman for whom there was a "fighting chance" of gaining several years of good health and high "quality of life" if radical and dangerous surgery were to be performed, while at the same time there was a serious risk that the operation itself would be fatal. The alternative was a few more years of living in a gravely incapacitated state where only a low "quality of life" would be possible. The surgeon's statement was his way of asserting the moral justification of deliberately risking his patient's life in favor of the chance of a really meaningful terminal sector – i.e., a chance of a period of "high quality" life as against a longer, more certain period of "low quality" life.

The broadening of the range of "concern" for medical decisions

At the same time that the medical profession is outspokenly reluctant to make such God-like decisions, it is also increasingly confronted with the inescapable obligation to use its "new controls over life and death in a responsible way."[47] One of the means by which medicine is dealing with this antinomy is through broadening its patterns of professional collaboration. In medical amphitheatres throughout the country, and in many conferences on medical ethical issues, physicians are discussing these aspects of their life-and-death responsibilities with psychiatrists, social workers, ethicists, theologians, lawyers, and social scientists, among others. Often, these discussions turn around general principles and concepts, and *ex post facto* analyses of decisions about patients that have already taken place. But, especially in university-affiliated medical institutions, it is also becoming more common for such consultations to be sought while the physicians entrusted with a particular case are still deliberating about the most rational and humane course of action to take. Widening the orbit of colleagues whose advice they seek enlarges the range of expertise available to physicians, and provides them with intellectual and moral support from professional circles that are more than "strictly medical."

But perhaps the deepest significance of these more inclusive collegial patterns lies in their relationship to the closer integration with our main societal value system towards which the "new" medicine seems to be struggling.[48] Partly independently of the basic shifts in these values, e.g., in the direction of their generalization, and partly as a consequence of them, medicine is now passing through a "time of troubles" and transition that centers on its growing capacity to sustain and abrogate life, its heightened tendency to raise questions of meaning, as well as of definition, about life and death, health and illness, and its greater concern with the equitable distribution of health care and scarce medical resources in our society. Through collaboration with other professionals, and also through the establishment of more collegial relations with patients and other consumers of health care, such as the families of patients, medicine seems to be reaching beyond the obtaining of counsel and consent on specific issues. A broader, more egalitarian moral consensus is being sought, that extends further than the "sacred trust" of traditional, one-to-one doctor–patient relationships, and the boundaries of what was previously defined as the medical professional community.[49]

Organ transplants and the gift complex

In our view, one of the therapeutic innovations that most dramatically exemplifies some of the overtly or covertly religious as well as moral problems with which modern medicine is grappling, is human organ transplantation.[50] For, central to transplantation is "the theme of the gift,"[51] a theme that we have shown to be fundamental to Judeo-Christian conceptions of life and death. With the possible exception of "giving birth," and to a lesser extent, donating blood, transplantation entails the most literal "gift of life" that a person can proffer or receive. The donor (a significant linguistic usage) contributes a vital part of his (her) body to a terminally ill, dying recipient, in order to save and maintain that other person's life. Because of the magnitude of this gift-exchange, and its symbolic, as well as biomedical implications, participating in a transplantation can be a transcendent experience for those involved, be it the live donor, the recipient, their relatives, the cadaver donor's family, or the members of the medical team. It may epitomize for them man's highest capacity to make the sacrificial gift of life-in-death, that is supreme love, commitment and communion. In this sense, regardless of how scientific the setting in which this transaction occurs may be, or how secularized the beliefs of those who take part in it, deep religious elements, some of them explicitly Christian, are at least latently present in the transplant situation.[52]

Nevertheless, here, as elsewhere, the properties of gift-exchange are such that transplantation confronts medicine and the larger society with a number of phenomena that are more troubling than transfiguring. To begin with, live-organ (kidney) transplantation involves both the donor and the medical team in an unprecedented act, whose morality is subject to question: the infliction of deliberate injury on a well person, in order to help another who is suffering from a fatal disease. However noble their motivation in performing major surgery on a healthy donor, the medical profession thereby compromises one of its basic, shall we say "absolute," ethical tenets: "to do no harm."[53]

Furthermore, under the circumstances in which live transplantations normally occur, the quality of consent obtained from the donor and recipient for this still experimental procedure is often strained. A family member is dying of renal disease, and his best chance for survival with a tolerable life is to be the recipient of a kidney from a relative whose tissue-type closely matches his own. No matter how scrupulously low-keyed and sensitive the medical team's process of screening candidates may be, the fact remains that, in this predicament, prospective donors are under very great inner and outer pressure to give an organ to their suffering relative who, in turn, is under extraordinary pressure to receive one. Thus, the norm of "voluntary informed consent" can only be imperfectly realized.

And what constitutes so-called healthy, positive motivation, either in life or in death, for someone to donate a part of his body to a known or unknown other? Here, the medical profession has been brought face to face with the question of how much faith they collectively have in the altruistic principle, and how much belief in the desire and capacity of human beings to relate to one another as their "brothers' keepers" and as their "strangers' keepers,"[54] which in Christian parlance may be phrased as "loving their neighbors."

Still another set of value-questions that transplantation has raised turns around the allocation of scarce resources. Who should be the beneficiaries of the limited supply of human organs for transplantation that are made available through donation? What criteria of choice, if any, would be compatible with the highest value-commitments of our society? More fundamentally still, ought we to be expending so many material and immaterial resources for this kind of confrontation with terminal illness and death, when we might be investing them in the more universalistically life-giving purpose of providing good health care for our entire citizenry?

But perhaps the most chastening discovery that medicine has made about the gift relationship established by transplantation is that it can bind donor, recipient and kin to one another, emotionally and morally, in ways that are likely to be as fettering as they are liberating. Giving and receiving life in this form can lock the participants into an encompassing creditor–debtor relationship that blurs their separate identities, and diminishes their ability to reach out to others. Herein lies the potential tyranny of the human gift, its paradox, and perhaps its ultimate religious mystery. Organ transplantation suggests that the only perfect, truly redemptive gifts are *divine* ones. These are gifts of life and death from God, which constitute the at once sacred and flawed materials on which medicine acts: our essential humanity. The threat is to compromise the universalistic thrust of modern values.

POR QUE?

Conclusion

We hope we have been able to draw certain lines of connection between some very ancient themes defining the human condition with reference to life and death, and some very immediate developments, with special reference to the orientations, functions and obligations of the contemporary medical profession.

Our primary theses are, first, that the problem of the meaning of death has been coming more and more explicitly to the fore in the recent development of our culture, and that a major focus of this salience has been in the medical world. Secondly we feel that, new as these developments are, they are not understandable except in reference to the great religious tradition of our culture, especially as expressed in the major constitutive "myths."

The theme of gift-exchange between God and man has been central to our analysis. In particular, we have emphasized the salience of the conception that human life is a gift from God. We have then, we think, been able to trace at least in outline the evolution of the conception that the death of the individual, at the close of a "full" life, not only *may* be, but in fact often *is*, interpreted as a reciprocal gift to God, the consummatory reciprocation of the gift of life. The emergence of this interpretation, we believe, has been enormously facilitated by medical control over the causes of adventitious death.

All of this has been occurring in the context of the development of a highly rationalized, technical, industrial society. "Scientific medicine" has been part and parcel of this society. The involvement, however, of the medical profession in the existential problems of the meaning of life and death, and at least its tentative movement in the direction of incorporating such a dimension, seems to us to be a striking example of the intimate interweaving of the more rationalistic and the more existential components in the development of modern society and culture. Far from there being a necessity to choose between the "scientific" attitude toward illness and health, life and death, and a "mystical" orientation, we hope that we have made a modest contribution to understanding the ways in which a synthesis of these two aspects of modern culture may be possible.

Notes

1 Talcott Parsons and Victor M. Lidz, "Death in American Society," in *Essays in Self-Destruction*, Edwin Shneidman, ed. (New York: Science House, 1967).

2 Peter Berger and Richard Lieban, "Kulturelle Wertstruktur und Bestattungsprakti-ken in den Vereinigten Staaten," *Kölner Zeitschrift für Soziologie und Sozialpsychologie*, No. 2, 1960.

3 Talcott Parsons, "Belief, Unbelief, and Disbelief," in Caporale and Grumelli, eds, *The Culture of Unbelief* (Berkeley: University of California Press, 1971), chapter 12. See also Robert N. Bellah, *Beyond Belief: Essays on Religion in a Post-Traditional World* (New York: Harper and Row, 1970), and his paper, "Between Religion and Social Science," in Caporale and Grumelli, eds, *op. cit.*, chapter 14.

4 Claude Lévi-Strauss, *Structural Anthropology* (New York: Basic Books, 1963). Edmund Leach's little book, *Genesis as Myth and Other Essays* (London: Jonathan Cape, 1971), has been of important substantive as well as methodological significance to us, as has Kenneth Burke's *The Rhetoric of Religion* (Boston: Beacon Press, 1961). See also Northrop Frye, "The Critical Path: An Essay on the Social Context of Literary Criticism," *Daedalus*, Spring 1970, pp. 268–342.

5 Renée C. Fox and Judith P. Swazey, *The Courage to Fail* (tentative title for a forthcoming book on organ transplant and hemodialysis, to be published by the University of Pennsylvania Press).

6 Marcel Mauss, *The Gift*, trans. by Ian Cunnison (Glencoe, IL: The Free Press, 1954).

7 *Op. cit.*, note 4.

8 *Op. cit.*, note 4.

9 Cf. "The Legitimacy of Solomon," in Leach, *op. cit.*

10 See also John, 1: 12. "But as many as received him, to them he gave the power to become the sons of God."

11 Cf. Talcott Parsons, "Christianity," in *International Encyclopedia of the Social Sciences*, David L. Sills, ed. (New York: The Macmillan Co. and The Free Press, 1968). Most explicit is the case of the soldier or martyr who, it is said, "gave his life for his country" or for a "cause."

12 Cf. Talcott Parsons, "Christianity," *op.cit.*

13 Perhaps the "bosom of Lenin" could be the equivalent of the "bosom of Abraham."

14 Talcott Parsons, "Belief, Unbelief, and Disbelief," *op. cit.*

15 Perhaps the slogan, "Never trust anyone over thirty," may be interpreted as symbolizing the "denial of death," since those living from age thirty on must become progressively more aware that the time will come when they will die.

16 Talcott Parsons, *The System of Modern Societies* (Englewood Cliffs, NJ: Prentice-Hall, 1971). See also Talcott Parsons and Gerald M. Platt, *The American University* (Harvard University Press, 1973).

17 Eric Lindemann, "Symptomatology and the Management of Acute Grief," in *American Journal of Psychiatry*, September, 1944, pp. 101–41.

18   Here the concept of reducible death is an adaptation of the idea of adventitious death discussed in T. Parsons and V. Lidz, "Death in American Society," *op. cit.*

19   Émile Durkheim, *The Elementary Forms of the Religious Life* (London: George Allen and Unwin, 1915).

20   This conception of moral authority is developed out of Durkheim's usage in *Moral Education* (New York: The Free Press, 1956) and *The Elementary Forms of the Religious Life*, *op. cit.* See also V. Lidz, "Moral Authority," in J. Loubser, R. Baum, A. Effrat, and V. Lidz, eds, *Explorations in General Theory in the Social Sciences* (New York: The Free Press, 1976).

21   Ibid.

22   Professor Lon L. Fuller has shown that the institution of adjudication performs this function in settling legal conflicts. See his *Anatomy of the Law* (New York: New American Library, 1969).

23   Cf. Henri Hubert and Marcel Mauss, *Sacrifice: Its Nature and Function* (Chicago: University of Chicago Press, 1964).

24   Here, as above, we use the traditional religious terminology. Let us, however, repeat our view that the relevance of these themes is not confined to religious "believers." Atheists or agnostics would simply phrase them differently.

25   This is the technical usage of "definition of the situation" employed in Talcott Parsons, "Some Problems of General Theory in Sociology," in J. McKinney and E. Tiryakian, eds, *Theoretical Sociology* (New York: Appleton-Century-Crofts, 1970).

26   Cf. Renée C. Fox and Judith P. Swazey, *The Courage to Fail, op. cit.*

27   D. Sudnow, *Passing On* (Englewood Cliffs, NJ: Prentice-Hall, 1967); Barney Glaser and Anselm Strauss, *Awareness of Dying* (Chicago: Aldine, 1965). Renée C. Fox, *Experiment Perilous* (New York: The Free Press, 1959) does not report the same conditions, or at least not in anything approaching the same degree. However, the patients in her study were gaining meaning for their deaths by being research subjects and, in dying, thereby contributing to the life of others in the future. This situation greatly affected their experiences of death as well as those of their physicians. Sudnow also reports conditions under which the stigmatization of dying patients by physicians and other hospital staff tended to bring about substantial relaxation of efforts to sustain the lives of dying patients. The strain also was manifest, e.g., in the "gallows humor" prevalent among the physicians.

28   Elisabeth Kubler-Ross, *On Death and Dying* (New York: The Macmillan Company, 1969).

29   Raymond Duff and August Hollingshead, *Sickness and Society* (New York: Random House, 1969).

30   Kubler-Ross, *op. cit.*

31   Duff and Hollingshead, *op. cit.*

32   Ibid.

33   Note the way in which President Nixon so strongly emphasized that Governor Wallace must be assured the very "finest" treatment and care after he had been shot.

34   The religious phrase, "His work is done," might function as one possible standard!

35   The process of technical advance brings an element of relativity into the conception of the "inevitability" of early death. As a striking example, one of us (Talcott Parsons) remembers years ago hearing, on the occasion of attending ward rounds at the Massachusetts General Hospital, Dr. Arlie Bock, who was the "visiting physician," tell that when he was a resident, he administered the first insulin given in that hospital to a patient in a diabetic coma. It was the first time that a

patient in a diabetic coma had ever recovered in the whole history of the hospital. In a certain sense this was almost literally bringing her "back from death."

36 Cf. Renée C. Fox, "A Sociological Perspective on Organ Transplantation and Hemodialysis," in *New Dimensions in Legal and Ethical Concepts for Human Research*, Annuals, New York Academy of Sciences, 169 (January 2, 1970), pp. 406–28.

37 It is an important feature of the process of differentiation under consideration here that an increasingly clear ethical distinction seems to be emerging between the moral status of contraception and that of abortion, at least beyond certain relatively early stages of pregnancy, although the boundary is not yet clearly defined. Even though the Catholic Church has so far refused to alter its historic position on either side, the change has gone very far indeed.

38 See Harold Garfinkel's study of a transsexual in his *Studies in Ethnomethodology* (Englewood Cliffs, NJ: Prentice-Hall, 1967).

39 Cf. Stephen B. Presser, "The Historical Background of the American Law of Adoption," *Journal of Family Law*, 1971.

40 Max Weber, *From Max Weber: Essays in Sociological Theory* (New York: Oxford, 1947). See also Talcott Parsons and Gerald M. Platt, *The American University, op. cit.*, ch. 5.

41 Kubler-Ross, *op. cit.*

42 We may recall the poignant words of Pope John XXIII when he clearly knew he was about to die, "My bags are packed, I am ready to go."

43 Cf. the conception of "social rights" developed in Talcott Parsons, "The Negro American," in his *Sociological Theory and Modern Society* (New York: The Free Press, 1967).

44 These are direct, participant observations about American medical school milieux in the 1950s, made by one of us (Renée Fox), in her role as field worker for a study of the education and socialization of medical students conducted during that period by the Columbia University Bureau of Applied Social Research. *The Student Physician*, edited by Robert K. Merton et al. (Cambridge, MA: Harvard University Press, 1957), was a product of that investigation.

45 This analysis and opinion were offered by Dr. Fletcher in the course of a keynote address that he delivered at the National Conference on the Teaching of Medical Ethics, held at the Tarrytown Conference Center, Tarrytown, New York, on June 1–3, 1972. The conference was co-sponsored by the Institute of Society, Ethics and the Life Sciences and the Columbia University College of Physicians and Surgeons.

46 Cf. Talcott Parsons, "Comparative Studies in Evolutionary Change," in Ivan Vallier, ed., *Comparative Methods in Sociology* (Berkeley: University of Calif. Press, 1971).

47 Joseph Fletcher, "Our Shameful Waste of Human Tissue: An Ethical Problem for the Living and the Dead," in Donald R. Cutler, ed., *The Religious Situation 1969* (Boston, MA: Beacon Press, 1969), p. 248.

48 This clearly requires careful definition and analysis. Perhaps the best reference we can give is to Parsons and Platt, *op. cit.*, ch. 2.

49 We conceive this, theoretically, to be a case of the complex which includes differentiation, upgrading, and the inclusion of new elements in the previously more restricted complex. We suggest that, in the recent phase, medicine is less inclined to "go it alone" without the help of other groups in the society. With respect to the changing structure within medicine itself, in the direction of a more ramified complex rather than a single diadic doctor–patient relationship, cf. Parsons and Platt, *op. cit.*, ch. 5.

50   This view of organ transplantation was first stated in R. C. Fox, "A Sociological Perspective on Organ Transplantation and Hemodialysis," *op. cit.* It is more fully developed in R. C. Fox and J. P. Swazcy, *op. cit.*

51   Marcel Mauss, *The Gift, op. cit.*, p. 66.

52   So far, especially in the more radical transplant situations, the relations of living donor and recipient have been mainly "particularized," i.e., occurring between close relatives. In the case of cadaver donors, the identity of whom is concealed from the recipients and their families, the possibility has begun to emerge of something like "organ banks" in which organ "deposits" would be made, and withdrawals from them would be wholly impersonal – merely "equating" the functional capacity of organs with recipients' needs. How far such a development can go and what its consequences might be are problems on the fringe of the present discussion.

53   This is perhaps to say that the striking increases in the potential to promote life at the same time imply risks and costs which may endanger life.

54   Richard M. Titmuss, *The Gift Relationship: From Human Blood to Social Policy* (New York: Pantheon Books, 1971), *in passim.*

Part III

Sociological Theory

8

Evolutionary Universals in Society

Slowly and somewhat inarticulately, emphasis in both sociological and anthropological quarters is shifting from a studied disinterest in problems of social and cultural evolution to a "new relativity" that relates its universals to an evolutionary framework.

The older perspectives insisted that social and cultural systems are made up of indefinitely numerous discrete "traits," that "cultures" are totally separate, or that certain broad "human" universals, like language and the incest taboo, should be emphasized. Varied as they are, these emphases have in common the fact that they divert attention from specific *continuities* in patterns of social change, so that either traits or culture types must be treated as discretely unique and basically unconnected, and a pattern, to be considered universal, must be equally important to *all* societies and cultures. Despite their ostentatious repudiation of "culture-boundness," these perspectives have been conspicuously anthropocentric in setting off problems of man's modes of life so sharply from questions of continuity with the rest of the organic world. But the emphasis on human universals has also had a kind of "levelling" influence, tending to restrict attention to what is generally and essentially human, without considering gradations within the human category.

The "new relativity" removes this barrier and tries to consider human ways in direct continuity with the subhuman. It assumes that the watershed between subhuman and human does not mark a cessation of developmental change, but rather a stage in a long process that begins with many pre-human phases and continues through that watershed into our own time, and beyond. Granting a wide range of variability of types at all stages, it assumes that levels of evolutionary advancement may be empirically specified for the human as well as the pre-human phases.

Evolutionary Universals

I shall designate as an evolutionary universal any organizational development sufficiently important to further evolution that, rather than emerging only once, it is likely to be "hit upon" by various systems operating under different conditions.

In the organic world, vision is a good example of an evolutionary universal. Because it mediates the input of organized information from the organism's environment, and because it deals with both the most distant and the widest range of information sources, vision is the most generalized mechanism of sensory information. It therefore has the greatest potential significance for adaptation of the organism to its environment.

The evidence is that vision has not been a "one shot" invention in organic evolution, but has evolved independently in three different phyla – the molluscs, the insects, and the vertebrates. A particularly interesting feature of this case is that, while the visual organs in the three groups are anatomically quite different and present no evolutionary continuity, biochemically all use the same mechanism involving Vitamin A, though there is no evidence that it was not independently "hit upon" three times.[1] Vision, whatever its mechanisms, seems to be a genuine prerequisite of *all* the higher levels of organic evolution. It has been lost only by very particular groups like the bats, which have not subsequently given rise to important evolutionary developments.

With reference to man and his biological potential for social and cultural evolution, two familiar evolutionary universals may be cited, namely the hands and the brain. The human hand is, of course, the primordial general-purpose tool. The combination of four mobile fingers and an opposable thumb enables it to perform an enormous variety of operations – grasping, holding, and manipulating many kinds of objects. Its location at the end of an arm with mobile joints allows it to be maneuvered into many positions. Finally, the pairing of the arm-hand organs much more than doubles the capacity of each one because it permits cooperation and a complex division of labor between them.

It is worth noting that the development of the hands and arms has been bought at a heavy cost in locomotion: man on his two legs cannot compete in speed and maneuverability with the faster four-legged species. Man, however, uses his hands for such a wide range of behavior impossible for handless species that the loss is far more than compensated. He can, for instance, protect himself with weapons instead of running away.

The human brain is less nearly unique than the hand, but its advantages over the brains of even anthropoids is so great that it is man's most distinctive organ, the most important single source of human capacity. Not only is it the primary organ for controlling complex operations, notably manual skills, and coordinating visual and auditory information, but above all it is the organic basis of the capacity to learn and manipulate symbols. Hence it is the organic foundation of culture. Interestingly, this development too is bought at the sacrifice of immediate adaptive advantages. For example the brain occupies so much of the head that the jaws are much less effective than in other mammalian species – but this too is compensated for by the hands. And the large brain is partly responsible for the long period of infantile dependency because the child must learn such a large factor of its effective behavior. Hence the burden of infant care and socialization is far higher for man than for any other species.

With these organic examples in mind, the conception of an evolutionary universal may be developed more fully. It should, I suggest, be formulated with reference to the concept of adaptation, which has been so fundamental to the theory of evolution since Darwin. Clearly, adaptation should mean, not merely passive "adjustment" to environmental conditions, but rather the capacity of a living system[2] to cope with its environment. This capacity includes an active concern with mastery, or the ability to change the environment to meet the needs of the system, as well as an ability to survive in the face of its unalterable features. Hence the capacity to cope with broad *ranges* of environmental factors, through adjustment or active control, or both, is crucial. Finally, a very critical point is the capacity to cope with unstable relations between system and environment, and hence with *uncertainty*. Instability here refers both to predictable variations, such as the cycle of the seasons, and to unpredictable variations, such as the sudden appearance of a dangerous predator.

An evolutionary universal, then, is a complex of structures and associated processes the development of which so increases the long-run adaptive capacity of living systems in a given class that only systems that develop the complex can attain certain higher levels of general adaptive capacity. This criterion, derived from the famous principle of natural selection, requires one major explicit qualification. The relatively disadvantaged system not developing a new universal need not be condemned to extinction. Thus some species representing all levels of organic evolution survive today – from the unicellular organisms up. The surviving lower types, however, stand in a variety of different relations to the higher. Some occupy special "niches" within which they live with limited scope, others stand in symbiotic relations to higher systems. They are not, by and large, major threats to the continued existence of the evolutionarily higher systems. Thus, though infectious diseases constitute a serious problem for man, bacteria are not likely to replace man as the dominant organic category, and man is symbiotically dependent on many bacterial species.

Two distinctions should be made here, because they apply most generally and throughout. The first is between the impact of an innovation when it is *first* introduced in a given species or society, and its importance as a continuing component of the system. Certain evolutionary universals in the social world, to be discussed below, initially provide their societies with major adaptive advantages over societies not developing them. Their introduction and institutionalization have, to be sure, often been attended with severe dislocations of the previous social organization, sometimes resulting in short-run losses in adaptation. Once institutionalized, however, they tend to become essential parts of later societies in the relevant lines of *development* and are seldom eliminated except by regression. But, as the system undergoes further evolution, universals are apt to generate major changes of their own, generally by developing more complex structures.

Unlike biological genes, cultural patterns are subject to "diffusion." Hence, for the cultural level, it is necessary to add a second distinction, between the conditions under which an adaptive advantage can develop for the first time, and those favoring its adoption from a source in which it is already established.

Prerequisites of the Evolution of Culture and Society

From his distinctive organic endowment and from his capacity for and ultimate dependence on generalized learning, man derives his unique ability to create and transmit *culture*. To quote the biologist Alfred Emerson, within a major sphere of man's adaptation, the "gene" has been replaced by the "symbol."[3] Hence, it is not only the genetic constitution of the species that determines the "needs" confronting the environment, but this constitution *plus* the cultural tradition. A set of "normative expectations" pertaining to man's relation to his environment delineates the ways in which adaptation should be developed and extended. Within the relevant range, cultural innovations, especially definitions of what man's life *ought* to be, thus replace Darwinian variations in genetic constitution.

Cultural "patterns" or orientations, however, do not implement themselves. Properly conceived in their most fundamental aspect as "religious," they must be articulated with the environment in ways that make effective adaptation possible. I am inclined to treat the entire orientational aspect of culture itself, in the simplest, least evolved forms, as directly synonymous with *religion*.[4] But since a cultural system – never any more an individual matter than a genetic pattern – is shared among a plurality of individuals, mechanisms of *communication* must exist to mediate this sharing. The fundamental evolutionary universal here is language: no concrete human group lacks it. Neither communication nor the learning processes that make it possible, however, is conceivable without determinately organized relations among those who teach and learn and communicate.

The evolutionary origin of *social organization* seems to be kinship. In an evolutionary sense it is an extension of the mammalian system of bisexual reproduction. The imperative of socialization is of course a central corollary of culture, as is the need to establish a viable social system to "carry" the culture. From one viewpoint, the core of the kinship system is the incest taboo, or, more generally, the rules of exogamy and endogamy structuring relations of descent, affinity, and residence. Finally, since the cultural level of action implies the use of brain, hands, and other organs in actively coping with the physical environment, we may say that culture implies the existence of technology, which is, in its most undifferentiated form, a synthesis of empirical knowledge and practical techniques.

These four features of even the simplest action system – "religion," communication with language, social organization through kinship, and technology – may be regarded as an integrated set of evolutionary universals at even the earliest human level. No known human society has existed without *all* four in relatively definite relations to each other. In fact, their presence constitutes the very minimum that may be said to mark a society as truly human.

Systematic relations exist not only among these four elements themselves, but between them and the more general framework of biological evolution. Technology clearly is the primary focus of the organization of the adaptive relations of the human system to its physical *environment*. Kinship is the social extension of the individual *organism's* basic articulation to the species through bisexual reproduction. But, through plasticity and the importance of learning, cultural and symbolic communications are integral to the human level of individual *personality* organization. *Social* relations among personalities, to be distinctively human, must be mediated by linguistic communication. Finally, the main *cultural patterns* that regulate the social, psychological, and organic levels of the total system of action are embodied (the more primitive the system, the more exclusively so) in the religious tradition, the focus of the use of symbolization to control the variety of conditions to which a human system is exposed.

Social Stratification

Two evolutionary universals are closely interrelated in the process of "breaking out" of what may be called the "primitive" stage of societal evolution. These are the development of a well-marked system of social stratification, and that of a system of explicit cultural legitimation of differentiated societal functions, pre-eminently the political function, independent of kinship. The two are closely connected, but I am inclined to think that stratification comes first and is a condition of legitimation of political function.

The key to the evolutionary importance of stratification lies in the role in primitive societies of *ascription* of social status to criteria of biological related-ness. The kinship nexus of social organization is intrinsically a "seamless web" of relationships which, in and of itself, contains no principle of boundedness for the system as distinguished from certain subgroups within it. Probably the earliest and most important basis of boundedness is the political criterion of territorial jurisdiction. But the economic problem of articulation with the envir-onment, contingent on kinship as well as other groups, is also prominent in primitive societies. In the first instance this is structured primarily through place of residence, which becomes increasingly important as technological develop-ment, notably of "settled agriculture," puts a premium on definiteness and permanence of location.

For present purposes, I assume that in the society we are discussing, the population occupying a territorial area is generally endogamous, with marriage of its members to those of other territorial groups being, if it occurs, somehow exceptional, and not systematically organized.[5] Given a presumptively endo-gamous territorial community, comprising a plurality of purely local groups, certain general processes of internal differentiation of the society can be explained. One aspect of this tends to be a prestige difference between central or "senior" lineage groups and "cadet" groups, whether or not the differentia-tion is on the basis of birth.[6] Quite generally, the latter must accept less advantageous bases of subsistence, including place of residence, than the for-mer. At least this is apt to be the case where the residence groups become foci for the control of resources and as such are sharply differentiated from more inclusive political groupings. Thus a second aspect of an increased level of functional differentiation among the structures of the society tends to be involved.

Typically, I think, kinship status, in terms of both descent criteria and relative prestige of marriage opportunities is highly correlated with relative economic advantage and political power. This is to say that, under the conditions postu-lated, a tendency toward *vertical* differentiation of the society as a system over-rides the pressure of the seamless web of kinship to equalize the status of all units of equivalent *kinship* character. This tendency is the product of two converging forces.

On the one hand, relative advantages are differentiated: members of cadet lineages, the kinship units with lesser claims to preferment, are "forced" into peripheral positions. They move to less advantaged residential locations and accept less productive economic resources, and they are not in a position to counteract these disadvantages by the use of political power.[7]

On the other hand, the society as a system gains functional advantages by concentrating responsibility for certain functions. This concentration focuses in two areas, analytically, the political and the religious. First, the increased complexity of a society that has grown in population and probably territory and has become differentiated in status terms raises more difficult problems of internal order, e.g. controlling violence, upholding property and marriage rules, etc., and of defense against encroachment from outside. Second, a cultural tradition very close to both the details of everyday life and the interests and solidarities of particular groups is put under strain by increasing size and diversity. There is, then, pressure to centralize both responsibility for the symbolic systems, especially the religious, and authority in collective processes, and to redefine them in the direction of greater generality.

For the present argument, I assume that the tendencies to centralize political and religious responsibility need not be clearly differentiated in any immediate situation. The main point is that the differentiation of groups relative to an advantage-disadvantage axis tends to converge with the functional "need" for centralization of responsibility. Since responsibility and prestige seem to be inherently related in a system of institutionalized expectations, the advantaged group tends to assume, or have ascribed to it, the centralized responsibilities. It should be clear that the problem does not concern the balance between services to others and benefits accuring to the advantaged group, but the convergence of *both* sets of forces tending to the same primary structural outcome.

The development of written language can become a fundamental accelerating factor in this process, because in the nature of the case literacy cannot immediately be extended to total adult populations, and yet it confers enormous adaptive advantages. It also has a tendency to favor cultural or religious elements over the political.[8]

The crucial step in the development of a stratification system occurs when important elements in the population assume the prerogatives and functions of higher status and, at least by implication, exclude all other elements. This creates an "upper," a "leading" or, possibly, a "ruling" class set over against the "mass" of the population. Given early, or, indeed, not so early conditions, it is inevitable that membership in this upper class is primarily if not entirely based on kinship status. Thus, an individual military or other leader may go far toward establishing an important criterion of status, but in doing so he elevates the status of his lineage. He cannot dissociate his relatives from his own success, even presuming he would wish to.

Stratification in the present sense, then, is the differentiation of the population on a prestige scale of kinship units such that the distinctions among such units, or classes of them, become hereditary to an important degree. There are reasons to assume that the early tendency, which may be repeated, leads to a *two*-class system. The most important means of consolidating such a system is upper-class endogamy. Since this repeats the primary principle which, along with territoriality, delineates the boundaries of early societies, the upper class constitutes a kind of subsociety. It is not a class, however, unless its counterpart, the lower class, is clearly included in the *same* societal community.

From this "primordial" two-class system there are various possibilities for evolutionary change. Probably the most important leads to a four-class system.[9] This is based on the development of urban communities in which political-administrative functions, centralized religious and other cultural activities, and territorially specialized economic action are carried on. Thus, generalized "centers" of higher-order activity emerge, but the imperatives of social organization require that these centers, as local communities – including, e.g., "provincial" centers – cannot be inhabited exclusively by upper-class people. Hence the urban upper class tends to be differentiated from the rural upper class,[10] and the urban from the rural lower class. When this occurs there is no longer a linear rank-order of classes. But so long as hereditary kinship status is a primary determinant of the individual's access to "advantages," we may speak of a stratified society; beyond the lowest level of complexity, every society is stratified.

Diffuse as its significance is, stratification is an *evolutionary* universal because the most primitive societies are not in the present sense stratified, but, beyond them, it is on two principal counts a prerequisite of a very wide range of further advances. First, what I have called a "prestige" position is a generalized prerequisite of responsible concentration of leadership. With few exceptions, those who lack a sufficiently "established" position cannot afford to "stick their necks out" in taking the responsibility for important changes. The second count concerns the availability of resources for implementing innovations. The dominance of kinship in social organization is inseparably connected with rigidity. People do what they are required to do by virtue of their kinship status. To whatever degree kinship is the basis of solidarity *within* an upper class, closure of that class by endogamy precludes kinship from being the basis of upper-class claims on the services and other resources of the lower groups. So long as the latter are genuinely within the same society, which implies solidarity across the class line, relations of mutual usefulness (e.g., patron–client relationships across class lines) on non-kin bases are possible – opening the door to universalistic definitions of merit as well as providing the upper groups with the resources to pursue their own advantages.

Social stratification in its initial development may thus be regarded as one primary condition of releasing the process of social evolution from the obstacles posed by ascription. The strong emphasis on kinship in much of the sociological literature on stratification tends to obscure the fact that the new mobility made possible by stratification is due primarily to such breaks in kinship ascription as that across class lines.

Stratification, of course, remains a major structural feature of subsequent societies and takes a wide variety of forms in their evolution. Since the general process of evolutionary change introduces a series of lines of differentiation on several bases, it is unlikely that a single simple prestige order will adequately represent the stratification system in more advanced societies. The "bourgeois" in the late European Middle Ages cannot be described simply as a "middle" class standing between the predominantly rural "feudal" classes and the peasantry. Nevertheless, stratification tends to exert a pressure to generalized hierarchization, going beyond particular bases of prestige, such as political power, special sources of wealth, etc. This is precisely because it brings these various advantages together in their relations to the diffuse status of the kinship group, and through kinship inheritance exerts pressure to continue them from generation to generation. Thus, in the transition to full modernity, stratification often becomes a predominantly conservative force in contrast to the opportunities it provides for innovation in the earlier stages.

Cultural Legitimation

Specialized cultural legitimation is, like stratification, intimately involved in the emergence from primitiveness, and certainly the two processes are related. Legitimation could, perhaps, be treated first; in certain crucial respects it is a prerequisite to the establishment of the type of prestige position referred to above. The ways in which this might be the case pose a major problem for more detailed studies of evolutionary processes. Our task here, however, is much more modest, namely to call attention to the fact that without both stratification and legitimation no major advances beyond the level of primitive society can be made.

The point of reference for the development of legitimation systems is the cultural counterpart of the seamless web of the kinship nexus with its presumptive equality of units. This is the cultural definition of the social collectivity simply as "we" who are essentially human or "people" and as such are undifferentiated, even in certain concepts of time, from our ancestors – except in certain senses for the mythical "founders" – and from contemporary "others." If the others are clearly recognized to be others (in an ideal type seamless web they would not be; they would be merely special groups of kin), they are regarded as not "really human," as strange in the sense that their relation to "us" is not comprehensible.

By explicit cultural legitimation, I mean the emergence of an institutionalized cultural definition of the society of reference, namely a referent of "we" (e.g., "We, the Tikopia" in Firth's study) which is differentiated, historically or comparatively or both, from other societies, while the merit of we-ness is asserted in a normative context. This definition has to be religious in some sense, e.g., stated in terms of a particular sacred tradition of relations to gods or holy places. It may also ascribe various meritorious features to the group, e.g., physical beauty, warlike prowess, faithful trusteeship of sacred territory or tradition, etc.[11]

This usage of the term legitimation is closely associated with Max Weber's analysis of political authority. For very important reasons the primary focus of early stages beyond the primitive is political, involving the society's capacity to carry out coordinated collective action. Stratification, therefore, is an essential condition of major advances in political effectiveness, because, as just noted, it gives the advantaged elements a secure enough position that they can accept certain risks in undertaking collective leadership.

The differentiation inherent in stratification creates new sources of strain and potential disorganization, and the use of advantaged position to undertake major innovations multiples this strain. Especially if, as is usually the case, the authors of major social innovation are already advantaged, they require legitimation for both their actions and their positions. Thus, a dynamic inherent in the development of cultural systems[12] revolves about the cultural importance of the question *why* – why such social arrangements as prestige and authority relations, and particular attendant rewards and deprivations, come about and are structured as they are. This cultural dynamic converges with the consequences of the stratification developments already outlined. Hence the crucial problem here is distributive, that of justifying advantages and prerogatives *over against* burdens and deprivations. Back of this, however, lies the problem of the meaning of the societal enterprise as a whole.

As the bases of legitimation are inherently cultural, meeting the legitimation need necessarily involves putting some kind of a premium on certain cultural services, and from this point of view there is clearly some potential advantage in specializing cultural action. Whether, under what conditions, and in what ways political and religious leadership or prestige status are differentiated from each other are exceedingly important general problems of societal evolution, but we cannot go into them here. A "God-King" may be the primary vehicle of legitimation for his own political regime, or the political "ruler" may be dependent on a priestly class that is in some degree structurally independent of his regime. But the main problems have to do with explicating the cultural basis of legitimation and institutionalizing agencies for implementing that function.

The functional argument here is essentially the same as that for stratification. Over an exceedingly wide front and relatively independently of particular cultural variations, political leaders must on the long run have not only sufficient power, but also legitimation for it. Particularly when bigger implementive steps are to be legitimized, legitimation must become a relatively explicit and, in many cases, a socially differentiated function. The combination of differentiated cultural patterns of legitimation with socially differentiated agencies is the essential aspect of the evolutionary universal of legitimation.

As evolutionary universals, stratification and legitimation are associated with the developmental problems of breaking through the ascriptive nexus of kinship, on the one hand, and of "traditionalized" culture, on the other. In turn they provide the basis for differentiation of a system that has previously, in the relevant respects, been undifferentiated. Differentiation must be carefully distinguished from segmentation, i.e., from either the development of undifferentiated segmental units of any given type within the system, or the splitting off of units from the system to form new societies, a process that appears to be particularly common at primitive levels. Differentiation requires solidarity and integrity of the system as a whole, with both common loyalties and common normative definitions of the situation. Stratification as here conceived is a hierarchical status differentiation that cuts across the overall seamless web of kinship and occurs definitely within a single collectivity, a "societal community." Legitimation is the differentiation of cultural definitions of normative patterns from a completely embedded, taken-for-granted fusion with the social structure, accompanied by institutionalization of the explicit, culture-oriented, legitimizing function in subsystems of the society.

Legitimation, of course, continues to present functional problems at later stages of evolution. The type associated with archaic religions is bound up with the relatively particularistic, arbitrary favor of divine patrons. A crucial step, represented by Bellah's "historic" religions, relates human society to a conception of supernatural order with which men must come to terms, rather than to particular divinities. Where a divinity is involved, like Jahweh, his relations with people are conceived in terms of an order which he makes binding on them, but to which, faith assures them, he will also adhere.[13]

Bureaucratic Organization

A second pair of evolutionary universals develop, each with varying degrees of completeness and relative importance, in societies that have moved considerably past the primitive stage, particularly those with well institutionalized literacy.[14] These universals are administrative bureaucracy, which in early stages is found overwhelmingly in government, and money and markets. I shall discuss bureaucracy first because its development is likely to precede that of money and markets.

Despite the criticisms made of it, mainly in the light of the complexities of modern organizations, Weber's ideal type can serve as the primary point of reference for a discussion of bureaucracy.[15] Its crucial feature is the institutionalization of the *authority of office*. This means that both individual incumbents and, perhaps even more importantly, the bureaucratic organization itself, may act "officially" for, or "in the name of," the organization, which could not otherwise exist. I shall call this capacity to act, or more broadly, that to make and promulgate binding decisions, *power* in a strict analytical sense.[16]

Although backed by coercive sanctions, up to and including the use of physical force, *at the same time* power rests on the consensual solidarity of a system that includes both the users of power and the "objects" of its use. (Note that I do not say *against* whom it is used: the "against" may or may not apply.) Power in this sense is the capacity of a unit in the social system, collective or individual, to establish or activate commitments to performance that contributes to, or is in the interest of, attainment of the goals of a collectivity. It is not itself a "factor" in effectiveness, nor a "real" output of the process, but a medium of mobilization and acquisition of factors and outputs. In this respect, it is like money.

Office implies the differentiation of the role of incumbent from a person's other role-involvements, above all from his kinship roles. Hence, so far as function in the collectivity is defined by the obligations of ascriptive kinship status, the organizational status cannot be an office in the present sense. Neither of the other two types of authority that Weber discusses – traditional and charismatic – establishes this differentiation between organizational role and the "personal" status of the incumbent. Hence bureaucratic authority is always rational-legal in type. Weber's well-known proposition that the top of a bureaucratic structure cannot itself be bureaucratic may be regarded as a statement about the modes of articulation of such a structure with other structures in the society. These may involve the ascribed traditional authority of royal families, some form of charismatic leadership, or the development of democratic associational control, to be discussed briefly below.

Internally, a bureaucratic system is always characterized by an institutionalized hierarchy of authority, which is differentiated on two axes: *level* of authority and "sphere" of competence. Spheres of competence are defined either on segmentary bases, e.g., territorially, or on functional bases, e.g., supply vs. combat units in an army. The hierarchical aspect defines the levels at which a higher authority's decisions, in case of conflict, take precedence over those of a lower authority. It is a general bureaucratic principle that the higher the level, the smaller the relative number of decision-making agencies, whether individual or collegial, and the wider the scope of each, so that at the top, in principle, a single agency must carry responsibility for *any* problems affecting the organization. Such a hierarchy is one of "pure" authority only so far as status within it is differentiated from other components of status, e.g., social class. Even with rather clear differentiation, however, position in a stratification system is likely to be highly correlated with position in a hierarchy of authority. Seldom, if ever, are high bureaucratic officials unequivocally members of the lowest social class.[17]

Externally, two particularly important boundaries pose difficulties for bureaucracies. The first has to do with recruiting manpower and obtaining facilities. In ideal type, a position in a bureaucratic organization constitutes an occupational role, which implies that criteria of eligibility should be defined in terms of competence and maximal responsibility to the organization, not to "private" interests independent of, and potentially in conflict with, those of the organization. Thus high aristocrats may put loyalty to their lineage ahead of the obligations of office, or clergymen in political office may place loyalty to the church ahead of obligation to the civil government. Also, remunerating officials and providing facilities for their functions presents a serious problem of differentiation and hence of independence. The "financing of public bodies," as Weber calls it,[18] cannot be fully bureaucratic in this sense unless payment is in money, the sources of which are outside the control of the recipients. Various forms of benefices and prebends only very imperfectly meet these conditions, but modern salaries and operating budgets approximate them relatively closely.[19]

The second boundary problem concerns political support. An organization is bureaucratic so far as incumbents of its offices can function independently of the influence of elements having special "interests" in its output, except where such elements are properly involved in the definition of the organization's goals through its nonbureaucratic top. Insulation from such influence, for example through such crude channels as bribery, is difficult to institutionalize and, as is well known, is relatively rare.[20]

In the optimal case, internal hierarchy and division of functions, recruitment of manpower and facilities, and exclusion of "improper" influence, are all regulated by universalistic norms. This is implicit in the proposition that bureaucratic authority belongs to Weber's rational-legal type. Of course, in many concrete instances this condition is met very imperfectly, even in the most highly developed societies.

Bureaucracy tends to develop earliest in governmental administration primarily because even a modest approximation to the essential criteria requires a considerable concentration of power, which, as noted above, depends both on prestige and on legitimation. In the very important cases, like the *polis* of antiquity, where power is widely dispersed, private units of organization are not likely either to be large enough or to command sufficient resources to become highly bureaucratized. Perhaps the *oikos* organization of the interests of important aristocratic lineages in late antiquity constitutes one of the most important relatively early examples approximating private bureaucracy. The Western Church is clearly another, as are modern business firms.

The basis on which I classify bureaucracy as an evolutionary universal is very simple. As Weber said, it is the most effective large-scale administrative organization that man has invented, and there is no direct substitute for it.[21] Where capacity to carry out large-scale organized operations is important, e.g., military operations with mass forces, water control, tax administration, policing of large and heterogeneous populations, and productive enterprise requiring large capital investment and much manpower, the unit that commands effective bureaucratic organization is inherently superior to the one that does not. It is by no means the only structural factor in the adaptive capacity of social systems, but no one can deny that it is an important one. Above all, it is built on further specializations ensuing from the broad emancipation from ascription that stratification and specialized legitimation make possible.

Money and the Market Complex

Immediate effectiveness of collective function, especially on a large scale, depends on concentration of power, as noted. Power is in part a function of the mobility of the resources available for use in the interests of the collective goals in question. Mobility of resources, however, is a direct function of access to them through the market. Though the market is the most general means of such access, it does have two principal competitors. First is requisitioning through the direct application of political power, e.g., defining a collective goal as having military significance and requisitioning manpower under it for national defense. A second type of mobilization is the activation of nonpolitical solidarities and commitments, such as those of ethnic or religious membership, local community, caste, etc. The essential theme here is, "as one of us, it is your duty..."

The political power path involves a fundamental difficulty because of the role of explicit or implied coercion – "you contribute, or else..." – while the activation of nonpolitical commitments, a category comprising at least two others, raises the issue of alternative obligations. The man appealed to in the interest of his ethnic group may ask, "what about the problems of my family?" In contrast, market exchange avoids three dilemmas: first, that I must do what is expected or face punishment for noncompliance; second, if I do not comply, I will be disloyal to certain larger groups, identification with which is very important to my general status; third, if I do not comply, I may betray the unit which, like my family, is the primary basis of my immediate personal security.

Market exchange makes it possible to obtain resources for future action and yet avoid such dilemmas as these, because money is a generalized resource for the consumer-recipient, who can purchase "good things" regardless of his relations to their sources in other respects. Availability through the market cannot be unlimited – one should not be able to purchase conjugal love or ultimate political loyalty – but possession of physical commodities, and by extension, control of personal services by purchase, certainly can, very generally, be legitimized in the market nexus.

As a symbolic medium, money "stands for" the economic utility of the real assets for which it is exchangeable, but it represents the concrete objects so abstractly that it is neutral among the competing claims of various other orders in which the same objects are significant. It thus directs attention away from the more consummatory and, by and large, immediate significance of these objects toward their *instrumental* significance as potential means to further ends. Thus money becomes the great mediator of the instrumental use of goods and services. Markets, involving both the access of the consuming unit to objects it needs for consumption and the access of producing units to "outlets" that are not ascribed, but contingent on the voluntary decisions of "customers" to purchase, may be stabilized institutionally. Thus this universal "emancipates" resources from such ascriptive bonds as demands to give kinship expectations priority, to be loyal in highly specific senses to certain political groups, or to submit the details of daily life to the specific imperatives of religious sects.

In the money and market system, money as a medium of exchange and property rights, including rights of alienation, must be institutionalized. In general it is a further step that institutionalizes broadly an individual's contractual right to sell his services in a labor market without seriously involving himself in diffuse dependency relationships, which at lower status levels are usually in some ways "unfree." Property in land, on a basis that provides for its alienation, presents a very important problem. Its wide extension seems, except in a very few cases, to be a late development. The institution of contract in exchange of money and goods is also a complex area of considerable variation. Finally, money itself is by no means a simple entity, and in particular the development of credit instruments, banking and the like, has many variations.[22]

These institutional elements are to a considerable degree independently variable and are often found unevenly developed. But if the main ones are sufficiently developed and integrated, the market system provides the operating units of the society, including of course its government, with a pool of disposable resources that can be applied to any of a range of uses and, within limits, can be shifted from use to use. The importance of such a pool is shown by the serious consequences of its shrinkage for even such highly organized political systems as some of the ancient empires.[23]

Modern socialist societies appear to be exceptional because, up to a point, they achieve high productivity with a relatively minimal reliance on monetary and market mechanisms, substituting bureaucracy for them. But too radical a "demonetization" has negative consequences even for such an advanced economy as that of the Soviet Union.

A principal reason for placing money and markets after bureaucracy in the present series of evolutionary universals is that the conditions of their large-scale development are more precarious. This is particularly true in the very important areas where a generalized system of universalistic norms has not yet become firmly established. Market operations, and the monetary medium itself, are inevitably highly dependent on political "protection." The very fact that the mobilization of political power, and its implementation through bureaucratic organization, is so effective generates interests against sacrificing certain short-run advantages to favor the enhanced flexibility that market systems can provide. This has been a major field of conflict historically, and it is being repeated today in underdeveloped societies. The strong tendency for developing societies to adopt a "socialistic" pattern reflects a preference for increasing productivity through governmentally controlled bureaucratic means rather than more decentralized market-oriented means.[24] But in general the money and market system has undoubtedly made a fundamental contribution to the adaptive capacity of the societies in which it has developed; those that restrict it too drastically are likely to suffer from severe adaptive disadvantages in the long run.

Generalized Universalistic Norms

A feature common to bureaucratic authority and the market system is that they incorporate, and are hence dependent on, universalistic norms. For bureaucracy, these involve definitions of the powers of office, the terms of access to it, and the line dividing proper from improper pressure or influence. For money and markets, the relevant norms include the whole complex of property rights, first in commodities, later in land and in monetary assets. Other norms regulate the monetary medium and contractual relations among the parties to transactions. Here relations between contracts of service or employment and other aspects of the civil and personal statuses of the persons concerned are particularly crucial.

Up to a point, the norms governing a bureaucratic organization may be regarded as independent of those governing property or those regulating the status of private persons in the same society. As noted, however, there are also certain intrinsic connections, such as that between bureaucratic organization and the mobility of resources.[25]

Although it is very difficult to pin down just what the crucial components are, how they are interrelated, and how they develop, one can identify the development of a general legal system as a crucial aspect of societal evolution. A general legal system is an integrated system of universalistic norms, applicable to the society as a whole rather than to a few functional or segmental sectors, highly generalized in terms of principles and standards, and relatively independent of both the religious agencies that legitimize the normative order of the society and vested interest groups in the operative sector, particularly in government.

The extent to which both bureaucratic organization and market systems can develop *without* a highly generalized universalistic normative order should not be underestimated. Such great Empires as the Mesopotamian, the ancient Chinese, and, perhaps the most extreme example, the Roman, including its Byzantine extension, certainly testify to this. But these societies suffered either from a static quality, failing to advance beyond certain points, or from instability leading in many cases to retrogression.[26] Although many of the elements of such a general normative order appeared in quite highly developed form in earlier societies, in my view their crystallization into a coherent system represents a distinctive new step, which more than the industrial revolution itself, ushered in the *modern* era of social evolution.[27]

The clear differentiation of secular government from religious organization has been a long and complicated process, and even in the modern world its results are unevenly developed. It has perhaps gone farthest in the sharp separation of Church and State in the United States. Bureaucracy has, of course, played an important part in this process. The secularization of government is associated with that of law, and both of these are related to the level of generality of the legal system.

Systems of law that are *directly* religiously sanctioned, treating compliance as a religious obligation, also tend to be "legalistic" in the sense of emphasizing detailed prescriptions and prohibitions, each of which is given specific Divine sanction. Preeminent examples are the Hebrew law of Leviticus, the later developments in the Talmudic tradition, and Islamic law based on the Koran and its interpretations. Legal decisions and the formulation of rules to cover new situations must then be based as directly as possible on an authoritative sacred text.

Not only does religious law as such tend to inhibit generalization of legal principle, but it also tends to favor what Weber called *substantive* over *formal* rationality.[28] The standard of legal correctness tends to be the implementation of religious precepts, not procedural propriety and consistency of general principle. Perhaps the outstanding difference between the legal systems of the other Empires, and the patterns that were developed importantly in Roman law, was the development of elements of formal rationality, which we may regard as a differentiation of legal norms out of "embeddedness" in the religious culture. The older systems – many of which still exist – tended to treat "justice" as a direct implementation of precepts of religious and moral conduct, in terms of what Weber called *Wertrationalität*, without institutionalizing an independent system of *societal* norms, adapted to the function of social control at the societal level and integrated on its own terms. The most important foci of such an independent system are, first, some kind of "codification" of norms under principles not *directly* moral or religious, though they generally continue to be grounded in religion, and, second, the formalization of procedural rules, defining the situations in which judgments are to be made on a societal basis. Especially important is the establishment of courts for purposes other than permitting political and religious leaders to make pronouncements and "examples."[29]

Something similar can be said about what I have called operative vested interests, notably government. Advantages are to be gained, on the one hand, by binding those outside the direct control of the group in question with detailed regulation, while, on the other hand, leaving maximum freedom for the group's leadership. This duality Weber made central to his concept of traditional authority, with its sphere of traditionalized fixity, on the one hand, and that of personal preorgative, reaching its extreme form in "sultanism," on the other.[30] Both aspects are highly resistant to the type of rationalization that is essential to a generalized universalistic legal system.

Though the Chinese Empire, Hindu law (*Manu*), Babylonia, and to some extent, Islam made important beginnings in the direction I am discussing, the Roman legal system of the Imperial period was uniquely advanced in these respects. Though the early *jus civilis* was very bound religiously, this was not true to the same extent of the *jus gentium*, or of the later system as a totality. While a professional judiciary never developed, the jurisconsults in their "unofficial" status did constitute a genuine professional group, and they systematized the law very extensively, in the later phases strongly under the influence of Stoic Philosophy.[31]

Though Roman law had a variety of more or less "archaic" features, its "failure" was surely on the level of institutionalization more than in any intrinsic defect of legal content. Roman society of that period lacked the institutional capacity, through government, religious legitimation, and other channels, to integrate the immense variety of peoples and cultures within the Empire, or to maintain the necessary economic, political, and administrative structures.[32] Roman law remained, however, the cultural reference point of all the significant later developments.

The next phase, of course, was the development of Catholic Canon Law, incorporating much of Roman law. A major characteristic of the Western Church, Canon Law was not only very important in maintaining and consolidating the Church's differentiation from secular government and society, but, with the Justinian documents, it also preserved the legal tradition.

The third phase was the revival of the study of Roman secular law in Renaissance Italy and its gradual adoption by the developing national states of early modern Europe. The result was that the modern national state developed as, fundamentally, a *Rechtsstaat*. In Continental Europe, however, one fundamental limitation on this development was the degree to which the law continued to be intertwined and almost identified with government. For example, most higher civil servants were lawyers. One might ask whether this represented a "legalization of bureaucracy" or a bureaucratization of the law and the legal profession. But with elaborate bodies of law, law faculties as major constituents of every important university, and the prominence of university-trained legal professions, Continental European nations certainly had well institutionalized legal systems.

In England, however, the development went, in a highly distinctive way, still farther. Although the differentiation of English Common Law from Continental Roman law had late Medieval roots, the crucial period was the early 17th century, when Justice Coke asserted the independence of the Common Law from control by royal prerogative. With this, the establishment of the organizational independence of the Judiciary was the crucial symbolic development. Substantially, the Common Law came to emphasize the protection of personal rights,[33] the institution of property in private hands, and both freedom of contract and protection of contractual interests far more strongly than did the Continental law. Common Law also emphasized the development of institutions, including both the adversary system, in which parties are highly independent of the Court, and procedural protections.[34]

Significantly, these Common Law developments were integral parts of the more general development of British institutions associated with the Puritan movement,[35] including the later establishment of the independence of Parliament and the development of physical science.

This development of English Common Law, with its adoption and further development in the overseas English-speaking world, not only constituted the most advanced case of universalistic normative order, but was probably decisive for the modern world. This general type of legal order is, in my opinion, the most important single hallmark of modern society. So much is it no accident that the Industrial Revolution occurred first in England, that I think it legitimate to regard the English type of legal system as a fundamental prerequisite of the first occurrence of the Industrial Revolution.[36]

The Democratic Association

A rather highly generalized universalistic legal order is in all likelihood a necessary prerequisite for the development of the last structural complex to be discussed as universal to social evolution, the democratic association with elective leadership and fully enfranchised membership. At least this seems true of the institutionalization of this pattern in the governments of large-scale societies. This form of democratic association originated only in the late 18th century in the Western world and was nowhere complete, if universal adult suffrage is a criterion, until well into the present century. Of course, those who regard the Communist society as a stable and enduring type might well dispute that democratic government in this sense is an evolutionary universal. But before discussing that issue, I will outline the history and principal components of this universal.

Surely it is significant that the earliest cases of democratic government were the *poleis* of classical antiquity, which were also the primary early sources of universalistic law. The democratic *polis*, however, not only was small in scale by modern standards (note Aristotle's belief that a citizen body should never be too large to assemble within earshot of a given speaker, of course without the aid of a public address system), but also its democratic associational aspects never included a total society. It is estimated that during the Periclean age in Athens, only about 30,000 of a total population of about 150,000 were citizens, the rest being metics and slaves. And, of course, citizen women were not enfranchised. Thus even in its democratic phase the *polis* was emphatically a two-class system. And under the conditions of the time, when Roman society increased in scale away from the *polis* type of situation, citizenship, at least for large proportions of the Empire's population, was bound to lose political functions almost in proportion to its gains in legal significance.

The basic principle of democratic association, however, never completely disappeared. To varying degrees and in varying forms, it survived in the *municipia* of the Roman Empire, in the Roman Senate, and in various aspects of the organization of the Christian Church, though the Church also maintained certain hierarchical aspects. Later the collegial pattern, e.g., the *college* of Cardinals, continued to be an aspect of Church structure. In the Italian and North European city-states of the late Middle Ages and early modern period, it had its place in government, for example in "senates," which though not democratically elected, were internally organized as democratic bodies. Another important case was the guild, as an association of merchants or craftsmen. In modern times there have, of course, been many different types of private association in many different fields. It is certainly safe to say that, even apart from government, the democratic association is a most prominent and important constituent of modern societies.

At the level of national government, we can speak first of the long development of Parliamentary assemblies functioning as democratic associations and legislating for the nation, whose members have been to some degree elected from fairly early times. Secondly, there has been a stepwise extension of both the franchise for electing legislative representatives and the legislative supremacy of their assemblies, following the lead of England, which developed rapidly in these respects after 1688. Later, the French and American Revolutions dramatized the conception of the total national community as essentially a democratic association in this sense.

There are four critically important components of the democratic association. First is the institutionalization of the leadership function in the form of an elective office, whether occupied by individuals, executive bodies, or collegial groups like legislatures. The second is the franchise, the institutionalized participation of members in collective decision-making through the election of officers and often through voting on specific policy issues. Third is the institutionalization of procedural rules for the voting process and the determination of its outcome and for the process of "discussion" or campaigning for votes by candidates or advocates of policies. Fourth is the institutionalization of the nearest possible approximation to the voluntary principle in regard to membership status. In the private association this is fundamental – no case where membership is ascribed or compulsory can be called a "pure" democratic association. In government, however, the coercive and compulsory elements of power, as well as the recruitment of societal communities largely by birth, modify the principle. Hence universality of franchise tends to replace the voluntary membership principle.

Formalization of definite procedural rules governing voting and the counting and evaluation of votes may be considered a case of formal rationality in Weber's sense, since it removes the consequences of the act from the control of the particular actor. It limits his control to the specific act of casting his ballot, choosing among the alternatives officially presented to him. Indirectly his vote might contribute to an outcome he did not desire, e.g., through splitting the opposition to an undesirable candidate and thus actually aiding him, but he cannot control this, except in the voting act itself.

Besides such formalization, however, Rokkan has shown in his comparative and historical study of Western electoral systems, that there is a strikingly general tendency to develop three other features of the franchise.[37] The first of these is universality, minimizing if not eliminating the overlap between membership and disenfranchisement. Thus property qualifications and, most recently, sex qualifications have been removed so that now the main Western democratic polities, with minimal exceptions, have universal adult suffrage. The second is equality, eliminating "class" systems, like the Prussian system in the German Empire, in favor of the principle, one citizen, one vote.[38] Finally, secrecy of the ballot insulates the voting decision from pressures emanating from status superiors or peers that might interfere with the expression of the voter's personal preferences.

Certain characteristics of elective office directly complementary to those of the franchise can be formulated. Aside from the ways of achieving office and the rules of tenure in it, they are very similar to the pattern of bureaucratic office. The first, corresponding to the formalization of electoral rules, is that conduct in office must be legally regulated by universalistic norms. Second, corresponding to the universality of the franchise, is the principle of subordinating segmental or private interests to the collective interest within the sphere of competence of the office. Third, corresponding to equality of the franchise, is the principle of accountability for decisions to a total electorate. And finally, corresponding to secrecy of the ballot, is the principle of limiting the powers of office to specified spheres, in sharp contrast to the diffuseness of both traditional and charismatic authority.

The adoption of even such a relatively specific pattern as equality of the franchise may be considered a universal tendency, essentially because, under the principle that the membership rightfully chooses both the broad orientations of collective policy and the elements having leadership privileges and responsibilities, there is, among those with minimal competence, no universalistic basis for discriminating among classes of members. As a limitation on the hierarchical structure of power within collectivities, equality of franchise is the limiting or boundary condition of the democratic association, corresponding to equality of opportunity on the bureaucratic boundary of the polity.[39]

Especially, though not exclusively, in national territorial states, the stable democratic association is notoriously difficult to institutionalize. Above all this seems to be a function of the difficulty in motivating holders of immediately effective power to relinquish their opportunities voluntarily despite the seriousness of the interest at stake – relinquishment of control of governmental machinery after electoral defeat being the most striking problem.[40] The system is also open to other serious difficulties, most notably corruption and "populist" irresponsibility, as well as *de facto* dictatorship. Furthermore, such difficulties are by no means absent in private associations, as witness the rarity of effective electoral systems in large trade unions.[41]

The basic argument for considering democratic association a universal, despite such problems, is that, the larger and more complex a society becomes, the more important is effective political organization, not only in its administrative capacity, but also, and not least, in its support of a universalistic legal order. Political effectiveness includes both the scale and operative flexibility of the organization of power. Power, however, precisely as a generalized societal medium, depends overwhelmingly on a consensual element,[42] i.e., the ordered institutionalization and exercise of influence, linking the power system to the higher-order societal consensus at the value level.[43]

No institutional form basically different from the democratic association can, *not* specifically *legitimize* authority and power in the most general sense, but *mediate consensus in its exercise* by particular persons and groups, and in the formation of particular binding policy decisions. At high levels of structural differentiation in the society itself and in its governmental system, generalized legitimation cannot fill this gap adequately. Providing structured participation in the selection of leaders and formation of basic policy, as well as in opportunities to be heard and exert influence and to have a real choice among alternatives, is the crucial function of the associational system from this point of view.

I realize that to take this position I must maintain that communist totalitarian organization will probably not fully match "democracy" in political and integrative capacity in the long run. I do indeed predict that it will prove to be unstable and will either make adjustments in the general direction of electoral democracy and a plural party system or "regress" into generally less advanced and politically less effective forms of organization, failing to advance as rapidly or as far as otherwise may be expected. One important basis of this prediction is that the Communist Party has everywhere emphasized its function in *educating* the people for the new society.[44] In the long run its legitimacy will certainly be undermined if the party leadership continues to be unwilling to *trust* the people it has educated. In the present context, however, to trust the people is to entrust them with a share of political responsibility. This can only mean that eventually the single monolithic party must relinquish its monopoly of such responsibility. (This is not to analyze the many complex ways in which this development might proceed, but only to indicate the *direction* in which it is most likely to move and the consequences it must bear if it fails in taking that direction.)

Conclusion

This paper is not meant to present even the schematic outline of a "theory" of societal evolution. My aim is much more limited: I have selected for detailed attention and illustration an especially important type of structural innovation that has appeared in the course of social change. I have attempted to clarify the concept "evolutionary universal" by briefly discussing a few examples from organic evolution, namely, vision, the human hands, and the human brain. I have interpreted these as innovations endowing their possessors with a very substantial increase in generalized adaptive capacity, so substantial that species lacking them are relatively disadvantaged in the major areas in which natural selection operates, not so much for survival as for the opportunity to initiate further major developments.

Four features of human societies at the level of culture and social organization were cited as having universal and major significance as prerequisites for socio-cultural development: technology, kinship organization based on an incest taboo, communication based on language, and religion. Primary attention, however, was given to six organizational complexes that develop mainly at the level of social structure. The first two, particularly important for the emergence of societies from primitiveness, are stratification, involving a primary break with primitive kinship ascription, and cultural legitimation, with institutionalized agencies that are independent of a diffuse religious tradition.

Fundamental to the structure of modern societies are, taken together, the other four complexes: bureaucratic organization of collective goal-attainment, money and market systems, generalized universalistic legal systems, and the democratic association with elective leadership and mediated membership support for policy orientations. Although these have developed very unevenly, some of them going back a very long time, all are clearly much more than simple "inventions" of particular societies.

Perhaps a single theme tying them together is that differentiation and attendant reduction in ascription has caused the initial two-class system to give way to more complex structures at the levels of social stratification and the relation between social structure and its cultural legitimation. First, this more complex system is characterized by a highly generalized universalistic normative structure in all fields. Second, subunits under such normative orders have greater autonomy both in pursuing their own goals and interests and in serving others instrumentally. Third, this autonomy is linked with the probability that structural units will develop greater diversity of interests and subgoals. Finally, this diversity results in pluralization of scales of prestige and therefore of differential access to economic resources, power, and influence.[45]

Comparatively, the institutionalization of these four complexes and their interrelations is very uneven. In the broadest frame of reference, however, we may think of them as together constituting the main outline of the structural foundations of modern society. Clearly, such a combination, balanced relative to the exigencies of particular societal units, confers on its possessors an adaptive advantage far superior to the structural potential of societies lacking it. Surely the bearing of this proposition on problems of rapid "modernization" in present "under-developed" societies is extremely important.

Certain cultural developments such as the "philosophic breakthroughs" that produced what Bellah calls the "historic" religions or the emergence of modern science in the 16th and 17th centuries, are of significance equal to the developments discussed above. Indeed, the level of institutionalization of scientific investigation and technological application of science in the present century has become a structural complex ranking in importance with the four I have described as essential to modernity.

In closing I wish to express the hope that the reader will not be too concerned with the details of my characterizations of particular evolutionary universals, my specific judgments about their concrete historical developments, or my detailed evaluations of their importance. These parts of the paper are meant primarily for illustration. I hope he will give particular attention to the *idea* of the evolutionary universal and its grounding in the conception of generalized adaptive capacity. If this idea is sound, empirical shortcomings in its application can be remedied by research and criticism.

Notes

1   George Wald, "Life and Light," *Scientific American*, 201 (October, 1959), 92–108.
2   Note that the species rather than the individual organism is the major system of reference here. See George Gaylord Simpson, *The Meaning of Evolution* (New Haven: Yale University Press, 1950).
3   Alfred Emerson, "Homeostasis and Comparison of Systems," in Roy R. Grinker (ed.), *Toward a Unified Theory of Behavior* (New York: Basic Books, 1956).
4   Cf. Émile Durkheim, *The Elementary Forms of the Religious Life* (London: Allen and Unwin, 1915).
5   See W. Lloyd Warner, *A Black Civilization* (2nd edn). (New York: Harper, 1958), for an analysis showing that such boundedness can be problematic.
6   This analysis has been suggested in part by Charles Ackerman who bases himself on a variety of the recent studies of kinship systems, but, perhaps, particularly on Rodney Needham's studies of the Purums; *Structure and Sentiment* (Chicago: University of Chicago Press, 1960).
7   I am putting forward this set of differentiating factors as an ideal type. Of course, in many particular cases they may not all operate together. For example, it may frequently happen that the outer lands to which cadet lineages move are more productive than the old ones. The net effect of these discrepancies is probably a tendency toward diversity of lines of development rather than the extinction of the main one sketched here. Indeed we can go farther and say that unless this advantage of economic resources comes to be combined with such structural advantages as incorporation in a stratification system it will not lead to further evolutionary developments.
8   See Talcott Parsons, *Societies: Evolutionary and Comparative Perspectives* (Englewood Cliffs, NJ: Prentice-Hall, 1966).
9   Cf. Gideon Sjoberg, *The Preindustrial City* (Glencoe, IL: The Free Press, 1960), ch. 5.
10   The upper class will be primarily rural in societies that take a more or less feudal direction.
11   For lack of space I shall not develop a series of examples here. Fortunately, Bellah's companion paper [*American Sociological Review*, vol. 29 (3), June 1964] covers much of the relevant ground in treating the transition from primitive to archaic religion and the principal features of the latter. The basic phenomena are gods conceived as acting and impinging on human society independently of the diffuse mythological order, priesthoods, whose members are expert in regulating relations to the gods, and cults organized in relation to the gods, but not yet, Bellah points

out, as bounded collectivities having memberships organized independently of "civil" status.

12 Claude Lévi-Strauss, *Totemism* (Boston: Beacon Paperbacks, 1963).

13 Another problem in this field concerns the implications of the dualism, so prominent in the historic religions, between the conceptions of this world and the otherworldly ideal order, and whether an empirical society and secular action within it may be considered religiously or morally "good" when set over against the otherworldly order. A transcendence of this dualism that permits a successful relation to the supernatural order through secular action, if it is highly moral, but which nevertheless maintains the transcendence of the supernatural order over this-worldly concerns, is central in developing legitimacy for modern social structures. Cf. Ernst Troeltsch, *Social Teachings of the Christian Churches* (New York: Harper Torchbooks, 1960).

14 As a predominantly cultural innovation, literacy is not discussed here. Cf. Parsons, *Societies, op. cit.*, ch. 1.

15 See "The Analysis of Formal Organizations," Part I of my *Structure and Process in Modern Societies* (Glencoe, IL: The Free Press, 1960); Peter M. Blau, "Critical Remarks on Weber's Theory of Authority," *American Political Science Review*, 57 (June, 1963), 305–16, and *The Dynamics of Bureaucracy* (2nd edn) (Chicago: University of Chicago Press, 1963); Carl J. Friedrich (ed.), *Authority* (Nomos I) (Cambridge, MA: Harvard University Press, 1958), especially Friedrich's own contribution, "Authority and Reason."

16 Cf. Talcott Parsons, "On the Concept of Political Power," *Proceedings of the American Philosophical Society*, 107 (June, 1963), 232–62.

17 The Ottoman Empire, where many high officials were "slaves" of the Sultan, is not an exception. In such circumstances slaves took on the status of their master's "household," and hence were outside the normal stratification system. See H. A. R. Gibb, *Studies on the Civilization of Islam* (Boston: Beacon Press, 1962).

18 Max Weber, "The Financing of Political Bodies," in *The Theory of Social and Economic Organization* (Glencoe, IL: The Free Press, 1947), pp. 310 ff.

19 Problems of this type have been exceedingly common over wide ranges and long periods. Eisenstadt gives many illustrations of the loss of fluidity of resources through aristocratization and similar developments. A very important one is the ruralization of the Roman legions in the later imperial period – they became essentially a border militia. At a lower level, a particularly good example is the difficulty of institutionalizing the differentiation of occupational from familial roles for the industrial labor force. S. N. Eisenstadt, *The Political Systems of Empires* (New York: The Free Press of Glencoe, 1963), especially ch. 3; Martin P. Nilsson, *Imperial Rome* (New York: Harcourt, Brace, 1926); Neil J. Smelser, *Social Change in the Industrial Revolution* (Chicago: University of Chicago Press, 1959).

20 The difficulty of mobilizing political support for bureaucratic regimes is exemplified by the particularly important case of the struggle between monarchs and aristocracies in early modern Europe. In spite of the obvious dangers of absolutism to the freedoms of the urban classes, the alliance between them and the monarchs was an essential way of developing sufficient support to counteract the traditionalizing influence of the aristocracies. The special place of the latter in military organization made the task of monarchies more difficult. Max Beloff, *The Age of Absolutism* (New York: Harper Torchbooks, 1962); John B. Wolf, *The Emergence of the Great Powers* (New York: Harper Torchbooks, 1962), especially chs 4 and 7.

21 Weber, *The Theory of Social and Economic Organization, op. cit.*, p. 377.

22   A useful typology of the organization of economic exchange relations, from an evolutionary point of view, is given by Neil J. Smelser, *The Sociology of Economic Life* (Englewood Cliffs, NJ: Prentice-Hall, 1963), pp. 86–8.

23   S. N. Eisenstadt, *op. cit.*, for example, makes a great deal of this factor, particularly in accounting for the gradual decline of the political power of the Byzantine Empire. This analysis is also closely related to Weber's thesis in his famous essay on the decline of the Roman Empire. Weber, however, particularly emphasized the mobility of manpower through slavery. Max Weber, "The Social Causes of the Decay of Ancient Civilization," *Journal of General Education* (October, 1950).

24   See Gregory Grossman, "The Structure and Organization of the Soviet Economy" in the *Slavic Review*, 21 (June, 1962), 203–22. The constriction of the market system may also have been a major factor in the difficulties suffered by the Chinese Communist regime in connection with the "Great Leap Forward" of 1958 and subsequent years. Audrey Donnithorne, "The Organization of Rural Trade in China since 1958," *China Quarterly*, No. 8 (October–December, 1961), 77–91, and Leo A. Orleans, "Problems of Manpower Absorption in Rural China," *China Quarterly*, No. 7 (July–September, 1961), 69–84.

25   It goes without saying that one of the largest channels of government spending in modern societies is for the purchase of goods and services in the markets, including the payment of civil servants and military personnel.

26   Eisenstadt, *op. cit.*, pp. 349 ff.

27   Parsons, *Societies, op. cit.*

28   Weber, *The Theory of Social and Economic Organization, op. cit.*, pp. 184ff, and *Max Weber on Law in Economy and Society* (Cambridge, MA: Harvard University Press, 1954), ch. 8.

29   Weber, *Max Weber on Law in Economy and Society, op. cit.*

30   Weber, *The Theory of Social and Economic Organization, op. cit.*

31   A handy summary of Roman legal development is "The Science of Law" by F. de Zulueta in Cyrus Balley (ed.), *The Legacy of Rome* (London: Oxford University Press, 1923).

32   Weber, "The Social Causes of the Decay of Ancient Civilization," *op. cit.*

33   A particularly clear analysis of the fundamental principles underlying this normative order is in the paper by John Rawls, "Constitutional Liberty and the Concept of Justice," in C. J. Friedrich (ed.), *Justice* (Nomos VI) (New York: Atherton Press, 1963). Rawls' discussion is not, however, specially oriented to legal problems.

34   See Roscoe Pound, *The Spirit of the Common Law* (Boston: Beacon Paperbacks, 1963), especially chs 2–4.

35   David Little, "The Logic of Order: An Examination of the Sources of Puritan–Anglican Controversy and of their Relations to Prevailing Legal Conceptions of Corporation in the Late 16th and Early 17th Century in England," unpublished Ph.D. Thesis, Harvard University, 1963.

36   It is exceedingly important here once more to distinguish the first occurrence of a social innovation from its subsequent diffusion. The latter can occur without the whole set of prerequisite societal conditions necessary for the former. Cf. my *Structure and Process in Modern Societies, op. cit.*, ch. 3.

37   Stein Rokkan, "Mass Suffrage, Secret Voting, and Political Participation," *The European Journal of Sociology*, 2 (1961), 132–52.

38   The recent decisions of the US Supreme Court on legislative reapportionment also constitute an important step in this process. In the majority opinion of the decision outlawing the Georgia county unit system of voting, Justice Douglas explicitly

stated that this was a direct application of the Constitutional principle of equal protection of the laws. See *The New York Times*, March 19, 1963.

39 Cf. Parsons, "On the Concept of Political Power," *op. cit.* and John Rawls, *loc. cit.*

40 In the 1920s and 30s the late Professor H. J. Laski was fond of saying that no "ruling class" would *ever* relinquish its position peacefully. Yet, in the late 1940s, the British Labor government both introduced the "welfare state" and set India free without a Conservative *coup d'état* occurring against them.

41 Seymour Martin Lipset, Martin Trow, and James Coleman, *Union Democracy* (Glencoe, IL: The Free Press, 1956).

42 Parsons, "On the Concept of Political Power," *loc. cit.*

43 Parsons, "On the Concept of Influence," *Public Opinion Quarterly*, 27 (Spring, 1963), 37–62.

44 Paul Hollander, "The New Man and His Enemies: A Study of the Stalinist Conceptions of Good and Evil Personified," unpublished Ph.D. dissertation, Princeton University, 1963. See also Allen Kassof's forthcoming book on Soviet youth.

45 Lest it be forgotten, what I have called the legitimation complex represents above all the differentiation between societal and cultural systems. The maintenance and extension of this differentiation is taken for granted in the present description of developments internal to the social system.

9

Pattern Variables Revisited: A Response to Robert Dubin

I am grateful to Professor Dubin for the careful attention he has given to the somewhat neglected pattern variables and for his considerable effort in exploring their potential usefulness. His article has led to a serious reconsideration of the problems he has raised – in particular, the relation between what he refers to as Model I (the pattern variables as formulated in *Toward a General Theory of Action*[1]) and Model II (the paradigm of four functional problems of systems of action from *Working Papers*,[2] and later publications). Dubin suggests that the usefulness of Model II is impaired by too drastic a condensation, and that it cannot be reconciled with Model I. The Editor's invitation to comment on his paper has given me the opportunity to work out an overdue clarification of the ways in which Model II builds on and goes beyond, rather than replaces, Model I.

Dubin is essentially correct in characterizing the pattern variables as a model that uses the unit act as its building block. The unit act involves the *relationship of an actor to a situation composed of objects,* and it is conceived as a choice (imputed by the theorist to the actor) among alternative ways of defining the situation. The unit act, however, does not occur independently but as one unit in the context of a wider system of actor–situation relationships; this system – including a plurality of acts – is referred to as an *action system.* The unit act is the logically minimal unit of analysis, but as such it can be conceived empirically only as a unit of an action system. Even for analysis of one discrete concrete act, an extended set of similar acts must be postulated as part of the action system – for example, those comprising a particular role. Figure 9.1 below is a paradigm for any such action system, not only the unit act.

The Frame of Reference

The pattern variables first emerged as a conceptual scheme for classifying types of roles in social systems, starting with the distinction between professional and business roles. In this sense, the concept "actor" referred to individual human beings as personalities in roles and the analysis – as Dubin puts it – " 'looks' out to the social system from the vantage point of the actor." In *Toward a General Theory,* the scheme was substantially revised and its relevance extended from role-analysis in the social system to the analysis of all types of systems of action.

Action is thus viewed as a process occurring between two structural parts of a system – actor and situation. In carrying out analysis at any level of the total action system, the concept "actor" is extended to define not only individual personalities in roles but other types of acting units – collectivities, behavioral organisms, and cultural systems. Since the term actor is used here to refer to any such acting unit, I attempt to avoid – except for purposes of analogy or illustration – psychological reference, for example, "motivation," attributed to actors as individuals. Thus "actor" can refer to a business firm in interaction with a household, or, at the cultural level, the implementation of empirical beliefs interacting with the implementation of evaluative beliefs.

Both the pattern variables and the four system-problems are conceptual schemes, or sets of categories, for classifying the components of action. They provide a frame of reference within which such classification can be made. The figures presented below indicate the methods, sets of rules and procedures, that state how these categories may be used analytically; they imply *theorems* – propositions that admit of logical, not empirical, proof – which state a set of determinate relationships among the categories and, in so doing, outline a *theory* of action. The theory, then, is a set of logical relationships among categories used to classify empirical phenomena and, in empirical reference, attempts to account for whatever may be the degree of uniformity and stability of such phenomena.

The pattern variables are a conceptual scheme for classifying the components of an action system – the actor–situation relational system which comprises a plurality of unit acts. Each variable defines one property of a particular class of components. In the first instance, they distinguish between two sets of components, *orientations* and *modalities*. Orientation concerns the actor's relationship *to* the objects in his situation and is conceptualized by the two "attitudinal" variables of diffuseness-specificity and affectivity-neutrality. In psychological terms, orientation refers to the actor's need for relating to the object world, to the basis of his interest in it. For other levels of analysis, of course this psychological reference must be generalized. Modality concerns the meaning *of* the object for the actor and is conceptualized by the two "object-categorization" variables of quality-performance and universalism-particularism. It refers to those aspects of the object that have meaning for the actor, given the situation. The orientation set of pattern variables "views" the relationship of actor to situation from the side of the actor or actors; the modality set views it from the side of the situation as consisting of objects. As Dubin suggests, the pattern variable of self-collectivity orientation does not belong at this level of analysis; it is placed in proper perspective below.

In classifying the components of the actor's relation to a situation, the pattern variables suggest propositions about any particular action system in terms of those components and the type of act their combination defines; thus a particular role can be characterized by the properties of universalism, performance, and so on. An action system, however, is not characterized solely by the actor's orientations and the modalities of objects significant to the actor; it is also a *structured* system with analytically independent aspects which the elementary pattern variable combinations by themselves do not take into account.

In such a structured system both actor and object share institutionalized norms, conformity with which is a condition for stability of the system. The relation between the actor's orientations and the modalities of objects in the situation cannot be random. The *Working Papers* established a nonrandom relationship between the two sets by matching the functionally corresponding categories on each side – universalism with specificity, particularism with diffuseness, performance with affectivity, and quality with neutrality. This matching yielded Dubin's Model II. It turned out that this arrangement converges with the classification of functional problems of systems that Bales had earlier formulated.[3] This convergence, the main subject of the *Working Papers*, opened up such a fertile range of possibilities that for several years my main attention has been given to their exploration rather than to direct concern with the scheme out of which it grew. However, it is now clear that "Model II" is not a substitute for the earlier version, in the sense that it represents the whole scheme, but rather a formulation of one particularly crucial part of a larger scheme. The following discussion places that part in the context of the larger scheme as the formulation of "integrative standards," those aspects of the action system shared by actor and object and that make the system a stable one.

In analyzing the components of any particular action system, one must also consider the larger system within which that action system is embedded. The action system is related to the "external system" beyond it, which I refer to here as the *environment* of the system, as distinguished from the *situation* of the acting unit. The following analysis treats this relation of action system to environment as mediated mainly through the adaptive subsystem. The combinations of pattern variable components in that subsystem were foreshadowed in the *Working Papers* by the "auxiliary" combinations of neutrality-performance, particularism-specificity, and so on.[4] The present paper, I believe, establishes the analytical independence of *these* combinations from those of the integrative standards in Model II, and goes considerably beyond the *Working Papers* in setting forth their significance for action systems.

Finally, the pattern variables – although they designate the *properties* of actor's orientations and objects' modalities in an action system – do not as such classify *types* of actors and objects. Such a typology cannot be derived from any particular action system, but only from the analysis of a range of such systems. It is this typology of actors and objects with which Dubin's left- and right-hand columns in his Table 1 is concerned. Figure 9.2 below has incorporated this important aspect of Dubin's problem.

With reference to Dubin's Table 1, the pattern variables themselves are discussed under what he terms the "actor's evaluation of objects." The column headed "Modalities of Objects" is admittedly redundant, for in addition to the redundancies noted by Dubin, the terms "classificatory" and "relational" are synonymous with "universalism" and "particularism," respectively, as I acknowledged in *The Social System*. In my Figure 9.2, Dubin's "motivational orientation" towards objects is covered by the pattern-maintenance or orientation subsystem; his "value-orientation" by the adaptive subsystem; and his "action-orientation" is characterized by the types of output of the system as a whole (see below).

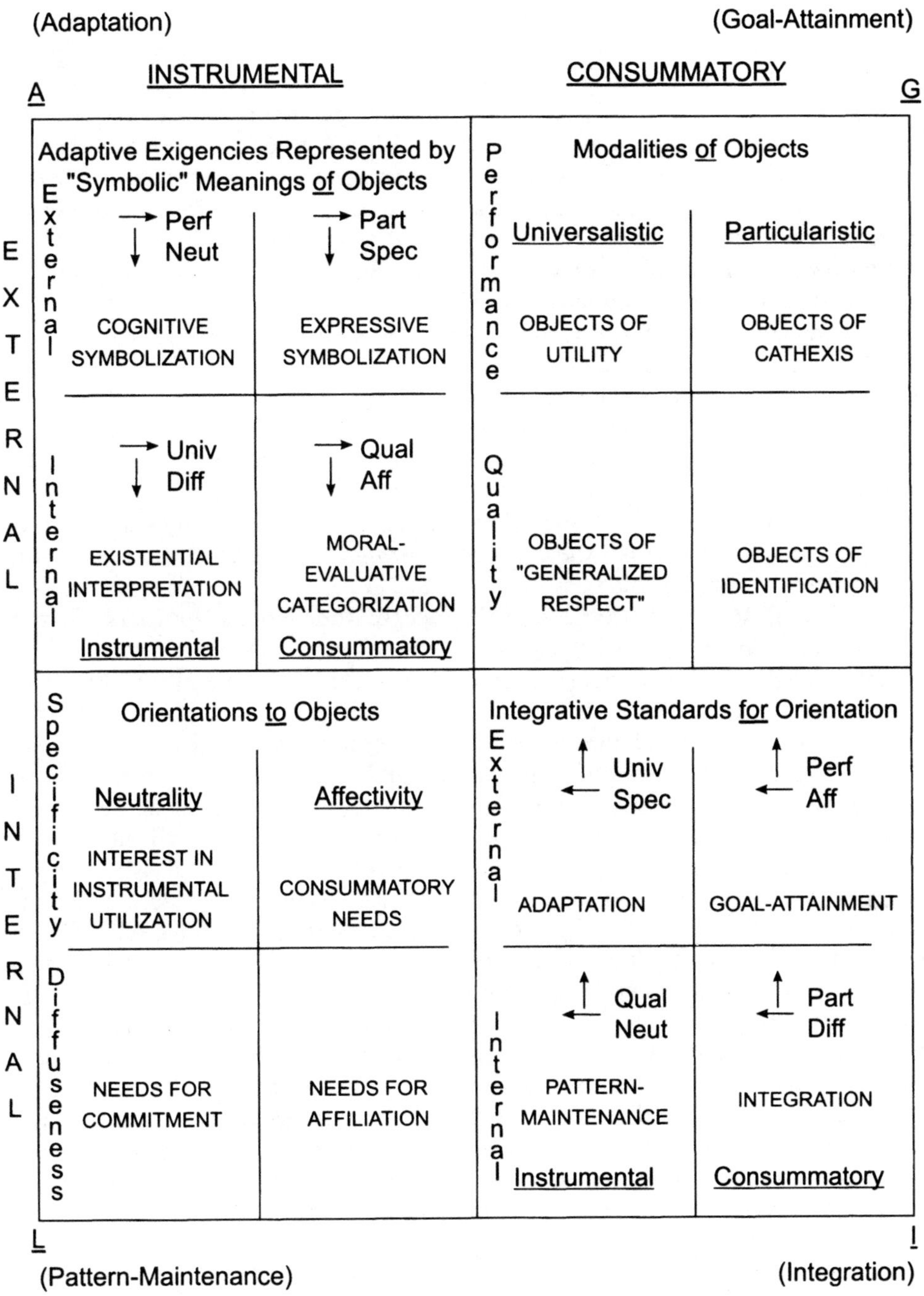

(Adaptation)   (Goal-Attainment)

A   INSTRUMENTAL   CONSUMMATORY   G

	Adaptive Exigencies Represented by "Symbolic" Meanings of Objects		Modalities of Objects	
E x t e r n a l	→ Perf ↓ Neut COGNITIVE SYMBOLIZATION	→ Part ↓ Spec EXPRESSIVE SYMBOLIZATION	**P e r f o r m a n c e** Universalistic OBJECTS OF UTILITY	Particularistic OBJECTS OF CATHEXIS
I n t e r n a l	→ Univ ↓ Diff EXISTENTIAL INTERPRETATION	→ Qual ↓ Aff MORAL- EVALUATIVE CATEGORIZATION	**Q u a l i t y** OBJECTS OF "GENERALIZED RESPECT"	OBJECTS OF IDENTIFICATION
	Instrumental	Consummatory		

E X T E R N A L

	Orientations to Objects		Integrative Standards for Orientation	
S p e c i f i c i t y	Neutrality INTEREST IN INSTRUMENTAL UTILIZATION	Affectivity CONSUMMATORY NEEDS	**E x t e r n a l** ↑ Univ ← Spec ADAPTATION	↑ Perf ← Aff GOAL-ATTAINMENT
D i f f u s e n e s s	NEEDS FOR COMMITMENT	NEEDS FOR AFFILIATION	**I n t e r n a l** ↑ Qual ← Neut PATTERN- MAINTENANCE	↑ Part ← Diff INTEGRATION
			Instrumental	Consummatory

I N T E R N A L

L   I

(Pattern-Maintenance)   (Integration)

Figure 9.1   The components of action systems

Thus the conceptual scheme of the four system-problems has added a set of rules and procedures – the basis of theorems – whereby the analysis of components of action in terms of pattern variables can be carried out by "looking down" on them, as Dubin has aptly put it, from the perspective of the action system. The action system is presented in Figure 9.1 above so as to establish the analytical independence of the four subsystems: orientations (pattern-maintenance); modalities (goal-attainment); their combination characterizing the conditions of internal stability of a relational system shared by both actor and object (integration); their combination characterizing the ways in which that system is stably related to the environment (adaptation).

Following the presentation of these four subsystems, the *same* information is displayed in tabular form different form the more familiar functional "layout." This second presentation (Figure 9.2) is designed to "look down" on any particular action system from the perspective of the more inclusive system. At this level, the analysis of types of actors and of objects can be carried out. In addition, Figure 9.2 highlights the distinction between the *control* of action – that is, the scale of priorities assigned to various ways of regulating action – and the *implementation* of action – the analytical relevance involved in the distinction between structure and process.

This then is the main frame of reference of the paper's approach to the classification and analysis of the components of action. We now turn to the paradigm itself, which is altogether newly formulated from the point of view of the internal relations between its components, and is presented in Figure 9.1. Its form is essentially that of Dubin's Table 4, which was derived from the *Working Papers*.[5] "Model II" is treated in the paradigm as the integration subsystem of the general system. The pattern variable scheme as formulated in *Toward A General Theory*, that is, the two "attitudinal" and "object-categorization" sets, are incorporated into the "pattern-maintenance" and the "goal-attainment" subsystems, respectively. To avoid terminological confusion we follow Dubin in referring to the two sets of pattern variables as the *orientation* set and the *modality* set. The fourth block of cells, representing the adaptation subsystem, is also entirely new, and is explicated below.

We have noted above that the primary reference of the concept "actor" is to the individual personality, but that in secondary respects, collectivities, behavioral organisms, and cultural systems may be conceived as actors. It is important to remember that our scheme concerns the *generalized* components of action, so that such psychological terms as "cathexis" and "identification" and "need," as used here, stand for more generalized concepts than would be applicable to actors and objects on these other levels; their reference is not confined to the personality level.

The Orientation Set (Pattern-Maintenance)[6]

The *orientation base* of a system of action may be categorized in terms of the two pattern variables, affectivity-neutrality and specificity-diffuseness. The relevant characteristic of the actor in defining his (or "its") orientation to an object or category of objects may be an "interest" in the object as a source of "consummation." This may be defined as an interest in establishing a *relation to* an object, which the actor has no incentive to change. In psychological terms, this may be phrased that the actor has a "need" for such a relationship, which can be "gratified" by its establishment. The alternative to the need for a consummatory relationship is the "need" for *help* toward the attainment of such a relationship to an object. Therefore, besides the consummatory, there is an instrumental basis of orientation to the object-world. At this point a pattern-variable "dilemma" arises because it is a fundamental assertion of our theory that consummatory and instrumental interests in objects *cannot* be maximized at the same time. The instrumental and consummatory bases are *analytically* independent.

The very discrimination of different bases of orientation of actors to objects implies that actors are conceived as systems; they are never oriented to their situations simply "as a whole," but always through specific modes of organization of independent components. From this point of view, it is always important whether the primary reference is to the *relation* of the acting system to its environment *or* to its own internal properties and equilibrium. The situation, or object-world, is in the nature of the case organized differently from the actor as system. Hence, in orientation *directly* to the situation, the specificities of differentiation among objects and their properties become salient. On the other hand, where internal "needs" of the acting system are paramount, the salience of these specificities recedes, and the orientation to objects becomes more diffuse. This is the setting in which the specificity-diffuseness variable fits. It indicates that where the "interaction surface" between actor and situation is approached, the actor's interests in objects must be more highly specified than where internal states of the acting system itself are in the forefront.

There is a pattern-variable dilemma here as well as in the instrumental-consummatory case. This is to say that the imperatives of specificity and of diffuseness cannot be maximally satisfied at the same time.

The cross-classification of these two orientational pattern-variables yields a four-fold table which is presented as the pattern-maintenance subsystem (L) of Figure 9.1. As distinguished from the pattern variables themselves, which are rubrics of classification, this constitutes a classification of *types* of orientation to objects. This distinction has not always been clear, I believe, neither in my own work nor in that of other writers.

It will be seen that the pure type of "consummatory needs" combines affectivity and specificity of interest; it is "pure" because it can focus on the actor's relation to the *specific* discretely differentiated object. But where the basis of interest is diffuse, there must be generalization to a broader *category* of objects, so the basis of the interest is the establishment of a relation between the acting system and a wider sector of the situational object-system. We have called this a "need for affiliation," for example, for a relation of mutual "solidarity" between diffuse sectors of the acting system and the object-system.

On the instrumental side, it is apparent that the same order of distinction applies to specifically differentiated bases of interest in objects and diffuser bases. *Manipulation* of objects in the interest of consummatory gratification or even passive adaptation to them requires concern with the specificities of their properties. Hence the "interest in instrumental utilization," though affectively neutral, is also specific; interest in the *category* is not enough. Where, however, the problem is not utilization, but the place of the orientation in the internal structure of the acting system, this level of the specification of interest not only is unnecessary but, because of the independent variability of the object-situation, becomes positively obstructive. *Commitment* to the specifics of object-situations introduces a rigidity of orientation which can be highly constrictive. Commitment can be and, functionally speaking, is better organized on a diffuser level. We therefore speak of "needs for commitment" as oriented to diffuse categories of objects and their properties rather than to specific objects and properties, and as engaging more diffuse sectors of the acting system than do "interests in instrumental utilization."

The Modality Set (Goal–Attainment)

With reference to the obverse side of the action relationship, that of the modalities of objects, the modality set of pattern variables constitutes the classificatory framework – particularism and universalism, and performance and quality. Particularism in this context means that from the point of view of the action system, the most significant aspect of an object is its relation of particularity to the actor: as compared with other objects which can "intrinsically" be classified as similar to it, the significance of *this* object to the actor lies in its *inclusion* in the same interactive system. In the contrasting case of universalistic modalities, the basis of an object's meaning lies in its universalistically defined properties, hence its inclusion in classes which transcend that particular relational system. For example, when a man falls in love, it is this *particular* woman with whom the love relationship exists. He may, like some other gentlemen, prefer blondes, but he is not in love with the category, but with one particular blonde. Thus the same kind of dilemma exists here as for the two pattern variables described above – it is impossible to maximize the particularistic meaning of objects and their universalistic meaning at the same time. A man sufficiently in love with blondeness as such, who therefore pursues any blonde, cannot establish a very stable love relationship with a particular woman. That there is an important "matching" between consummatory bases of interest and particularistic meaning of objects is clear; its significance is discussed below.

A basic postulate of action theory is that the status of acting systems and those of the situational object-world in which they act are independently variable. At their "interface," then, an especially important property of objects is their probable *performance* in respect to the actors oriented to them. Recall that the prototype of the actor-object relation is social interaction, in which the "object" is also in turn an actor who does something. Thus physical objects, which do not "act," are the limiting case of objects to which the term "performance" is inherently inapplicable.

In contrast with this situation, is the meaning of objects in terms of what they "are," of their qualities defined independently of performances, which are inherently relative to situations. The internal reference of the acting system matches with interest in the qualities of objects rather than their performances, since these are presumptively more independent of direct situational exigencies.

These two classificatory rubrics – performance-quality and universalism-particularism – yield a four-fold typology of objects (or of components), seen from the perspective of their meaning to actors. This is the goal-attainment subsystem (G) in Figure 9.1. This terminology is also adopted from the proto-typical case of interaction of persons. Thus an object whose primary meaning is particularistic and based on its actual and expected performances, following psychoanalytic usage, may be called an "object of cathexis." It is "looked at" in terms of its potentialities for gratifying specific consummatory needs. However, if an object is defined in universalistic terms, but at the same time as a source of performances significant to the actor, it can be said to be an "object of utility," for it is viewed with respect to its potentialities in helping to bring about consummatory states of the acting system.

In contrast with both these types, objects may be treated as "objects of identification" if their meaning is both particularistic and refers essentially to what they "are" rather than what they "do." Here the objects' meaning to actors is not subject to the more detailed fluctuations which go with the meaning of cathexis.

Finally, the universalistic case, the fourth type, is called an "object of generalized respect." Here the object is categorized by the actor in universalistic terms, but also with relation to its qualities. This is the type of object which in a social context Durkheim speaks of as generating attitudes of "moral authority."[7]

Problems of Integration and Adaptation

The argument so far may be summarized: We have outlined, in terms of the present conceptual scheme, the elementary components of action and certain aspects of their interrelations. Essentially these are the components of unit acts but do not yet comprise systems of action.

First, we have assumed that all action involves the *relating* of acting units to objects in their situation. This is the basis for the fundamental distinction between components belonging to the characterization of *orienting* actors and those belonging to the *modalities* of the objects to which they are oriented – that is, between the two "sets" of elementary pattern variables. Second, we have used the elementary variables to classify types of elementary combination. The underlying assumption here is that on this level they are always analytically independent; hence the orientation set (cluster L of Figure 9.1) and the modality set (cluster G) are treated as mutually exclusive, each type being composed of components drawn only from one of the two sets. Third, each cell within each cluster is composed of *only* two pattern variable designations. Fourth, what elsewhere are defined as "pattern variable opposites" never occur in the same cell. Subject to these rules, the classifications designated by the four cells in each cluster are logically exhaustive of the possibilities. We consider the fourth assumption to be the application of a fundamental theorem concerning the conditions of the stability of orientation, namely, that neither the same orientation nor the same object can be successfully defined, in a particular context or orientation, in terms of *both* alternatives without discrimination, for example, universalistically and particularistically or specifically and diffusely at the same time.

Subject to these constraints, however, we see no reason why the composition of possible types of unit acts do not exhaust the range of logically possible independent variation of the components thus formulated. But such a definition does not tell us anything about the conditions of the existence of a *system* of such unit acts other than that there are such limiting circumstances as physical and biological conditions of survival. In other words, this level of analysis describes a *population* of action-units and certain of the ways in which they are empirically ordered in relation to each other. It cannot provide an analysis of the relations of their *interaction*, which constitute a system subject to mechanisms of equilibration and change as a system through "feedback" processes – in one sense, the *organization* of the system.

To take the step to this organizational level, it is necessary to attempt to conceptualize two basic sets of "functions" which cannot be treated either as the orientations of actors or as the meanings or modalities of the objects to which they are primarily oriented. These are, first, the modes of internal *integration* of the system, that is, of the interrelations of the elementary actor-object units. This means, within our frame of reference, the normative standards on the basis of which such relations can be said to be stable. Second, there are the mechanisms by which the system as a whole is *adapted to the environment* within which it operates. Since from the point of view of orientation this environment must consist in some sense of objects, the problem is that of conceptualizing the relation between objects internal to the system and those (albeit in some sense meaningful) external to the system.

To repeat, those reviewed above constitute the full complement of elementary components of action systems. Therefore, in dealing with these two additional system functions or subsystem clusters, we do not propose to introduce additional elementary components, but rather to suggest new *combinations* of these components. On this basis the I and A clusters of cells in Figure 9.1 are constructed on the hypothesis that each cell of the two clusters should be defined by *one* pattern variable component drawn from each of the two elementary subsets. If this policy and the general rules formulated above are followed, the combinations represented in the two clusters will be logically exhaustive of the possibilities.

Within these rules the problem is that of the basis of allocation of the components as between the two clusters, and within each as between the cells. The governing principles for treating this problem are more fully elucidated below, following a review of the allocations themselves and some problems of the system as a whole. Here, suffice it to say, first, that internal integration is dependent on the *matching* of the function of the object for the "needs" of the orienting actor with the functional meaning with which the object is categorized. Thus in some sense the gratification of consummatory needs is dependent on the possibility of categorizing appropriate objects as objects of cathexis, and so on. Why only two of the four components which might define this matching are involved, and which two, are also explained below.

Secondly, the significance of objects external to the system is not their *actual* meaning *in* the system, but rather their *potential* meaning *for* the system – the ways in which taking cognizance of this meaning or failing to do so *may* affect the functioning of the system. With these preliminaries, we may now review schematically the actual content suggested for the cells.

The Integrative Subset

How are the formal characteristics of the I and A cells in Figure 9.1 to be interpreted? The integrative subset states the primary conditions of internal stability or *order* in an action system. These conditions may be formulated as follows: (1) In so far as the primary functional problem of the system, conceived either in terms of structural differentiation or temporal phases, is *adaptive*, stability is dependent on the *universalistic* categorization of the relevant objects, regardless of whether or not they have certain particularistic meanings, *and* on sufficient *specificity* in the basis of interest in these objects to exclude more diffuse considerations of orientation. (2) In so far as the primary functional problem is the *attainment* of a *goal* for the system, stability is dependent on attention to the potentialities of *performance* of the object in its relation to the actor, *and* on affective engagement of the actor in the establishment of the optimal (consummatory) relation to the object – hence the lifting of "inhibitions" on such engagement. (3) In so far as the primary functional problem is integration of the system, stability is dependent on particularistic categorization of the relevant objects (that is, to the extent that they are also actors, their inclusion in the system), *and* the maintenance of a *diffuse* basis of interest in these objects (that is, one which is not contingent on fluctuations in their specific performances or properties). (4) In so far as the primary functional problem for the system is the *maintenance* of the *pattern* of its units, stability is dependent on maintaining a categorization of the objects in terms of their *qualities* independently of their specific performances, *and* an affectively *neutral* orientation, one that is not alterable as a function of specific situational rewards.

In terms of the regulation of action, these combinations of pattern variable components define categories of *norms* governing the interaction of units in the system. Norms themselves must be differentiated. It is in the nature of an action system to be subject to a plurality of functional exigencies; no single undifferentiated normative pattern or "value" permits stability over the range of these different exigencies. Hence norms constitute a differentiated and structured subsystem of the larger system. They constitute the structural aspect of the *relational nexus* between actors and objects in their situations.

Precisely because the above propositions state conditions of stable equilibrium involving the *relations between* a plurality of elementary components, I believe that they go beyond description to state, implicitly at least, certain theorems about the consequences of variations in these relations. These theorems are considered following the discussion of the system itself.

The Adaptive Subset

In the adaptive subset, the formal bases of selection of the component combinations, as we have noted, are antithetical to those used in the integrative subset. This is to say that they combine both external and internal references, and both instrumental and consummatory references.

We have termed these combinations as defining "mechanisms" for ordering the adaptive relations of a system of action to the environment in which it functions. To clarify this problem an important distinction must be made. When we referred above to the orientation of actors to objects and the related modalities or meanings of objects, we were indicating components *internal* to a system of action. Objects that are *constituents* of the system must, however, be distinguished from objects that are part of the *environment* of the system. The boundary concept which defines this distinction is "particularism;" an object categorized particularistically is defined as belonging to the system. Adaptation concerns the relations of the whole system to objects which, as such, are *not* included in it.

Adaptive mechanisms, then, must be conceived as ways of categorizing the meanings of objects universalistically, that is, independently of their actual or potential inclusion in a given system. These mechanisms are "symbolic" media, including language as the prototype, but also empirical knowledge, money, and so on. Use of the media for referring to objects and categories of objects does not *ipso facto* commit the actor to any particular relation of inclusion or exclusion relative to the objects concerned. By use of the media, however, *meanings* may be treated as *internal* to the system, whereas the objects themselves may or may not remain external. This is the basic difference from modalities, which are meanings wherein the objects themselves are defined as internal.

In this context, the pattern variable combinations of the adaptive subset may be explicated as follows: (1) In order to symbolize the *adaptive* significance of objects in the environment of an action system (for example, to "understand" them cognitively), it is necessary to categorize them in terms of what actually or potentially they "do" (*performance*), *and* to orient to them with affective *neutrality*, that is, independently of their potentialities for gratifying the actor. This "pattern" is defined as a condition for stability of an orientation to the *external* environment which can maximize "objective" understanding of the objects comprising it; adopting a term from personality analysis we may term the pattern empirical "cognitive symbolization." (2) In order to symbolize and categorize objects that are external to the system according to their significance for goal-attainment, it is necessary to focus their possible meaning on specific bases of interest or "motivation" (specificity), *and* on their potential "belongingness" in a system of meanings which also defines the system of action (particularism). This we call "expressive symbolization," the generalization of particularistic meanings to a universalistic level of significance. (3) In order to symbolize and categorize the significance of *norms* that are external to the system, it is necessary to treat them as aspects of an objectively "given" state of affairs or "order" (quality), *and* to treat them with affectivity – that is, the actor cannot be emotionally indifferent to whether or not he feels committed to the norms in question. This we name "moral-evaluative categorization." (4) In order to symbolize and categorize the significance of "sources of normative authority," it is necessary to combine a universalistic definition of the object, as having properties not dependent on its inclusion in the system, with a *diffuse* basis of interest, so that the meaning in question cannot be treated as contingent on the fluctuating relations between the orienting actor and the environment. This we call "existential interpretation."

Here another version of the external–internal distinction is important. For the first two of these – the adaptive and goal-attainment categories – refer to objects considered as such, irrespective of whether or not they are included with the acting system within a more comprehensive system. In the latter two cases, however, this question of common membership in a more comprehensive system is central. A norm is binding on a unit only in so far as the unit shares common membership with other units similarly bound. An object is a source of normative authority only so far as its authority extends to other units, defined universalistically as similarly subject to that authority. It is on these grounds that we emphasize "symbolization" in the first two cases and "categorization" in the second two.

Note that the differentiation of symbolic media according to functional significance parallels the differentiation of integrative standards. They too are results of a process of differentiating the components involved in the elementary pattern-variable sets and of integrating the selected components across the orientation–modality line. As distinguished from the *internal* integration of the system, the adaptive subset refers to the system's integration with its environment as part of a more comprehensive system of action.

The Perspective of the System as a Whole

So far we have considered the elementary components which make up a system of action and two main ways in which they are related across the orientation–modality line. These components and relations, however, constitute a system which in turn functions in relation to what we call an "environment." We now consider a few aspects of the properties of this system in its environmental context. The main reference point for this analysis is a rearrangement or transformation of the items of Figure 9.1, as presented in Figure 9.2.

The components in Figure 9.2 are the same sixteen pattern variable combinations represented in Figure 9.1. However, there are two new features of the arrangement: First, each of the four major blocks of cells of Figure 9.1 is set forth as a column of Figure 9.2. Within each column the cells in turn are arranged from top to bottom in the order L–I–G–A. This constitutes a cybernetic hierarchy of control,[8] that is, each cell categorizes the necessary but not sufficient conditions for operation of the cell next above it in the column, and in the opposite direction, the categories of each cell control the processes categorized in the one below it. For instance, definition of an end or goal controls the selection of means for its attainment.

	STRUCTURAL CATEGORIES		CATEGORIES OF PROCESS		
	Units of Orientation to Objects (L) (Properties of Actors)	Integrative Standards (I)	Symbolic Representation of External Objects (A)	Internal Meanings of Objects (G) (Inputs–Outputs)	Outputs to Environment
L	Neut Diff NORMATIVE COMMITMENTS	Qual Neut Ground-of-meaning Anchorage PATTERN-MAINTENANCE	Diff Univ EXISTENTIAL INTERPRETATION	Univ Qual "RESPECT"	
I	Aff Diff AFFILIATIONS	Part Manifold of Diff evaluative selections INTEGRATION Allocative selection	Aff Qual MORAL-EVALUATION	Part Qual IDENTIFICATION	Responsible Action
G	Aff Spec CONSUMMATORY NEEDS	Perf Range of Aff action-choice GOAL (attainment) SELECTION	Spec Part EXPRESSIVE SYMBOLIZATION	Perf Part CATHEXIS	Expressive Action
A	Neut Spec INSTRUMENTAL CAPACITIES	Empirical- Univ cognitive Spec field ADAPTATION Means-Selection	Neut Perf COGNITIVE SYMBOLIZATION	Perf Univ UTILITY	Instrumental Action

Direction of Limiting Conditions ↑

Direction of Implementation *vis-à-vis* Environment ———→

←——— Direction of Environmental "Stimulation"

Figure 9.2 The action system in relation to its environment

The second difference from Figure 9.1 is the arrangement of the columns from left to right in a serial order which, stated in functional terms, is L–I–A–G. The two left-hand columns designate the structural components of the system. The L column formulates the properties of units conceived as actors; the I column formulates the structural aspect of the relational nexus between units, that is, the norms which function as integrative standards. The two right-hand columns categorize the elements of *process* by which the system operates. The G column shows the modalities of objects from the point of view of *change* of meaning as a process of relating inputs and outputs; it brings *into* the system meaning-categorizations generated by the system. The A column formulates the components involved in the symbolic mechanisms mediating the adaptive aspect of process. Whereas the hierarchy of control places the A subset at the bottom of each column, as a column itself it is placed "inside" the system because it consists of a set of symbolized *meanings* (or "representations") of the environmental object-world outside the system, or the categorization of objects independently of their inclusion in or exclusion from the system. It therefore constitutes the *internal environment* of the system, the environment to which *units* must adapt in their relations to each other, but the actual objects symbolized constitute the external environment to which the *system* as a whole must adapt.

We have suggested that the outputs of action systems *consist in* changes in the meanings of objects. It follows that the inputs also consist in meanings of objects. What the process of action accomplishes, then, is *change* in these meanings. We assume of course that new objects and categories of objects are created in the process; these presumably are themselves action systems and their "cultural" precipitates. The distinction between changing the meaning of an old object and creating a new object thus appears to depend on the point of observation.

The modalities of objects in the G column of Figure 9.2 therefore may be treated as a classification of the outputs of *internal* action process, in a sense similar to the usage in economics of "value-added."[9] Thus action process, so far as it is effectively *adaptive* internally, may be said to add utility to objects – for example, utility in the economist's sense, the relevant category for social systems, also is a category of meaning in the present context. Action which is successfully oriented internally to *goal-attainment* leads to the enhanced cathectic value of objects in the system. Action which is successfully *integrative* leads to increased "identification-meaning" – in social systems, to solidarity with and among objects. Finally, processes of "pattern-maintenance" maintain or restore the "respect" in which the relevant system itself is held as an object in the social system; here is Durkheim's "the integrity of moral authority."

The designations to the right of the G column in Figure 9.2 are the "action-orientations" in the Orientation column of Dubin's Table 1. We suggest that these can be treated as categories of output *to its environment* of the *system as a whole* (as distinguished from the outputs of internal process). Thus instrumental action by a system may be treated as resulting in increase in the instrumental values to it of objects *within* its environment or more inclusive system. Similarly, expressive action produces enhanced cathectic meaning of objects in the environment; and responsible action increases the integrative identification category of meaning (for example, in the social system, "moral" value). In accord with principles we have used consistently,[10] we suggest that there is no category of output for the L subsystem except in cases of change in the structure of the system.

The Classification of Objects

One further set of categories which play a part in Dubin's Table 1 needs to be accounted for – the classification of types of object as physical, social, and cultural. This problem can most conveniently be treated at the environmental level. If a given system is conceived as an actor or an action system, then a system with which it *inter*acts is a social object. We have explained why this category should be differentiated into at least two subcategories: the system organized about the single human individual, namely, personality; and the social system constituted by the interaction of a plurality of individuals. A *physical* object, then, is one with which the system does not in this sense interact, and which, standing below the action system in the hierarchy of control, is conditional to it; a *cultural* object is also one with which it does not interact, but which stands above it in the hierarchy of control, and therefore is a focus of its own control system.

However, a further principle is involved, not developed here, of *interpenetration* of systems.[11] The crucial case of physical systems with which the personality interpenetrates is the behavioral organism, the physical system which constitutes the fundamental facility-base for the operation of the personality system. At the other extreme are "acting" cultural systems, implemented through social and personal actions, which constitute the operating normative control systems of social systems. At each "end" of the control series, then, is a set of limiting conceptions of nonaction "reality." At the lower end is "purely physical" reality with which the action system does not interpenetrate, but which is only conditional to it. At the upper end is "nonempirical," perhaps "cosmic," reality with which, similarly, there is no significant interpenetration, and which is thus conceived only as an "existential ground" of operative cultural systems.

A similar classification can be worked out for the alternative case where the system in question is conceived as acting, and not as an object. Here it seems that the parallel to a cultural object is the conception of the "subject" as "knowing, feeling, and willing." At the social level, this is our concept of "actor" in the sense of participation in *interaction*. At the interpenetrating subsocial level, it is the concept of organism, as "functioning" in relation to an environment. Perhaps at a still lower level should be placed the "hereditary constitution" of a species (as distinguished from the particular organism in phylogenetic, not ontogenetic terms).

Combinations of the Components

We now return to the question of the bases of combination and allocation of the pattern variable components. A maximum number of types could be generated of course by treating the potential combinations as all those randomly possible. This procedure, however, would mean the sacrifice of connections referred to above as the *organization* of systems of action and the determinate theoretical generalizations associated with them.

We have restricted random combinations, first, by composing two cell clusters (L and G) exclusively from one or the other of the elementary sets; second, by never placing both members of a "dilemma" pair in the same cell; third, by placing only *one* component from each elementary set in each cell of the I and A clusters; and, finally, by drawing these from "functionally cognate" cells of the elementary combination paradigms. (See Figures 9.1 and 9.2.) Within these rules of organization we have followed a further policy of selection in the allocations to the I and A clusters. In terms of the "geometry" of Figure 9.1, this policy involves two procedures: (1) for the I cluster, the distribution of the modality components is derived by keeping the "functionally cognate" reference constant and then rotating clockwise the modality axes one quarter turn, and the distribution of the orientation components is similarly decided by rotating the orientation axes in the counterclockwise direction; (2) for the A cluster, the direction of rotation is the reverse in each case. Thus, in the G cluster the distinction between universalism and particularism defines the *horizontal* axis of the paradigm, in the I cluster it assumes the *diagonal*. Put otherwise: of the *two* occurrences of each component in the G table only *one* of each is included in the I table, and these are placed in a diagonal position. The effect of this is to "shift" the relevant category from one to the other of the two positions in which it could be placed in the elementary set. The procedure never leads to "crossing over" into a "forbidden" cell; for example, universalism and particularism never "change places."

What is the meaning of these patternings? It is inherent in the organization of Figure 9.2 that integrative functions stand higher in the order of control than either goal-attainment or adaptive functions, which follow in that order. On grounds that cannot be fully explained here, I suggest that the horizontal and vertical axes of the paradigm state the location of the processes, conceived as inter-unit interchanges, which, respectively, have primarily internal adaptive significance in providing facilities to the units in question, and internal goal-attainment significance in providing rewards. Thus, the "rotation" brings about an involvement of the pattern variable components in integrative interchanges along the axes of Durkheim's "mechanical" (L–G) and "organic" solidarity (A–I).[12]

The suggestion, then, is that, relative to the elementary clusters, both I and A clusters have integrative significance. The I set states internal integrative *standards*, departure from which is associated with those realistic internal consequences known in interaction theory as "negative sanctions." The A set states standards of *meanings* of external objects ("cultural standards"), departure from which is associated with cultural selectivity and distortion, although not with immediately felt "sanctions."

What of the obverse "directions" of rotation? There is a double incidence of these directionalities. *Within* the clusters the rotations of the axes of the orientations and of the modalities are in opposite directions. The modalities of objects, from the point of view of a system of action, constitute ways of relating not only the acting unit but the system to the environment external to it. Hence it is an imperative of integration that, from the modality side, priority should be enjoyed by the category of meaning of the object (internally, as defining the actor–object relation) which is of primary functional significance *for the system* in the relevant context. From the orientation side, the imperative is that priority goes to the mode of orientation of primary significance to the actor in terms of its "needs." Thus, if the system function in question is adaptive, universalistic meanings take precedence over particularistic. For the actor, then, the primacy of specificity may be regarded as protecting his interest in *other* contexts of meaning of the same and other objects by limiting his commitments to the more immediately important ones.

These two designations are "functionally cognate" in that they share the characteristics of external orientation and instrumental significance. Here the rotation means that on the A–I axis of the integrative cluster (not of the system as a whole) the modality component in the adaptive cell is related to what in the G cluster is its *consummatory* "partner," whereas the orientation component is related to its *internal* partner. This is simply another way of stating the obverse directions of rotation. Put in general functional terms: the obverse relationship protects the system by giving primacy to instrumental over consummatory considerations in the adaptive context, while it protects the actor by giving primacy to external over internal considerations.

Another example from the adaptive cluster pairs the integrative cell with affectivity. From the viewpoint of the system, the significance of the object as "internalized" or institutionalized must clearly take precedence over its varying performances as oriented to the external situation. For it to serve as a standard of moral-evaluative categorization, however, there must also be affective involvement. The rotation in this case means that categorization in terms of quality is specifically distinguished from the performance component in its application to cognitive symbolization, whereas affectivity is contrasted (and thus integrated) with neutrality in the cognitive context. The formula for evaluative categorization on the modality side therefore designates internal significance, on the orientation side, consummatory significance.

The "diagonal" relations of the pattern variable pairs in the I and A clusters thus formulate the relations of combined discrimination and balance between the modality components and the orientational components. In each case the balance "protects" the categorization from confusion with its pattern variable opposite.

The same essential principles hold when the functioning of the system as a whole is considered. Here rotation in the clockwise direction designates what psychologists often call "performance" process, that is, change in the relations of the system to its environment on the assumption that its internal structure remains unchanged. The primary focus of change in this case lies in the adaptive subsystem. The counterclockwise direction of process designates "learning" processes. Here the primary focus of change centers in the internal structure of the system, in the first instance in the integrative system producing a change in its standards.

Types of Action and the Organization of Components

Another theoretical issue requires brief comment. This concerns the fact that the present analysis is mainly an analytical classification of *components* of *any* system of action, including the "unit act" as the most elementary building block of action systems.[13] Dubin, however, speaks of *types* of act. From the present point of view types must be constructed of varying combinations of components. In addition to *composition* – in terms of the presence or absence of components, or different "weights" assigned to them – there is organization of these components. We interpret the restrictions on random combination, and the clustering of pattern variable combinations in the four functional sets, to be statements of organization. The state of a system is never, in our opinion, adequately described by its "composition" – that is, by what components are present in what quantities; the patterns of their relationships are equally essential. These considerations should be taken into account in attempts to develop a typology of acts from a classification of components in the act.

Another relevant point concerns the status of the pattern variable, self *versus* collectivity orientation. My present view is that this was an unduly restricted formulation of an element in the organization of action components at the level next above that designated by the primary pattern variables. In fact, Figure 9.1, I believe, documents four levels of organization. The first of these is represented by the L and G cells, characterized by pairs of elementary pattern-variable components – resulting in orientations and modalities, respectively. The second level is represented by the cross-combinations of elements from each pattern variable set, as shown in the I and A cells; as noted above, these are necessitated by the exigencies of differentiation and integration of the elementary combinations. The third level is the combination in turn of all of these elements into the four subsystems which have functional significance for the system as a whole, while the fourth is the organization *of* the system as a whole in relation to its environment.

The problem of the self-collectivity variable arises at the point where the I and A cells are organized into their respective subsystems. Subunits are organized into higher order "collective" units, the prototype being the organization of "members" into social collectivities. This organization takes place along the axis which distinguishes the "external" and "internal" foci in these cells. The inference is that there is another concept-pair which formulates the other axis of differentiation. In the I and A cells this is termed the "instrumental-consummatory" axis, which should be placed on the same analytical level of generality as the former pattern variable.

The difference, I believe, between the two primary pattern variable sets and this other "secondary" set – internal-external and instrumental-consummatory – is one of level of organization. The secondary set formulates the bases of relationship *across* the two primary sets, as distinguished from relations *within* each.

Some Theoretical Propositions

These restrictions on combinatorial randomness logically imply certain general propositions about the modes of inter-connecting the components of a system of action. As distinguished from the exposition of a frame of reference, these are *theoretical* propositions or theorems. We are not sure that all propositions which can be derived from the logical structure of the system have been exhaustively worked out, even at this very high level of generality. But the following propositions seem to be the most significant:

1. The nature of the hierarchy of control, running from the cultural reference at the top of Figure 9.2 to the physical at the bottom, indicates that the *structure* of systems of action is conceived as consisting in *patterns of normative culture*. The ways in which types of action system are differentiated, then, means that these patterns may be conceived as *internalized* in personalities and behavioral organisms, and as *institutionalized* in social and cultural systems.

2. It follows from this first proposition, plus the exposure of any system of action to plural functional exigencies, that the normative culture which constitutes its structure must be *differentiated* relative to these functional exigencies. These differentiated parts must then be integrated according to the four standards formulated in the I cells of Figure 9.1, and action oriented to the four different standards must be appropriately balanced, if the system is to remain stable. This is to say that process in the system, if it is to be compatible with the conditions of stability, must conform in some degree with the rules of a normative *order*, which is itself both differentiated and integrated.

3. For this "compliance" with the requirements of normative order to take place, the "distance" must not be too great between the structure of the acting unit and the normative requirements of its action necessitated by the functional exigencies of the system. It follows that the structure of acting units (which are objects to each other), as well as of norms, must incorporate appropriate elements of the system of normative culture – involving the internalization of "social object systems" in personalities, and the institutionalization of culturally normative systems in social systems.

4. Coordinate with the importance of order as formulated in the hierarchy of control and the place of normative culture in action systems, is the pattern of *temporal* order imposed by the functional exigencies of systems. Coordinate with the normative priority of ends is the temporal priority of means; only when the prerequisities of a consummatory goal-state have been established in the proper temporal order can the goal-state be realistically achieved. In both Figures 9.1 and 9.2 process is thus conceived in temporal terms as moving from left to right, the direction of "implementation."

5. A "law of inertia" may be stated: Change in the rate or direction of process is a consequence of *disturbance in the relations* between an actor or acting system and its situation, or the meanings of objects. If this relational system is completely stable, in this sense there is no process which is problematical for the theory of action. Whatever its source, such disturbance will always "show up" in the form of "strain" or difficulty in the attainment of valued goal-states. From this point of reference may be distinguished two fundamental types of process:

(a) *"Performance" processes:* These are processes by which the disturbance is eliminated or adequately reduced through adaptive mechanisms, leaving the integrative standards – the most directly vulnerable aspect of the structure of the system – unchanged. The process may be adaptive in either the passive or the active sense, that is, through "adjusting to" changes in environmental exigencies or achieving "mastery" over them. The basic paradigm of this type of process is the means-end schema. In Figure 9.1 the directionality of such process is clockwise relative to the goal-focus, from A to G.

(b) *"Learning" processes* or processes of structural change in the system: Here, whatever its source, the disturbance is propagated to the integrative standards themselves and involves shifts in their symbolization and categorization and in their relative priorities. Whereas in performance processes goals are *given*, in learning processes they must be *redefined*. Relative to the goal-focus, then, the directionality of such process is counterclockwise, from I to G in Figure 9.1.

6. To be stable in the long run, a system of action must establish a generalized adaptive relation to its environment which is relatively emancipated from the particularities of specific goal-states. To preserve its own normative control in the face of environmental variability, it must be related *selectively* to the environment. There are two primary aspects of this adaptive relationship: (a) the level of generality of symbolic or "linguistic" organization of the orientation to environmental object-systems (the higher the level of generality the more adequate the adaptation); and (b) the ways in which the boundary of the system is drawn in terms of inclusion-exclusion of objects according to their meanings. The latter is synonymous with the conception of "control" in relevant respects. Control can thus be seen to be the active aspect of the concept of adaptation. The generalization here is that only controllable elements can be included in a system. The criterion for inclusion within an organized action system state is the action theory version of the famous "principle of natural selection." This is a fundamental generalization about all living systems, and particularly important for action systems because they constitute a higher order of such systems.[14]

Concluding Remarks

The whole of the preceding exposition sets out a conceptual scheme, as frame of reference and as theory. It in no way purports to be an empirical contribution. Dubin, however, speaks of the importance of empirical verification of these concepts, and of their promise in this respect. There is no feature of his discussion with which I more fully agree; but the reader should not be misled to suppose that this presentation contributes to that goal. Certainly a good deal has been accomplished in this direction at various levels in my own work and in that of my collaborators as well as of many others, above all through codification with various bodies of empirical material and the conceptual schemes in terms of which they are analyzed.[15]

It should be kept in mind that the six propositions stated above are couched at a very high level of generality, deliberately designed to cover all classes of action system. Therefore it is unlikely that these propositions as such can be empirically verified at the usual operational levels. Such verification would require *specification* to lower levels, for example, the conditions of small experimental groups as a subtype of social system. Only in so far as codification reveals uniformities in the cognate features of many different types of operationally studied system do the more general theorems have a prospect of approaching rigorous empirical verification.

This specification should not be assumed to be capable of being carried out by simple "common sense;" it requires careful technical analysis through a series of concatenated steps. I believe, however, that the theory of action in its present state provides methods for successfully carrying out this specification, and conversely, generalization as well *from* lower-level uniformities to higher levels. Perhaps the most important key to this possibility is the conception of *all* systems of action as systematically articulated with others along system-subsystem lines. The basic system types designated here as organisms, personalities, social systems, and cultural systems must be regarded as *sub*systems of the general category of action system. Each of these in turn is differentiated into further subsystems at different levels of elaboration. Any subsystem is articulated with other subsystems by definable categories of input-output interchange, the processes, in sufficiently highly differentiated subsystems, being mediated by symbolic-type mechanisms such as those discussed above.

In many respects, this possibility of dealing with *multiple* system references and of keeping straight the distinctions and articulations between them, has turned out to be the greatest enrichment of theoretical analysis developed from Dubin's "Model II." A "flat" conception of a single system reference which must be accepted or rejected on an all-or-none basis for the analysis of complex empirical problems, cannot possibly do justice to the formidable difficulties in the study of human action.

Notes

1 Talcott Parsons and Edward A. Shils, eds, *Toward a General Theory of Action* (Cambridge: Harvard University Press, 1951).
2 Talcott Parsons, Robert F. Bales, and Edward A. Shils, *Working Papers in the Theory of Action* (Glencoe, IL: Free Press, 1953).
3 Robert F. Bales, *Interaction Process Analysis* (Cambridge: Addison-Wesley, 1950), ch. 2.
4 Cf. Parsons, Bales, and Shils, *op. cit.*, ch. 5, figure 2, p. 182.
5 Ibid., p. 182.
6 There is a pattern-maintenance subsystem *below* the adaptive subsystem in the hierarchy of control of any system of action and another *above* the integrative subsystem in the series. In figure 9.1 we define L as the *lower*-level case, on the basis parallel to the usage employed in relating the household to the firm in Talcott Parsons and Neil J. Smelser, *Economy and Society* (Glencoe, IL: Free Press, 1956), ch. 2.
7 Particularly in *L'Education Morale* (Paris: Alcan, 1925). Cf. Parsons, *The Structure of Social Action* (New York: McGraw-Hill, 1937), ch. 10. This classification of meanings of objects has been more fully set forth in Talcott Parsons, Edward A. Shils, Kaspar D. Naegele, and Jesse R. Pitts, eds, *Theories of Society* (Glencoe, IL: Free Press, 1961), Introduction to Part IV.
8 Cf. Parsons *et al.*, eds, *Theories of Society, op. cit.*, General Introduction, Part II.
9 See Parsons and Smelser, *op. cit.*, ch. 4, for a discussion of this concept; it is further developed by Smelser in *Social Change in the Industrial Revolution* (Chicago: University of Chicago Press, 1959).

10   Cf. Parsons and Smelser, *op. cit.*

11   Cf. Talcott Parsons, "An Approach to Psychological Theory in Terms of the Theory of Action," in Sigmund Koch, ed., *Psychology: A Study of A Science* (New York: McGraw-Hill, 1959), vol. 3.

12   On the general problem of interchanges and their paradigmatic location, see Parsons and Smelser, *op. cit.* On the relation of the integrative interchanges to Durkheim's two types of solidarity, see Talcott Parsons, "Durkheim's Contribution to the Theory of Integration of Social Systems," in Kurt H. Wolff, ed., *Émile Durkheim 1858–1917* (Columbus: Ohio State University Press, 1959).

13   The most important attempt to use essentially this conceptual scheme at the level, as I see it, of the "unit act" of the behavioral organism is James Olds' interpretation of the S-R-S sequence which has figured so prominently in behavior psychology, in action theory terms; see Olds, *The Growth and Structure of Motives* (Glencoe, IL: Free Press, 1956), ch. 4. Another paradigm which seems to be more generalized, but even more precisely corresponding in logical structure with the unit act, is the TOTE unit presented by George A. Miller, Eugene Galanter, and Karl H. Pribram in *Plans and the Structure of Behavior* (New York: Holt, 1960).

14   These propositions represent a further development of the set of "laws" of action systems tentatively stated by Parsons, Bales, and Shils, *op. cit.*, ch. 3.

15   For example: Bales' work on small groups; the work on family structure and socialization, including codification with psychoanalytic theory presented in Parsons, Robert F. Bales *et al.*, *Family, Socialization and Interaction Process* (Glencoe, IL: Free Press, 1955); codification with economic theory in Parsons and Smelser, *op. cit.*; and with certain problems of economic development in Smelser, *op. cit.*; codification with learning theory in Olds, *op. cit.*; the analysis of voting behavior in Parsons, " 'Voting' and the Equilibrium of the American Political System," in Eugene Burdick and Arthur Brodbeck, eds, *American Voting Behavior* (Glencoe, IL: Free Press, 1958), pp. 80–120; the relation to various aspects of psychological theory in Koch, *op. cit.*; and the recent essays published in Parsons, *Structure and Process in Modern Societies* (Glencoe, IL.: Free Press, 1960), the bibliography of which contains further references.

Part IV

American Society and the World Order

10

Social Strains in America

To the relatively objective observer, whether American or foreign, it seems clear that the complex of phenomena that have come to be known as "McCarthyism" must be symptoms of a process in American society of some deep and general significance. Some interpret it simply as political reaction, even as a kind of neofascism. Some think of it as simply a manifestation of nationalism. The present paper proposes to bring to bear some theoretical perspectives of sociology in an attempt to work out an interpretation which goes beyond catchwords of this order.

McCarthyism can be understood as a relatively acute symptom of the strains which accompany a major change in the situation and structure of American society, a change which in this instance consists in the development of the attitudes and institutional machinery required to implement a greatly enhanced level of national political responsibility. The necessity for this development arises both from our own growth to an enormous potential of power, and from the changed relation to the rest of the world which this growth in itself, and other changes extraneous to American development, have entailed. The strains to which I refer derive primarily from conflicts between the demands imposed by the new situation and the inertia of those elements of our social structure which are most resistant to the necessary changes.

The situation I have in mind centers on the American position in international affairs. The main facts are familiar to all. It is not something that has come about suddenly, but the impact of its pressures has been cumulative.

The starting point is the relative geographical isolation of the United States in the "formative" period of its national history, down to, let us say, about the opening of the present century. The Spanish-American War extended our involvements into the Spanish-speaking areas of the Caribbean and to the Philippines, and the Boxer episode in China and our mediation of the Russo-Japanese War indicated rapidly growing interests in the Orient. Then the First World War brought us in as one of the major belligerents, with a brief possibility of taking a role of world leadership. From this advanced degree of international involvement, however, we recoiled with a violent reaction, repudiating the Treaty of Versailles and the League of Nations.

In the ensuing period of "normalcy," until the shock of Pearl Harbor settled the question, it could still be held that the "quarrels" of foreign powers beyond the Americas were none of our concern, unless some "arbitrary" disturbance impinged too closely on our national interests. By the end of the Second World War, however, this attitude could not again be revived by any body of opinion which pretended to depend upon a realistic appraisal of our situation. Our own strength, in spite of our massive disarmament and demobilization, had grown too great; the defeat of France and the disorganization of Germany destroyed such Continental European balance of power as had existed; Britain, though victorious, was greatly weakened in the face of world-wide commitments; and Soviet Russia emerged as a victorious and expanding power, leading with a revolutionary ideology a movement which could readily destroy such elements of stability favorable to our own national values and interests as still remained in the world. Along with all this have come developments in military technology that have drastically neutralized the protections formerly conferred by geographical distance, so that even the elementary military security of the United States cannot now be taken for granted apart from world-wide political order.

The vicissitudes of American foreign policy and its relations to domestic politics over this period show the disturbing effect of this developing situation on our society. We have twice intervened militarily on a grand scale. With a notable difference of degree, we have both times recoiled from the implications of our intervention. In the second case the recoil did not last long, since the beginnings of the Cold War about 1947 made it clear that only American action was able to prevent Soviet domination of the whole continent of Europe. It can, however, be argued that this early and grand-scale resumption of responsibility imposed serious internal strains because it did not allow time for "digesting" the implications of our role in the war.

The outstanding characteristic of the society on which this greatly changed situation has impinged is that it had come to be the industrial society par excellence – partly because the settlement of the continental area coincided with the later industrial revolution, partly because of the immense area and natural resources of the country, but partly too because of certain important differences between American and European society. Since the United States did not have a class structure tightly integrated with a political organization that had developed its main forms before the industrial revolution, the economy has had a freedom to develop and to set the tone for the whole society in a way markedly different from any European country or Japan.

All highly industrialized societies exhibit many features in common which are independent of the particular historical paths by which their developments have taken place. These include the bureaucratic organization of the productive process itself, in the sense that the roles of individuals are of the occupational type and the organizations in which they are grouped are mainly "specific function" organizations. Under this arrangement the peasant type of agricultural holding, where farming is very closely bound up with a kinship unit, is minimized; so too of small family businesses; people tend to look to their productive function and to profit as a measure of success and hence of emancipation from conflicting ties and claims; the rights of property ownership are centered primarily in the organization which carries functional responsibility, and hence permits a high degree of segregation between private life and occupational roles for production purposes; contract plays a central part in the system of exchange, and para-economic elements tend to be reduced in importance.

Outside the sphere which touches the organization of the economy itself, industrialism means above all that the structures which would interfere with the free functioning of the economy, and of their adaptation to it, are minimized. The first of these is family and kinship. The American family system, chiefly characterized by the isolation of the nuclear or conjugal family, has gone farther than in any European society toward removing all interferences with the occupational roles of the breadwinning members, and with occupational mobility. A second field is religion. The American combination of federalism and the separation of church and state has resulted in a system of "denominational pluralism" which prevents organized religion from constituting a monolithic structure standing in the way of secular social developments. The third field concerns the matter of social stratification. The United States of course has a class structure; but it is one which has its primary roots in the system of occupational roles, and in contrast to the typical European situation it acts as no more than a brake on the processes of social mobility which are most important to an industrial type of occupational system. Under an effective family system there must be some continuity of class status from generation to generation, and there cannot be complete "equality of opportunity." In America, however, it is clearly the occupational system rather than kinship continuity that prevails.

Linked to this situation is our system of formal education. The United States was among the pioneers in developing publicly supported education; but this has taken place in a notably decentralized way. Not only is there no Department of Education in the Federal government, but even the various state departments are to a large extent service organizations for the locally controlled school systems. Higher education further has been considerably more independent of class standards which equate the "scholar" with the "gentleman" (in a class sense) than has been the case in Europe. Also a far larger proportion of each age-group attends institutions of higher education than in European countries.

Politically the most important fact about American industrialism is that it has developed overwhelmingly under the aegis of free enterprise. Historically the center of gravity of the integration of American society has not rested in the political field. There came to be established a kind of "burden of proof" expectation that responsibilities should not be undertaken by government unless, first, the necessity for their being undertaken at all was clearly established, and second, there was no other obviously adequate way to get the job done. It is therefore not surprising that the opening up of vast new fields of governmental responsibility should meet with considerable resistance and conflict.

The impact of this problem on our orientation to foreign relations has been complicated by an important set of internal circumstances. It is a commonplace that industrialism creates on a large scale two sets of problems which uniformly in all industrialized countries have required modifications of any doctrinaire "laissez-faire" policy: the problems of controlling the processes of the economy itself, and of dealing with certain social repercussions of industrialization.

As the process of industrialization has developed in America there has been a steady increase in the amount of public control imposed on the economy, with the initiative mainly in the hands of the Federal government. This trend was accelerated in the latter years of the nineteenth century, and has continued, with interruptions, through the New Deal. The New Deal, however, was more concerned with the social repercussions of industrialization, rather than with more narrowly economic problems. The introduction of a national system of social security and legislation more favorable to labor are perhaps the most typical developments. This internal process of government intervention has not gone far enough to satisfy European socialists, but it certainly constitutes a great modification of the earlier situation. Moreover, in broad lines it can be regarded as firmly established. It is significant that the major political parties now tend to view with each other in promoting the extension of social security benefits, that there is no likelihood of repeal of the Federal Reserve Act, and that there is no strong movement to place the unions under really severe legal restraints.

On the whole, business groups have accepted the new situation and co-operated to make it work with considerably more good faith than in Continental Europe. Nevertheless, these internal changes have been sufficiently recent and far-reaching to keep the strains attendant on them from being fully resolved. Moreover they have created an important part of the problems with which this examination is chiefly concerned, problems touching the composition of the higher strata of the society, where the primary burden of responsibility must fall.

By contrast with European countries, perhaps in some ways particularly Britain, the United States has been conspicuous for the absence or relative weakness of two types of elite elements. The first of these is a hereditary upper class with a status continuous from pre-industrial times, closely integrated with politics and public service. The second is an occupational elite whose roots are essentially independent of the business world – in the independent professions, the universities, the church, or government, including civil and military services.

In America the businessmen have tended to be the natural leaders of the general community. But, both for the reasons just reviewed and for certain others, this leadership has not remained undisputed. On the whole the business community has, step by step, resisted the processes of internal change necessitated by industrialization rather than taken the leadership in introducing them. The leadership that has emerged has been miscellaneous in social origin, including professional politicians, especially those in touch with the urban political machines, leaders in the labor union movement and elements in close touch with them. An important part has been played by men and women who may be said to exhibit a more or less "aristocratic" tinge, particularly in the Eastern cities, President Roosevelt of course having been among them. An important part has been played by lawyers who have made themselves more independent of the business connection than the typical corporation lawyer of a generation ago. Under the pressure of emergency, there has been a tendency for high military officers to play important roles in public life.

Another important group has been composed of "intellectuals" – again a rather miscellaneous assembly including writers, newspapermen, and members of university faculties. In general the importance of the universities has been steadily enhanced by the increasingly technical character of the operations of the economy; businessmen themselves have had to be more highly educated than their predecessors, and have become increasingly dependent on still more highly trained technicians of various kinds.

The important point is that the "natural" tendency for a relatively unequivocal business leadership of the general community has been frustrated, and the business group has had to give way at many points. Nevertheless, a clearly defined non-business component of the elite has not yet crystallized. In my opinion, the striking feature of the American elite is not what Soviet propaganda contends that it is – the clear-cut dominance by "capitalists" – but rather its fluid and relatively unstructured character. In particular, there is no clear determination of where political leadership, in the sense including both "politics" and "administration," is to center.

A further feature of the structure of American society is intimately related to the residual strains left by recent social changes. There is a continuing tendency for earlier economic developments to leave a "precipitate" of upper groups, the position of whose members is founded in the achievements of their ancestors, in this case relatively recent ones. By historical necessity these groups are strongest in the older parts of the country. Hence the cities of the Eastern seaboard have tended to develop groups that are the closest approach we have – though still very different from their European equivalent – to an aristocracy. They have generally originated in business interests, but have taken on a form somewhat similar to the mercantile aristocracies of some earlier European societies, such as the Hanseatic cities. In the perspective of popular democratic sentiments, these groups have tended to symbolize at the same time capitalistic interests and social snobbery. In certain circumstances they may be identified with "bohemianism" and related phenomena which are sources of uneasiness to traditional morality.

As the American social and economic center has shifted westward, such groups in the great Middle Western area and beyond have been progressively less prominent. There the elites have consisted of new men. In the nature of the case the proportional contribution to the economy and the society in general from the older and the newer parts of the country has shifted, with the newer progressively increasing their share. But at the same time there is the sense among them of having had to fight for this share against the "dominance" of the East. A similar feeling permeates the lower levels of the class structure. A major theme of the populist type of agrarian and other radicalism had combined class and sectional elements, locating the source of people's troubles in the bankers and railway magnates of the East and in Wall Street. It must not be forgotten that the isolationism of the between-the-wars period was intimately connected with this sectional and class sentiment. The elder La Follette, who was one of the principal destroyers of the League of Nations, was not a "conservative" or in any usual sense a reactionary, but a principal leader of the popular revolt against "the interests."

It must also not be forgotten that a large proportion of the American population are descendants of relatively recent immigrants whose cultural origins are different from the dominant Protestant Anglo-Saxon elements. A generation and more ago the bulk of the new immigration constituted an urban proletariat largely dominated by the political machines of the great cities. By now a great change has taken place. The children of these immigrants have been very much Americanized, but to a considerable degree they are still sensitive about their full acceptance. This sensitivity is if anything heightened by the fact that on the whole most of these elements have risen rapidly in the economic and social scale. They are no longer the inhabitants of the scandalous slums; many have climbed to lower middle class status and higher. They have a certain susceptibility to "democratic" appeals which are directed against the alleged snobbery of the older dominant elements.

Finally, the effect of the great depression of the 1930s on the leading business groups must not be forgotten. Such a collapse of the economy could not fail to be felt as a major failure of the expectation that business leaders should bear the major responsibility for the welfare of the economy as a whole and thus of the community. In general it was not the businessmen but the government, under leadership which was broadly antagonistic to business, which came to the rescue. Similarly, the other great class of American proprietors, the farmers, had to accept governmental help of a sort that entailed controls, which in turn inevitably entailed severe conflicts with the individualistic traditions of their history. The fact that the strains of the war and postwar periods have been piled so immediately on those of depression has much to do with the severity of the tensions with which this analysis is concerned.

My thesis, then, is that the strains of the international situation have impinged on a society undergoing important internal changes which have themselves been sources of strain, with the effect of superimposing one kind of strain on another. What responses to this compound strain are to be expected?

It is a generalization well established in social science that neither individuals nor societies can undergo major structural changes without the likelihood of producing a considerable element of "irrational" behavior. There will tend to be conspicuous distortions of the patterns of value and of the normal beliefs about the facts of situations. These distorted beliefs and promptings to irrational action will also tend to be heavily weighted with emotion, to be "overdetermined" as the psychologists say.

The psychology of such reactions is complex, but for present purposes it will suffice to distinguish two main components. On the negative side, there will tend to be high levels of anxiety and aggression, focused on what rightly or wrongly are felt to be the sources of strain and difficulty. On the positive side there will tend to be wishful patterns of belief with a strong "regressive" flavor, whose chief function is to wish away the disturbing situation and establish a situation in phantasy where "everything will be all right," preferably as it was before the disturbing situation came about. Very generally then the psychological formula tends to prescribe a set of beliefs that certain specific, symbolic agencies are responsible for the present state of distress; they have "arbitrarily" upset a satisfactory state of affairs. If only they could be eliminated the trouble would disappear and a satisfactory state restored. The role of this type of mechanism in primitive magic is quite well known.

In a normal process of learning in the individual, or of developmental change in the social system, such irrational phenomena are temporary, and tend to subside as capacity to deal with the new situation grows. This may be more or less easily achieved of course, and resolution of the conflicts and strains may fail to be achieved for a long period or may even be permanently unsuccessful. But under favorable circumstances these reactions are superseded by an increasingly realistic facing of the situation by institutionalized means.

Our present problem therefore centers on the need to mobilize American society to cope with a dangerous and threatening situation which is also intrinsically difficult. It can clearly only be coped with at the governmental level; and hence the problem is in essence a matter of political action, involving both questions of leadership – of who, promoting what policies, shall take the primary responsibility – and of the commitment of the many heterogeneous elements of our population to the national interest.

Consequently there has come to be an enormous increase in pressure to subordinate private interests to the public interest, and this in a society where the presumptions have been more strongly in favor of the private interest than in most. Readiness to make commitments to a collective interest is the focus of what we ordinarily mean by "loyalty." It seems to me that the problem of loyalty at its core is a genuine and realistic one; but attitudes toward it shade all the way from a reasonable concern with getting the necessary degree of loyal cooperation by legitimate appeals, to a grossly irrational set of anxieties about the prevalence of disloyalty, and a readiness to vent the accompanying aggression on innocent scapegoats.

Underlying the concern for loyalty in general, and explaining a good deal of the reaction to it, is the ambivalence of our approach to the situation: The people in the most "exposed" positions are on the one hand pulled by patriotic motives toward fulfillment of the expectations inherent in the new situation; they want to "do their bit." But at the same time their established attitudes and orientations resist fulfillment of the obligation. In the conflict of motives which ensues it is a natural consequence for the resistance to be displaced or projected on to other objects which function as scapegoats. In the present situation it is precisely those parts of our population where individualistic traditions are strongest that are placed under the greatest strain, and that produce the severest resistances to accepting the obligations of our situation. Such resistances, however, conflict with equally strong patriotic motives. In such a situation, when one's own resistance to loyal acceptance of unpalatable obligations, such as paying high taxes, are particularly strong, it is easy to impute disloyal intentions to others.

Our present emotional preoccupation with the problem of loyalty indicates above all that the crisis is not, as some tend to think, primarily concerned with fundamental values, but rather with their implementation. It is true that certain features of the pattern of reaction, such as tendencies to aggressive nationalism and to abdication of responsibilities, would, if carried through, lead to severe conflict with our values. But the main problem is not concerned with doubts about whether the stable political order of a free world is a goal worth sacrificing for, but rather with the question of how our population is rising or failing to rise to the challenge.

The primary symbol that connects the objective external problem and its dangers with the internal strain and its structure is "Communism." "World Communism" and its spread constitute the features of the world situation on which the difficulty of our international problem clearly centers. Internally it is felt that Communists and their "sympathizers" constitute the primary focus of actual or potential disloyalty.

With respect to the external situation, the focus of the difficulty in the current role of Soviet Russia is of course reasonable enough. Problems then arise mainly in connection with certain elements of "obsessiveness" in the way in which the situation is approached, manifested for instance in a tendency to subordinate all other approaches to the situation exclusively to the military, and in the extreme violence of reaction in some circles to the Chinese situation, in contrast to the relative tolerance with which Yugoslavia is regarded.

Internally, the realistic difficulty resides mainly in the fact that there has indeed been a considerable amount of Communist infiltration in the United States, particularly in the 1930s. It is true that the Communist Party itself has never achieved great electoral success, but for a time Communist influence was paramount in a number of important labor unions, and a considerable number of the associations Americans so like to join were revealed to be Communist-front organizations, with effective Communist control behind the public participation of many non-Communists. Perhaps most important was the fact that considerable numbers of the intellectuals became fellow-travelers. In the days of the rise of Nazism and of the popular front, many of them felt that only Soviet Russia was sincere in its commitment to collective security; that there was a Franco-British "plot" to get Germany and Russia embroiled with each other, etc. The shock of the Nazi-Soviet pact woke up many fellow-travelers, but by no means all; and the cause was considerably retrieved by Hitler's attack on Russia.

Two other features of the Communist movement which make it an ideal negative symbol in the context of the present loyalty problem are the combination of conspiratorial methods and foreign control with the progressive component of its ideological system. On the one hand the party has drastically repudiated the procedures of constitutional democracy, and on this issue has broken with all the democratic socialist parties of Europe; it claims the protection of democratic procedures and civil liberties, but does not hesitate to abuse them when this seems to be advantageous. There has further never been any question of the American party determining its own policies by democratic procedures. Perhaps in fact the knowledge of the extent to which the "front" organizations have been manipulated from behind the scenes has been the most disillusioning aspect for liberal Americans of their experience with Communism at home.

At the same time the movement had a large content of professed idealism, which may be taken to account for the appeal of Communism before the Cold War era for such large elements of liberal opinion in the United States, as in other Western countries. Marx was, after all, himself a child of the Enlightenment, and the Communist movement has incorporated in its ideology many of the doctrines of human rights that have formed a part of our general inheritance. However grossly the symbols of democracy, of the rights of men, of peace and brotherhood, have been abused by the Communists, they are powerful symbols in our own tradition, and their appeal is understandable.

Hence the symbol "Communism" is one to which a special order of ambivalence readily attaches. It has powerful sources of appeal to the liberal tradition, but those who are out of sympathy with the main tradition of American liberalism can find a powerful target for their objections in the totalitarian tactics of Communism and can readily stigmatize it as "un-American." Then, by extending their objections to the liberal component of Communist ideology, they can attack liberalism in general, on the grounds that association with Communist totalitarianism makes anything liberal suspect.

These considerations account for the anti-Communist's readiness to carry over a stereotype from those who have really been party members or advanced fellow-travelers to large elements of the intellectuals, the labor movement, etc., who have been essentially democratic liberals of various shades of opinion. Since by and large the Democratic Party has more of this liberalism than has the Republican, it is not surprising that a tendency to label it as "sympathizing" with or "soft toward" Communism has appeared. Such a label has also been extended, though not very seriously, to the Protestant clergy.

But there is one further extension of the association that is not accounted for in these terms, nor is the failure to include certain plausible targets so accountable. The extension I have in mind is that which leads to the inclusion as "pro-Communist" of certain men or institutions that have been associated with political responsibility in the international field. Two symbols stand out here. The first is Dean Acheson. Mr. Acheson has for years served the Democratic Party. But he has belonged to the conservative, not the New Deal wing of the party. Furthermore, the coupling of General Marshall with him, though only in connection with China, and only by extremists, clearly precludes political radicalism as the primary objection, since Marshall has never in any way been identified with New Deal views. The other case is that of Harvard University as an alleged "hot-bed" of Communism and fellow-traveling. The relevant point is that Mr. Acheson typifies the "aristocrat" in public service; he came of a wealthy family, he went to a select private school (Groton) and to Yale and Harvard Law School. He represents symbolically those Eastern vested interests, against whom antagonism has existed among the new men of the Middle West and the populist movement, including the descendants of recent immigrants. Similarly, among American universities Harvard has been particularly identified as educating a social elite, the members of which are thought of as "just the type," in their striped trousers and morning coats, to sell out the country to the social snobs of European capitals. It is the combination of aristocratic associations – through the Boston Brahmins – and a kind of urban-bohemian sophistication along with its devotion to intellectual and cultural values, including precisely its high intellectual standards, which makes Harvard a vulnerable symbol in this context.

The symbol "Communism," then, from its area of legitimate application, tends to be generalized to include groups in the population who have been associated with political liberalism of many shades and with intellectual values in general and to include the Eastern upper-class groups who have tended to be relatively internationalist in their outlook.

A second underlying ambivalent attitude-structure is discernible in addition to that concerning the relation between the totalitarian and the progressive aspects of Communism. On the one hand, Communism very obviously symbolizes what is anathema to the individualistic tradition of a business economy – the feared attempt to destroy private enterprise and with it the great tradition of individual freedom. But on the other hand, in order to rise to the challenge of the current political situation, it is necessary for the older balance between a free economy and the power of government to be considerably shifted in favor of the latter. We must have a stronger government than we have traditionally been accustomed to, and we must come to trust it more fully. It has had in recent times to assume very substantial regulatory functions in relation to the economy, and now vastly enhanced responsibilities in relation to international affairs.

But, on the basis of a philosophy which, in a very different way from our individualistic tradition, gives primacy to "economic interests," namely the Marxist philosophy, the Communist movement asserts the unqualified, the totalitarian supremacy of government over the economy. It is precisely an actual change in our own system in what in one sense is clearly this direction that emerges as the primary focus of the frustrations to which the older American system has been subjected. The leaders of the economy, the businessmen, have been forced to accept far more "interference" from government with what they have considered "their affairs" than they have liked. And now they must, like everyone else, pay unprecedentedly high taxes to support an enormous military establishment, and give the government in other respects unprecedentedly great powers over the population. The result of this situation is an ambivalence of attitude that on the one hand demands a stringent display of loyalty going to lengths far beyond our tradition of individual liberty, and on the other hand is ready to blame elements which by ordinary logic have little or nothing to do with Communism, for working in league with the Communist movement to create this horrible situation.

Generally speaking, the indefensible aspect of this tendency in a realistic assessment appears in a readiness to question the loyalty of all those who have assumed responsibility for leadership in meeting the exigencies of the new situation. These include many who have helped to solve the internal problems of the control of the economy, those who in the uneasy later 'thirties and the first phase of the war tried to get American policy and public opinion to face the dangers of the international situation, and those who since the war have tried to take responsibility in relation to the difficult postwar situation. Roughly, these are the presumptively disloyal elements who are also presumptively tainted with Communism. Here again, admittedly, certain features of our historical record and attitudes provide some realistic basis for this tendency. In fact many elements in both parties have failed lamentably to assess correctly the dangers of the situation, both internally and externally. New Dealers have stigmatized even the most responsible elements of the business world as economic royalists and the like, while many elements in business have clung long past a reasonable time to an outmoded belief in the possibility of a society with only a "night watchman" government. In foreign affairs, some members of the Democratic Party have been slow to learn how formidable a danger was presented by totalitarian Communism, but this is matched by the utopianism of many Republicans about the consequences of American withdrawal from international responsibilities, through high tariffs as well as political isolationism. The necessity to learn the hard realities of a complex world and the difficulty of the process is not a task to be imposed on only part of the body politic. No party or group can claim a monopoly either of patriotic motive or of competent understanding of affairs.

In a double sense, then, Communism symbolizes "the intruder." Externally the world Communist movement is the obvious source of the most serious difficulties we have to face. On the other hand, although Communism has constituted to some degree a realistic internal danger, it has above all come to symbolize those factors that have disturbed the beneficent natural state of an American society which allegedly and in phantasy existed before the urgent problems of control of the economy and greatly enhanced responsibility in international affairs had to be tackled.

Against this background it can perhaps be made clear why the description of McCarthyism as simply a political reactionary movement is inadequate. In the first place, it is clearly not simply a cloak for the "vested interests" but rather a movement that profoundly splits the previously dominant groups. This is evident in the split, particularly conspicuous since about 1952, within the Republican Party. An important part of the business elite, especially in the Middle West and in Texas, the "newest" area of all, have tended in varying degrees to be attracted by the McCarthy appeal. But other important groups, notably in the East, have shied away from it and apparently have come to be more and more consolidated against it. Very broadly, these can be identified with the business element among the Eisenhower Republicans.

But at the same time the McCarthy following is by no means confined to the vested-interest groups. There has been an important popular following of very miscellaneous composition. It has comprised an important part of those who aspire to full status in the American system but have, realistically or not, felt discriminated against in various ways, especially the Mid-Western lower and lower middle classes and much of the population of recent immigrant origin. The elements of continuity between Western agrarian populism and McCarthyism are not by any means purely fortuitous. At the levels of both leadership and popular following, the division of American political opinion over this issue *cuts clean across the traditional lines of distinction between "conservatives" and "progressives,"* especially where that tends to be defined, as it so often is, in terms of the capitalistic or moneyed interests as against those who seek to bring them under more stringent control. McCarthyism is *both* a movement supported by certain vested-interest elements *and* a popular revolt against the upper classes.

Another striking characteristic of McCarthyism is that it is highly selective in the liberal causes it attacks. Apart from the issue of Communism in the labor unions, now largely solved, there has been no concerted attack on the general position of the labor movement. Further, the social program aimed toward the reduction of racial discrimination has continued to be pressed, to which fact the decision of the Supreme Court outlawing segregation in public education and its calm reception provide dramatic evidence. Nevertheless, so far as I am aware there has been no outcry from McCarthyite quarters to the effect that this decision is further evidence of Communist influence in high circles – in spite of the fact that eight out of nine members of the present court were appointed by Roosevelt and Truman.

Perhaps even more notable is the fact that, unlike the 1930s, when Father Coughlin and others were preaching a vicious anti-Semitism, anti-Semitism as a public issue has since the war been very nearly absent from the American scene. This is of course associated with full employment. But particularly in view of the rather large and conspicuous participation of Jewish intellectuals in the fellow-traveling of the 1930s, it is notable that Jewishness has not been singled out as a symbolic focus for the questioning of loyalty. A critical difference from German Nazism is evident here. To the Nazis the Jew was the *primary* negative symbol, the Communist the most prominent secondary one. But it must also be remembered that capitalism was symbolically involved. One of the functions of the Jew was to *link* Communism and capitalism together. This trio were the "intruders" to the Nazis. They symbolized different aspects of the disturbance created by the rapid development of industrialism to the older pre-industrial *Gemeinschaft* of German political romanticism. It was the obverse of the American case – a new economy destroying an old political system, not new political responsibilities interfering with the accustomed ways of economic life.

Negatively, then, the use of the symbol "Communism" as the focus of anxiety and aggression is associated with a high order of selectivity among possibly vulnerable targets. This selectivity is, I submit, consistent with the hypothesis that the focus of the strain expressed by McCarthyism lies in the area of political responsibility – not, as Marxists would hold, in the structure of the economy as such, nor in the class structure in any simple, Marxian-tinged sense.

The same interpretation is confirmed by the evidence on the positive side. The broadest formula for what the McCarthyites positively "want" – besides the elimination of all Communist influence, real or alleged – is perhaps "isolationism." The dominant note is, I think, the regressive one. It is the wishful preservation of an old order, which allegedly need never have been disturbed but for the wilful interference of malevolent elements, Communists and their sympathizers. The nationalistic overtones center on a phantasy of a happy "American way" where everything used to be all right. Naturally it is tinged with the ideology of traditional laissez-faire, but not perhaps unduly so. Also it tends to spill over into a kind of irritated activism. On the one hand we want to keep out of trouble; but on the other hand, having identified an enemy, we want to smash him forthwith. The connection between the two can be seen, for example, in relation to China, where the phantasy seems to be that by drastic action it would be possible to "clean up" the Chinese situation quickly and then our troubles would be over.

The main contention of these pages has been that McCarthyism is best understood as a symptom of the strains attendant on a deep-seated process of change in our society, rather than as a "movement" presenting a policy or set of values for the American people to act on. Its content is overwhelmingly negative, not positive. It advocates "getting rid" of undesirable influences, and has amazingly little to say about what should be done.

This negativism is primarily the expression of fear, secondarily of anger, the aggression which is a product of frustration. The solution, which is both realistically feasible and within the great American tradition, is to regain our national self-confidence and to take active steps to cope with the situation with which we are faced.

On the popular level the crisis is primarily a crisis of confidence. We are baffled and anxious, and tend to seek relief in hunting scapegoats. We must improve our understanding and come to realize our strength and trust in it. But this cannot be done simply by wishing it to be done. I have consistently argued that the changed situation in which we are placed demands a far-reaching change in the structure of our society. It demands policies, and confidence, but it demands more than these. It demands above all three things. The first is a revision of our conception of citizenship to encourage the ordinary man to accept greater responsibility. The second is the development of the necessary implementing machinery. Third is national political leadership, not only in the sense of individual candidates for office or appointment, but in the sense of social strata where a traditional political responsibility is ingrained.

The most important of these requirements is the third. Under American conditions, a politically leading stratum must be made up of a combination of business and nonbusiness elements. The role of the economy in American society and of the business element in it is such that political leadership without prominent business participation is doomed to ineffectiveness and to the perpetuation of dangerous internal conflict. It is not possible to lead the American people *against* the leaders of the business world. But at the same time, so varied now are the national elements which make a legitimate claim to be represented, the business element cannot monopolize or dominate political leadership and responsibility. Broadly, I think, a political elite in the two main aspects of "politicians" whose specialities consist in the management of public opinion, and of "administrators" in both civil and military services, must be greatly strengthened. It is here that the practical consequences of McCarthyism run most directly counter to the realistic needs of the time. But along with such a specifically political elite there must also be close alliance with other, predominantly "cultural" elements, notably perhaps in the universities, but also in the churches.

In the final sense, then, the solution of the problem of McCarthyism lies in the successful accomplishment of the social changes to which we are called by our position in the world and by our own domestic requirements. We have already made notable progress toward this objective; the current flare-up of stress in the form of McCarthyism can be taken simply as evidence that the process is not complete.

11

The Distribution of Power in American Society

(Review of C. Wright Mills, *The Power Elite*, New York, Oxford University Press, 1956.)

I

It has been remarked that it is relatively rare, in the United States at least, for social scientists to attempt interpretive analyses of major aspects of the total society in which they live. This is particularly true of sociologists,[1] unlike economists, who have made notable attempts in recent years to interpret their societies – for example, Schumpeter's *Capitalism, Socialism and Democracy* and Galbraith's *American Capitalism*. If for this reason alone, the present book of Professor Mills, which must be understood as one of a series as yet far from complete, would be worthy of serious attention.

In the nature of the case, to produce such a study is a very difficult enterprise. However operationally useful precise data may be – and Mr. Mills makes copious and, with some exceptions, relatively good use of them – they cannot suffice for a full empirical grounding of interpretive conclusions, not only because on their own level they are fragmentary and incomplete, but because many of the crucial empirical questions arise on a level at which available operational procedures are not of much or any use. This is not in the least to say that observation is not feasible, but rather that it cannot be precise observation in the usual operational sense.

I am referring to questions of the type which are central to Mr. Mills' argument, as to whether and in what sense a relatively small group of the occupants of "command posts" in the society has acquired a paramount position of power, as to whether the relative power of such a group has greatly increased in the last twenty years, as to how unified such a group is, and the like.

There are technical ways of reducing the element of arbitrariness in such judgments and protecting them against at least the grosser sorts of ideological distortion. Checking against all the available precise data is one such method; viewing the problem from the perspective given by wide and deep knowledge, not only of our own society but of others, is another. But I think the most important is exercising control through the use of a relatively well-integrated and technical theoretical scheme. Undertaking as a professional sociologist to review Mr. Mills' book, I am motivated largely by the opportunity to test some of his main conclusions against expectations derived from a type of technical theory that is at best only partially shared by the author of the book. In these terms I wish to take serious issue with Mr. Mills' position on a number of very important points and to outline an alternative interpretation of what I take to be the salient facts of the situation. There are some points at which I differ from Mills on simple questions of fact, but for the most part my criticisms will deal with empirical generalizations and their theoretical background.[2] These generalizations concern not only the facts he chooses to state and emphasize but others he omits or treats as unimportant.

What is the gist of Mills' argument? I am able here to give only a very brief summary. The reader should not depend on this review alone for his information about the contents of the book itself, but should go directly to Mills' own statement of his case.

Mills' central theme is the contention – in contrast to what he refers to as the traditional view of the political pluralism of American society – that there has developed to an unprecedented degree in the last generation or so a concentration of power in the hands of a small, relatively tightly integrated group of people. These are defined as the people occupying the institutional "command posts" of the society, the places where the decisions are made that have the greatest immediate and direct influence on the course of events in the society and on the shaping of its future and that of the rest of the world, so far as that future is dependent on what happens in the United States. Mills argues that the power of this group has grown disproportionately to the growth in size and power of the society as a whole.

The "command posts" in question are centered in large-scale organizations, which are certainly a prominent feature of American society. The power elite are in general those who occupy the decision-making positions in these large organizations. Mills identifies these in only two basic areas, business and government – although for his purposes the field of government is subdivided into the military and the political sectors; indeed, he almost tends to treat the military as independent of the rest of government. He clearly is thinking of the centralized type of organization where a few "top executives" exercise the main immediate decision-making power, in contrast to the democratic association with a somewhat more decentralized structure of authority and influence. It seems to be largely on this ground that he contends that the executive branch of the federal government has gained a pronounced ascendancy over the legislative. He relegates Congress – even the most influential group of Senators – to what he calls the "middle level" of the power structure; such people do not belong to the "power elite."

Mills broadly identifies the power elite with the "upper class." But he does not agree with Lloyd Warner and his group that the primary element of this upper class is a hereditary group of families or lineages; its position clearly depends on occupational status, though there is also emphasis on the importance within it of the "very rich," the majority of whom have inherited their wealth. Contrary to most sociological usage, Mills restricts the term "class" to an economic meaning, so that by "upper class" he means, essentially, the rich. But this still leaves open the question of the substantive relations between inherited and newly acquired wealth, family status relatively independent of at least very large wealth, occupational status within various income ranges, and similar problems.

Generally, Mills is rather vague on the relations between the power elite and other elements which in some sense enjoy rather high prestige. He emphasizes the prominence of lawyers among the "political directorate," but there is no clear analysis of the role of professional groups in the occupational structure generally; one presumes that except for a few lawyers who are successful in politics or business, and perhaps some engineers, professional people do not belong to the power elite. Similarly he emphasizes that members of the power elite have more than the average amount of education, and in particular he stresses the proportion who have been to select private schools and to "Ivy League" colleges. In general, he is greatly concerned about the fact that the power elite are not "representative" of the population as a whole in the sense of constituting a random sample by socio-economic origin, by education, by ethnic group, etc. This is a point to which I shall return.

Neither the "higher circles" generally nor the component of the "very rich" (Mills' term) are a leisure class in Veblen's sense; many, if not most of them, "work" in various fields of business and financial management. Furthermore, the processes of recruitment are about what social scientists have come to expect. Mills does not give any exact criteria for what he considers to be "upper class" as a category of social origin, but I have the impression that he puts the line somewhat lower than most sociologists would. But, however that may be, it is clear that there is a considerable element of stability from generation to generation in the higher-status groups in American society. Thus if, to employ a pattern used by Mills, we take a group of prominent persons, the family origin of from two-thirds to three-fourths of them will be the upper third of the American status structure. It is not these essential facts but the interpretation placed upon them which raises questions for us. The only point of fact I would question is whether the recruitment of the very rich has shown a sharper increase through the process of inheritance than through self-earning. It is possible that this is so, but I am inclined to doubt it, and in any case their position does not depend only on the process which Mills calls "cumulative advantage."

Mills radically denies that the group he calls the "very rich" and the "corporate rich" are distinct "classes," in his sense. He explicitly lumps them together and on the whole gives the very rich a greater position of influence than they are usually accorded or than, I think, they actually enjoy. This is in line with his thesis that there is a single, unified power elite. Clearly, it is his contention that the base of the (business) group as a whole lies in command of the very large business enterprises – somewhat erroneously, or at least ambiguously, he puts the primary emphasis on control of property in accounting for this power.

Of the three main subgroups, Mills treats the "political directorate" as by far the weakest. It has, according to him, been greatly infiltrated by the business element, so that it can scarcely be treated as independent. Hence virtually the only element independent of what might be called the business oligarchy is the military – and this, he holds, is coming increasingly to fuse with the business group, or at least to form a close community of interest with it.

The pluralistic components of our older political traditions, Mills feels, are rooted primarily in local groupings – partly, of course, through the constitutional provisions which establish federalism and make Congressional representation dependent on local constituencies. But the operations of the big organizations have become national in scope, and often international. Hence structures rooted in localism have simply been pushed into a secondary position.

But at the same time Mills contends that the structural base of authentic localism has been progressively atrophied through the development of what he calls the "mass society." The most conspicuous phenomena of the mass society are the prevalence and characteristics of the media of mass communication, which tend to serve as instruments of the power elite out of the reach of locally based "publics" and influential elements in them. The theory of the mass society is only very sketchily presented in one chapter near the end of the book, but is clearly meant to provide one of the main components of the total picture of American society which Mills is presenting.

In terms of recent history, one of Mills' main contentions is that the New Deal period did not represent a turning point in social development, but rather a superficial flurry which only momentarily disturbed the process of emergence of the power elite and the dominance of the business contingent within it. Thus Mills speaks of the economic elite as in due course coming "to control and to use for their own purposes the New Deal institutions whose creation they had so bitterly denounced" (pp. 272–3).

Mills repeatedly disavows any intention of presenting a "conspiratorial" interpretation of American social and political development. He stresses the institutional positions occupied by his elite rather than their personalities and conspiratorial activities. Nevertheless he often comes very close to this implication because of his special theory that a peculiar irresponsibility attaches to the elite and their actions. By this he seems to mean the absence or relative ineffectiveness of formal legal restraints or of a system of "checks and balances" of the sort which has traditionally been associated with our political system. His contention thus is that the power elite has been freed from the historic restraints of our society and uses its power in terms of what he calls a "higher immorality" – a conception which is not very clearly explained.

Finally, it should be mentioned that in this, as in some of his previous writings, Mills' general tone toward both men and institutions is sharply caustic. *The Power Elite* certainly purports to be an exposition and an explanation of what has been happening in American society, but it is equally an indictment. There is no pretense of even trying to maintain a scientific neutrality; the book is a fiery and sarcastic attack on the pretensions of the "higher circles" in America either to competence in exercise of their responsibilities or to moral legitimation of their position. In such a case, the critic must ascertain the moral position from which the indictment is formulated; I shall have something to say about this later. In his combination of often insightful exposition and analysis, empirical one-sidedness and distortion, and moral indictment and sarcasm, Mills reminds one more of Veblen than of any other figure; that he has attained the stature of Veblen I question, but the role he is cutting out for himself is similar.

II

As I have said, the Mills analysis presents what, to me, is a subtle and complex combination of acceptable and unacceptable elements. Let me now attempt, at some of the most important points, to unravel these elements from each other. I want to try this first on the level of empirical generalization and then to raise one or two more strictly theoretical problems. I shall do so more in my own terms than in those employed by Mills.

In my opinion, two salient sets of processes have been going on in American society during the past half-century, the combination of which encompasses the main facts which are essential to our problem. The first of these is the dynamic of a maturing industrial society, including not only the highly industrialized economy itself but its setting in the society as a whole – notably, its political system and class structure (in a wider sense of the term "class" than Mills') – and the repercussions of the industrial development on the rest of the society. The second concerns the altered position of the United States in world society, which is a consequence in part of our own economic growth, in part of a variety of exogenous changes, including the relative decline of the Western European powers, the rise of Soviet Russia, and the break-up of the "colonial" organization of much of the non-white world. The enormous enhancement of American power and responsibility in the world has taken place in a relatively short time and was bound to have profound repercussions on the characteristics of our own society. Our old political isolation has disappeared and given way to the deepest of involvements.

My first thesis is that these two processes *both* work in the direction of increasing the relative importance of government in our society and, with it, of political power. But their impact has been all the greater because of the extent to which the United States has been an almost specifically non-political society. This has been evidenced above all in the institutions and tradition of political decentralization already mentioned, one aspect of which is the localism which Mills discusses. A second, however, has been a cultural tradition which has emphasized economic values – an emphasis on enterprise and production in an activist sense, not a merely passive hedonistic valuation of the enjoyment of material well-being. Moreover, the virtually unimpeded process of settlement of a continent in political isolation from the main system of world powers has favored maintenance of this emphasis to a greater extent than would otherwise have readily been possible.

At some points in his discussion, Mills seems to look back to the Jeffersonian picture of a system of economic production consisting mainly of small farmers and artisans, with presumably a small mercantile class mediating between them and consumers. Clearly this is not a situation compatible with high industrial development, in either of two respects. First, the order of decentralization of production where the standard unit is a family-size one is incompatible with either the organization or the technology necessary for high industrialism. Second, the "Jeffersonian" economy is not one in which economic production is differentiated from other social functions in specialized organizations; instead, the typical productive unit is at the same time a kinship unit and a unit of citizenship in the community.[3]

In all salient respects, the modern economy has moved very far from the Jeffersonian ideal. The pace-setting units have become both large and specialized. Their development has been part of a general process of structural differentiation in the society which has led to greater specialization in many fields. An essential aspect of the process of development of the economy as a system in *both* these senses is greater specialization on at least three levels: first, the specialization of organizations in the functions of economic production as distinguished from other functions; second, the specialization of functions within the economy; and third, the specialization of the roles of classes of individuals within the organization.

Leadership is an essential function in all social systems, which with their increase of scale and their functional differentiation tend to become more specialized. I think we can, within considerable limits, regard the emergence of the large firm with operations on a nation-wide basis as a "normal" outcome of the process of growth and differentiation of the economy. Similarly, the rise to prominence within the firm of specialized executive functions is also a normal outcome of a process of growth in size and in structural differentiation. The question then arises whether the process of concentration of firms, and of executive power within firms, has "gone too far" because it has been greatly influenced by factors extraneous to the process of economic development itself.

Mills makes the assertion that the size of the large firm has exceeded the limits of economic efficiency. He presents no evidence, and I think most competent persons would regard this as an exceedingly difficult question. There is, however, one line of evidence not cited by Mills which has a bearing on it. It is true that the absolute size of firms has steadily increased – General Motors today is larger than any firm of the 1920s. But the *relative* share of the largest firms in the production of the economy has remained essentially stable for more than a generation, a fact which points to some kind of equilibrium condition with respect to the degree of concentration in the system as a whole.

A cognate question is whether the power of the executive or managerial class within industry, and particularly within the large firms, has increased inordinately, which if true would indicate that factors other than the functional needs of the productive process were operating to skew the internal power structure of firms in favor of the executive groups.

Generally speaking, Mills' argument is that the power of the very rich and the corporate rich *within* the economy is inordinately great and, by virtue of the factor of cumulative advantage, is becoming continually greater. At the very least, I think it can be said that his case is not proved and that there is equally good, if not better, evidence for an alternative view, particularly with reference to the trend.

First, I am not able to accept Mills' close identification of the very rich (i.e., the holders of "great fortunes") with the "corporate rich" (the primary holders of executive power in business organizations) as a single class in any very useful sense. Certainly, in the "heroic age" of American capitalism, from the Civil War to just after the turn of the century, the dominant figures were the entrepreneurs who, mainly as the founders of great enterprises and as the bankers and promoters concerned with mergers and reorganizations and the like, came to control these great organizations. But the dominant sociological fact of the outcome of that era was that these owning groups did not, as a group, succeed in consolidating their position precisely *within* their own enterprises and in the economy. It is a notorious fact that the *very* large enterprise still largely under family control through property holdings is much more the exception than the rule. Instead, the control has passed – by no means fully, but for the most part – to professional career executives, who have not reached their positions through the exercise of *property* rights but through some sort of process of appointment and promotion.

Mills concedes the main facts of this situation but fails, in my opinion, to evaluate them properly. It seems to be clear that the original "captains of industry," the makers of the great fortunes, *failed* to achieve or to exercise sufficient cumulative advantages to consolidate control of the enterprises in their families and their class ("class" in a sociological, not an economic, sense). This came about essentially because there were factors operating contrary to that of cumulative advantage, which Mills stresses so heavily. The main factor was the pressure to link executive responsibility with competence in such a way that the ascriptive rights of property ownership have tended to give way to the occupational functions of "professionals."

There are, above all, two ways in which Mills' treatment obscures the importance and nature of this shift. First, he continues to speak of power *within* the economy as based on property. To a considerable degree, of course, this is legally true, since the legal control of enterprise rests with stockholders. But, as Berle and Means first made abundantly clear, very generally it is not substantively true. In the old-style family enterprise, still predominant in the small-business sector of the economy, the functions of management and ownership are fused in the same people. In the larger enterprise they have by and large become differentiated. The fact that executives receive large salaries and bonuses is not to be twisted into an assumption that they control, so far as they do, through their property rights. Paradoxical as it may seem, a relatively backward industrial economy like that of France is far more *property*-based than is the case with the United States. In general, property holdings have not, of course, been expropriated, except for their diminution through inheritance and income taxes, which are not as negligible as Mills maintains. What has happened is that their relation to the *power* structure of the economy has been greatly altered. Mills almost entirely passes over this change.

The second problem concerns the process of recruitment in the higher occupational reaches of the economy. It is entirely clear that the process operates in the higher reaches overwhelmingly by appointment, i.e., the decisions of superiors as individuals or in small groups as to who should occupy certain positions. It is also true that the process is relatively unformalized – e.g., there are no competitive examinations and few, if any, formal qualifications of training. But from these facts Mills concludes, and again and again reiterates, that executive competence has very little, if anything, to do with the selection, that it is an overwhelmingly arbitrary process of choosing those who are congenial to the selectors, presumably because they can be counted upon to be "yes men." At the very least this contention is unproved, and I seriously doubt its correctness. There are certainly many difficulties and imperfections in the selection process. But I think it almost certain that higher levels of competence are selected than would on the average be the case through kinship ascription, and that, as such processes go, the levels selected are relatively high.

One final point in this field. It does seem probable that the factor of cumulative advantage has a good deal to do with the high levels of financial remuneration of the higher executive groups and with the discrepancies between their incomes and those of governmental and professional people on comparable levels of competence and responsibility. But this is very far from the great fortune level of the founding entrepreneur type, and the evidence seems to be that the discrepancy has not been cumulatively increasing to an appreciable degree, particularly relative to wages at the labor levels; cases like that of the academic profession are somewhat special.

So far I have been speaking about the nature and power position of the elite *within* the economy. The general tenor of my argument has been that, given the nature of an industrial society, a relatively well-defined elite or leadership group *should be expected to develop* in the business world; it is out of the question that power should be diffused equally among an indefinite number of very small units, as the ideal of pure competition and a good deal of the ideology of business itself would have it. But first I question whether the position of power of the business leadership groups is such that a heavy operation of the factor of cumulative advantage must be invoked to account for it. Secondly, I must stress that the business elite is no longer primarily an elite of *property*-owners, but that its center of gravity has shifted to occupationally professional executives or managers. Differential advantages of family origin, etc., are about the same for admission to this group as to other groups requiring educational and other qualifications. Again the evidence is that the proportion of its members recruited from the upper economic and social groups is and remains relatively high, but it has not, in recent times, been increasing, as the theory of cumulative advantage would lead us to expect.

The problem of an elite within the economy must, however, be clearly distinguished from that of an elite in the society as a whole and the power position occupied by such an elite. There are two main orders of questions bearing on the transition from one to the other. Though a thorough consideration of this transition would lead into very far-reaching questions, for present purposes one can be treated rather briefly. Mills gives us the impression that "eliteness" in any society, including our own, is overwhelmingly a question of the power that an individual or a group can command. By this, he means (I shall further discuss his concept of power presently) influence on the "big" decisions directly affecting what happens in the society in the short run. But there are many elements in the society which are relatively powerless in this sense, but nevertheless of the greatest functional importance. Our society has almost divested kinship units as such of important power in this sense. But this does not mean at all that the family has ceased to be important. Closely linked with this is the question of the feminine role. Women qua women by and large do not have a position of power comparable to that of men; but this is not to say that they are unimportant – otherwise how can we account for the extent of our national preoccupations with questions of sexuality? Finally, there is a *distinct* difference between the rank-order of occupations – which, relative to other role-types, are closely involved with decision-making in a society like ours – by power and by prestige. The most striking case is the relatively high position of the professions relative to executive roles in business, as revealed by the famous North-Hatt data. Physicians as a group do not exercise great power, but there is no reason to question their very high prestige, which has been demonstrated in study after study.

The second main context, however, directly concerns the question of power. In a complex society the primary locus of power lies in the political system. There are many subtle analytical problems involved in the delineation of this system and its functions in the society which cannot be gone into here; this formula will have to suffice. Two questions are, however, primary for our purposes: the degree of differentiation of the political system from other systems; and its own internal structure. These two problems, it will be noted, parallel those raised with reference to the economy.

For historical reasons it seems clear that the development of the American political system, since the breakdown of the first synthesis associated with the "founders of the Republic," has lagged behind that of the economy. This is a function primarily of the two factors already noted – the economic emphasis inherent in our system of values, and the relative lack of urgency of certain political problems because of our especially protected and favored national position. Relative to the economic structure, which had by that time grown enormously, the political was at its weakest in the period from the Civil War to the end of the century; this situation is sketched by Mills in broadly correct terms. Since then, both internal exigencies and the exigencies of our international position have been stimuli for major changes.

Internally, beyond the more elementary provisions for law and order and essential minimum services – much of this, of course, on a local basis – the main focus of the development of our political system has been *control* of economic organization and processes, and coping with some of the social consequences of economic growth and industrialization. The process started well before the turn of the century with the Interstate Commerce legislation and the Anti-Trust Act and continued through the New Deal era, not steadily but with waves of new measures and levels of political control.

A major problem in relation to Mills' analysis is whether this is "genuine" control. His view seems to be that at times it has been, but that on balance it is the business power-holders who control government, not vice versa; the above quotation about the outcome of the New Deal puts it succinctly. In my opinion this is a misinterpretation. If genuine and in some sense effective controls had not been imposed, I find it impossible to understand the bitter and continuing opposition on the part of business to the measures which have been taken.[4] Even some of those most completely taken for granted now, like the Federal Reserve system, were bitterly fought at the time. It therefore seems to me to be the sounder interpretation that there has been a genuine growth of autonomous governmental power – apart from the military aspect, which will be discussed presently – and that one major aspect of this has been relatively effective control of the business system. This control and the growth of "big government" have been generally accepted in the society as a whole. The participation of big-business men in governmental processes is by no means to be interpreted as a simple index of their power to dominate government in their own interests, as Mills often seems to maintain.

To me, another indication of Mills' biased view of the governmental situation is his almost complete failure even to mention the political parties, or to analyze their differences. It seems to me broadly true that the Republican party, though a coalition, is more than any other single thing the party of the bigger sector of business. Four years of a Republican administration – two of them without control of Congress – is certainly not enough to indicate that big business through its favorite party organ controls the government on a long-run basis. So Mills is practically forced to the view that the alleged control operates above and beyond the party system. This seems to be connected with his relegation of the legislative branch to the "middle level" of power. I have strong reservations about this, but also it must not be forgotten that the presidency is the biggest prize of all in party politics, and it is its importance which forms the primary integrating focus of our particular type of party system. Surely the presidency is not simply the football of an inner clique which manipulates the executive branch independently of the party.[5]

Mills, of course, recognizes that the aftermath of two world wars, the rise of Communist power, and the relative decline of the older Western Great Powers provide the occasion for the increasing prominence of the military group in our governmental system. Before these changes – and, indeed, to a remarkable extent, as late as the 1930s – the military played a far smaller role in this country than in any other society of comparable scale and organizational and techno-logical development. Part of the change may be interpreted as simply the redressing of a balance. But it seems to me correct to say that for the last ten years there has been a special situation attributable to the extremely unsettled condition of the world at large and to the difficulties entailed for the American system, given its background, in meeting the problem on its own terms. There is thus a sense in which it is true that the higher military officers have tended to fill a vacuum in the field of national decision-making. There are two main points to be made about Mills' treatment of the matter. First, more in this field than perhaps any other, Mills' discussion is marred by a hasty tendency to generalize from very recent short-run developments to the long-run prospects of the structure of the society. Even here he fails to mention that in certain crucial questions the recommendations of the military have been overruled by civilian authority, although the President is a former military man. Secondly, the tone of indictment, particularly evidenced by the quite unnecessary and, I think, in-appropriate parading of the term "warlord," is stronger in his discussion of this area than in any other, except perhaps the "mass society."

Related to the position of the higher military officers is what Mills calls the "military metaphysic," meaning the definition of international problems in terms of the primacy of military force. That there has been such a tendency, and that it has gone beyond the objective requirements of the situation, seem to be unquestionable. But I very much doubt whether it is as absolute as many of Mills' statements make it appear, and a swing in another direction is discernible already.[6] This seems to be another case of Mills' tendency to make large generalizations about major trends from short-run experience.

Finally, let us say a word about what Mills calls the "political directorate" – that is, the non-military component in the groups most influential in the affairs of government and politics. Again I think there is a certain correctness in his contention that a definite weakness exists here, and that the high participation both of business and of military elements in the exercise of power is related to this. But a difficulty arises in terms of the perspective on American society which I have been emphasizing throughout. Both the non-political stress in American social structure and values generally, and the recency and intensity of the pressures to build up this aspect of our structure, would lead one to predict that it would be a major focus of strain. American society has not developed a well-integrated political-government elite, in the sense that it has developed a relatively well-integrated business-executive group. For this reason responsibility has been carried – imperfectly, of course – by a very miscellaneous group which includes members of the business and military groups, as would be expected, but also "politicians," in the usual sense of people making an at least partial career out of elective office and the influencing of elections; professional people, particularly lawyers but also economists, political scientists, and even natural scientists (e.g., John von Neumann as Atomic Energy Commissioner); journalists; and, a very important element, upper-class people in more than the purely economic sense that Mills employs, of whom Franklin Roosevelt was one and Adlai Stevenson, though also a lawyer, is another. In my opinion, the structure of the American political leadership group is far from a settled thing. It certainly is not settled in terms of the long-run dominance of a business-military coalition.

Mills holds that the United States has no higher civil service at all, in the European sense, and seems to imply that we should have. There is relative truth in his empirical contention, though I think he tends to underestimate the real influence of "non-political" government officials on longer-run policy.[7] At least it seems highly probable that in the nature of the case the tendency will be toward a strengthening of the element of professional governmental officials who are essentially independent both of short-run "politics" and of elements extraneous to the structure of government and its responsibilities. In fact, the military officer is a special case of this type, and though his role is not stabilized, it presumably must come to be more important than it traditionally has been. However, it is questionable how far the specific models of civil service organization either of Britain or of Continental Europe – particularly, certain of their special connections with the class structure and the educational system – are appropriate to American conditions. Such connections in the American case would accentuate rather than mitigate the prominence of the Ivy League element to which Mills so seriously objects.[8]

Above all, I do not think that Mills has made a convincing case for his contention that the power structure impinging directly on American government is in process of crystallizing into a top business-military coalition with a much weaker political "junior partner" whose main function presumably is, by manipulation of the mass media and the political process in the narrower sense, to keep the great majority of Americans from protesting too loudly or even from awakening to what allegedly is "really" going on. On a number of counts which have been reviewed, there is a case on a short-run basis for part of his interpretation. But I think that the kinds of factors brought out in the previous discussion make it extremely dubious that even the partial correctness of his interpretation of a current situation will prove to be a sound indicator of what is to be expected over such longer periods as a generation or more.

My conviction on this point is strengthened by a variety of other considerations which, for reasons of space, cannot be discussed here, but may be mentioned. First, I am extremely skeptical of Mills' interpretation of what he calls the "mass society," which includes the structural position of the great majority of the American population. In this he ignores both kinship and friendship, and the whole mass of associational activities and relationships. One example is the spread of church membership – which I suppose Mills would dismiss as simply an escape from the boredom of white-collar life, but in my opinion is of considerable positive significance.

Another very important complex which Mills either treats cavalierly or ignores completely involves education at the various levels, and with it the enormous development, over a century, of science and learning and the professions resting upon them. It is true that the people rooted in these areas of the social structure are not prominent in the power elite, and are even subject to some conflicts with it; but they would not be expected to be prominent in this way – their functions in the society are different. Nonetheless, they must be taken very seriously into account in a diagnosis of what has been happening to the society as a whole. One of the most important sets of facts concerns the ways in which the services of technical professional groups have come to penetrate the structures both of business and of government, a circumstance which over a period of time has greatly enhanced the role of the universities as custodians of learning and sources of trained personnel.

Finally, there is one special case of a professional group whose role Mills treats with serious inadequacy – namely, lawyers. First, he dismisses the judicial branch of government as just "trailing along," with the implication that with a slight lag it simply does the bidding of the "real" holders of power. This seems to be a most biased appraisal of the role of the courts. Not to speak of the longer-run record, the initiative taken by the courts in the matter of racial segregation and in the reassertion of civil liberties after the miasma of McCarthyism does not appear to me to be compatible with Mills' views. Similar considerations seem to apply to various aspects of the role of the private legal profession, notably with respect to the *control* of processes in the business world. Mills tends to assume that the relation between law and business is an overwhelmingly one-way relation; lawyers are there to serve the interests of businessmen and essentially have no independent influence. This, I think, is an illusion stemming largely from Mills' preoccupation with a certain kind of power. His implicit reasoning seems to be that since lawyers have less power than businessmen, they do not really "count."

III

The last problem I wish to raise, therefore, concerns Mills' conception of power and its use as a category of social analysis. Unfortunately, the concept of power is not a settled one in the social sciences, either in political science or in sociology. Mills, however, adopts one main version of the concept without attempting to justify it. This is what may be called the "zero-sum" concept; power, that is to say, is power *over* others. The power A has in a system is necessarily and by definition at the expense of B. This conception of power then is generalized to the whole conception of the political process when Mills says that "Politics is a struggle for power."

Within limits, every student of social affairs is free to define important concepts the way he prefers; there is no canonically "correct" definition. But choosing one alternative will have consequences which differ from those implied in another, and this is the case with Mills' conception of power. The essential point at present is that, to Mills, power is not a facility for the performance of function in and on behalf of the society as a system, but is interpreted exclusively as a facility for getting what one group, the holders of power, wants by preventing another group, the "outs," from getting what it wants.

What this conception does is to elevate a secondary and derived aspect of a total phenomenon into the central place. A comparison may help to make this clear. There is obviously a distributive aspect of wealth and it is in a sense true that the wealth of one person or group by definition cannot also be possessed by another group. Thus the *distribution* of wealth is, in the nature of the case, a focus of conflicts of interest in a society. But what of the positive functions of wealth and of the conditions of its production? It has become fully established that the wealth available for distribution can only come about through the processes of production, and that these processes require the "co-operation" or integration of a variety of different agencies – what economists call the "factors of production." Wealth in turn is a generalized class of facilities available to units of the society – individuals and various types and levels of collectivities – for whatever uses may be important to them. But even apart from the question of what share each gets, the fact that there should be wealth to divide, and how much, cannot be taken for granted as given except within a very limited context.

Very similar things can be said about power in a political sense. Power is a generalized facility or resource in the society. It has to be divided or allocated, but it also has to be produced and it has collective as well as distributive functions. It is the capacity to mobilize the resources of the society for the attainment of goals for which a general "public" commitment has been made, or may be made. It is mobilization, above all, of the action of persons and groups, which is *binding* on them by virtue of their position in the society. Thus within a much larger complex Mills concentrates almost exclusively on the distributive aspect of power. He is interested only in *who* has power and what *sectoral* interests he is serving with his power, not in how power comes to be generated or in what communal rather than sectoral interests are served.

The result is a highly selective treatment of the whole complex of the power problem. There is, in the first place, a tendency to exaggerate the empirical importance of power by alleging that it is only power which "really" determines what happens in a society. Against this, I would place the view that power is only one of several cognate factors in the determination of social events. This bias of Mills is particularly evident in his tendency to foreshorten social processes and emphasize overwhelmingly short-run factors. There is, secondly, the tendency to think of power as presumptively illegitimate; if people exercise considerable power, it must be because they have somehow usurped it where they had no right and they intend to use it to the detriment of others. This comes out most conspicuously in Mills' imputation of irresponsibility to his "power elite" and the allegation, vaguely conceived and presented with very little evidence, that they are characterized by a "higher immorality." It is notable that as he approaches the climax indicated by the title of his final chapter the tone of indictment becomes shriller and shriller and the atmosphere of objective analysis recedes.

Back of all this lies, I am sure, an only partly manifest "metaphysical" position which Mills shares with Veblen and a long line of indicters of modern industrial society. I would call it a utopian conception of an ideal society in which power does not play a part at all.

This is a philosophical and ethical background which is common both to utopian liberalism and socialism in our society and to a good deal of "capitalist" ideology. They have in common an underlying "individualism" of a certain type. This is not primarily individualism in the sense that the welfare and rights of the individual constitute fundamental moral values, but rather that *both* individual and collective rights are alleged to be promoted only by *minimizing* the positive organization of social groups. Social organization as such is presumptively bad because, on a limited, short-run basis, it always and necessarily limits the freedom of the individual to do exactly what he may happen to want. The question of the deeper and longer-run dependence of the goals and capacities of individuals themselves on social organization is simply shoved into the background. From this point of view, both power in the individual enterprise and power in the larger society are presumptively evil in themselves, because they represent the primary visible focus of the capacity of somebody to see to it that somebody else acts or does not act in certain ways, whether at the moment he wants to or not.

There are, in contemporary society, three main versions of this individualistic utopianism, which may be called "liberal" and "capitalist" and "socialist" – I place all three terms in quotation marks deliberately. The liberal version is mainly "humanistically" oriented to the *total* welfare of the individual as a person, and in American terms it is very likely to assume a Jeffersonian cast, to hold up the vision of a simpler and hence almost by definition "better" society against the inhumanities and impersonalities of large-scale modern industrialism and all its concomitants.

The capitalist version is, with all the qualifications which such an assertion must occasion, *primarily* production-oriented. Essentially it says that, whatever the cost to individuals – including even businessmen themselves, or especially so

– production must be achieved, carried on, and so far as possible increased. This is the focus of what has been called the "business creed."[9] Understandably it has been highly sensitive to "interferences" on both fronts, from liberal sources which would sacrifice productivity to humanistic values, and from government-alist sources which would "interfere" with the businessman's primary respons-ibility for production. Social organization beyond the level of the firm is thus presumptively a limitation of its freedom.

The socialist version has been a secondary theme in American ideology largely because of the apolitical character of American society, which, as I have noted, has been prominent historically. The opposition to capitalism has centered on two fronts, the control of the economy in the interests of preventing abuses of power and the steering of the benefits of productivity in the humanis-tic direction of "welfare." But the socialist questions whether *control* of the abuses of private enterprise is possible at all; to him, for the state to take over production directly is the only way. From this perspective, furthermore, the "Jeffersonian" version of romantic utopianism seems particularly unrealistic and unacceptable.

From one point of view, the socialist romanticizes the state and the political process. Whereas he distrusts private interests almost totally and feels that they cannot be entrusted with any responsibility, he romantically believes that if public authority alone is entrusted with all responsibilities, all will be well – because some mystical "popular will" or "public interest" controls it – forget-ting that public authority, like other forms of social organization, is administered by human beings. And that he does not fundamentally trust even public author-ity is evidenced by his ultimate ideal that the state should "wither away" and the spontaneous co-operation of institutionally unorganized human beings should take over. The socialist has been put in a particularly difficult position in the contemporary world by the development of communism which, while still paying lip service to the eventual withering-away of the state, carries the en-forcement of its predominance over all private interests, including the liberties of its citizens, to the totalitarian extreme.

Mills does not make his own position explicit in this book. As noted, at times he speaks like a nostalgic Jeffersonian liberal. I understand, however, that he professes to be a socialist – non-Communist, of course. But a basic strain of his thinking is consistent with both wings of the liberal-socialist dilemma on the basically *individualistic* premises that I have outlined: either that social organiza-tion beyond the level of the family and the local community is a bad thing *in toto*, or that it is instrumentally justified only to get society over a particular hump, the threat of the capitalist evil.

Mills seems to be suggesting that the development of the power elite is bringing that capitalist evil to a climax, to a situation which is intolerable to liberals and socialists alike. I suggest an alternative view: that, though of course accompanied by a whole range of "abuses," the main lines of social develop-ment in America are essentially acceptable to a humanistic ethic which in my case is closer to the liberal than to either of the other two outlined here. But it differs in not being in the older sense an individualistic liberalism. If the individualistic assumptions are modified in favor of a set which not only admit the necessity but assert the desirability of positive social organization, much of the ideological conflict between the three positions as total "systems" evaporates. Above all, it can be positively asserted that power, while of course subject to abuses and in need of many controls, is an essential and desirable component of a highly organized society. This position, in asserting and justifying the increased importance of government, thus grants that there is a grain of truth in the "socialist" theme. There is, however, also some justification for the existence of "capitalism," if by that is meant the institutionalization of responsibility for the larger part of economic production in the hands of a variety of private, non-governmental agencies. To my mind, there is no more reason why all important economic production should be controlled by government than why all scientific research should be.

Hence, in my opinion, many of the difficulties of Mills' analysis of a crucial problem in American society arise from his failure to transcend the dilemmas inherent in much of the individualistic tradition in American and, more broadly, in Western thought. It seems to me that he is clearly and, in the degree to which he pushes this position, unjustifiably anti-capitalist. He is partly pro-liberal and probably even more pro-socialist. But in the American scene a choice between these old alternatives of ideological orientation is no longer enough. It is necessary not only to criticize existing conditions from the older philosophical or ideological points of view, but to take serious stock of the ideological assumptions underlying the bulk of American political discussion of such problems as power.

Notes

1   The main exception here is Robin M. Williams' excellent *American Society* (New York, 1951), which has received far less general attention than it deserves, perhaps because of its somewhat textbookish orientation.

2   Mr. Mills is clearly writing only partly for an audience of technical social scientists. Though my own argument will be largely based on considerations of technical theory, I shall not introduce explicit justification of my theoretical judgments into this review, but will try to state my case in relatively non-technical terms.

3   How far this "Jeffersonianism" thus represents the moral position from which Mills launches his indictment is a question I will discuss at the end of the article. It provides a convenient reference point in terms of contrast both for Mills' characterization of the current society and for my own very different one.

4   Cf. F. X. Sutton, *et al.*, *The American Business Creed* (Cambridge, MA, 1956), for an excellent analysis of the point of view of business toward its relations to government. The authors make it clear that the present state of affairs is far from being fully accepted in business circles even now.

5   Somewhat curiously, though tending to suggest that President Eisenhower's elevation to the presidency is symptomatic of the alliance between the "warlords" and the upper business group, Mills does not even mention Adlai Stevenson as a significant figure in the American political scene. To be sure, his book appeared before Stevenson's second nomination. But where does Stevenson fit?

6   Whatever may be thought of it in other respects, Mr. Dulles' reluctance to join Britain and France in military measures against Egypt was hardly an expression of the "military metaphysic" now allegedly dominating the government.

7   Good examples are the Department of Agriculture and the Reclamation Service of the Department of the Interior – and now, increasingly, the Public Health Service. I think that this is even true of the Foreign Service, and that Mills here, as in so many other connections, seriously exaggerates the probable long-run consequences of the McCarthyites' intervention in the affairs of the State Department.

8   I think it correct to say that five years of Labour government in Britain, far from lessening the prominence of Oxford and Cambridge educations as qualifications for the civil service, in fact increased their relative importance, by increasing the national importance of the civil service itself.

9   Cf. Sutton, *et al.*, *op. cit.*

12

Order and Community in the International Social System

This brief paper must necessarily begin on a note of apology. It is an essay in a field in which the author is in no sense an expert. There has, in recent years, been an immense amount of work in this field which has produced an extensive literature. [...] My knowledge of this literature is fragmentary indeed, and it has not been possible to take time to familiarize myself with it to even a minimum degree of desirability. Under these limitations, the best that can be done is to attempt to mobilize concepts and propositions which have proved useful in the more general theory of social systems and its fields of empirical application, with which I am more familiar, in order to throw light on this particularly important and urgent subject.

The problem of the basis of order in social systems has been a classic focus for theoretical analysis, and one which is of particular importance to sociology. Because of its evident centrality in the international field, this seems to be a particularly appropriate point of reference for the present discussion.

In most current sociological theory, order is conceived as the existence of normative control over a range of the action of acting units, whether these be individuals or collectivities, so that, on the one hand, their action is kept within limits which are compatible with at least the minimum stability of the system as a whole and, on the other hand, there is a basis for at least certain types of concerted action when the occasion so requires. The essential normative components can be conceived as *values*, which concern the most general level of conception of the desirable type of social system, but without reference either to internal functional differentiation or to particularities of the situation, and *norms*, which are generalized formulations – more or less explicit – of expectations of proper action by differentiated units in relatively specific situations.

These normative components of a social system are also part of what, in analytical terms, we call the cultural system, but they become part of the social system insofar as they are *institutionalized*. Institutionalization, as that concept is used here, is a mode of integration of the appropriate cultural elements with the "interests" of acting units, whose action is oriented in terms of these normative components. Institutionalization is conceived as the phenomenon in social systems which is parallel to the internalization of values and social objects in the personality of the individual – a conception which has become relatively familiar to social scientists.

The crucial cultural component here is *evaluative orientation*. For full institutionalization, however, there must be three other components, namely, (a) an
adequately precise cognitive conception of the nature of the desirable object (in
this case the *type* of social system) in relation to its type of environment; (b) the
goal-commitments of units of the system to "doing their part" in maintaining
such a system (for the individual, "motivational" commitment); and (c) evaluative ideas concerning the conditions of operation of the system and the benefits
and costs involved in the alternatives of success and failure (this is broadly the
field of ideology in a nonpejorative sense).[1]

The basic consequence of the institutionalization of normative culture is to
produce an area of *coincidence* of normative obligation, on the one hand, and
"interest," on the other. That is to say, for acting units it comes to pass that it is
to their interest to do what, in terms of the normative order, they *ought* to do. In
this sense, institutionalization is not an either–or proposition, but a matter of
degree. At one pole, is the Hobbesian state of the war of all against all, whether
the units at war be individuals or nation-states. At the other pole, is a state of
complete integration, where any action which deviates from the normative
order, which itself is presumed to be completely consistent and explicit, is
unthinkable. Obviously *both* are theoretical limiting cases, and neither is
descriptive of *any* empirical state of affairs. If international affairs were in fact
a Hobbesian state of nature, none of us would be here to write about them, and
we are all too painfully aware of the flaws in its state of integration. Here,
however, it is relevant to remark that breakdown of order into war does not
analytically imply that there are *no* forces which tend to support order, but
rather that they have not proved strong enough to prevent a specific breakdown
for the occasion in question. The very prevalence of ideological justifications for
resorting to war may itself be regarded as evidence of the presence of the
normative components under discussion.

The normative elements of a social system do not stand alone, of course. The
reason for emphasizing them here is their involvement in the problem of order.
Perhaps the best single term in general usage for the non-normative components
is the term *interests*, of which, in turn, the most important subcategories are
political and economic. Order as here conceived is order among interests. These
may be conceived as related in one or a combination of the following ways: (a)
as integrated in the sense in which a well-led collectivity, effectively achieving a
well-defined goal, is integrated; (b) as competing when there is effective normative regulation of competitive relations without having a collective goal imposed
on the regulated system (the market is the prototypical case); or (c) as conflicting when the lack of regulation tends toward a disequilibrium in the system,
whether through polarization, or through various forms and levels of what may
be called fragmentation.

It is essential to the treatment of the relations between components of normative order, on the one hand, and interests, on the other, to keep the relativity
of this relation in mind continually. The distinction is analytical and does not
represent a classification of concrete entities. It is primarily a matter of the level
of system-reference at which analysis is carried out. Thus, religious ethics
certainly constitute a component of normative order in one system reference,

but at the same time a church, in its own conception of its position as a trustee of ethics, may also function as an "interest group," either positively integrated with others, competing with them, or in conflict with them. It is clearly the relation between the play of interests and the potential components of normative order which constitutes the core of our problem in this paper.

Of the two great categories of interests, the political category is most directly relevant to the present argument. For reasons which cannot be gone into here, political interests tend to come to focus in the problem of power as the generalized capacity to attain the goals of the unit in question. Where territorially organized political units are in question, the focus of the primary problem is, above all, the margin between a conflicting type of relation and one which can become competitive in the regulated sense. Economic interests are certainly important and will be mentioned at certain points, but there would probably be general agreement that the focus of the problem of international order lies in the regulation of the potential conflicts of political power interests. Given the political organization of territorial units, economic interests tend to be funneled, though not with uniform intensity, into competitive or conflicting power-interests.

Our central problem then may be defined as the need to identify the principal elements of normative order which are present in contemporary international relations, and to suggest their potentialities and limitations for being strengthened at cultural levels and for meeting the basic conditions of minimal institutionalization.

The concept of a society provides a convenient approach. In sociological tradition, this has tended to refer to the highest-order social system, one which fulfills the prerequisites of a level of order that permits a relatively complete and stable development, within its boundaries, of *all* the important types of structure and process with which the analyst of social systems is concerned. Perhaps the Aristotelian concept of self-sufficiency has served as the fundamental model.

One particular tendency evident in various treatments of the concept of society is especially important in the present context. This is the emphasis on the relation between a pattern of normative order and the effective control of action within a territorial area. In terms of the structure of complex societies, this refers to the relation between political organization, on the one hand, and a legal system, on the other. The legal system is the most explicit and formal aspect of the normative order. Not only to secure compliance, but, as Durkheim noted, also to assert the seriousness with which the normative order is taken, it is essential that there should be attempts at *enforcement* of the obligations defined in the order, and that some machinery should be entrusted with this enforcement function. In cases of resistance, the tendency is to resort to increasingly drastic measures. The element of territoriality becomes particularly crucial because, at least in the negative, preventive context, physical force becomes the ultimate sanction – the end of the line. Though it has crucial limitations as a stimulator of desired action, it is the ultimate preventive; sufficient force, properly applied, can prevent any human action, if only because dead men do not act. Hence, there can be no certainty of implementation of a normative order, unless the employment of physical force can be controlled – and controlled within a territorial area – because force must be applied to the object in the *place* where it is located. Of course, in many respects the threat of force, as a deterrent, is more important than is its actual application.

The same general idea of relativity which was applied to the distinction between elements of normative order and interests may be used here. The organization of order with regard to territorial jurisdictions is a common element of all societal organization. But the nation-state (or something like it), as seen in comparative perspective, is not an isolated and unique phenomenon. Organization of order on a territorial basis clearly continues to be important for many subunits of a politically organized society, including, of course, many units not ordinarily thought of as political; the relative immunity from interference within one's own residential premises – the famous "Englishman's castle" – is a case in point. This surely is one main reason why real estate is somewhat different from other objects of property rights. This becomes even more conspicuous with respect to what are explicitly considered units of local government as such, and is most fully institutionalized in the case of federal organization, where territorial units below the top level certainly have very important elements of institutionalized autonomy. With respect to the United States, the use of the word "state" for the federal unit rather than for the national government is surely significant. In certain respects, the importance of these autonomies, with territorial as well as other references, has necessarily increased as a result of the generally increasing differentiation of modern society, which carries with it an increasingly prominent pluralism of group structures.[2]

If this is true when one looks from the national state "downward" in the series of levels of organization, there is no reason why it should not also be true when one looks in the opposite direction. A relevant consideration here is the historical trend, very broadly conceived. With various important breaks and discontinuities, this is, of course, the progressive extension of the magnitude of territorial range of relatively stable political order. It would be hard to conceive of the process by which these extensions had taken place without reference to the prior existence of components of normative order which transcended the area of effective institutionalization at any given time. However important sheer conquest and forcible enforcement may have been in the extension process, the fact that many of the most important religious movements, for instance, have extended well beyond the political boundaries of any one society identified with them is surely relevant in this connection.

Thus, it can be seen that the strictures on the doctrine of absolute sovereignty, which were particularly emphasized by the late Professor Lask, in his pre-Marxist period, should be interpreted as applying in both directions. The case of a "state" which is completely sovereign internally, in the sense that only the "top" political authority can make any decisions in case of conflict, is clearly a limiting case, incompatible not only with any genuine federalism, but also with a variety of other modes of more or less pluralistic social organization. Similarly, whatever the level of centralization of the internal control of order, absolute sovereignty in the external sense (which postulates a state of war of all against all between such sovereign units) is a theoretical limiting case, which at most is only approximated in reality. At the very least there will be a component of competition mitigating conflict, and this implies some normative order.

These considerations are relevant to the question of how the concept of a social system should be understood in the present context. The essential point concerns the kind and degree of normative integration. I should regard the famous Hobbesian state of war as the limiting concept, the statement of the limit at which the concept of social system becomes meaningless. Short of this, there is an indefinite range of gradations in the direction of progressively higher levels of integration, with, of course, qualitative differences of type being involved as well. From this point of view, the national state represents a social system characterized by a relatively high level of integration in one respect, namely, capacity to control activity within a territorial area and to act concertedly as an "interest group" *vis-à-vis* other territorial units. But there is no implication either that its existence is incompatible with other elements of normative control over territorial areas, transcending those of its "sovereignty" (though the nature of such controls is of course problematic), or that elements of order which have other than primarily territorial-political references are negligible. On this basis I think we can quite legitimately consider an international order as a social system, however precarious the element of normative control may be. The problems of degree and conditions should be treated as empirical problems, not as problems of definition in an abstract theoretical sense.

Roscoe Pound's notion of the relation between law and "politically organized society" can, with proper qualifications, be taken as a central concept. It should not, however, be absolutized. With the development of the modern nation-state, the tightness of its control over the use of force within its boundaries has increased, partly because force has become more formidable, both technologically and organizationally, and hence more dangerous if not controlled. But the nation-state is, with some qualifications, the product of a process of social differentiation; hence it may be argued that by and large there are more – and more important – elements within a modern society which are essentially independent of the principal controllers of the use of force than there are in less differentiated societies. Thus, a military establishment which is predominantly professional and under civilian control, rather than fused with the higher echelons of government, as was recently the case in Imperial Germany and Japan, is one index.[3] Another is the structural independence of the legal system from operative government. In such a situation, there is, in addition to government and law, the immense ramification of social structures and groups in cultural, economic, and other fields which are characteristic of highly differentiated societies; pluralism in this sense is a basic immanent trend.[4]

The most important exception is the modern more or less "totalitarian" state, which tries not merely to enforce a monopoly of force in the traditional political sense, but beyond this a basic subordination, in other respects, of potentially independent structural elements in the society. In spite of its prominence on the contemporary scene, I think it is legitimate to regard this as a special case, one which will have to be discussed further below.

All social systems, including societies (except for limiting cases), are *open* rather than closed systems. It would be expected that the trend of the process of differentiation just referred to would be to increase, rather than decrease, their openness. This is to say that the obverse of the independence of many internal structural elements from the political authority, which in one sense (but *only* one) "controls," would be both the permission and the encouragement of the establishment of connections which extend across national boundaries. A prototypical example, and one of very critical significance, is international trade.

The relations of international trade to the political actions and relations of governments have, of course, been very complex. It has sometimes been tempting to reduce them to such slogans as "trade follows the flag," and, in fact, there have been plenty of cases of "economic imperialism." Nevertheless, a certain level of independence of trade relations from the governments of the principals has existed for a long time and has probably been growing. The fact that governments, as well as business groups within their territories, have often had an interest in promoting trade, as well as in preventing or controlling competition, does not invalidate the preceding assertion. The essential question is whether this has been a field of activity in which there were components of *order* which were not a simple function of the political policies of governments. That this has in fact been the case is attested by the relatively extensive development of international law in this field.

Of course, this independence from governments should not be exaggerated. Very generally, governments have been in a position to limit, or even stop, their nationals in these activities, and have done so on occasion through tariffs, embargoes, and various other devices. But it would certainly be going too far to say that in no sense have governments respected international law and the interests of groups other than their own nationals in these fields; within certain limits it would be considered undesirable politically to go too far in these respects.

Closely connected with trade, but distinguishable from it, there has existed a normative order relative to freedom and security of persons and of communications as between political jurisdictions. One of the most important illustrations of this phenomenon is the code regulating conduct on the high seas where ships are out of range of national controls. Still another concerns freedom to travel, and with this the whole complex of norms regarding the rights of aliens present within the jurisdiction of a government, either as temporary visitors or as residents on various bases. Of course, the matters of passports and visas play a role here. It is significant that before World War I travel within the whole Western world was possible without passports or visas, and that this is now being revived. Another interesting tendency throughout much of Western Europe is to waive customs inspection in the matter of the personal belongings of travellers. Connected with these issues are such matters as international copyright conventions and, of course, freedom of communication through broadcasting, magazines, newspapers, etc.

All of these factors and many more involve elements of international order which, to be sure, are likely to break down under the stress of war, and sometimes during crises short of war, but which are very much present and not to be neglected. It is true that they are regulated by governments, but this does not mean that they are entirely the "creatures" of governments. It is also true that insofar as they do respect them or participate in their extensions, governments are by no means always wholly "disinterested"; they may well see a national interest involved in these procedures. But this is not the point. We have already noted that it is the hallmark of institutionalization that self-interest comes to be bound up with conformity with a normative order. Hence, the fact that a unit finds it to be in its self-interest to act in a certain way by itself says nothing one way or the other about whether the action is or is not in accord with a normative order. Only one point is certain, namely, that a normative order which laid down requirements which were in serious conflict with the self-interests of all the units related to it could not be upheld for very long.

Within frameworks such as these, there has developed a widely ramified system of private associations and solidarities across national boundaries. Those in the field of trade are probably on the largest scale. However, economic relations, because of the inherent competitive element, are perhaps in themselves more precarious with respect to order than some others. A very important category is that having to do with cultural interests. For example, almost all associations built around scientific disciplines have extensive international connections, hold frequent technical meetings and conferences, and, of course, engage in much exchange of information through publications which are mutually available.

Considering the fact that, historically, religion has been involved so prominently in social conflicts, not infrequently to the point of war, it is worthwhile to call attention to the extent to which religious adherence and, indeed, formal religious organization transcend national boundaries. In the Western world the largest single example is the Roman Catholic church, but on a smaller scale "international" Judaism and the various Protestant denominations have a similar character; for the latter group, the recent emergence of the World Council of Churches is a significant development.

Even in the nationalistically sensitive area of law there is one little noted, but remarkable, phenomenon. Some Americans have taken delight in twisting the Lion's tail, but the legal profession in this country has quietly but consistently treated decisions in British courts, either current or made long after American independence, as providing valid precedents for American judicial process in areas not covered by legislation. Common Law is thus a common heritage of normative order not merely in the sense that American law is historically derived from English law, but in the sense that today, in significant degree, Common Law is a *single* corpus which is treated as legally valid and subject to legal growth with little reference to national boundaries (at least in Great Britain itself, the United States, and the British Commonwealth). I am sure that similar statements can be made of Continental Roman Law.

Hence, my view is that there is already a very considerable scope of international normative order and of solidarities operating under it in private spheres, which, to be sure, are subject to governmental influence, but which are not in any sense simply agencies of governments. This is particularly important because the tendency toward pluralism of social structures, referred to above, creates a situation in which governments – and the political parties which compete for power in such governments and which seek support in this competition – tend to represent more or less integrated combinations of the various interest groups involved, to be dependent on them, and to try to further their interests. The long-run presumption is that the strengthening of private international solidarities should strengthen the interest of governments in protecting or even extending these solidarities. The essential point here is the existence, in the nature of modern societies, of a nexus of solidary relationships which crosscut the divisions on the basis of "national" interest.

What now of the nation-state itself? The essential point, which has of course been made many times, is that it is by no means such a monolithic either–or unit as it has often been held to be. Just as there are many internal private groups with interests which cut across national lines, so the idea of the absolute sovereignty of governments is at best only an approximation of the truth. Since nationalism has been so prominent in the immediate historical background, there has been a strong ideological, and perhaps somewhat less a practical, sensitivity to any suggestion of surrendering elements of sovereignty. However, the boundary between international engagements which are "purely contractual" (in line with the usual interpretation of most treaties) and somewhat stronger bonds is difficult to draw.

Even in the purely contractual field, it is not irrelevant to point out that Durkheim's basic analysis of the conditions of functioning of a contractual system between individuals ought to apply as well in a system where national governments are the contracting parties. International relations in this field may appear to be highly unstable; but the important point here is that this is a *relative* matter. I, for one, do not believe that such stability as has existed would have been possible without a substantial "noncontractual element of contract,"[5] that is, a normative order regulating the content and procedures of contract. That this is so is indicated in the first instance by the immense body of tradition and protocol which governs the status of embassies and consulates and the conduct of diplomacy, but it clearly extends beyond this to values having to do with national independence and honor, with defining limits of legitimate pressures in securing assent to treaties, and the like.

Whether by formal contractual agreement or in various other ways, the international system is clearly not simply an aggregate of atomistic sovereign units; rather, these units are organized in complex ways into various kinds of "communities of interest" and the like. The British Commonwealth, the West European combinations (which, in certain respects, are now divided into the "six" and the "seven"), NATO, SEATO, and – by no means least – the Communist bloc are familiar examples.

Perhaps the most crucial question here is the difficult one as to the extent to which such combinations are a simple function of "power" relations. It is my view that for ideological reasons the current tendency, perhaps particularly evident in the United States, is to exaggerate the extent to which this is the case. For example, there is the contention that the English-speaking community is not a genuine one at all, but that Britain and her dominions are attached to the United States *only* because of our predominant – in the last analysis, military –

power position; in other words, that there is no alternative in the face of such power but to submit in the interests of elementary security. Similarly, on the side of the Communist bloc it is alleged that the dominant military power of the Soviet Union is the only significant factor. The alternative interpretation is that not only do the positions of the United States and the Soviet Union respectively contain elements of sheer power – which of course is there – but that they also contain elements of genuine *leadership*. Leadership in this sense exists only when there is political support for the position, backed by interests other than the most elementary security and subject to an accepted (i.e., institutionalized) normative order. In my opinion, the element of sheer power is more prominent in the Communist case, but it is dangerous to assume that other elements are negligible. If this is so, the noncoercive elements on the "other" side are clearly of substantially greater weight. To take one well-known example, it seems very difficult to believe that the integrity of the British Commonwealth could be understood as a simple function of the predominant power of the United Kingdom.

It is also of particular importance to note that these solidarities which exist between formally "sovereign" states do not occur entirely in mutually exclusive groups, but that there are important cross-cutting elements. One of the most striking cases, of course, is that of Canada, which is a member of the Commonwealth, and which by virtue of geographical and power factors, but not these alone, also stands in a very special relation to the United States. The broad conclusion seems to be that, to a considerable extent, a *pluralistic* international system has been developing. This means that the most significant nearly "ultimate" units do not function simply as "individual" units, or as a "mass," but are involved in a complex network of solidary associations which, however, are not completely monolithic but cross-cut each other in significant respects.[6]

Two further points about the international system should be made. The first is the very commonplace one that we *do* have a world-wide international organization in the United Nations. Quite obviously, this is not a "world government," with effective powers to legislate bindingly and to coerce the losing parties in disputes into acceptance of its decisions. However, these limitations do not mean that its presence in the situation is of negligible importance; it is a common fallacy of "liberals" to suppose that an element not strong enough to meet the most extreme stresses is so unimportant as scarcely to be there at all (e.g., since civil rights are not completely and literally enforced in the United States in all contexts, the vaunted American commitment to civil rights is of no importance and, moreover, is sheer "hypocrisy"). Apart from its many unobtrusive "routine" operations, the role played by the United Nations in the Middle Eastern crisis in 1956, and more recently in the Congo crisis, shows that it can have a very appreciable effect, particularly in *legitimizing* the establishment of elementary political order under auspices *other* than those of the most powerful outside interests immediately involved.

The second focal phenomenon is the *polarization* of the world political system as between the Communist bloc and the "free world," with a substantial "uncommitted" contingent. This clearly is the focus of the danger of breakdown into general war. It has, however, another aspect, namely, the sense not only in which the whole world has come to be a single political system, but also in which it is coming to be structured as something resembling, however remotely, a two-party system. A two-party system is clearly dangerous to order precisely because it polarizes allegiances, though not without residue in favorable cases. But on the other hand, there is the sharp focus on the *problem* of order, of creating a basis on which the conflict can be contained. Experience in relation to the two-party system within countries seems to indicate that two primary sets of conditions underlie the integrative stability of such a system.[7] One of these concerns the underlying structure of cross-cutting solidarities, referred to above under the heading of the problem of pluralism. The important point to note here is the asymmetry as between the free world and the Communist bloc in this respect, the latter clearly being far more nearly "monolithic," both within itself and in its external relations. This, however, is a matter of degree; probably the infrastructure of pluralistic solidarities within the bloc is in fact far more ramified and important than the current image of the Communist system would readily indicate.

The more obvious – and more immediately acute – problem concerns another level, that of "constitutional" order standing "above" the party conflict. Here the question centers on the *legitimacy* of each major party group from the point of view of the other. The dominant public impression in the cold war period has undoubtedly been that on this level the conflict was absolute and irreconcilable, an impression documented by highly authoritative statements on both sides. The essential question is to what degree this represents an ideological and short-term set of positions, and, hence, whether it is possible that it is more in the nature of the internal partisan conflict in an electoral campaign than of a genuine "state of war." The most obvious indications that something of the sort may be involved concern the extent to which the "parties" are sensitive to the impact of not only their words, but of their actions, on "world opinion." Essentially, this constitutes an appeal beyond unit-interest to a basis for legitimacy common to both sides. From one point of view this is the instrumental exploitation of men's irrational "sentiments," but from another it is an index finger, pointing toward a set of normative factors of primary importance.

That there is some trend in this direction is the most plausible interpretation of a number of features of recent behavior across the line of the Iron Curtain. Two of these features are particularly noteworthy. One is the visits of prominent politicians from each side, including heads of state and of government, to neutral or semi-neutral territory. Examples would be the visits of Khrushchev and Eisenhower to India, the interpretation of which could surely be applied to the visits of two presidential candidates during a campaign to New York, for example. The other is the fact that, in spite of the debacle of the Summit meeting in May, 1960, the United Nations Assembly was used as a forum for debate, patently oriented to the influencing of "world opinion." Even though observance of the etiquette of parliamentary procedure is far from perfect, the Assembly is treated as a forum in which the point of view of one group is advocated within some sort of "constitutional" order, both of procedure and of definition of the rights of member states. Perhaps most important of all, conflict is fought out at the verbal level, rather than at the level of overt hostile acts.

This is the point at which the famous stalemate of mutual nuclear deterrence becomes most significant. We have stressed that, given the institutionalization of a normative order, it is to be expected that there will be a relative coincidence of the structure of interests in conformity with it. It would be most unlikely that this would be an entirely one-way relationship. It is therefore reasonable to hypothesize that if circumstances exist by virtue of which there is a realistic coincidence of interests over any important area, and given the presence of other essential factors, a relatively favorable situation will be created for the development of a normative order to govern these interests. A highly important historical example is the institutionalization of contract relative to economic exchange. Though by no means the only factor, it is certainly reasonable to suppose that one of the factors involved was the enhanced appreciation of the mutual advantage of exchange relationships, and with it, of course, appreciation of the mutual disadvantages, in a market of opportunities, of exploitation by some participants to gain at the expense of other parties (e.g., through fraud).[8]

The nuclear stalemate thus creates a situation in which, in highly dramatic form, there seems to be an element of mutual, *two*-sided interest in the stability of the system. The beneficial effect of polarization, along with its danger, is the tendency to dramatize the problem of stability, to focus responsibility for actions disturbing to it, and, with sufficient imaginativeness, to open up positive opportunities for formulating elements of normative order.

However, such elements of order are not likely to be created completely *ad hoc*, out of thin air; indeed, if they were not grounded in existing deeper-lying cultural traditions, it is unlikely that they could take hold. The next important question, therefore, is whether any *common* normative factors exist in the world situation which, by extension and further specification, might provide a basis for a stronger normative order, particularly at the "constitutional" level, as I have called it.

In the social sciences in the past generation, perhaps most particularly in anthropology, there has been a strong emphasis on cultural relativity which, however justified for certain purposes, has at times been interpreted to imply that there were no common factors at the value level. More recently there has been a reaction to this and a search for common elements, which, as will be evident, have to be our primary point of reference, and which are the subject of the present brief inquiry.

For the present paper, though by no means for all purposes, the keynote must, I think, be set in certain fundamental universal significances of Western culture.[9] In the present connection it is vital to note that, culturally, Communism is a product of Western civilization; after all, Karl Marx was a German Jew, who spent most of his productive life in England and who synthesized elements drawn primarily from English Utilitarianism and German Idealism. The adoption of Communism in Russia was certainly part of the westernization of Russia, the most important of the Christian areas which had been least touched by European developments dating from the Renaissance and the Reformation; further extension to China is even more obviously an aspect of

"Westernization." But, of course, the impact of Western civilization at cultural levels has been far broader than the spread of the Communist movement; it has operated, in particular, through the role of the "intellectuals" in those non-Western societies which have had important literature traditions.[10]

With Weber as our principal guide, I think we can delineate those features of Western culture which are of primary significance in this context. They have to do with the development of normative institutional frameworks for the higher-order organization of secular society, whereas most of the important non-Western cultures had left a far greater sphere of "traditionalism" in these respects, as evidenced by predominantly peasant economies, by the special social position of hereditary aristocracies, by the relatively low level or complete absence of formal education of all but a very small elite group, etc.[11]

Whatever the deeper cultural bases of these emphases of Western values (and to me they are ultimately rooted in religious orientations), the primary consequence of present significance is an immense emphasis on the importance of the two primary levels of the *operative* organization of modern societies, of "modernization," namely, the political structure of the society and the economy. In the former case the drive is toward the development of a "modern state," with, above all, effective administrative organization of a "bureaucratic" character, which has meant the elimination or sharp reduction of the influence of "traditional" power groups. The involvement of anything approaching political democracy has, of course, been extremely uneven. The other main context is the modernization of the economy, which has meant a more or less close approach to industrialization as we understand it, with its use of bureaucratic organization, of a mobile and technically trained labor force, extension of monetary transactions and market organization, and various other familiar features.

Viewed in this context, and against the background of the conception of cultural relativity, there has emerged in the modern world the phenomenon of a remarkable world-wide consensus. For the sociologist this must be clearly understood in its societal relevance as located at the *value* level. Looked at in the twin perspectives of the developmental trend and a comparison with the advanced nations of the West, the primary "reference group," it may be called the valuation of *modernization*. It has in turn two primary foci, namely, the political – the development of a "strong" and viable political organization – and the economic, which has come to mean above all industrialization. Clearly, nationalism and its relation to political independence, particularly in respect to the history of Western "imperialism," is involved and is the aspect especially relevant to our present concern. Also, of course, one major basis of the interest in industrialization is its potential contribution to the power base of a strong national government.

Though precarious at many points and very unevenly diffused among populations, this is, in my opinion, a genuine value-consensus and one which runs deep. Its incompleteness lies not so much at this level as in the very serious problems involved in its integration with other components of the culture in two respects. One of these concerns the highest-level historic cultures of the various societies concerned. To take one example, in the considerable range of countries where Islam has figured prominently, there are acute problems in the threat of modernization to the traditional role of Islam, centering in the relations between new political and economic elites and the guardians of religious tradition and in the relationship of these new factors in the internal normative order to the traditions of religious law. Strains and potential conflicts of a similar order operate in very different ways, of course, in such countries as India and China.

The second major problem consists of the step in specification from values to what we have been calling norms. One of the main sources of difficulty in this field lies in the fact that in "traditional societies" norms are usually couched at rather low levels of generalization; they involve very detailed prescriptions. For the most part, the circumstances which originally made these details meaningful have been, or are in the course of being, radically changed by the modernization process itself. Such measures as the more or less wholesale adoption of Western law, which has happened to a considerable extent, create serious strains and difficulties which take a long time to resolve.

In my opinion, even the difference between the Communistic and the "liberal" versions of westernization lies primarily at these levels, not at the level of values, in the sense in which that concept is used here. In connection with the "cultural premises" of values, what Communism does is to shunt out the problems in this area altogether by making its special version of "materialism" a political religion. By becoming a Communist, a person renounces Islam, Confucianism, Hinduism or Buddhism, *ipso facto*, to say nothing of Christianity, and pretends that the historic problems which cluster around such movements are pseudo-problems which enlightened modern men find unworthy of concern. It seems unlikely that in the very long run such problems will remain so conveniently dormant, but this complicated subject cannot be entered into here.

As to institutionalization of secular social norms, Communism introduces a similarly convenient truncation of the complexity of the problems involved. The essential point is the attempt to maximize, under the aegis of the semi-religious party, the centralization of political power and with it the *direct* political control of the society, particularly of the process of economic development. Above all, if it can harness the broad impetus we call "nationalism," this can in the short run (the shortness of which should not be overestimated) be a powerful combination, in that it can combine an impressive effectiveness with the channeling of very deep sentiments. The most formidable of these seem to be, on the one hand, the negative complex focusing about the resentments generated by the now rapidly passing political and economic ascendancy of the Western powers; the primary ideological symbols here are colonialism and imperialism, both of which are considered as unequivocally evil. Social psychologists will see here an important case for application of the idea of relative deprivation; the very vehemence of the feelings expressed regarding colonialism is an index of lessened, rather than enhanced, subjection to it.

The other primary simplification centers about the ideological opposition between capitalism and socialism. Capitalism has come to symbolize a threat to the general integrity of the traditional community involved in the modernization process, and in particular to its economic aspects. It is questionable whether the actual strains are greater under politically controlled "socialistic" auspices or under those which allow a wider scope for "free enterprise," but that is not the point. Rather, the point is that the *symbol* of socialism permits the psychological security of belief in the continuity between the traditional community, which is conceived as coming into its own through national independence, and the emerging "modern" community; allegedly, there are no disruptive "self-interested" elements to threaten this integrity, above all, perhaps, to collaborate with the still dangerous "imperial" powers or those who, like Western businessmen, are symbolically identified with them, though they operate privately.

By virtue of the fact that, in its original Western core, economic modernization occurred largely under the aegis of free enterprise, and that this fact became ideologically crystallized as delineating the "right" way, the West has been saddled with the burden of vulnerability to the ideological derogation of being wickedly "capitalistic." The parallelism, as ideological symbols, of capitalism and socialism in the economic sphere, and imperialism and national independence in the political sphere, is patent. It is clearly the combination of the two contrasts that constitutes the primary ideological polarization in the world today.

If the above interpretation is correct, and I believe it is, the proposition that there exists a genuine value consensus underlying the various current differences, and *even* the ideological and interest-focused polarization of the cold war, is of the utmost importance in the present context. Equal importance must be attached to the assertion that there *is* a fundamental point of reference for the institutionalization of a system of normative order in the international field. There is a basis on which it is possible to recognize the *legitimacy* of the interests of various parties to conflicts and disputes, and to reduce the problems at issue to differences *within* a legitimized framework, rather than altogether outside it.

In visualizing this possibility, it is important to bear in mind that in situations of conflict there are tendencies both to ideological exaggeration and to what may be called overgeneralization. The first is perhaps most important in estimations of the "real" situation, e.g., estimates of the power and the drastic intentions of the opposition. Ambivalence in these fields is clearly indicated by oscillation between expressions of anxiety and boastfulness about one's own invincibility. ("Rocket-rattling," including the not-so-distant American threats of "massive retaliation," is very likely to involve at least an element of "whistling in the dark.") The second is clearly expressed in the tendency to insist on the absoluteness and inclusiveness of the conflict at the allegedly highest levels of "principle," which again has been prominent on both sides. From each point of view the other becomes the incarnation of an "absolute evil" with which no compromise of any sort is morally acceptable.

Members of democratic societies are familiar with the fact that in the heat of political campaigns (and under other conditions of strain), things are often said which imply an absolute condemnation of the opposition; such statements are usually forgotten in cooler moments.

It should be clear from the above that I contend that there can be value consensus which does not cover the *whole* range of social and cultural orientations. A good historical example of a relative resolution between bitterly opposed camps on such a basis is the religious conflicts in Europe following the Reformation. A *relative* order in the European system was in fact achieved, not by the definitive victory of either the Protestants or the Catholics, nor by their coming to terms on the level of theology. The reconciliation was on the level of *civil* polity, and it occurred in two main steps. The first invoked the famous formula of *cuius regio, eius religio*, thus permitting the enforcement of religious uniformity within the political unit, but not for the European *system* of units. Gradually, then, in varying degrees, religious toleration came to be institutionalized – although still in only rudimentary form in such countries as Spain – so that every such society became a religious mixture. It would be my view that there is genuine prospect of attaining a resolution of the cold war conflict on this basis, which involves a genuine institutionalization of the valuation of the rights of individuals to religious freedom and of the rule of law. There is no prospect whatever of a resolution of the conflict through the definitive victory of one side over the other, or through "demonstrating" the errors of Communism to the Communist world, or vice versa. If the conflict at this "politically religious" level is ever resolved, it will be because the *issues* have ceased to be significant, not because of the cultural "victory" of one side over the other.

One further point may be made in conclusion. I have argued that there exists a genuine consensus at a certain level of values. It should, however, be equally clear that the implications of this consensus are institutionalized at the level of norms only in the most fragmentary fashion, and that much further specification of these implications is necessary before even a moderately stable international order can be expected to emerge. It would lead us too far afield to attempt to go into these problems. However, it is perhaps correct to say that there are two main types of process by which the range of normative order has been extended to include wider participation. One of these is the establishment of "authority" which can, with varying degrees of consent on the part of the governed, undertake direct leadership and implement collective goals. The other is the process by which parties with conflicting interests in a situation have come to accept mediation (which may eventually develop into adjudication). The latter process has been associated historically with relatively autonomous legal developments. Often, though not necessarily, this has occurred under the "umbrella" of a political authority, although the important groups do not always act simply as agents of that authority.

A good deal of this type of institutionalization already exists in the various fields of international law and in a number of other contexts. Its extension is likely to be relatively slow and less dramatic than the policies of an international organization which is the center of world attention and the scene of confrontations of conflicting interests at the most explicit level. In the long run, however, this type of extension of order is potentially of great importance.

The above discussion has self-consciously stressed those elements in the current international situation which provide some basis for hope of the gradual evolution of a more stable international order. One major reason for this emphasis is that much of current discussion stresses the alternative – the absolute decisiveness of military power, the depth of the conflict of values, etc. There is very often a tendency for the factors stressed herein to be lost from sight or to be treated as of purely incidental significance. I do not, however, wish to state – or even imply – a concrete judgment of actual prospects in this area. This has been meant to be a *theoretical* essay on the analytical problems of international order. The assessment of empirical probabilities is another task, beyond the scope of this endeavor.

Notes

1   Talcott Parsons, paper on "The Sociology of Knowledge," read at the Fifth World Congress of the International Sociological Association, 1959.

2   See William Kornhauser, *The Politics of Mass Society*, and my review article, *World Politics*, October, 1960.

3   See Morris Janowitz, *The Professional Soldier* (Glencoe, 1960).

4   Kornhauser, *op. cit.*, and my review article.

5   Émile Durkheim, *The Division of Labor in Society*, Book I, Chapter VII.

6   Kornhauser, *op. cit.*

7   Talcott Parsons, " 'Voting' and the Equilibrium of the American Political System," in Eugene Burdick and Arthur J. Brodbeck, eds, *American Voting Behavior* (Glencoe, 1959).

8   See Max Weber's treatment of the English stock exchange, as discussed in Reinhard Bendix, *Max Weber: An Intellectual Portrait* (New York, 1960).

9   See Max Weber's remarks on this subject in his general introduction to his studies in the sociology of religion published in this country as the Introduction to the *Protestant Ethic and the Spirit of Capitalism*.

10   See various papers by Edward Shils, especially "The Intellectuals and the Powers: Some Perspectives for Comparative Analysis," *Comparative Studies in Society and History* (October, 1958).

11   On the concept of "traditional society" from the point of view of the process of economic development, see W. W. Rostow, *The Stages of Economic Growth* (Cambridge, 1960).

13

Polarization of the World and International Order

The greatest and most immediate danger to world peace stems from the bipolarization of the world community. It is wholly understandable, therefore, that this situation has been subjected to the most intensive discussion, and that, moreover, its threatening aspects have stood overwhelmingly at the center of attention. In this brief paper, I should like to explore the other side of this coin. For it is my contention that in certain respects these "most threatening" aspects may present an opportunity, however tenuous, to achieve a more stable system of international order.

The most obvious point of reference for the elaboration of this view is the fact that for the first time in history, we must acknowledge the existence of a world political community, at least in a relative sense. Through the development of mass media of communication, the nations of the world have become increasingly aware of their interdependence. Inevitably, important events in any major country will have rapid repercussions in all others. Indeed, any attempt to isolate a subsystem, unless that system is of minor intrinsic significance, must rely on special insulating mechanisms which impose rather rigid controls. With rapidly diminishing exceptions, we are all members of the world political community – for better or worse. In the United States, there has been a growing recognition of this phenomenon during the last three decades. Interestingly, "isolationism," which was formerly a major area of debate, was not even an issue in the recent Presidential campaign; American "involvement" was taken for granted by both parties.

I am aware, of course, that the very propriety of my use of the term "world community" may be questioned, since it implies at least a rudimentary element of order. However, I maintain that polarization, in itself, implies the existence of such an element of order. While it is conceivable, of course, that this element of order is inherent in certain geopolitical constellations which have been wholly independent of the main trends in social development, the enormous diversity of societies and cultures would seem to argue against this view. "East" and "West" may merely be geographical symbols, but these symbols refer to an emergent patterning of sociocultural organization, rather than an inevitable geographically or even ideologically based conflict of interest. Indeed the ideological "battle for men's minds" constitutes a crucial factor in this argument, for an ideological conflict presupposes a common frame of reference in terms of which the ideological differences make sense.

Insofar as a conflict of orientation can be defined as "political," and insofar as it occurs within a pattern of order rather than a Hobbesian state of nature, polarization bears some similarity to the intranational two-party system. This is not to imply that such a party system now exists in the world political community. However, it does not seem beyond the realm of possibility to suggest that some of the ingredients for such a system are present.

Some Basic Components of International Order

Certain major clues emerge as to the nature of those components of international order which are currently most significant. These concern, first, the position which the Western countries have occupied in relation to the rest of the world, particularly since the eighteenth century; and second, the designation of "modernization" as the primary goal of the non-Western sector, along with various subgoals, such as industrialization, economic development, political independence and autonomy, and the like. These developments stem from a crucial historic event, namely, the emergence in the Western world of what is known today as "industrial society" ("capitalism" is clearly too narrow a term) – in Great Britain, the United States, and Germany in the main – which came almost to full flower in the latter half of the last century, although there have been very important further developments during this century as well. Apart from the powerful "material" influence which industrialism exerts on society (whether this influence is regarded as "exploitative" or not), the concept of industrialism and its implications have been accepted almost universally.

The Implementation of a Common Set of Values

From the point of view of values, economic productivity would appear to be at the core of this pattern. Productivity has been evaluated in a variety of contexts, but a few themes have been particularly prominent. For one, economic productivity enables an improvement in living standards, along with certain concomitant benefits, in the form of higher levels of consumption, greater economic security, better health, and the like. Secondly, economic productivity has been related to autonomy, to emancipation. At this level, it has appealed to "dependent" groups; and it is in this context that it is connected with nationalism. A third and similar theme focuses on equality. As might be expected, this has involved a general challenge to the superior status of traditional elites. On the one hand, this theme has had an "internal" frame of reference, in that it pertains to territorial societies; on the other, it pertains to a demand for equal status as societies, with its bearing on political independence. The fourth important theme has been concerned with education, more specifically, its instrumental function, with respect to productivity as well as its intrinsic value.

Clearly, this broad value complex is common to both of the ideologies which today are engaged in a bitter struggle for ascendancy. Marxism grew out of Western culture during the era of emancipation from the traditionalism and "legitimism" of the European Old Regime. Its concepts stem largely from utilitarian liberalism, especially in the economic sphere; they include the political heritage of the French Revolution. The basic differences between Marxist ideology and that of the "free world" center on two points. The first, of course, involves the concept of socialism as distinguished from capitalism or free enterprise, namely, the relationship between productive organization and public authority. The second involves the interpretation of the concept of democracy, namely, the "liberal" principle of political enfranchisement and open electoral alternatives in the choice of political leadership, as opposed to guidance by a single party which assumes the trusteeship of the interests of the people. Obviously, there are other basic differences as well, such as the hostility of Communism to traditional religion, at least in principle, but important elements in the liberal world may be similarly characterized. However, on the whole, we are impressed by the fact that both of these widely divergent ideologies which, presumably, gave rise to polarization, emerged during various stages of development in the process of industrialization.

It is widely acknowledged that the recent history of the Communist movement constitutes a drastic invalidation of Marx's prediction that the revolution would originate within the most highly industrialized societies (clearly, he had England and Germany in mind). Indeed, evidence has been accumulating which would appear to indicate that the appeal of the radical left in a given society bears an inverse relation to the degree of industrialization of that society.[1] In general, the more successful industrial economies have been able to integrate their working classes into the society – with varying degrees of success, of course, and with many residual strains. In any event, this integration carries with it the legitimation of the appropriate role and status of organizational leadership and responsibility, and the recognition and reward of technical competence. The development of the Soviet Union has been in accord with these fundamental trends. On the other hand, the leftist appeal has been most effective in those instances where the structured inferiority of status, with its concomitant resentment against discrimination, exploitation, imperialism, etc., involves not classes in the Marxian sense, but societies in the territorial-political sense.

In one sense, this phenomenon is in accord with the character and significance of Marxism, although it may not conform to its original intentions. Viewed in the perspective of later developments, I consider the most important feature of Marxism to be its assertion of the inherent fusion of economic and political factors in human societies; from the perspective of our Western society, this might be interpreted as the doctrine of politization of the economy. A process of differentiation has in fact been in progress, in more highly industrialized societies, which has decreased the relative importance of the area of such fusion. The fact that such a large proportion of the working-class vote in the United States is split between the major parties is very much a case in point. It is interesting to speculate as to what might be expected in this connection in an industrially "mature" Soviet Union, if a system of plural parties were permitted there.

As mentioned earlier, the strong interest in economic development in underdeveloped societies can be linked directly to the powerful force of nationalism.

There is no question, of course, that the working classes in Western societies were more "underdeveloped" economically in Marx's time than they are at present. But the economic interests of these groups were said to cut across the main, nationally defined lines, which denoted the cleavage of political interests, whereas in present so-called underdeveloped countries, economic and political interests more nearly coincide.

Theoretically, then, economics and politics comprise the two major categories of "interests." We have yet to consider their relation to systems of normative order, however. For it is a fundamental proposition of social science that no system of the "play of interests" can be considered stable, unless these interests are pursued within an institutionalized normative system – a common framework of values, of generalized norms, and of the structuring of the interests themselves.

As suggested above, there is a certain plausibility in the view that the primary achievement of modern industrial societies has been the resolution of the class conflict (as defined by Marx), in the sense that, insofar as they may be said to operate, internal political polarizations do not simply follow the lines of cleavage dictated by the economic interests of particular classes. Indeed, there is no clear-cut dichotomization of economic interest itself. Our problem, then, may be stated as follows: First, in the newly emergent world community, is it inevitable that the cleavage between "have" and "have-not" nations must lead to polarization? Second, is this phenomenon susceptible to those integrative processes which have, in fact, operated within successfully industrialized societies? Since the earlier Marxist assumption that integration was impossible without violent revolution has proved invalid, is it not reasonable to discount the neo-Marxist assumption that "war" – whether military or economic – between the "imperialist" nations and the "people's democracies" is equally inevitable? If we accept this view, we must then attempt to identify the mechanisms which may facilitate this integrative process.

From a sociological point of view, the process of industrialization within national societies can be interpreted as most essentially one of structural differentiation. This concept, in turn, presupposes a common normative framework, primarily at the level of values. Our first concern, then, is whether there is a common value system which at least to some extent extends across the line which separates the contemporary antagonists. Despite the older ideal of a generalized cultural relativity, and an attendant ideological conflict, if the problem is defined with sufficient care there seems to be little question of the validity of this hypothesis. In each case, economic productivity on the one hand and political power (including autonomy) on the other, are the foci of concern. In societies where the status of these value components cannot be based on historical tradition, something approaching their Western evaluation has emerged, in terms of a very general set of commitments, very broadly conceived. Clearly this is historically intimately related to the overwhelmingly predominant position of the West in the areas of productivity, power, and prestige, precisely during the "imperialist" era. In other words, even in those societies where hostility toward the West has been particularly prominent, the social equivalent of a process of identification has taken place, which might be likened to "identification with the aggressor" or what Rostow has termed the "demonstration effect."[2] In addition, there have been varying kinds and degrees of reinforcement of the existing components of other value systems.[3]

Obviously, this can hardly be said to constitute a consensus on the valuation of basic goals or meanings. Rather, it represents an instrumental consensus on the valuation of capacities, at various levels of the organization of the society, to undertake whatever activities may be deemed most important to the welfare of that society. It involves the recognition that the economic productivity of the community and its political integration – the capacity to mobilize community resources for the pursuit of collective goals without external constraints – enable new levels of possible achievement in a variety of directions. There is a hierarchical element involved here as well, in that economic "opportunity" depends on political order in a more immediate sense than political order depends on the economic status of a society. Therefore, the normative ordering of the political sphere takes a certain precedence over the regulation of its economy. I consider this the primary reason for the fact that present major conflicts are conceptualized in political terms, in spite of the ideological prominence of economic considerations.

The achievement of autonomy is clearly central to this issue. Autonomy at the national level obviously removes certain constraints which are inherent in the status of colonial dependency. However, it also creates new problems, since the potentialities of "autarchic" self-sufficiency are clearly limited. Moreover, the smaller the unit, relative to the potential system of which it may be a part, the more limited are its potentialities. These limitations can be diminished only if relevant values are institutionalized in a community which is wider than the autonomous unit. In other words, parochial interests must be subordinated to those of a more extensive (and more efficient) system. Once this subordination has been institutionalized, it enables a higher level of value implementation within a framework of order than would be possible if each of the subsystems involved had to go it alone as radically autonomous units. Basically, polarization may be said to stem from this phenomenon.

Given the valuation of a major type of achievement, functioning, or whatever, greater gains can be attained in the short run by freezing the problem within a relatively restricted framework of order, and insulating the system of immediate concern from the interferences and potentialities of involvement in a wider system. To adopt an economic term, the tendency to exploit this possibility of short-run effectiveness may be called "protectionism."

In this sense, the alternative to protectionism involves the risks which are a concomitant to commitment to a higher-level, more extensive system of order. In large measure, this greatly enhanced level of risk may be attributed to competitive activities, which might otherwise be excluded. Understandably, there is strong motivation to avoid such competition by operating only within the limits of a less extensive system. On the other hand, however, the potentialities of higher value implementation are equally valid arguments in favor of the more extensive system in the long run, provided certain conditions of their implementation can be realized.

In any event, we cannot fail to recognize the presence of the primary ingredient of integration as opposed to polarization: common values obtain at a certain level of the general societal system. Moreover, it is a genuinely common, albeit incomplete, system of values at the level where main conflicts come to a head. However, values constitute only one component of institutionalized order; the problem, therefore, is to strengthen the other components to the point where they begin to outweigh the divisive elements.

With regard to values, at present polarization involves those parts of the world community which have reached certain levels of attainment, as opposed to those which have not yet achieved these levels of attainment. Thus, the have-nots are faced with the problem of catching up with the haves. With respect to political power, the Communist bloc has in fact caught up, at least to some extent. With special reference to the command of military force, it is now for all practical purposes the equal of the free world. However, there is a considerable gap between the West and the Communist bloc in the economic sphere, and this is particularly evident in the standard of living of their respective populations.

In summary, then, insofar as polarization is structured about national political units, the leadership of the have-not (Communist) bloc has achieved substantial equality with respect to one component of a larger system of productivity and political effectiveness, namely, with respect to military power. But it has accomplished this by following a protectionist policy, in that other potentialities – both internal and external – have been subordinated to a restricted goal. Internally, on an economic level, the Communist bloc has used authoritarian trusteeship to concentrate its resources on building up the ingredients of national power, at the expense of the living standards of the masses,[4] and it has denied subgroups within its society a share of the power which they could exercise in a pluralistic political system. Externally, it has become oriented to protective control within its own sphere of influence, in terms of the doctrine of absolute sovereignty. However, this dual protectionism has been counteracted on the non-Communist front by a strong measure of what might be called "defensive protectionism," which is not only military, but ideological and political in the large sense, and to some extent economic as well.

In terms of ideology, the greatest threat of Communist protectionism stems from its all-encompassing goal of definitive ultimate victory for the socialist cause (although Khrushchev's famous dictum, "We will bury you," has been interpreted to imply economic superiority rather than military conquest). The counter ideology, of course, postulates the necessity of stamping out the "Communist evil." Clearly, definitive victory for either side is not the only possible choice. We have another alternative, namely, the eventual integration of both sides – and of uncommitted units as well – in a wider system of order.

In addition to common values, there are three other essential components of institutionalized order.[5] The first of these comprises a set of minimum rules through which the implications of these values are defined in practice within the system. The second component is the structure of interests, which must be differentiated at appropriate levels. The third is an ideology in which the system of reference is defined as an empirical entity, rather than an ideology concerned merely with value patterns which define directions of desirability.

The existence of a common set of values may be considered the focal point for change. Three principal factors concerning these values may have a bearing on the direction of policy. The first of these is the failure to recognize the existence of such a value consensus. This lack of awareness may be due to the fact that value commitments have come to be fused with the protectionist elements of respective ideologies and practical policies. Thus, the opposition contends that only a rigid formula of socialist organization is morally acceptable; on our own side, "free enterprise" is said to be the basic moral issue with which there can be no compromise.

Obviously, this is a fundamental and delicate problem. Essentially, the task of disentangling values from other components implies that many issues which have at some point been treated as fundamental moral issues must be downgraded. Once again, the internal party system may provide a helpful point of reference. A political party may, with justification, be committed to the particular policies it favors, which are in direct contrast to those advocated by the opposition. But, in a broader sense, the party system also implies the existence of a set of value commitments of a higher order which are shared by both parties; moreover, institutional considerations must supersede party differences. In the United States, for example, loyalty to the Constitution presumably supersedes party interests, no matter how important. Admittedly it is extremely difficult to maintain this perspective in the midst of a highly emotional ideological conflict. However, it is an easier task for those whose superior positions have been established than it is for groups in the process of achieving status. My first policy recommendation, therefore, is that every effort be made to promulgate carefully considered statements of value commitments which may provide a basis for consensus among both have and have-not nations. This would require that such statements be dissociated from the specific ideological position of either of the polarized camps.

In all probability, this will also require increasing recognition of the significant status of a rather large and growing neutral group of political units not firmly committed to either side. When a nation withdraws its potential support from the forces with which it has previously been allied, whether tacitly or overtly, it is inevitable that this action must permit – and promote – neutralism. And, of course, neutralism itself can fulfill a protectionist function, in that it may incorporate a cynical approach which may have the effect, whether deliberate or not, of playing one side off against the other. At the same time, under the proper conditions, neutral forces may evince more interest than would be possible for so-called committed factions in those elements of order which transcend polarization. Although this opinion requires substantial qualification, it would seem that in this frame of reference India has come closer to achieving the position of a moral leader than any other national unit, with the possible exception of Sweden. Here again, the intranational system may serve to point up the significance of neutralism. In successful two-party systems there is likely to be an important uncommitted sector of the electorate, an independent vote. As has been noted frequently, this uncommitted sector can serve as an important check on tendencies toward extremism on either side, since the effect of such extremism is to alienate the neutral groups, and hence to throw the balance in the direction of the opposition. In summary, then, we must clarify the nature of universally held value commitments, and promulgate their effective recognition. This in turn involves maximal dissociation from the defensive ideological positions and practical policies specific to either side. Admittedly, the accomplishment of such dissociation will depend on a high level of national self-criticism and self-discipline. The proper application of social science should prove valuable in this connection.

The third factor concerns the level at which value commitments are stated. Throughout this paper I have emphasized the fact that the Communist bloc and the nations of the free world do, in fact, share certain values in common. However, this should not be interpreted to imply that these common values have ultimate standing. At present, they might best be considered as relative; however, the repudiation of value absolutism does not imply the kind of relativity which would rule out the possibility of a common measure.

To illustrate, at one phase of Western history, religion (in the historic-formal sense) was the primary focus of political conflict. Beginning with the Thirty Years War, Western Christendom has undergone a gradual process, in the course of which religious tolerance has come to be institutionalized. I cannot describe the various stages of this process here, but I think my readers will agree that it has made its greatest progress in the United States, with denominational pluralism and the separation of church and state. In a sense, the recent election of a Roman Catholic to the presidency has put a seal on the pattern.

One of the notable facts about the world situation is the broad renunciation on the part of religious groups of any attempt to further their interests through proselytizing crusades. Even in the nineteenth century the degree to which Christian missions were politically implemented by Western interests requires careful examination. Whatever level of support did exist at that time has diminished notably since; nor is this development due entirely to anticolonialism. Conversely, acceptance of the Hindu or Buddhist religion by the West is not considered a prerequisite for the maintenance of friendly relations with India or Burma. Even Islam, the non-Christian religion which is most predisposed to militant proselytizing, has not stressed this. Many other issues are involved, but the significant fact is that current polarization has taken shape at secular political levels, with only one side making a point of militant secularism. There is a lesson to be learned here, namely, that it is somewhat dangerous to be dogmatic about the exact level at which a relatively stable value consensus can be attained. It is my opinion that this value consensus will vary with time and circumstances. In addition, I think an important parallel can be drawn between the present situation and the tensions which grew out of the Peace of Westphalia, at which time the formula *cuius regio, eius religio* was established, which provided for the institutionalization of religious liberty between political units, but not within them.

To return to our present concern with political liberty, and more specifically with the generalization of the implications of a value commitment to this end, it has been claimed vociferously that autonomy is the fundamental right of territorial political units. Why should such autonomy be confined to this level of social organization, and not be extended to liberties within the political unit?

Indeed, I do not believe that such a limitation is really defensible as a value position on any terms; and in fact it is not defended by the Communists on those grounds, but on ideological grounds. Their argument, which stems from the Marxist concept of stage of development, is based on the allegation that the masses cannot be permitted freedom from the tutelage of the party until the final stage of the revolution. Presumably, the "withering away of the state" (and also of the party) will bring with it a level of individual freedom – both political and in other contexts as well – which will far exceed the freedom attained by bourgeois societies. We are all familiar with this theoretical approach; I have restated it here to bring into focus one essential point, namely, that freedom is valued, however distorted the means for attaining it. We can therefore conclude that political freedom at the associational and individual levels – subject, of course, to adequate institutional regulation – constitutes an essential component of the central value complex under discussion, and that the failure of the Communist camp to recognize this component in internal matters represents a basic ideological issue which merits special treatment. From a practical point of view, we are confronted with overwhelming evidence of the importance of emphasis on the existence of a value consensus. We can establish this fact effectively only if we enunciate these values directly and if we are particularly careful to avoid ideological commitments, which are specific to particular levels of society.

The Common Observance of Procedural Norms

In the present frame of reference, norms may be defined as patterns of desirable behavior which implement values in a variety of contexts, which are differentiated according to the particular functions of the agencies concerned and the specific situations in which they operate. The agencies of primary importance for purposes of this discussion are governments; the specific situation with which we are concerned is their relationship to each other, as this bears on the question of international order or, in its broadest sense, on the question of international law.

By way of preliminary comment, I would point out that there has been considerable development, and relatively good implementation, of norms in a wide variety of spheres other than those which involve the more direct relationships between governments. I refer to the regulation of international trade, to the conventions which enable the international circulation of persons and information and the like, and to the rules which have been established for conduct on the high seas, which is outside the territorial jurisdiction of any single government. There have been certain breaks in this legal order across the line of the Iron Curtain, of course, and recently censorship regulations and restrictions have been imposed on persons leaving the Union of South Africa. Nevertheless, this is a component of existing order which is not to be underestimated, and which is capable of gradual extension, without incurring major controversy in the process. One of the positive heritages of colonialism lies in the fact that European standards have been extended rather widely. Perhaps in this light the restrictive policies maintained by the Communist countries[6] may be viewed as a defensive maneuver. Thus, it becomes all the more important for the countries of the free world to maintain high standards in this respect. The McCarthy episode in American history was severely damaging precisely for this reason. The continuing presence of such protectionist elements in the nations of the free world should be overhauled very thoroughly.[7]

However, our discussion of the more immediately relevant category of norms – those which concern direct relations between governments – must encompass the whole complex of diplomatic usage, protocol, and immunities. Of course, under extreme stress, these break down.

The organization of the United Nations (and I refer to the League of Nations as well) may be viewed as an extension of a trend with deep historical roots. The central characteristic of this trend is the attempt to establish consensus at the procedural level. That is, the institutionalization of procedures is considered the focal growing point of systems of order at the level of norms, a feature which is shared both by legal systems, in the more technical sense, and by political systems. This is not to say that the common observance of general procedural norms will inevitably obviate conflicts as to standards of fairness, or those which refer to opportunity or methods of treatment of the case. Of course, such a procedural system undercuts the absolutism of commitment to goals by introducing problems attendant to settlement or compromise. However, there are different kinds of compromise. For our purposes, the important type is the promotion of integration, in terms of a higher normative level.

Of course, in part, procedural systems also enable coercive sanctions to enforce their norms. But coercive sanctions constitute only one component of the sanction system, and our crucial concern here does not involve the identification of specific sanctions. Rather, I wish to underscore a more basic issue, namely, the acceptance of procedural obligations.

I believe that this willingness on the part of its members to abide by the rules of procedure constitutes the central significance of the United Nations. For, in this sense, it is the embodiment of the world community. Clearly, the range within which one might compare the United Nations to a court of law is still very limited (though it certainly should be capable of extension). But, short of a court of law, the United Nations may be likened to a forum in which the participants are obliged to provide for the public statement of a case, and to permit a hearing for the opposition's objections to the case, as stated. Participation at either level implies recognition of the legitimacy and power of judgment by world opinion.

It is to be expected that those who are deeply committed to particular goals will be extremely ambivalent about the acceptance of procedural norms, for such acceptance carries with it the risk of defeat without all-out struggle. In light of the reluctance of the Communist bloc to compromise, the behavior of Khrushchev and his cohorts in the early fall of 1960 was significant, not because of their attempts to disturb the orderly procedure of the United Nations, but because they deemed it so important to play the game. They demanded that structural changes be made in the procedural system and in fact threatened to walk out if these demands were not met. Quite apart from the validity of these demands, I believe that the fact that polarized conflict was brought within the framework of orderly procedure was of fundamental significance, and that every effort should be made to maintain and develop this pattern. Of course, this will require shrewd assessment of the degree to which pressure can be exerted without precipitating an explosion which might wreck the whole system. Despite the problem it may pose, the existence of a procedural forum to which there is an important degree of commitment on both sides constitutes one of our most precious assets.

The significance of the United Nations as a forum will emerge in sharper focus if its similarity to a democratic electoral system and a court of law is underscored. The latter does not guarantee a satisfactory outcome for either party, or even a just outcome, but rather a fair trial. The former does not guarantee that the outcome of an election will be good for the country from the point of view of either party, but rather that the incoming administration will have the adequate support of the electorate, according to procedural rules, and thereby be enabled to take the crucial step from the status of party leadership to leadership of the polity as a whole.

Obviously, then, reliance on procedural norms inevitably means increased risk to particular partisan goals. If we expect the Communist camp to submit their vital interests to procedural norms, we must, as a corollary, accept the possibility that adherence to these norms will result in the defeat of our own interests in many instances.

In other words, the development of new systems of norms of a higher order necessarily involves the institutionalization of a willingness to take risks relative to particular goals, even very important goals. Although these risks can be confined with certain limits, they cannot be eliminated entirely. Nevertheless, this is the price we must pay for increased freedom, for the resolution of the impasse which results from the protectionist policies of antagonistic elements.[8]

The Pluralistic Structure of Interests

The third basic component of the institutionalization of a new system of order derives from the structure of what I referred to earlier as "interests." My speculations regarding this component bear a close relationship to the preceding discussion of the role of procedural norms. However, other considerations are involved as well. We are concerned here with the level of differentiation within the system of interests, with the so-called problem of pluralism.[9]

The core of the problem is contained in one facet of the contrast between the Communist system, as it operates within the current climate of polarization, and the free world. I refer to the monolithic tendency of the Communist system, that is, its tendency to include as many aspects as possible of the society in question within a single system of highly centralized control, and hence to conceive of policy as an all-or-none commitment to complete success, as defined in terms of its broad goals, rather than as a commitment to attempt to integrate differentiated subinterests either internally or externally. The applicability of this definition to a national society, such as the Soviet Union, and particularly with regard to its relationship with other members of the Communist bloc, requires extensive qualification. Nevertheless, when one considers the quality of the international coalition of the free nations, whose solidarity is continually in question, the difference is striking. Furthermore, in this sense, the liberal societies are far more pluralistic internally, in ways which are undoubtedly familiar to the reader.

One of the basic attributes of a political system which has achieved a minimum level of stability is its capacity to resolve conflicts of interests; this in turn involves the structure of the system of interests. Typically, situations which require political decision-making are continually shifting. Policy issues hinge on a particular element, specific to a given situation; hence, issues change as a consequence of situational change.

In such a system, a monolithic bloc which is capable of staking its whole position on a particular issue, which has grown out of a specific situation, has a built-in short-run advantage because it can afford to apply a kind of pressure that less monolithic systems cannot risk. But this short-run advantage is gained at the expense of an element of instability in the large system which is essentially a feature of rigidity, on the one hand, and of an unreadiness to contemplate drastic change, with the knowledge that such change may cause the breakdown of the whole system, on the other.

Polarization in a stable two-party system does not constitute a fundamental threat because any such disruptive tendency is counteracted by an underlying structure of pluralistic, and hence cross-cutting, solidarities. As a function of shifting situations which need to be dealt with, different balances among these structured interests can be mobilized; in other words, the sponsorship and motivation of a party are not constant, but vary, within limits, according to the situation. Interest components are enfranchised in that they have a realistic choice among a variety of alternatives to which they can lend their support. Consequently, it is exceedingly important to distinguish between polarization within monolithic blocs and polarization within a pluralistic infrastructure.

The cold war might be likened to the former type of polarization. On the one hand, the goal of the Communists is limited to the achievement of equal status. At the same time, however, in line with their deep ambivalence, they claim the right to achieve complete supremacy over the other camp. If this radical polarization is to be mitigated, our major task is to identify the process which might enable a shift in the direction of the pluralistic type of polarization, as conceptualized by the party system, and to determine the extent to which such a shift is in fact in progress.

In such a system issues must be dealt with one at a time, without too frequently posing broad questions of "confidence." Of course, in certain situations, it is possible for pluralization to operate directly between the principal protagonists. For example, in the field of cultural exchange, there has been a genuine mutual appreciation of the achievements of both sides in the natural sciences and the arts. In this area, solidarity stems from a devotion to, and recognition of, common standards. Quite possibly, the use of scientific experts to thresh out the technical problems of nuclear arms inspection would constitute a valuable application of this principle.

However, in all probability, it is with respect to pluralism that the existence of a substantial neutral bloc is most important. The process of decision-making in the world community requires that particular emphasis be placed on the expectation that the combinations in favor of one policy will differ from those which favor another. For example, it is inevitable that a major unit, such as the United States, will find itself allied with certain nations with respect to certain issues, and that these same allies may become their opponents on other issues. Ultimatums ("you are either for or against us all along the line") must be avoided at all costs. The direction of development should be pluralistic in this sense. To paraphrase the wording used by one important group of students of internal political process, the flexibility essential to the orderly adaptation of a system to variant situations involves the phenomenon of "cross-pressuring"; that is, it requires the participation of groups which have predilections in either of two alternative directions, and with respect to which the balance of interest may be expected to shift.[10]

What I have called the pluralistic structure of interests is an important ingredient of stability because it fragments the pressures which can influence the system at any one political decision point. In other words, a strong vested interest in the functioning of the larger system, as well as normative commitments, will serve to prevent untenable situations which require an ultimate and irreversible decision – in the extreme case, a declaration of war. Clearly, this implies the acceptance of the risk which is a concomitant of the subservience of individual interests to the procedural system.

One aspect of the significance of mutual nuclear deterrence is particularly relevant at this point. Nuclear war, with all of its implications of destruction for both sides, may well be the price to be paid for pressing a partisan case to the limit, so to speak. When relatively extreme measures are under consideration, a process does seem to obtain wherein the costs are counted – however subtle this process may be. Policy is thus deflected away from impulsive ultimatums to more particularized issues. This process can therefore be considered to represent one factor operating in the direction of the fragmentation which favors a pluralistic structure of interests. Moreover, it is applicable to neutral nations as well, in that the efforts on the part of the major parties to gain the allegiance of neutrals lead to a sort of stalemate which, in turn, prevents them from pushing coercive threats to extremes. Thus, competition is oriented toward the advantages of alliance for neutral nations, rather than threats of the dire consequences of political or ideological divergence.

The Positive Function of Ideology

For present purposes, ideology refers to the formulation of an evaluative, empirical, cognitive picture of the system in question, including the form this system may possibly take in the future. It is prerequisite of stable institutionalization that there exist a strong correlation between the implications of the value system and the diagnosis of the empirical system. Moreover, those processes which will enable a closer relationship between the empirical system and value requirements must be clearly envisioned.[11]

Those who tend to treat realistic interests as the primary basis of conflict also tend to downgrade ideology to the status of an epiphenomenon which can be safely ignored. While in some respects the Communist camp appears to assert this view with great vehemence, at the same time, in another context, they insist with equal vehemence on the importance of maintaining ideological correctness. However, among the "free" nations, too, there is a school of so-called realists who profess to believe that ideology is of little consequence. In my opinion, this constitutes a serious error.

Ideology has a dual functional significance. On the one hand, it is an educational mechanism. By enlisting the fervor which accompanies a sense of mission, it greatly facilitates the process of commitment which is an essential ingredient of institutionalization. With respect to the Communists, this involves institutionalization of the values described above, which may be summarized as the trend toward modernization. That is, a radical break with the reactionary past of the societies in the enemy camp is emphasized and dramatized. Indeed, Lenin advocated the extension of this function well beyond the earlier Marxist position, in that he stressed the importance of moving directly from what Marxists called feudalism to socialism, and omitting the intermediate bourgeois capitalism stage. In this light, Communist ideology may be interpreted as a statement of the symbolic values of modernization in which symbolic, covert gestures of reconciliation are made toward both the past and the future, within the framework of expected conflict.

The first of these gestures involves the attempt to preserve the integrity of the premodern system; and I believe that this is the primary significance of the symbol, socialism. In essence, the purpose of this device is to assure us that the process of differentiation which is inherent in modernization need not jeopardize the integrity of preindustrial community solidarity, provided the transition is carried out in such a way as to prevent the aggressive maneuvers of private interests, which are not bound by loyalty to such a community. Thus, this mechanism may be considered to facilitate recognition and acceptance of the risk-taking necessary for industrialization by asserting that these risks are limited to spheres of a lower order.

I would further interpret this aspect of Communist ideology as primarily defensive or protectionist in character, and hence to apply in a context which is not directly relevant to the polarized conflict. It is also very closely associated with basic anxieties about political democracy, since presumably this democracy would weaken preventive control over centrifugal tendencies in the community. The obverse of this, of course, is the defensive component of the counterideology, that is, the compulsive attachment to the free-enterprise formula, the fear of "creeping socialism," and the tendency to invoke authoritarian political measures, allegedly in order to safeguard our freedom.

The second component of the dual function of ideology concerns the inferior status of the rising elements, relative to those elements which are already well established. In a psychological sense, the attitude of these rising elements might be viewed as defensive; in our own frame of reference, it might be considered a variation of protectionism. Here, precisely because the core elements of the free world have already at least partially achieved the goals to which the developing nations aspire, there is a strong motivation to derogate these attainments. In ideological terms, the aim of these underdeveloped nations is not to achieve parity, but to supplant certain well-established elements of the "superior" society, for example, to substitute socialism for capitalism. The primary function of ideology in this instance is to emphasize the unique character of the socialist contribution. One rather oversimplified solution immediately comes to mind, namely, the use of opposition to maximize motivation, to define achievement as victory rather than mere goal attainment. Of course, here again the reaction of the counterideology must be considered, that is, the automatic tendency to define the success of those developing societies which are Communistically oriented as a defeat for the free world.

The direction of desirable change seems clear: ideological stresses must be minimized; those aspects of the situation which demonstrate an interest in order which transcends polarity must be underscored. One of the main themes here concerns those features which all industrial societies share in common, in contrast with previous economic and social organizations. An exposition of such features would necessarily focus on the standard of living of the masses – for obvious reasons a very sensitive area for the Communists. The features of social organization as such, particularly the differentiation of collectivities and roles, would constitute another area of focus. Still another concerns common elements at the cultural level, notably science and the arts.

This discussion has been based on an important assumption, which may seem rather vulnerable at this point. I refer to the assumption that one side has achieved a position of relative superiority in relation to the important values. The Communist goals, in terms of catching up and surpassing, may be taken as tacit proof of the validity of this assumption; however, on the other hand, their vehement assertions of the superiority of socialism and their irrational accusations of imperialism would appear to deny such gains. Thus, we must consider whether there is any prospect of dissociating these values from partisan considerations. If no such possibility exists, we must accept the fact that partisanship (as opposed to the mutual unmasking of ideological biases) cannot be transcended.

The fact that common values exist which have deep roots in the great traditions of all Western culture is one focus of leverage for such dissociation. Procedural norms and the pluralistic differentiation of interests constitute mechanisms which operate in the same direction. And we have another very important resource, namely, the contribution of social science. Insofar as the development of knowledge in this sphere is genuine and not spurious, it involves the institutionalization of norms of technical competence and genuine objectivity. To date, this process has been slow, halting, and difficult, but significant progress has been made and, hopefully, will continue in the future. On the basis of a realistic assessment of the current status of industrial societies and possible future trends of development, we can detect an element of common ground. Obviously, this mechanism will not produce dramatic consequences in immediate crisis situations, but its long-run importance should not be underestimated.[12]

Summary and Conclusions

The foregoing discussion may be summarized in a series of propositions:

1. Polarization, which is the salient characteristic of the world community at present, constitutes the primary threat to peace. However, at the same time, polarization attests to the existence of a world community and thus presents certain opportunities for the development of a more stable order within that community.

2. An effective two-party system within a relatively stable national polity constitutes a theoretical model which, while it is far from precisely applicable, is sufficiently similar to world bipolarity to provide significant clues as to methods for achieving world order.

3. The formulation of common value commitments which transcend partisan differences is one of the most important prerequisites of international order. It is my contention that, at a certain level, such a base does in fact exist in the world community, specifically with regard to the importance attached to economic development and political autonomy. This basic uniformity needs to be clearly asserted in contexts which can be dissociated from divisive ideological particularities.

4. As they are presently conceived, value concepts are too general to influence political behavior. They must be spelled out in concrete terms. Moreover, it is particularly important that they be defined in terms of norms at the level of the procedures through which they can best be implemented. A consent on the part of the opposing factions to adhere to the rules of procedure implies the assumption of risk that one's particular goal may be jeopardized, that one's adversary may be victorious with respect to particular issues. Obviously, the stronger the commitment to a particular goal, the more difficult it will become to accept this procedural risk. However, there are considerable compensations for the acceptance of such risks; these risks enable gains which would be prohibited, or at least greatly deterred, by a go-it-alone policy. At many different points in the development of social structures, this has been accomplished by processes of differentiation. It can be promoted deliberately in many ways.

5. One of the main threats to stability stems from the monolithic concentration of interests on partisan all-or-none goal striving. The mitigation of this threat is, in part, dependent on the differentiation of interests in a pluralistic direction, so that a sufficiently important proportion will cut across the lines of partisan division. Procedural mechanisms tend to favor this process of differentiation and hence to increase pluralism. In this connection, the existence of sufficiently strong neutral elements which can form particularized ties in either direction is important. Under the proper conditions, neutralism should not be deplored, but welcomed.

6. Ideology is essentially a defensive or protective mechanism. However, it does have important positive functions in a world community, in that it cushions the inevitable severe strains which are inherent in the process of modernization. However, its tendency toward intransigence must be counteracted. This may be

accomplished by dissociating value consensus from ideological difference, on the one hand, and, on the other hand, by objective scientific diagnosis of empirical situations, which tend to be presented in selected and distorted versions in ideological discussion.

7. Progress toward institutionalizing the normative framework of the world community, and the attendant web of pluralistic interests, depends on a balanced combination of various measures which are in accord with inherent trends, rather than one dramatic set of measures. Acute crises may be handled by single dramatic measures, but this balance is essential to our prospects over the long term.

It is my opinion, therefore, that Western policy should include each of the four components formulated in propositions 3 through 6 above. These include, first, the assertion of common values in ways which minimize the self-righteous implication that only we are true to these values, that our opponents are not; second, the promotion of procedural innovations, even though by so doing we are likely to suffer defeat on particular issues; third, the promotion of those opportunities which are likely to develop ties of solidarity both with Iron Curtain countries on specific divergent issues, and, above all, with neutral nations, even though they may be dealing simultaneously with the opposition in regard to other issues; and, finally, the use of social science to develop the most competent analyses possible at the present state of our knowledge of social and political systems throughout the world.

The hypothesis put forth in this paper lacks specificity because it stresses the balance between a plurality of factors. Moreover, it must be regarded as a preliminary sketch, rather than the sum of a carefully developed set of proposals. I have stated repeatedly that under the proper conditions a given factor, such as the establishment of procedural norms, or the pluralization of interests through the appeal to neutral elements, might be expected to work in the desired direction. A few suggestions as to these "proper conditions" have been delineated in the course of the discussion. But space forbids a full description of such conditions at the desired level of concreteness. (To a great extent, they probably are not known and can only be elucidated through further research.) In conclusion, then, the foregoing discussion does not purport to provide an infallible prescription for effective foreign policy. Rather, it purports to outline a theoretical framework within which, given the proper specification, a type of policy which has a better chance for success could be formulated. The careful delineation of such a policy would require a great deal of theoretical and empirical groundwork, which would obviously extend far beyond the limits of this paper.

Notes

1   Cf. S. M. Lipset, *Political Man* (Garden City, NY: Doubleday, 1960), and my review article in *World Politics* (October, 1960).
2   See Walt W. Rostow, *Theory of Economic Growth* (Cambridge: Cambridge University Press, 1960).

3   See Robert N. Bellah, *Tokugawa Religion* (Glencoe, IL: The Free Press, 1958).

4   See Alexander Gerschenkron, "Problems and Patterns of Russian Economic Development" in Cyril Black (ed.), *The Transformation of Russian Society: Aspects of Social Change Since 1861* (Cambridge, MA: Harvard University Press, 1960), pp. 42–72.

5   This is a scheme developed by the author in various publications. See, in particular, "An Approach to the Sociology of Knowledge," *Proceedings of the Fourth World Congress of Sociology, IV* (1959).

6   For example, their refusal to participate in the international copyright convention.

7   For example, the proposed repeal of the Connally amendment to the World Court Statute.

8   An excellent example of a suggestion for a procedural device outside the framework of the United Nations is T. C. Schelling's proposal of a "special surveillance force." See pp. 87–105 of Q. Wright et al. (eds), *Preventing World War III* (New York: Simon & Schuster, 1961).

9   See William Kornhauser, *The Politics of Mass Society* (Glencoe, IL: The Free Press, 1959), and my review article in *World Politics* (October, 1960).

10   See Bernard Berelson, Paul F. Lazarsfeld, and William McPhee, *Voting: A Study of Opinion Formation in a Presidential Campaign* (Chicago: University of Chicago Press, 1954).

11   See Parsons, "An Approach to the Sociology of Knowledge," *op. cit.*

12   At the International Sociological Congress at Stresa, Italy, in September, 1959, the leader of the Soviet Delegation, Professor P. N. Fedoseav, stated that his colleagues proposed to demonstrate the superiority of socialism by empirical research. This constitutes submitting one's case to an objective judgment, that of competent peers, with the implicit possibility that one may be shown to be wrong. It is another version of the supercession of intransigent assertion of particular goal-commitments, by acceptance of a procedural mechanism, including exposure to the risks inherent in such a system.

14

Youth in the Context of American Society

The passage of time has recently been symbolized by the fact that we have elected the first President of the United States to be born in the twentieth century – indeed, well inside it. It is perhaps equally relevant to remark that we have recently entered an era in which a substantial proportion of current youth (rather than children) will experience a major part of their active lives in the twenty-first century. Thus a sixteen-year-old of today will be only fifty-five at the coming turn of the century.

It is possible that the twentieth century will be characterized by future historians as one of the centuries of turmoil and transition – in the modern history of the West, perhaps most analogous to the seventeenth. It is also likely, however, that it will be judged as one of the great creative centuries, in which major stages of the process of building a new society, a new culture, will have occurred. The tremendous developments in the sciences and in the technologies deriving from them, the quite new levels of industrialization, and the spread of the industrial pattern from its places of origin, together with the long series of "emancipations" (e.g., women's suffrage and the rapid decline of colonialism) will presumably figure prominently among its achievements. At the same time, it clearly has been and will probably continue to be a century of turmoil, not one of the placid enjoyment of prior accomplishment, but of challenge and danger. It is in this broad perspective that I should like to sketch some of the problems of American youth, as the heirs of the next phase of our future, with both its opportunities and its difficulties.

In the course of this century, the United States has emerged at the forefront of the line of general development, not only because of its wealth and political power but also – more importantly in the present context – because it displays the type of social organization that belongs to the future. Since during the same period and only a little behind our own stage of progress a somewhat differing and competing version has also emerged in the Communist societies, it is not surprising that there is high tension at both political and ideological levels. Obviously, the meaning of American society presents a world-wide problem, not least to its own citizens and in turn to its younger ones: since they have the longest future ahead of them, they have the most at stake.

Some Salient Characteristics of American Society

Before we take up the specific situation of youth, it will be best to sketch a few of the main features of our society and the ideological discussions about them, with special reference to their effect on youth. The structural characteristic usually emphasized is industrialism. It is certainly true that the United States has developed industrial organization and productivity farther than any other society in history. Not only has it done this on a massive scale, both as regards population and area, but it has also attained by far the highest levels of per-capita productivity yet known. The salience of industrialism in turn emphasizes the economic aspects of social structure: a high evaluation of productivity, the free enterprise system, with the private, profit-oriented business firm as a conspicuous unit of organization, and with private consumption prominent in the disposal of the products of industry. This last feature includes both the high levels of current family income and what may be called the "capitalization" of households through the spread of home ownership, the development of consumer durable goods, and the like.

It would be misleading, however, to overstress this economic aspect. Economic development itself depends on many noneconomic conditions, and economic and noneconomic aspects are subtly interwoven in many ways. The same period (roughly, the present century) which has seen the enormous growth of industrial productivity has also seen a very large relative, as well as absolute, growth in the organization and functions of government. The largest growth of all, of course, is in the armed services, but by no means only there. State and local governments have also expanded. Another prominent development has been that of the legal system, which is interstitial between governmental and nongovernmental sectors of society. I mean here not only legislation and the functioning of courts of law but also the private legal profession, with professional lawyers employed in government in various capacities.

A consideration of the legal profession leads to one of the learned professions in general, the educational organizations in which men are trained, and the cultural systems that form the basis of their competence. The most important development has been the growth of the sciences and their application, not only in industry and the military field but also in many others, notably, that of health. Though they are behind their physical and biological sister disciplines, the sciences dealing with human behavior in society have made very great advances, to an altogether new level. To take only the cruder indices, they have grown enormously in the numbers of trained personnel, in the volume of publications, in the amount of research funds devoted to their pursuit, and the like. All this would not have been possible without a vast expansion of the educational system, relatively greatest at the highest levels. By any quantitative standard, the American population today is by far the most highly educated of any large society known to history – and it is rapidly becoming more so.

Furthermore, this has become in the first instance a society of large organizations, though the tenacious survival of small units (in agriculture, but more broadly in retail trade and various other fields) is a striking fact. (It is important to note that the large organization has many features that are independent of whether it operates in private industry, in government, or in the private non-profit sector.) It is also a highly urbanized society. Less than ten percent of its labor force is engaged in agriculture, and more than half the population lives in metropolitan areas, urban communities that are rapidly expanding and changing their character.

It is also a society with a great mobility as to persons, place of residence, and social and economic status. It is a society that within about eighty years has assimilated a tremendous number of immigrants, who, though overwhelmingly European in origin, came from a great diversity of national, cultural, and religious backgrounds. Their descendants have increasingly become full Americans, and increasingly widely dispersed in the social structure, including its higher reaches. After all, the current President of the United States is the grandson of Irish immigrants and the first Catholic to occupy that office.

Overriding all these features is the fact that this is a rapidly developing society. There are good reasons for supposing that rapid change is generally a source of unsettlement and confusion, particularly accentuated perhaps if the change is not guided by a set of sharply defined master symbols that tell just what the change is about. The American process of change is of this type; but we can also say that it is not a state of nearly random confusion but in the main is a coherently directional process. Since it is not centrally directed or symbolized, however, it is particularly important to understand its main pattern.

There has been the obvious aspect of growth that is expressed in sheer scale, such as the size of the population, the magnitude and complexity of organization. At the more specifically social levels, however, I should like to stress certain features of the process that may help to make the situation of American youth (as well as other phenomena of our time) more understandable. On the one hand, at the level of the predominant pattern, our value system has remained relatively stable. On the other hand, relative to the value system, there has been a complex process of change, of which structural differentiation is perhaps the most important single feature. It is associated, however, with various others, which I shall call "extending exclusiveness," "normative upgrading," and "an increasing conceptualization of value patterns on the general level." These are all technical terms which, if they are not to be regarded as sociological jargon, need to be elucidated.

Values generally are patterned conceptions of the qualities of meaning of the objects of human experiences; by virtue of these qualities, the objects are considered desirable for the evaluating persons. Among such objects is the type of society considered to be good, not only in some abstract sense but also for "our kind of people" as members of it. The value patterns that play a part in controlling action in a society are in the first instance the conceptions of the good type of society to which the members of that society are committed. Such a pattern exists at a very high level of generality, without any specification of functions, or any level of internal differentiation, or particularities of situation.

In my own work it has proved useful to formulate the dominant American value pattern at this very general level as one of *instrumental activism*. Its cultural grounding lies in moral and (eventually) religious orientations, which in turn derive directly from Puritan traditions. The relevance of the pattern extends through all three of the religious, moral, and societal levels, as well as to others that cannot be detailed here. It is most important to keep them distinct, in particular, the difference between the moral and the societal levels.

In its religious aspect, instrumental activism is based on the pattern Max Weber called "inner-worldly asceticism," the conception of man's role as an instrument of the divine will in building a kingdom of God on earth. Through a series of steps, both in internal cultural development and in institutionalization (which cannot be detailed here), this has produced a conception of the human condition in which the individual is committed to maximal effort in the interest of valued *achievement* under a system of normative order. This system is in the first instance moral, but also, at the societal level, it is embodied in legal norms. Achievement is conceived in "rational" terms, which include the maximal objective understanding of the empirical conditions of action, as well as the faithful adherence to normative commitments. It is of great importance that, once institutionalized, the fulfillment of such a value pattern need not be motivated by an explicit recognition of its religious groundings.

One way of describing the pattern in its moral aspects is to say that it is fundamentally individualistic. It tends to maximize the desirability of autonomy and responsibility in the individual. Yet this is an institutionalized individualism, in that it is normatively controlled at the moral level in two ways. First, it is premised on the conception of human existence as serving ends or functions beyond those of physical longevity, or health, or the satisfication of the psychological needs of the personality apart from these value commitments. In a sense, it is the building of the "good life," not only for the particular individual but also for all mankind – a life that is accounted as desirable, not merely desired. This includes commitment to a good society. Second, to implement these moral premises, it is necessary for the autonomous and responsible achievements of the individual to be regulated by a normative order – at this level, a moral law that defines the relations of various contributions and the patterns of distributive justice.

The society, then, has a dual meaning, from this moral point of view. On the one hand, it is perhaps the primary field in which valued achievement is possible for the individual. In so far as it facilitates such achievements, the society is a good one. On the other hand, the building of the good society (that is, its progressive improvement) is the primary goal of valued action – along with such cultural developments as are intimately involved in social progress, such as science. To the individual, therefore, the most important goal to which he can orient himself is a contribution to the good society.

The value pattern I am outlining is activistic, therefore, in that it is oriented toward control or mastery of the human condition, as judged by moral standards. It is not a doctrine of passive adjustment to conditions, but one of active adaptation. On the other hand, it is instrumental with reference to the source of moral legitimation, in the sense that human achievement is not conceived as an end in itself but as a means to goals beyond the process and its immediate outcome.

This value pattern implies that the society is meant to be a developing, evolving entity. It is meant to develop in the direction of progressive "improvement." But this development is to be through the autonomous initiative and achievements of its units – in the last analysis, individual persons. It is therefore a society which places heavy responsibilities (in the form of expectations) on its individual members. At the same time, it subjects them to two very crucial sets of limitations which have an important bearing on the problem of youth.

One of these concerns the "moralism" of the value system – the fact that individualism is bound within a strongly emphasized framework of normative order. The achievement, the success, of the individual must ideally be in accord with the rules, above all, with those which guarantee opportunity to all, and which keep the system in line with its remoter values. Of course, the more complex the society, the greater the difficulty of defining the requisite norms, a difficulty which is greatly compounded by rapid change. Furthermore, in the interest of effectiveness, achievement must often be in the context of the collective organization, thus further limiting autonomy.

The second and for present purposes an even more crucial limitation is that it is in the nature of such a system that it is not characterized by a single, simple, paramount goal for the society as a system. The values legitimize a *direction* of change, not a terminal state. Furthermore, only in the most general sense is this direction "officially" defined, with respect to such famous formulae as liberty, democracy, general welfare, and distributive justice. The individual is left with a great deal of responsibility, not only for achieving *within* the institutionalized normative order, but for his own interpretation of its meaning and of his obligations in and to it.

Space forbids detailing the ramifications of this value system. Instead, it is necessary to my analysis to outline briefly the main features of the process of social change mentioned above. The suggestion is that the main pattern of values has been and probably will continue to be stable, but that the structure of the society, including its subsystem values at lower levels, has in the nature of the case been involved in a rapid and far-reaching process of change. This centers on the process of differentiation, but very importantly it also involves what we have referred to as inclusion, upgrading, and increasing generalization. I shall confine my discussion here to the structure of the society, though this in turn is intimately connected with problems concerned with the personality of the individual, including his personal values.

Differentiation refers to the process by which simple structures are divided into functionally differing components, these components becoming relatively independent of one another, and then recombined into more complex structures in which the functions of the differentiated units are complementary. A key example in the development of industrial society everywhere is the differentiation, at the collectivity level, of the unit of economic production from the kinship household. Obviously, in peasant economies, production is carried out by and in the household. The development of employing organizations which are structurally distinct from any household is the key new structural element. This clearly means a loss of function to the old undifferentiated unit, but also a gain in autonomy, though this in turn involves a new dependency, because the household can no longer be self-subsistent. The classical formula is that the productive services of certain members (usually the adult males) have been alienated from the organization directly responsible for subsistence and thus lost to the household, which then depends on money income from occupational earnings and in turn on the markets for consumers' goods.

These losses, however, are not without their compensations: the gain in the productivity of the economy and in the standard of living of the household. This familiar paradigm has to be generalized so as to divest it of its exclusively economic features and show it as the primary characterization of a very general process of social change. First, it is essential to point out that it always operates simultaneously in both collectivities and individual roles. Thus, in the example just given, a new type of productive organization which is not a household or (on more complex levels) even a family farm has to be developed. The local community no longer consists only of farm households but also of nonproducing households and productive units – e.g., firms. Then the same individual (the head of the household) has a dual role as head of the family and as employee in a producing unit (the case of the individual enterpreneur is a somewhat special one).

By the extension of inclusiveness, I mean that, once a step of differentiation has been established, there is a tendency to extend the new pattern to increasing proportions of the relevant population of units. In the illustrative case, the overwhelming tendency that has operated for well over a century has been to reduce the proportion of households which are even in part economically self-sufficient, in the sense of a family farm, in favor of those whose members are gainfully employed outside the household. This is a principal aspect of the spread of industrialization and urbanization. The same logic applies to newly established educational standards, e.g., the expectation that a secondary-school education will be normal for the whole age cohort.

Normative upgrading means a type of change in the normative order, to which the operation of units, both individual and collective, is subject. It is a shift from the prescription of rules by a special class or unit in a special situation to more generalized norms having to do with more inclusive classes of units in wider ranges of situations. Thus the law that specifies that a railway engine must be equipped with a steam whistle to give warning at crossings has by court interpretation been generalized to include any effective warning signal (since oil-burning locomotives are not equipped with steam).[1] But in a sense parallel to that in which differentiation leads to alienation from the older unit, normative upgrading means that the unit is left with a problem, since the rules no longer give such concretely unequivocal guidance to what is expected. If the rule is general enough, its application to a particular situation requires interpretation. Such upgrading, we contend, is a necessary concomitant of the process of differentiation.

When we speak of norms, we mean rules applying to particular categories of units in a system, operating in particular types of situations. For example, individual adults may not be employed under conditions which infringe on certain basic freedoms of the individual. The repercussions of a step in differentiation, however, cannot be confined to this level; they must also involve some part of the value system; this is to say, the functions of the differentiated categories of units, which are now different from one another, must not only be regulated but also legitimized. To use our example again, it cannot be true that the whole duty of the fathers of families is to gain subsistence for their households through making the household itself productive, but it becomes legitimate to support the household by earning a money income through work for an outside employer and among other things to be absent from the household many hours a week. At the collectivity level, therefore, a business that is not the direct support of a household (such as farming) must be a legitimate way of life – that is, the unit that employs labor for such purposes, without itself being a household, must be legitimate. This requires defining the values in terms sufficiently general to include both the old and the new way of life.

The values must therefore legitimize a structural complex by which economic production and the consumption needs of households are met simultaneously – that is, both the labor markets and the markets for consumers' goods. For example, this structural complex is of focal importance in the modern (as distinguished from medieval) urban community. The value attitude that regards the rural or the handicraft way of life as morally superior to the modern urban and – if you will – industrial way (a common attitude in the Western world of today) is an example of the failure of the adequate value generalization that is an essential part of institutionalizing the process of structural change.

To sum up, we may state that both the nature of the American value pattern and the nature of the process of change going on in the society make for considerable difficulties in the personal adjustment of individuals. On the one hand, our type of activism, with its individualistic emphases, puts a heavy responsibility for autonomous achievement on the individual. On the other hand, it subjects him to important limitations: he must not only be regulated by norms and the necessity of working cooperatively, in collective contexts; he must also interpret his own responsibilities and the rules to which he is subject. Beyond that, ours is a society which in the nature of its values cannot have a single clear-cut societal goal which can be dramatically symbolized. The individual is relegated to contributions which are relatively specialized, and it is not always easy to see their bearing on the larger whole. Furthermore, the general erosion of traditional culture and symbols, which is inseparable from a scientific age, makes inadequate many of the old formulae once used to give meaning and legitimation to our values and achievements. This is perhaps true in particular of the older religious grounding of our values.

Not unrelated to these considerations is the very fact of the *relative* success of the society in developing in relation to its values. Not only is there a high general standard of living, which, it should be remembered, means the availability of facilities for *whatever* uses are valued; e.g., increased income may allow for attending prize fights or symphony concerts – a not inconsiderable amount has been going into the latter channel. There is certainly a much better standard of minimum welfare and general distributive justice now than in our past. However much remains to be done, and it is clearly considerable, it is no longer possible to contend that poverty, misery, preventable illness, etc., are the primary lot of the average American. Indeed, the accent has shifted to our duty to the less favored portions of the world. Furthermore, for the average individual, it is probable that opportunity is more widely open than in any large-scale society in history to secure education, access to historically validated cultural goods, and the like. But perhaps it can be seen that, in the light of this all too brief analysis, the great problem has come to be, what to do with all these advantages – not, as has so often been true, how to avoid the worst disasters and take a few modest little steps forward.[2] To be sure, there is a very real danger of the collapse of all civilization through nuclear war; but somehow that danger fails to deter people from making significant investments in the future, not only for themselves as individuals, but also for the society as a whole.

The Position of American Youth

It is in this broad picture of the American social structure and its development that I should like to consider the position of American youth. Contrary to prevalent views that mainly stress the rising standard of living and the allegedly indulgent and easy life, I think it is legitimate to infer that the general trend of development of the society has been and will continue to be one which, by and large, puts greater rather than diminished demands on its average individual citizen – with some conspicuous exceptions. He must operate in more complex situations than before. He attempts to do many things his predecessors never attempted, that indeed were beyond their capacities. To succeed in what he attempts, he has to exercise progressively higher levels of competence and responsibility. These inferences seem to me inescapable when full account of the nature of the society and its main trends of development is taken.

If capacities and relevant opportunities developed as rapidly as do demands, it would follow that life on the average would be neither more nor less difficult. There seems reason to believe that if anything demands have tended somewhat to outrun the development of capacities – especially those for orienting to normatively complex situations – and in some respects even opportunities, and that this is a major source of the current unrest and malaise. My broad contention, taking due account of the process of change just outlined, is that this society, however, is one that is relatively well organized and integrated with reference to its major values and its major trends of development. If those values are intact and are by and large shared by the younger generation (there seems to be every indication that they are), then it ought to be a society in which they can look forward to a good life. In so far as their mood is one of bewilderment, frustration, or whatever, one should look for relatively specific sources of difficulty rather than to a generalized malintegration of the society as a whole.

It may be well to set the tone of the following analysis by an example of the ways in which current common sense can often misinterpret phenomena that raise distressing problems. American society, of course, is known for its high divorce rate. Until the peak following World War II, moreover, the trend was upward throughout the century, though since then it has appreciably declined. This divorce rate has widely been interpreted as an index of the "disintegration of the family" and, more importantly, of the levels of moral responsibility of married persons.

That it results in increased numbers of broken families is of course true, though the seriousness of this is mitigated by the fact that most divorces occur between childless couples and that most divorced persons remarry, a large proportion stably. In any case, the proportion of the population of marriageable age that is married and living with their spouses is now the highest it has been in the history of the census.

The main point, however, is that this point of view fails to take into account the increased strain put on the marriage relationship in the modern situation. In effect, it says, since an increased proportion fail in a difficult task relative to those who previously failed in an easier task, this increased rate of failures is an index of a declining level of responsibility; seen in this light, this interpretation is palpably absurd, but if the underlying situation is not analyzed, it is plausible.

The increased difficulty of the task has two main aspects. One is the increased differentiation of the nuclear family from other structures in which it was formerly embedded, notably the farm and other household or family enterprises from which economic support was derived. This differentiation deprives the family and the marriage relationship within it of certain bases of structural support. This is clearly related to the component of freedom mentioned above; the freedom of choice of marriage partners is clearly related to the spread of the view that really serious incompatibility may justify breaking the marriage tie.

The other factor is the enhanced level of expectation in functioning outside the family for both adults and children. For adults, particularly men, the central obligation concerns the levels of responsibility and competence required by their jobs; for children, these requirements of growing up in a more complex and competitive world, going farther in education, and undertaking substantially more autonomous responsibility along the way impose greater demands than before. It is my impression that the cases in which marriage was undertaken irresponsibly are no more numerous than in any other time, and that divorce is not often lightly resorted to but is a confession of failure in an undertaking in which both parties have usually tried very hard to succeed.[3]

I cite this example because it is a conspicuous special case of the more general considerations I wish to discuss. The first keynote here is the rising general level of expectations. The primary reference point, of course, is that of adult roles at their peak of responsibility in middle age. The most prominent example is that of the higher levels of masculine occupational roles, in which (in those with technical emphasis) the requisite levels of training and technical competence are continually rising. With respect to managerial roles, the size and complexity of organizations is increasing, and hence the requirements necessary for their successful management also. Similar things, however, are true in various other fields. Thus the whole range of associational affairs requires membership support for leadership as well as responsible leadership itself, both of which involve complicated responsibilities. These range from the many private associations and "good causes" through participation on boards and staffs (including university departments and faculties) to participation through voting and other forms of exercising public responsibility.

The family in this context is a further case. The feminine role is typically anchored in the first instance in the family. Family duties may not be more onerous in such senses as drudgery and hard work than they were, but they involve a higher level of competence and responsibility, particularly, though not exclusively, in the field of the psychological management of both children and husbands, as well as of selves – the latter because wives are now far more autonomous on the average than they were. What we may call the independence training of children is more delicate and difficult than was the older type of training in strict obedience – that is, if autonomy for the young is to be accompanied by high levels of self-discipline and responsibility. But in addition, the typical married woman participates far more extensively outside the home than she formerly did, and in particular she forms a rapidly increasing propor- tion in the labor force.

Perhaps the central repercussion of this general upgrading of expectations (and hence of the norms with which conformity is expected) on the situation of youth is in the field of formal education. Here, of course, there has been a steady process of lengthening the average period of schooling, with the minimum satisfactory norm for all approaching the completion of high school, while nearly forty percent of the total age cohort now enter college, and a steadily increasing percentage complete college. Finally, by far the most rapidly growing sector has been that of postgraduate professional education. Uneven as standards are, and unsatisfactory as they are at many points, there is no solid evidence of a general tendency to deterioration and much evidence of their improvement, especially in the best schools at all levels.[4]

It seems fair, then, to conclude that in getting a formal education the average young American is undertaking a more difficult, and certainly a longer, job than his father or mother did, and that it is very likely that he is working harder at it. A growing proportion is prolonging formal education into the early adult years, thus raising important problems about marriage, financial independence, and various other considerations.

Furthermore, he is doing this in a context in which, both within and outside the school, he must assume more autonomous responsibility than did his pre- decessors. In the school itself – and in college – the slow though gradual trend has been in the direction of a mildly "progressive" type of education, with a diminution of the amount of drill and learning by rote. In certain respects, parents have grown distinctly more permissive within the family and with regard to their children's activities outside. This throws an important stress on the child's relations to his age peers, one that becomes particularly important in adolescence. This is the area least under adult control, in which deviant ten- dencies can most readily be mutually reinforced, without being immediately checked by adult intervention. This is to say that in general the educational process puts increased demands on the younger group.

Three other factors seem involved in this situation of strain from the com- bination of enhanced expectations and autonomy. They concern one aspect of the psychological preparation for the tasks of maturing, one aspect of the choices that are open, and one aspect of the situation with reference to normat- ive regulation.

First, with respect to psychological preparation, there seems to have been a trend within the family to *increase* the dependency of the young pre-oedipal child, particularly on the mother, of course. This trend is the consequence of the structural isolation of the nuclear family. There is less likelihood of there being close relatives either directly in the home or having very intensive and continual contact with the family. For middle-class families, the virtual disappearance of the domestic servant has also left less room for a division of responsibility for child care. Further, the proportion of very large families with five or more children has been sharply decreasing, while those with three and four children have been increasing. All these factors contribute to a concentration of relationships within the family and of the parents' (especially the mother's) sanctioning powers – both disciplinary and rewarding.

Psychological theory, however, indicates that under the proper circumstances this enhanced dependency contributes to developing motivations for high levels of achievement. These circumstances include high levels of aspiration for the child on the part of the parents and the use of the proper types of discipline. The essential point is that high dependency provides a very strong motivation to please the parent. This in turn can be used to incite him to learn what the parent sets him, if he is suitably rewarded by parental approval. The general findings of studies on the types of discipline used in middle-class families – the use of the withdrawal of love and approval as the predominant type of negative sanction – seem to fit in this picture.

The dependency components of motivation, however, are seldom if ever fully extinguished. The balance is so delicate in their relation to the autonomous components that it is easily upset, and in many cases this is a source of considerable strain. Attempting to maintain this balance, for example, may very well contribute to the great increase in the practice of "going steady" and its relation to the trend to early marriages. Emerging in adolescence, the dyadic heterosexual relation is the main component of the relational system of youth that articulates most directly with the earlier dependency complex – though some of it may also be expressed in same-sex peer groups, and indeed in "crushes" on the teacher. It is striking that the main trend seems to be toward intensive, and not merely erotic but diffuse, dyadic relations, rather than to sexual libertinism. This is in turn reflected in the emotional intensity of the marriage relationship and hence in the elements of potential strain underlying the problem of divorce.

This brings me to the second of the factors mentioned above, the range of choices open. A progressive increase in this range is a consequence of the general process of social change sketched above, namely, differentiation in the structure of the society. As this process goes on, types of interest, motivation, and evaluation that were embedded in a less differentiated complex come to be separated out, to become more autonomous and more visible in that they are freed from more ascriptive types of control. Ties to class and family, to local community and region become more flexible and hence often "expendable" as more choices become available.

One of the most conspicuous cases in relation to the present interest is the erotic component of sex relations. In an earlier phase of our society, it was rather rigidly controlled even within marriage, indeed, not infrequently it was partially suppressed. The process by which it has become differentiated, allowing much greater freedom in this area, is closely related to the differentiation of function and the structural isolation of the nuclear family.[5] In a society in which autonomous freedom is so widespread, there is much greater freedom in this field as in many others, not only in practice but also in portrayals on the stage, in the movies and television, and in the press, magazines, and books.

In this connection, since much of the newer freedom is illegitimate in relation to the older standards (normative upgrading and value generalization take time), it is very difficult to draw lines between the areas of new freedom in process of being legitimated and the types which are sufficiently dysfunctional, even in the new state of society, so that the probability is they will be controlled or even suppressed. The adolescent in our society is faced with difficult problems of choice and evaluation in areas such as this, because an adequate codification of the norms governing many of these newly emancipated areas has not yet been developed.

The third factor, that of normative regulations, is essentially a generalization of the second factor. We have maintained (though of course without documentation) that, contrary to various current opinions, the basic pattern of American values has not changed. Value patterns, however, are only part of the normative culture of the society. At the lower levels, both at the more specific levels of values and of what we technically call norms, it is in the nature of the type of process of change we have been discussing that there should be a continual reorganization of the normative system. Unfortunately, this does not occur as an instantaneous adjustment to the major innovations, but is a slow, uneven, and often painful process. In its course, at any one time (as we have noted), there are important elements of indeterminacy in the structure of expectations – not simply in the sense that there are areas of freedom in which autonomous decision is expected, but also in the sense that, where people feel there ought to be guidance, it is either lacking altogether, or the individual is subject to conflicting expectations that are impossible to fulfill all at once. This is the condition that some sociologists, following Durkheim, call *anomie*.

There seems to be an important reason why this source of strain and disturbance bears rather more heavily on the younger generation than on others. This is owing to the fact that the major agents for initiating processes of change lie in other sectors of the society, above all, in large-scale organization, in the developments of science and technology, in the higher political processes, and in the higher ranges of culture. Their impact tends to spread, and there is a time lag in change between the locations of primary change and the other parts of the social structure.

Though there is of course much unevenness, it seems correct to say that, with one major exception, the social structures bearing most directly on youth are likely to be rather far down the line in the propagation of the effects of change. These are the family and the school, and they are anchored in the local residential community. The major exception is the college, and still more, the university, which is one of the major loci of innovation and which can involve its students in the process more directly.

By and large, it seems fair to suggest that adults are on the average probably more conservative in their parental roles than when their children are not involved, and that this is typical of most of their roles outside the family. Similarly, schools, especially elementary and secondary schools, are on the whole probably more conservative in most respects than are the organizations that employ the fathers of their children. In the present phase of social development, another important institution of the residential community, the parish church or synagogue, is probably distinctly on the conservative side as a rule.

This would suggest that, partly as a matter of generation lag, partly for more complex reasons of the sort indicated, the adult agencies on which the youth most depends tend to some extent to be "out of tune" with what he senses to be the most advanced developments of the time. He senses that he is put in an unfair dilemma by having to be so subject to their control.

If we are right in thinking that special pressures operate on the younger generation relative to the general pressures generated by social change, on the other side of the relationship there are factors which make for special sensitivities on their part. The residua of early dependency, as pointed out above, constitute one such factor. In addition, the impact on youth of the general process of social differentiation makes for greater differences between their position and that of children, on the one hand, and that of adults, on the other, than is true in less differentiated societies. Compared to our own past or to most other societies, there is a more pronounced, and above all (as noted) an increasingly long segregation of the younger groups, centered above all on the system of formal education. It may be argued especially that the impact of this process is particularly pronounced at the upper fringe of the youth period, for the rapidly increasing proportion of the age cohort engaged in higher education – in college, and, very importantly, in postgraduate work. These are people who are adults in all respects except for the element of dependency, since they have not yet attained full occupational independence.

The Youth Culture

The question may now be raised as to how young people react to this type of situation. Obviously, it is a highly variegated one and therefore occasions much diversity of behavior, but there are certain broad patterns which can be distinguished. These may be summed up under the conception, now familiar to social scientists, of a relatively differentiated "youth culture." Perhaps S. N. Eisenstadt is its most comprehensive student, certainly in its comparative perspective.[6]

It is Eisenstadt's contention that a distinctive pattern of values, relationships, and behavior for youth tends to appear and become more or less institutionalized in societies that develop a highly universalistic pattern of organization at the levels of adult role involvements. Since all lives start in the family, which is a highly particularistic type of structure, there is not only the difficulty of rising to higher levels within the same type of relationship system, but also of learning to adjust to a very different type. What has been discussed above as the enhancement of dependency in early childhood is a special case of this general proposition. Totalitarian societies attempt to bring this period under stringent centralized control through officially organized, adult-directed youth organizations such as the Soviet *Komsomols,* or earlier, the *Hitlerjugend.* In democratic societies, however, it tends to be relatively free, though in our own it is rather closely articulated with the system of formal education through a ramifying network of extracurricular activities.

As a consequence of youth's being exposed to such strains, it might be expected that youth culture would manifest signs of internal conflict and that it would incorporate elements of conformity as well as of alienation and revolt. In nonrational, psychological terms, rather than in terms of rational aims, youth culture attempts to balance its need for conforming to the expectations of the adult agencies most directly involved (parents and the local residential community) with some kind of outlet for tension and revolt and with some sensitivity to the winds of change above and beyond its local situation.

For two reasons, one would expect to find the fullest expression of these trends at the level of the peer group. For one thing, this group is the area of greatest immunity to adult control; indeed, the range of its freedom in this respect is particularly conspicuous in the American case. The other reason is that this is the area to which it is easiest to displace the elements of dependency generated in early experience in the family – on the one hand, because the strong stress on autonomy precludes maintaining too great an overt dependence on parents or other adult agencies, and, on the other, because the competitive discipline of school achievement enforces autonomous responsibility in this area. The peer group then gradually differentiates into two components, one focusing on the cross-sex relationship and one focusing on "activities," some of which occur within the one-sex group, others, relatively nonerotic, in mixed groups.

In general, the most conspicuous feature of the youth peer group is a duality of orientation. On the one hand, there tends to be a compulsive independence in relation to certain adult expectations, a touchy sensitivity to control, which in certain cases is expressed in overt defiance. On the other hand, within the group, there tends to be a fiercely compulsive conformity, a sharp loyalty to the group, an insistence on the literal observance of its norms, and punishment of deviance. Along with this goes a strong romantic streak. This has been most conspicuous in the romantic love theme in the cross-sex relationship, but it is also more generalized, extending to youth-culture heroes such as athletes and group leaders of various sorts, and sometimes to objects of interest outside the youth situation.

It is my impression (not easy to document) that important shifts of emphasis in American youth culture have occurred in the last generation. For the main trend, notably the increasingly broad band we think of as middle class, there has been a considerable relaxation of tension in both the two essential reference directions, toward parents and toward school expectations – though this relaxation is distinctly uneven. In the case of the school, there is a markedly greater acceptance of the evaluation of good school work and its importance for the future. This, of course, is associated with the general process of educational upgrading, particularly with the competition to enter good colleges and, at the next level, especially for students at the better colleges, to be admitted to graduate schools. The essential point, however, is that this increased pressure has been largely met with a positive response rather than with rebellion or passive withdrawal. The main exception is in the lowest sector, where the pattern of delinquency is most prominent and truancy a major feature. This is partly understandable as a direct consequence of the upgrading of educational expectations, because it puts an increased pressure on those who are disadvantaged by a combination of low ability, a nonsupportive family or ethnic background.

As to youth's relation to the family, it seems probable that the institutionalizing of increased permissiveness for and understanding of youth-culture activities is a major factor. The newer generation of parents is more firmly committed to a policy of training serious independence. It tolerates more freedom, and it expects higher levels of performance and responsibility. Further, it is probably true that the development of the pattern of "going steady" has drained off some tension into semi-institutionalized channels – tension formerly expressed in wilder patterns of sexual behavior. To be sure, this creates a good many problems, not only as to how far the partners will go in their own erotic relations, but also possibly premature commitments affecting future marriage. It may be that the pendulum has swung too far and that adjustments are to be expected.

Within this broad framework, the question of the content of peer-group interests is important. What I have called the romantic trend can be broadly expressed in two directions; the tentative terms "regressive" and "progressive" are appropriate, if not taken too literally. Both components are normally involved in such a situation, but their proportions and content may vary. They derive specifically from the general paradigm of social change outlined above, the former, at social levels, tending to resist change, the latter to anticipate and promote it.

One of the most striking interests of American youth culture has been in masculine physical prowess, expressed in particular in athletics. It seems quite clear that there has been a declining curve in this respect, most conspicuous in the more elite schools and colleges, but on the whole it is a very general one, except for the cult of violence in the delinquent sector. The cult of physical prowess has clearly been a reflex of the pressure to occupational achievement in a society in which brains rather than brawn come increasingly to count. From this point of view, it is a regressive phenomenon.

The indication is that the lessened concentration on this cult is an index of greater acceptance of the general developmental trend. Alcohol and sex are both in a somewhat different category. For the individual, they are fields of emancipation from the restrictions of childhood, but they are definitely and primarily regressive in their significance for the adult personality. However, as noted above, the emancipation of youth in this respect has been connected with a general emancipation which is part of the process of differentiation in the adult society, which permits greater expressiveness in these areas. I have the impression that a significant change has occurred from the somewhat frenetic atmosphere of the "flaming youth" of the 1920s and to some extent of the 1930s. There is less rebellion in both respects, more moderation in the use of alcohol, and more "seriousness" in the field of sexual relations. Youth has become better integrated in the general culture.

On the other side, the progressive one, the most important phenomena are most conspicuous at the upper end of the range, both in terms of the socio-cultural level and of the stage of the life cycle. This is the enormous development of serious cultural interests among students in the more elite colleges. The most important field of these interests seem to be that of the arts, including highbrow music, literature, drama, and painting.

The first essential point here is that this constitutes a very definite upgrading of cultural standards, compared with the philistinism of the most nearly corresponding circles in an earlier generation. Second, however, it is at least variant and selective (though not, I think, deviant) with respect to the main trends of the society, since the main developments in the latter are on the "instrumental" rather than the "expressive" side. As to the special involvement of elite youth in the arts, it may be said that youth has tended to become a kind of "loyal opposition" to the main trends of the culture, making a bid for leadership in a sphere important to a balanced society yet somewhat neglected by the principal innovating agencies.

The question of youth's relation to the political situation is of rather special interest and considerable complexity. The susceptibility of youth groups to radical political ideologies, both left and right, has often been remarked. It appears, however, that this is a widely variant phenomenon. It seems to be most conspicuous, on the one hand, in societies just entering a more "developed" state, in which intellectuals play a special role and in which students, as potential intellectuals, are specially placed. In a second type of case, major political transitions and instabilities are prominent, as in several European countries during this century, notably Germany.

Seen in this context, American youth has seemed to be apathetic politically. During the 1930s and 1940s, there was a certain amount of leftist activity, including a small Communist contingent, but the main trend has certainly been one of limited involvement. Recently, there seems to have been a kind of resurgence of political interest and activity. It has not, however, taken the form of any explicit, generalized, ideological commitment. Rather, it has tended to focus on specific issues in which moral problems are sharply defined, notably in race relations and the problems of nuclear war. It does not seem too much to say that the main trend has been in accord with the general political characteristics of the society, which has been a relatively stable system with a strong pluralistic character. The concomitant skepticism as to generalized ideological formulae is usually thought deplorable by the moralists among our intellectuals. In this broad respect, however, the main orientation of youth seems to be in tune with the society in which they are learning to take their places.

The elements in youth culture that express strain because of deviations from the main standards of the adult society are by no means absent. One such deviation is what we have called the "romantic," the devotion to expectations unrealistically simplified and idealized with respect to actual situations. A particularly clear example has been the romantic love complex. It is interesting, therefore, that a comparable pattern seems to have appeared recently in the political field, one that is connected with a pervasive theme of concern: the "meaningfulness" of current and future roles in modern industrial society.

In the field of politics, one not very explicit interpretation of a meaningful role for youth in general is to exert a major personal influence on determining the "big" political decisions of our time. The realistic problem, of course, is the organization of large-scale societies on bases that are not rigidly fixed in tradition, not authoritarian, and not unduly unstable. In this respect, public opinion (though in the long run extremely important) is necessarily diffuse and, with few exceptions, unable to dictate particular decisions. The main policy-making function is of necessity confined to relatively few and is the special responsibility of elected representatives who, in large-scale societies, become professionalized to a considerable degree. The average adult citizen, even if high in competence and responsibility, is excluded from these few. Yet this is not to say that in his role as citizen his responsibilities are meaningless or that his life in general can become meaningful only if his principal concerns (e.g., his non-political job) are sacrificed to the attempt to become a top "influential" in national politics. If this were true, representative democracy as we know it would itself be meaningless. The alternative, however (if large-scale society is to exist at all), is not populistic direct democracy but dictatorship.

This particular syndrome, of course, is a part of a larger one: the general difficulty of accepting the constraints inherent in large-scale organizations – in particular, the "instrumental" aspect of roles other than those at the highest levels. We have already pointed out some of the features of our developing social system that make this a focus of strain. Equally, through the development of institutionalized individualism, there is a whole series of factors making for an increasing rather than a diminishing autonomy. The question, however, concerns the spheres in which the autonomy of various categories of individuals can operate. Differentiation inevitably entails mutual dependence: the more differentiation, the more dependence. In a system characterized by high levels of differentiation, it is to be expected that organizational policy making will also become differentiated. Hence, only a few will become very intimately concerned with it. The problem of what mechanism can control these few is indeed a complex one which cannot be analyzed here. The political role, however, seems to provide particularly striking evidence of a romantic element in current youth ideology.

Perhaps the most significant fact about current youth culture is its concern with meaningfulness. This preoccupation definitely lies on the serious and progressive side of the division I have outlined. Furthermore, it represents a rise in the level of concern from the earlier preoccupation with social justice – even though the problem of race relations is understandably a prominent one. Another prominent example is the much discussed concern with problems of "identity." This is wholly natural and to be expected in the light of *anomie*. In a society that is changing as rapidly as ours and in which there is so much mobility of status, it is only natural that the older generation cannot provide direct guidance and role models that would present the young person with a neatly structured definition of the situation. Rather, he must find his own way, because he is pushed out of the nest and expected to fly. Even the nature of the medium in which he is to fly is continually changing, so that, when he enters college, there are many uncertainties about the nature of opportunities in his chosen field on completing graduate school. His elders simply do not have the knowledge to guide him in detail.

It is highly significant that the primary concern has been shifting since early in the century from the field of social justice to that of meaningfulness, as exemplified by the problem of identity – except for the status of special groups such as the Negro. In terms of the social structure, this enhances the problem of integration, and focuses concern more on problems of meaning than on those of situation and opportunity in the simpler sense. It is a consequence of the process of social change we have outlined.

It is also understandable and significant that the components of anxiety that inevitably characterize this type of strained situation should find appropriate fields of displacement in the very serious, real dangers of the modern world, particularly those of war. It may also be suggested that the elite youth's resonance to the diagnosis of the current social situation in terms of conformity and mass culture should be expected.[7] Essentially, this diagnosis is an easy disparagement of the society, which youth can consider to be the source of difficulty and (so it seems to them) partially unmanageable problems.

Conclusion

The above analysis suggests in the main that contemporary American society is of a type in which one would expect the situation of youth to involve (certainly, by the standards of the society from which it is emerging) rather special conditions of strain. As part of the more general process of differentiation to which we have alluded, youth groups themselves are coming to occupy an increasingly differentiated position, most conspicuously, in the field of formal education. Though an expanding educational system is vital in preparing for future function, it has the effect of segregating (more sharply and extensively than ever before) an increasing proportion of the younger age groups. The extension of education to increasingly older age levels is a striking example.

The other main focus of strain is the impact on youth of the pace and nature of the general process of social change. This is especially observable in the problem of *anomie*. In view of this change, youth's expectations cannot be defined either very early or very precisely, and this results in considerable insecurity. Indeed, the situation is such that a marked degree of legitimate grievance is inevitable. Every young person is entitled in some respects to complain that he has been brought into "a world I never made."

To assess the situation of American youth within the present frame of reference presents an especially difficult problem of balance. This is an era that lays great stress, both internally and externally, on the urgencies of the times, precisely in the more sensitive and responsible quarters. Such a temper highlights what is felt to be wrong and emphasizes the need for change through active intervention. With reference to the actual state of society, therefore, the tendency is to lean toward a negative evaluation of the status quo, because both the concrete deficiencies and the obstacles to improvement are so great.

That this tendency should be particularly prominent in the younger age groups is natural. It is both to be expected and to be welcomed. The main feature of the youth situation is perhaps the combination of current dependence with the expectation of an early assumption of responsibility. I think that evidence has been presented above that this conflict is accentuated under present conditions. The current youthful indictments of the present state of our society may be interpreted as a kind of campaign position, which prepares the way for the definition of their role when they take over the primary responsibilities, as they inevitably will.

It seems highly probable that the more immediate situation is strongly influenced by the present phase of the society with respect to a certain cyclical pattern that is especially conspicuous in the political sphere. This is the cycle between periods of "activism" in developing and implementing a sense of the urgency of collective goals, and of "consolidation" in the sense of withdrawing from too active commitments and on the whole giving security and "soundness" the primary emphasis. There is little doubt that in this meaning, the most recent phase (the "Eisenhower era") has been one of consolidation, and that we are now involved in the transition to a more activistic phase.

Broadly speaking, youth in a developing society of the American type, in its deepest values and commitments, is likely to be favorable to the activistic side. It is inculcated with the major values of the society, and strongly impressed with the importance of its future responsibilities. At the same time, however, it is frustrated by being deprived of power and influence in the current situation, though it recognizes that such a deprivation is in certain respects essential, if its segregation for purposes of training is to be effective – a segregation which increases with each step in the process of differentiation. A certain impatience, however, is to be expected, and with it a certain discontent with the present situation. Since it is relatively difficult to challenge the basic structure of the youth situation in such respects (e.g., as that one should not be permitted to start the full practice of medicine before graduating from college), this impatience tends to be displaced on the total society as a system, rather than on the younger generation in its specific situation. From this point of view, a generous measure of youthful dissatisfaction with the state of American society may be a sign of the healthy commitment of youth to the activist component of the value system. However good the current society may be from various points of view, *it is not good enough to meet their standards*. It goes almost without saying that a fallibility of empirical judgment in detail is to be expected.

The task of the social scientist, as a scientific observer of society, is to develop the closest possible approach to an objective account of the character and processes of the society. To him, therefore, this problem must appear in a slightly different light: he must try to see it in as broad a historical and comparative perspective as he can, and he must test his judgments as far as possible in terms of available empirical facts and logically precise and coherent theoretical analyses.

Viewed in this way (subject, of course, to the inevitable fallibilities of all cognitive undertakings), American society in a sense appears to be running a scheduled course. We find no cogent evidence of a major change in the essential pattern of its governing values. Nor do we find that – considering the expected strains and complications of such processes as rapid industrialization, the assimilation of many millions of immigrants, and a new order of change in the power structure, the social characteristics, and the balances of its relation to the outside world – American society is not doing reasonably well (as distinguished from outstandingly) in implementing these values. Our society on the whole seems to remain committed to its essential mandate.

The broad features of the situation of American youth seem to accord with this pattern. There are many elements of strain, but on the whole they may be considered normal for this type of society. Furthermore, the patterns of reaction on the part of American youth also seem well within normal limits. Given the American value system we have outlined, it seems fair to conclude that youth cannot help giving a *relative* sanction to the general outline of society as it has come to be institutionalized. On the other hand, it is impossible for youth to be satisfied with the status quo, which must be treated only as a point of departure for the far higher attainments that are not only desirable but also obligatory.

Clearly, American youth is in a ferment. On the whole, this ferment seems to accord relatively well with the sociologist's expectations. It expresses many dissatisfactions with the current state of society, some of which are fully justified, others are of a more dubious validity. Yet the general orientation appears to be, not a basic alienation, but an eagerness to learn, to accept higher orders of responsibility, and to "fit," not in the sense of passive conformity, but in the sense of their readiness to work within the system, rather than in basic opposition to it. The future of American society and the future place of that society in the larger world appear to present in the main a *challenge* to American youth. To cope with that challenge, an intensive psychological preparation is now taking place.

Notes

1 Willard Hurst, *Law and Social Process in United States History* (Ann Arbor: University of Michigan Press, 1960), ch. 2.

2 To sociologists, the frustrating aspects of a favorable situation in this sense may be summed up under the concept of "relative deprivation." See Robert K. Merton and Paul Lazarsfeld, *Continuities in Social Research: Studies in the Scope and Method of The American Soldier* (Chicago: The Free Press of Glencoe, Illinois, 1950).

3 See Talcott Parsons, Robert F. Bales, et al., *Family, Socialization and Interaction Process* (Chicago: The Free Press of Glencoe, Illinois, 1955), especially ch. 1.

4 For example, I am quite certain that the general level of academic achievement on the part of students of Harvard College and the Harvard Graduate School has substantially risen during my personal contact with them (more than thirty years).

5 The emancipation of components that were previously rigidly controlled by ascription is of course a major feature of the general process of differentiation, which could not be detailed here for reasons of space.

6 S. N. Eisenstadt, *From Generation to Generation* (Chicago: The Free Press of Glencoe, Illinois, 1956).

7 For an analysis of this complex in the society, see Winston R. White, *Beyond Conformity* (New York: The Free Press of Glencoe, 1961).

15

Death in American Society – a Brief Working Paper

The aim of this paper is to delineate certain aspects of attitudes toward death in American society, and to analyze the cultural roots of these attitudes as they relate to the social structure. It is hoped that this effort may help to clarify or to suggest problems for research. The subject is not only of interest and importance in itself, but it is one which should throw new light on many of the basic problems of our society and culture. Most directly related, of course, are our attitudes toward aging, the increasing proportion of older people in the population, the problem of having children, and rates of population growth.

Perhaps the best way to begin is in terms of a foil. A widely current belief which seems to be open to criticism is the view that American society is characterized by a kind of "denial" of the reality of death. Phenomena in the practice of undertaking – the dressing of the corpse in ordinary clothes, the use of cosmetics, the very special concern with the impermeability of coffins – are all cited as evidence.

The general tendency of interpretation is the thesis of "going soft." Americans are allegedly coming to be progressively less capable of facing the harsh realities of the actual world. Unpleasant things tend to be regarded as not very "real." We are said to live in a kind of world of illusion; to construct an elaborate system of defenses to protect ourselves against the intrusion of reality into this world. The problem of death becomes only one, though a particularly striking, manifestation of this general tendency.

Consideration of the problem presented by this view leads one immediately into some of the salient demographic facts which may be considered to bear on it. The demographic revolution of the past century in "modern" societies has been characterized by passage from a high-birth-rate, high-death-rate balance to one of vastly lower death rates, and where something of a balance is maintained, necessarily much lower birth rates. From an expectation of life at birth of not much over thirty years, it has gone well into the sixties in the Western world.

Combined with this is the fact that the maximum *span* of life has not greatly changed, if indeed at all. Also there has been a sharp decrease in what might be regarded as premature deaths, particularly in infancy, but very importantly in the younger and middle mature years.[1] It is also notable that this broad demographic picture holds for a century which has been severely plagued by wars, the consequences of which, of course, are included in the longevity figures.

Perhaps the most conspicuous factor in this change is to be found in the public health branch of modern medicine, particularly in the control of infectious diseases. On the other hand, rising standards of living with better diets and more adequate housing have certainly contributed to the change.

Most generally we may say that this change has been a result of a very broad development of active instrumental controls over the physical environment. While medicine and public health are particularly important in the present context, they are but part of a larger movement.

This raises an important question for the view with which we started the discussion. Does "facing death" mean avoiding any attempt to control circumstances which might eventuate in death, as well as avoiding mitigation of the generally unpleasant and distressing aspects of death?

With regard to the first part of the question, it is well known that many societies take a much more fatalistic attitude than our own, both toward illness and toward death, not only in old age, but throughout the life cycle. Thus the loss of a large proportion of young children before maturity is, in some societies, considered normal, and it would even be thought of as interfering with Divine Providence to attempt to save them. The line between the inevitable in disaster, and the possibilities and rightness of its avoidance, is a subtle one.

The attitude conspicuous in the United States is one of bringing to bear every possible resource to prolong active and healthy life. It would seem, then, that a clue to the development of some aspects of our attitudes toward death might be found in the whole complex of health and the tendency to prolong life in good health. There would seem to be scarcely any doubt of the deep grounding of this complex in our culture. Although the scientific basis of modern medicine and public health was largely laid in Europe, its development since early in this century and its organized practical application constitute a major American achievement.

Three points in particular deserve emphasis. The first is an inference from the effort to prolong life, i.e. we do not like to accept the fact of death *unless* it is felt to be inevitable. (This is one of the bases on which war presents very complicated attitudinal problems to Americans.)

The second point is that, where death is felt to be inevitable, there is a strong tendency to mitigate its connection with suffering. Even in the extreme case of execution, deliberate torture preliminary to death would arouse deep revulsion, however heinous the crime. Certainly there is no widespread objection to the use of sedatives to reduce physical pain in fatal illnesses or accident cases.

These two connections suggest the third which, in turn, will open up an important theme for this paper. This is that the trend of American development has been to differentiate from the "death complex" of previous human experience a central aspect from two adventitious ones. The central one is the inevitability of death at the completion of a full life cycle and the patterning of attitudes associated with it. The two adventitious ones are, first, the fact of premature death, which in terms of the "modern temper" very often cannot be treated as anything but man-made, whether it be by preventable disease, by accident, crime, or war. It is this which is treated as undesirable, and though its reality is not denied, its inevitability and desirability are denied, at a very deep level. The second adventitious component is the association of death with suffering, not only in the physical sense of pain, but also in the frustrations of disability and the various aspects of "mental suffering" which may be involved. Suffering, like premature death, is not treated either as inevitable or as an inherently desirable aspect of the ordering of the human condition, except in certain cases of the imposition of punishments.

This is not to say that in either case there is a fact or prospect of complete elimination. Doubtless there will always be an important residuum in both respects. But in recent times the quantitative change has been so great as to constitute a change in quality. We will still exhort people to endure the sufferings to which they are subjected, including their own premature deaths – if foreseeable – and those of persons close to them, with fortitude. But it seems unlikely that any Spartan conception of virtue which makes a point of inviting suffering and the risk of death just to show one can "take it like a man" will have a prominent place in the values of our type of society in the foreseeable future. Rather, one can expect an asymptotic pattern of gradual reduction of such adventitious elements, combined with institutionalized provision for coping with the remaining cases.

The consequence of this is to confront us with the problem of the meaning of death as the termination of a normal life cycle in what is probably a new state of relative purity in human experience. A number of facets of the new situation may be brought to mind. First, on a demographic basis, a rapidly increasing proportion of the population have reached an age where their more obvious life-tasks by the ordinary criteria have been completed. Perhaps the most important of these changes bear on occupational careers and family roles. To put it schematically, such persons have retired from occupational jobs, and their children are grown with families of their own. Whatever the complex problems of the roles this group of "oldsters" are to assume, or have already assumed, they are a group who, by the nature of their position in the society, are living "in the shadow of death," since they have entered what is by all institutional criteria, a terminal period of their lives.[2] These people have, of course, survived the risks of premature death, and also since they are likely to be in better health than their counterparts of earlier generations, it may be presumed that the considerable majority are relatively free of the grosser forms of suffering.

Combined with this demographic fact is the failure of the maximum span of human life to increase. This underlines the inevitability of death, and though it does not fix its time precisely, it narrows the range of its probable occurrence; for example, for people over 80 it is quite clear that they cannot have many more years to live.

Another aspect of the situation is such as to encourage enhanced awareness of death and hence in some sense concern with it. This is true both for old people themselves and for a much wider group because, there being so many more old people than before, more younger ones are closely associated with them, particularly perhaps with aging parents.

Not least of the features of the American, as of the Western situation generally in these respects, is the fact of very rapid and extensive changes in the larger society. It seems likely that many features of our attitudes and practices in relation to death are in part at least consequences of these processes of change and the conflicts engendered by them. In order to sort these out, however, it is necessary to have a clear picture of the major relevant features of the cultural orientation which lies in the background.

Before entering upon a more detailed discussion of this, certain considerations which bear on the possibility of an alternative to the "denial" hypothesis may be suggested. The first is that American society has institutionalized the values of science to a high degree. On the other hand, scientific attitudes cannot cover more than a fraction of the range of problems which must be confronted in a society. Furthermore, where science is relevant there is much imperfection in implementing such orientations. Nevertheless, a certain realism in facing the facts of the world is characteristic of the scientific attitude. It would seem, therefore, to be anomalous that such a society should be characterized by a fundamental attitude which is so drastically at variance with that of science.

A second point concerns a phenomenon which has come to be well known to social scientists in a number of fields, but most clearly perhaps in that of voting behavior. Thus the phenomenon of "apathy" need not mean basic indifference to problem areas but is rather a manifestation of a conflicted state.[3] And since conflicted states are especially likely to be widespread in periods of rapid change, it may therefore very well be that some of our tendency to be silent about problems of the meaning of death is related to phenomena of conflict. This form of "apathy" is related to denial but is not quite the same thing.

There is a third point of considerable interest. There is a range of areas in American society in which privacy of the individual is institutionally protected. This includes his sex life to a large degree, in certain respects his personal financial affairs, and not least his religious convictions. It seems to us that certain phenomena in contemporary treatment of the problem of death belong in the context of this "privatization." It is considered to be a private affair into which others should not casually probe.

The Problem of the Meaning of Death

It is axiomatic to the sociologist that the orientation of action takes place within a *definition of the situation*. This consists in the "diagnosis" of the empirical aspects of the situation of action, including the nature of acting units, and a set of normative and other nonempirical cultural expectations or commitments. The definition of the situation is inherently a cultural component of the action system.

We may take as our starting point that death is not only inevitable but is a normal phenomenon which must be treated in some sense as functionally important in an order of nature which as a whole is accepted as meaningful.[4]

This would seem to imply that there is a strong urge to "round out" a life by being as sure as possible that it ends with a record of creditable achievements. If this basic orientation remains intact, the most acceptable death is that which comes at the end of a full life in which the individual can be said to come somewhere near having maximized the opportunities given him by his capacities and his situation.

It is our view that this should indeed be considered the ideal-type orientation to death, but that the bases of such an attitude and the possibilities of its impairment need clarification.

If this conclusion that the fact of death be considered normal and, under the proper circumstances, in some senses desirable, constitutes an ideal type, it is also true that the situation is one inherently fraught with strains. That this should be so scarcely needs further argument. Can we, however, say anything about possible reactions to these strains, and apply our knowledge of reaction to social strains generally to this problem?

The most important possibilities of different types of reaction to strain, for present purposes at least, seem to lie in the distinction between what may be called regressive and utopian patterns. In monetary systems, for example, these correspond to the well-known patterns of deflationary and inflationary disturbances of the system. Let us discuss the deflationary case first.

It has been noted that in our kind of orientation system the individual faces greater risk than in a less differentiated system. If there is sufficient pressure, and controls fail to operate, he may attempt to enhance his sense of security by falling back on primitive patterns which seem safer, but also leave less degrees of freedom open. We are all familiar with this in the economic sense. The individual places his assets in "liquid" form, distrusting the usual credit instruments. He moves successively to government securities, to cash, to gold or even to commodities as the only things not exposed to the hazards of a ramified monetary-market system.

In the moral-religious case the parallel may be said to lie in "fundamentalism." Although in the economic case we stressed the flight into "real assets," there is an alternative, namely to influence the higher-order agencies which control markets, the proximal one in a modern economy being government. Moral-religious fundamentalism also has this dual possibility. The analogue of real assets lies in attempting to reduce the complexity of the societal reference system within which moral responsibility has to be assumed. This path leads eventually to giving overwhelming moral priority to the more primordial social ties, especially of kinship.[5] In the moral sphere it is sometimes found in movements of what in some circles passes for moral rigorism demanding punishment and cessation of acts which have generally come to be accepted in society. But just as in a banking system which is functioning properly, even though they have the formal right, it is strictly impossible to pay all depositors in cash immediately; so in moral systems everyone is in some sense by fundamentalist standards, guilty, and to call them all to account at one time will do nothing but destroy the functioning moral order.[6]

The other alternative leading to the possibility of deflationary breakdown is the renunciation of the moral responsibility of the individual in favor of his complete dependence on "higher authority." In the religious case this means the kind of theistic fundamentalism which attributes everything to Divine Will, leaving little or no scope for human responsibility.

The type of orientation to the American death complex which was used as a foil at the beginning of this paper seems to be a case of this "fundamentalist" attitude, which is associated with a tendency to "deflate" the main orientation pattern, and liquidate the moral "investments" which have been entered into under it. The aspect of the "reality" of death which is denied, is characterized mainly by its fear and horror-producing features – those exemplified by Durer's famous *Ritter, Tod und Teufel*. Emphasis on this is calculated to minimize the activation of moral guilt about shortcomings in this life – if its end is so horrible, how can its substance be good? It also maximizes the motivation to throw the fate of the dead exclusively on Divine mercy with the implication that they cannot possibly "deserve" to die in peace and with a good conscience. This, of course, has been one major set of themes in the history of Christianity.

We can perhaps gain additional perspective on what we are calling the normal orientation pattern, by a brief consideration of the opposite type of deviation from it. This, in terms of the economic analogy, is "inflationary." We referred to it, by contrast with fundamentalism, as "utopian." It is this which more nearly earns the epithet of "denial." Indeed, Norman Vincent Peale is sometimes held to exemplify the central tendency of the American orientation. On an impressionistic appraisal of Peale's attitude I think the characterization is oversevere, but not entirely unjustified. What I would challenge, however, is the contention that this is indeed the central tendency.

This may well be a matter for research. The present concern is rather for typology, and I think this line of deviation can be characterized typologically in relation to the other two. Perhaps its most important trait would be a tendency to play down systematically the possibilities both of the moral and of the religious insecurity of the individual. It would suggest that there are no really serious moral dilemmas in modern life, and in accepting responsibility there is no serious risk of incurring moral guilt. Religiously the conception of God is one of unfailing beneficence without the element of imposition of discipline and trouble, the hard taskmaster and, indeed, the punisher. Perhaps the most ubiquitous symbol of this attitude in the death complex is the famous Forest Lawn of Los Angeles.

Pushed far enough, of course, this tendency completely undermines genuine moral responsibility and makes death, not a consummatory ending including a sense of possible reward for work well done, but only a relatively meaningless cessation. The conception of "positive thinking" shares with so many idealisms the illusion that serious achievement is not dependent on coping with the realistic difficulties and obstacles of complex situations, but is only a matter of the "right attitude." It makes the element of reward (and of genuine frustration) meaningless, since it is not conceived to be necessary to achieve in order to gain it.

The Problem of Symbolization

We have suggested that there is a central ideal type of American orientation toward the problem of the meaning of death, and that there are two main types of deviation from this central type. We think that this analysis should be empirically verifiable through research, including the identification of sectors of the society in which one or another of the three main types predominates.

The prevalence of the two types we have spoken of as deviant, and of their unresolved conflict with each other and with what we have called the central type, suggests that major processes of restructuring at the level of cultural symbolization may be going on.

The most obvious one to a social scientist centers about the theme of differentiation which we have briefly outlined above. It is striking that the central symbolic definition of the problem of death in our cultural heritage is that of the crucifixion, which is not only the death of the mortal Jesus, but the death of a young man, under conditions of maximum suffering. The suggestion is that at the highest level of religious symbolization these independent components will have to be still further differentiated from each other. Until a new symbolic structure which gives more meaning to the ultimate outcome for the individual of the positive moral responsibilities of an achievement-oriented ethic has become formulated and institutionalized, continued oscillations between "hell-fire and damnation" fundamentalism – and perhaps its intellectual equivalent, existentialist "despair" – and the sugary sentimentality of "positive thinking" are to be expected. The stabilization of modern society requires more than effective control of nuclear armaments; it requires cultural reconstruction of the most thoroughgoing sort.

In conclusion, it may be worthwhile to mention a range of phenomena which, because of their connections with themes of death, would appear to merit special study. The first is the very obvious one of the more or less ritualized mortuary customs and observances. Here a particularly important set of considerations concern the consequences of the mobility and structural pluralism of our society. These sociological facts are conspicuously incompatible with mortuary customs which are organized primarily about the primordial solidarities of kinship and local associations.

Second, there is an immense proliferation of phenomena where death themes play a part on phantom levels. This is very true indeed of certain categories of literature, and of content broadcast over the mass media. This pure phantasy field shades over into attitudes toward the realistic risks of war and the complex of public anxieties which characterizes this problem.

Finally, an important set of problems concern study of the special occupation groups which have occasion to deal with situations of death. In the ordinary course of events three are especially involved, namely, the physician, the undertaker and the clergyman. Two other occupations, the police and most especially the military, have the duty of contingent killing of people if they are deemed to be a sufficient threat to public order or national security. Finally life insurance agents are occupationally concerned with persuading people to plan for the contingency of death, as are lawyers who draw wills for their clients. The impact of this involvement on the attitudes of members of all these groups presents important problems, extending even to the motivations of entry into them.

Notes

1 Particularly striking examples are the lowering of maternal mortality and the reduction of death from tuberculosis.

2 Though there is nothing necessarily permanent about the age of 65, it is the commonest age of occupational retirement at present. It is notable that the proportion of the American population over 65 has about doubled in the present century, from about 4% to about 8%, and will increase still further. On the family side the most striking datum is perhaps the fact that, even allowing for divorce and separation, now more than one third of the marriage period of an American couple is spent after the youngest child has left home and become independent.

3 Thus the findings by Berelson and Lazarsfeld that voters in process of shifting party allegiance were least interested in or active with respect to the campaign. The phenomenon has also been analyzed by Barber.

4 There are, of course, schools of thought which regard the whole order of nature as chaotically meaningless or in other respects fundamentally antithetical to all the higher interests of man. This can, however, certainly not be claimed to be the main attitude institutionalized in American culture.

5 The famous Oedipus story of Greek mythology, classically structured in the triology of Sophocles, may be interpreted as dramatizing the struggle to get free of the fundamentalist societal-moral order organized in kinship terms. The inexorable punishment of Oedipus for parricide and incest, both committed in circumstances where there could be no possibility of personal moral responsibility, seems to be demanded by the Gods and this demand is exploited by such characters as Cleon, whereas the apotheosis of Oedipus and his protection by Theseus represents the conviction that there is a higher moral order within which Oedipus' moral qualities can be recognized and his guilt absolved.

6 This is something like what Luther attempted to do. Cf. R. H. Tawney, *Religion and the Rise of Capitalism* (New York: Harcourt, Brace and Co., 1926).

16

Religion in Postindustrial America: The Problem of Secularization

The present paper is in some respects a sequel to "The 'Gift of Life' and Its Reciprocation," which appeared in the Autumn 1972 issue of *Social Research*.[1] I begin with the presentation and explication of a schematic paradigm of the symbolic structure of medieval Christianity, indicating the principal modifications that must be introduced to accommodate the development of Protestantism. I then turn to two major developments of the post-Reformation era: the process sometimes called secularization, and that which has led to the ecumenical movement of recent times. Within the framework of these two developments, I briefly discuss two phenomena that do not fit into what has traditionally been called religion: civil religion and Marxian socialism, which may be called a secularized religion. Finally, I consider the current religious situation, with special reference to the United States, and the appearance of what must be called post-Marxian themes in certain dissident social and cultural movements in the United States.

A Paradigm of Christian Symbolism

Figure 16.1 represents the main structure of Christian symbolism as found in the medieval Roman Catholic Church. It reflects some of the ideas put forward in "The 'Gift of Life' and Its Reciprocation," in which my colleagues and I sought to explicate some aspects of the meaning of death in the Western religious tradition. We there adopted the concept of life as a gift, and utilized ideas of gift-giving and gift-exchange formulated a generation ago by Marcel Mauss.[2] The formulation of the paradigm was greatly facilitated by certain writings of Edmund Leach and Kenneth Burke as well as by the original biblical texts.[3]

The figure presents the two-level system of Christian symbolism: the temporal and the transcendental, or the secular and the sacred. In the figure, the inner rectangle, designated "The Human Level," is organized about two reference concept pairs. First is the one that has figured so prominently in anthropological and sociological thinking, namely, sex and age. It should be remembered that I am speaking in symbolic terms, though in some cases the symbolic figures are referred to in canonical documents with quite definite sex identity and sometimes with generation identity. In this respect the category of

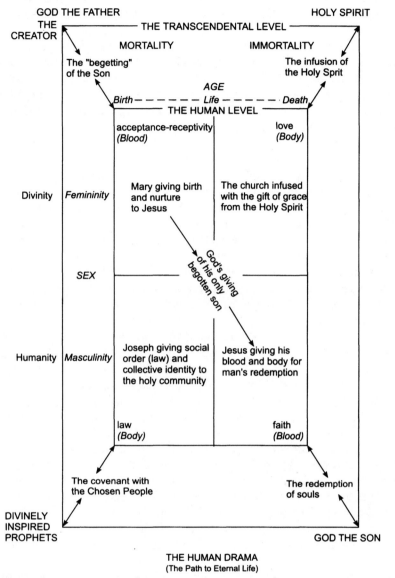

Figure 16.1   The human condition as symbolically organized about age and sex: the Christian syndrome as gift complex

sex is relatively straightforward. For what social scientists have called age, I have substituted the life course as a whole with special reference to its beginning and its end, birth and death. The symbolization, then, has to do with certain relations between the cultural conceptions of what it means to be born and what it means to die.[4]

The second reference concept pair is taken from the symbolization of kinship relations as analyzed by David Schneider.[5] The most obvious of these symbols is blood, as habitually used in the expression "blood relationship." It is striking that in perhaps the most intimate relation of kinship, that of mother and child, a common bloodstream is not physiologically shared. Nevertheless, blood has become a primary symbol of this type of relatedness. The other concept that Schneider uses is that of relationship in law, organized not about blood but about what is in some sense a contract. The prototypical empirical kinship case is the relation of the parties in a marriage.

In religion as in kinship, the symbol blood plays a central part. This is true in many religious traditions but particularly in Christianity, where the blood of Christ is symbolized by the wine in the central Christian ritual, the eucharist. The other primary component of the eucharist, the bread, symbolizes the body of Christ. In "The 'Gift of Life,'" my colleagues and I argued that body as a symbol is very closely related to a relation of law in Schneider's sense, and indeed this turns up in a variety of cultural traditions other than the American.

I have structured the inner rectangle to yield a fourfold table, the two dichotomized dimensions of which are (in the vertical axis) femininity and masculinity, and (in the horizontal axis) birth and death – that is, the old categories of sex and age in the appropriate modifications as just explained. In New Testament tradition, three of the four cells are related to symbolic individuals, and they are related to each other and to other human beings through a gift relationship. The fourth I think of as symbolizing the church, which, in the words of the eucharist, constitutes the mystical body of Christ. The two left cells are what Leach would call the "sociological" parents of Jesus, of whom, in the religiously symbolic sense, clearly the more important is Mary, the "Mother of God." Leach, however, aptly refers to Joseph as Jesus's "sociological" father. Symbolically, the figure of Joseph seems to represent continuity between the Christian group and the Jewish community within which Christianity arose. Thus, in the gospel according to Matthew, there is an elaborate genealogy which traces Joseph's descent from the patriarchs and prophets and strongly asserts his belonging – and therefore his sociological son Jesus's belonging – to the "House of David." This in turn we may associate with the continuity in some sense of the Jewish law, despite the profound alteration of the meaning of that law by Jesus and Paul.

It will be noted that Mary is depicted as *giving* birth and nurture to Jesus. Jesus himself, then, having been given birth by a human mother, in his sacrificial death on the cross is symbolized as *giving* his blood and body for man's redemption. Finally, the church is conceived as infused with the gift of grace from the Holy Spirit.

Whereas the vertical axis of the inner rectangle is conceived in terms of the sex dichotomy, the horizontal axis is concerned with a dichotomized version of the age variable, focusing on the two extreme points of the life course, birth and death. From this point of view, it is highly symbolic that in a certain sense the founding act of Christianity was Jesus's sacrificial death. The church, then, particularly in the Catholic tradition, was conceived as the agency through which the transcending of death and the achievement of eternal life could come about.

The other two primary reference symbols – namely, blood and body – are depicted as characterizing the diagonals of the inner rectangle. Blood is involved not only in Jesus's sacrifice but also in his relation as blood child to Mary. It therefore symbolizes both a religious event and a terrestrial kinship. The other diagonal axis is associated with the symbol of body, but interestingly in both cases not specifically an individual's body but corporate bodies. If my interpretation is correct, the relatively secular community that has been sanctified through its relation to the heritage of Israel is a necessary substratum for the religion. This, in turn, is related to the church as the mystical body of Christ with all its well known meanings. Here the gift theme appears again in the concept of grace as the instrument of human salvation.

The outer rectangle in the figure is designated "The Transcendental Level." At three of its corners I have placed the three persons of the Trinity. The concept of God the Father, which is placed at the upper left corner, gained a new meaning in Christianity in contrast to Judaism through the symbolic act of God's "begetting" a son, Jesus, through the human woman Mary. This act of begetting is quite different from that of creation as portrayed in Genesis. God created Adam and Eve, but he begat Jesus. Among other things, begetting symbolizes the continuity of the human species, which began with an act of creation.

The second main act of God in the drama of salvation was the "giving of his only begotten son" for the redemption of mankind. The upper right corner represents the concept of the Holy Spirit, which has a special relationship to the church and the gift of grace. The lower right corner is the locus of God the Son, the personal agent of redemption.

The lower left corner does not involve a person of the Trinity but rather the Christian inheritance from the Jewish tradition. I have focused it about the divinely inspired patriarchs and prophets, notably Moses and David, as establishing a particularly sanctified human community, the "Chosen People." It will be remembered that the concept of the covenant, which was central to the Old Testament, was carried over into Christianity in various forms and is particularly important in the Puritan branch of Protestantism.

Finally, at the bottom of the figure, outside either rectangle, is a schematic notation about the human drama that I have labeled "The Path to Eternal Life." The duality is present in the spiritual conception of Jesus and his actual physical birth. Jesus, standing in a certain symbolic sense for mankind, was by that set of circumstances the receiver of what I have called the gift of life. According to Mauss, the acceptance of a gift calls for its reciprocation. Part of that reciprocation is living a religiously acceptable life, the consummation of which is dying in the faith, which completes the reciprocation of the gift.

The paradigm omits reference to two particularly important features of the Catholic system. The first is the sacraments. Besides the eucharist, already mentioned, the church instituted several other sacraments, notably penance, baptism, marriage, and extreme unction. The sacraments were considered to be consequences of the gift of grace coming to the church through Jesus's sacrifice and through the Holy Spirit. The church claimed a monopoly of the legitimate use of the sacraments. It became its policy, contrary to practices of early Christianity, that the sacraments could be administered only by ordained priests deriving their authority through apostolic succession from St. Peter, whose direct successor as the head of the church was the bishop of Rome, the pope.

A second important feature omitted from the paradigm is the religious order, whose members took vows of perpetual devotion to the religious life. Although in early Christianity there were individual anchorites, collective monasticism did not develop until the third century. Members of the religious orders, the regular clergy, were the true "upper class" of the church, with – to pursue the metaphor – the secular clergy serving as a kind of middle class and the laity constituting, religiously speaking, the unprivileged "masses."

There has been a remarkable stability in the main Catholic pattern down to the present day. Mention should be made, however, of two important developments. After the outbreak of the Reformation, which will be discussed presently, the Catholic Church reacted by tightening discipline, particularly over the clergy, and by more strictly defining the sacramental system. For the laity it insisted on full doctrinal conformity and maintenance of prescribed religious practices. The spirit of this Counter-Reformation is embodied in the Society of Jesus, founded by St. Ignatius Loyola in 1540. From the start, the Jesuits were militant servants of the papacy rather than monks absorbed in devotional exercises.

The second important development is a much more recent one. In a sense, the main pattern of the Counter-Reformation endured into the present century: only a century ago, in 1870, Pius IX promulgated the doctrine of papal infallibility. The recent period, however, has seen increased participation of the Roman Catholic Church in what has come to be called the ecumenical movement. The brief papacy of John XXIII and the Second Vatican Council precipitated a critical situation within the church. For example, there has been since then a vastly increased demand for the termination of the requirement of celibacy for the secular clergy, and there have been many resignations from the priesthood over this issue.

Changes Introduced by the Protestant Movement

The Reformation revolutionized the religious constitution of Europe. Although the outcome was long uncertain, by the Peace of Westphalia (1648) it had become evident that the change was irreversible. There would never again be religious unity in Western Europe under the aegis of the Roman Church.

Of the many religious changes introduced by Protestantism, perhaps the most significant was the elimination of the conception of the sacraments as the actual quasi-magical operation of divine grace. In Max Weber's terms, this deprived the church – that is, in its Protestant version – of the status of a *Gnadenanstalt*.[6] The church was no longer the mediator of the mystical-transcendental transactions between God and man. For Protestantism the so-called visible church became essentially an association of believers with a common interest in fulfilling the conditions for salvation prescribed in the Bible, including especially cognitive understanding of those conditions. The clergy were no longer manipulators of divine grace but became teachers, leaders of congregations, missionaries to the lay public exhorting it to commitment to and steadfastness in the faith. To be sure, the sacraments were maintained, but with profoundly altered meaning. They became merely symbolic affirmations of faith and commitment to the Christian message. In its modified form the eucharist remained the central ritual. But marriage, for example, increasingly lost its sacramental quality, a loss which underlay later toleration of divorce.

Another important change was the elimination of the religious orders in favor of a kind of democracy of all Christians. With this went the famous shift, beginning in Luther's own writings, of which Max Weber made so much in his essay *The Protestant Ethic and the Spirit of Capitalism*[7] – the shift to the view that religious obligations in the fullest sense could be discharged by laymen and specifically in lay occupations (*Berufe*) rather than by clergy in segregated monastic communities. Associated with this shift was the legitimation of clerical marriage. This was dramatically symbolized by Luther's own decision to marry in violation of his monastic vows and by the fact that the woman he married was a former nun.

This change has often been interpreted as reflecting a relaxation of standards of religious rigor. Indeed, this is the beginning of a line of argument about secularization of which I shall have more to say below, and it represents one – possibly the prevalent – view. There has, however, been another interpretation of the change. This is to the effect that the change was not primarily a downgrading (religiously speaking) of the clergy, both regular and secular, but rather an upgrading of the laity. Luther's marriage, from this point of view, symbolized his conviction that the fully religious life could be lived in the ordinary status of the lay citizen and not only as a monk or priest. Weber quotes a religious notable of the period, Sebastian Franck, to the effect that, as a consequence of the Reformation, "every man was expected to be in essence a monk."[8]

The Reformation was an exceedingly complex religiosocial movement. Weber, nevertheless, suggests that it can be divided into two principal branches, the Lutheran and the Calvinist. The Lutheran branch represented the more inward, spiritualistic interpretation of emancipation from the institutionally "objective" Catholic Church. Its primary concern was with the soul of the individual Christian believer. The Calvinist branch, on the other hand, emphasized the Christian community as a corporate entity, a fully legitimized descendant of the early and medieval churches and the bearer of the main Christian heritage. Calvinism prevailed in northwestern Europe, notably in Holland and Great Britain, and eventually in North America. It also had a profound impact on France. Calvin himself was a Frenchman, and in the religious wars of the seventeenth century the Calvinist party only narrowly missed achieving political control of France.

Protestant rulers, like Catholic, initially assumed that their subjects would adhere to their religion. Indeed, *cuius regio, eius religio* was the formula by which the Peace of Westphalia brought at least a provisional end to the wars of religion. Before that, however, notably in Holland and England, limited religious toleration had developed. In England, nonconformist sects existed beside the established Anglican Church. Although religious uniformity was enforced within several of the English-speaking American colonies, as was the case in Massachusetts, different colonies were of different religious persuasions, so the thirteen colonies taken together presented a picture of religious pluralism.

Generally speaking, what might be called the liberal tendency of Protestant development within the original Calvinist framework has prevailed. This is true of England and Holland, although the Church of England has never been disestablished and as late as the 1870s only those who subscribed to the Thirty-nine Articles, the official creed of the Church of England, were eligible for membership in the universities of Oxford and Cambridge, whether as students or teachers. Only the United States insisted on a thoroughgoing separation of church and state. The First Amendment to the Constitution forbade Congress to "establish religion" or "to interfere with the free exercise thereof." The United States thus became the leader in the movement toward religious toleration and denominational pluralism. This first occurred on a substantial scale within the Protestant movement itself. Only later, with the advent of large bodies of Roman Catholic immigrants, first from Ireland and then from Continental Europe, did there arise an important problem as to the status of Catholics. Still later, the status of considerable numbers of religious Jews presented a problem. The outcome has been a denominationally pluralistic and increasingly ecumenical religious situation in both Western Europe and America. The situation in Communist-controlled countries is, of course, different.

The Problem of Secularization

From one point of view, the development just sketched constituted an individualization or "privatization" of the religious situation. Religious freedom, of course, included the freedom to abstain from formal religious participation, and I think it can be said that increasing numbers from all three religious backgrounds have taken this course. We might therefore add to the three – Protestants, Catholics, and Jews – a fourth category, secular humanists.

In view of the sociocultural background, this individualization does not, however, represent the whole story. Nor is the story fully told in the usual sense of the term "secularization" as used even by so sensitive a student as Peter L. Berger.[9] The key to the complexities of that concept lies not so much at the level of individual belief and religious practice as in what has happened to the various societies as corporate entities with the privatization of religion and abstention from traditional religious organizations.

An extremely important clue is to be found in Robert Bellah's conception, put forward a decade ago, of what he called the civil religion.[10] Bellah's analysis of this concept constitutes a landmark in the understanding of the American religious situation, for civil religion seems to represent one of the two primary alternatives confronting modern Protestantism.

Ascetic Protestantism always affirmed that the primary field for action prompted by authentic religious impulse was the secular world. Indeed, the collective aim of the Puritan movement was the establishment of the kingdom of God on earth. From the point of view of earlier Christian tradition, this would seem to be almost by definition an impossible task. The Puritans' sustained commitment to this goal, however, testifies to their belief that success of some sort was possible. And, in fact, with the establishment of an independent American republic, there was something of a conviction in elite circles that a major part at least of this extraordinary task had been accomplished.

Well before the achievement of independence, the development of American Protestantism had clearly taken an individualistic direction. The most important consequence was the establishment of the voluntary principle with respect to the more formal aspects of religious obligation, notably church membership. This in turn was closely associated with the high development of religious toleration and the conception of colonial society as denominationally pluralistic. The constitutional provision for the separation of church and state merely ratified the existing situation.

These developments seem to me to have constituted a differentiation between levels of religious significance. The process referred to above as individualization had rendered untenable the old coincidence of the individual's concern with personal salvation and the collective conception of the church as a social entity – a *Gnadenanstalt*, in Weber's sense. In Puritan doctrine, however, the great task was the collective one of constructing the kingdom of God on earth. It is my view that the roots of the civil religion in America lie in the attempt to validate the legitimacy of the Puritans' claim to have achieved a measure of success. The "new nation," as Lipset called it, was interpreted from the very first canonical document, the Declaration of Independence, to be a sacred entity.[11]

The development of the civil religion was a way by which two crucial themes of American cultural and social history could be combined. One of these was secularization in the usual sense which denied traditional denominational bodies any official status. The new society became a secular society in which religion was relegated to the private sphere. The other theme is no less important: the building of the kingdom of God on earth. The establishment of the new American nation was a culmination of this process. The very facts of independence and a new constitution "conceived in liberty and dedicated to the proposition that all men are created equal" were developments that could not fail to carry with them a religious dimension. This took a form that was relatively consistent with traditional Christian conceptions and definitions, and it is this that is the core of what Bellah calls the American civil religion. There was no radical break with the primary religious heritage, though there was a careful avoidance of any attempt to define the new civil religion as Christian in a specifically dogmatic sense. Bellah documents, for example, how the many official statements – notably presidential inaugural addresses – that use the term "God" or various synonyms such as "Supreme Being" carefully avoid reference to Christ.

This civil religion must be sharply contrasted with the religious outcome of the French Revolution. French society had developed under a particularly stringent form of monarchical absolutism. Furthermore, the Catholic Church in France was extremely conservative. Thus the general background of presumptive religious freedom that had been so important to the development of the American colonies during the eighteenth century was missing in Catholic monarchical France. In making a sharp break with the past, the French revolutionary movement not only bitterly opposed the monarchy but was also strongly anticlerical. The civil religion deliberately established by the French revolutionaries – worship of the Supreme Being – was, as Bellah points out, very different from that which developed in America. Its conflict with traditional French Catholicism was acute indeed.

The most influential thinker in the background of the French Revolution was Rousseau. Rousseau contrasted in the sharpest possible way a romantically conceived state of nature with a completely unitary civil society. The central mechanism of this unitary entity was the General Will, which in principle had to be shared in by the whole population of citizens. There was no place for the political pluralism that was so characteristic of American society. The very radicalism of the French model of a revolutionary society proved fatal to the maintenance of its integrity. After the Terror, a reaction set in that brought a succession of regimes not easily identified with the revolutionary ideal. These culminated in the Empire of Napoleon I and, after his fall, in the Bourbon restoration. France did develop a certain type of bourgeois society somewhat similar to England's. However, throughout the nineteenth century and well into the present one, French society remained deeply divided between the revolutionary tradition, republican and militantly anticlerical, and the conservative tradition based on the monarchy, the army, and the Catholic Church. In a sense, nineteenth-century France provided the most extreme pattern of the internal conflicts that were general throughout Europe.

The most important politicocultural movement to emerge in Europe after the French Revolution was socialism, whose ideological leadership was provided by Karl Marx. Marx was a German who spent the most important part of his productive life as an exile in London. Lipset has shrewdly observed that Marx's economic data were derived from English developments while his political ideas were shaped by developments in France.[12] In the second half of the nineteenth century, Marxism became a "secular religion." As such, it could claim a direct cultural descent from the thought of Rousseau and the traditions of the French Revolution. Furthermore, given the essential disestablishment of the traditional Christian churches, Marxism was the most important alternative to the American version of the civil religion.

Let us start with the striking resemblance between Marxism and traditional Christian doctrine. From its earliest beginnings to the Protestant Reformation, Christianity conceived of secular society as inherently depraved. Only through divine intervention could men be quite literally saved, that is, rescued from the sin and death that were the natural condition of temporal man. This view was profoundly altered by Calvinism and other influences. Because American Protestants believed they had succeeded in setting up a truly Christian commonwealth, it was impossible to accept the traditional Christian view of the utter corruption of secular society. Any nondenominational religious orientation that could survive in this situation had to give a positive sanction to the newly institutionalized social order.

The situation in Europe as a result of the French Revolution was very different. The Revolution had pursued a highly romanticized conception of an ideal society characterized by the total absence of individual self-interest. With the ebbing of the revolutionary élan, however, the maintenance of this ideal proved to be impossible, and society reverted to a state of Rousseauian corruption in which self-interest figured very prominently indeed. In the revolutionary tradition there remained the memory of the Revolution's short-lived victory over the evils of corrupt society, and some of those who were deeply imbued with that tradition maintained that only revolution could eliminate the corruption of traditional society.

The French revolutionaries had located the corruption of the old regime in the monarchy, aristocracy, and church. With the vast weakening of monarchies and aristocracies in the course of the nineteenth century, and with the development of the fruits of the Industrial Revolution, Marxists found the source of the trouble in the system of economic organization – capitalism. Correspondingly, the saving element could no longer, at least initially, be the people as a whole, as in the main French revolutionary tradition, but had to be that part of the people who were allegedly uncorrupted by the capitalist system. This pointed rather obviously to the exploited and – in the Marxian sense – alienated working class.

The Marxian secular religion and, more broadly, the socialist movement generally took on an eschatological orientation very similar to that of traditional Christianity. Men of good will were condemned to suffer the humiliations and deprivations of a corrupt society until such time as the revolution could occur. With the revolution would come liberation, that "leap into freedom" from the coercion and slavery of capitalism. The socialist movement thus not only resembled the main Christian tradition in its pessimistic diagnosis of the contemporary secular world, but was characterized by a very similar pattern of eschatological hope. The new society was to be brought about not by a last judgment but by a political revolution. And the revolution was to be brought about not by the second coming of an individual savior but by the intervention of a collective savior – the proletariat.

The fundamental changes in the religious constitution of Western society which culminated in the later eighteenth century thus did not lead to the destruction of the influence of religion but rather to the development of two strikingly important new types and levels of religion. The antagonism between them finally came to something of a head in the present century with the Russian Revolution. There was, of course, considerable tension before then, but it has been particularly acute in the more than fifty years since that event. The vicissitudes have been many and complex, notably complicated by the rise of Nazi Germany in the 1930s with its common threat to both the West and the Soviet Union. This produced in the Second World War what in certain respects was an unnatural alliance between the Soviet Union and the Western democracies, paralleling in some ways the eighteenth-century alliance between Catholic France and Protestant Prussia which underlay the basic religious changes of that period.

In any case, I think it is legitimate to interpret what has often been called the "cold war" as in a very important aspect constituting a set of wars of religion which are not without their relation to the wars of religion that followed the Reformation. Although the tensions remain very strong, there seems some reason to believe that the most acute phase of this particular polarization of the Western world has begun to come to an end. The primary task of the rest of this paper is to outline a diagnosis of the implications of this changed situation for a phase of religious development onto which we have barely begun to enter.

Some Aspects of the Contemporary Situation

The two syndromes reviewed in the preceding section may in my opinion properly be called civil religions in Bellah's sense. In the American case, the civil religion was from the beginning part of the constitutive structure of the new nation. It can be considered a direct and legitimate descendant of the orientation of the Puritan colonists, particularly as their position has been presented and analyzed in the work of Perry Miller.[13]

Marxian socialism was originally the civil religion of an alienated opposition movement. In this respect, it clearly resembled early Christianity before it became the official religion of the Roman Empire. The resemblance is even closer if we consider, not the Empire as a whole, but only the Jewish community, which by the time of the appearance of Christianity was already a diaspora. Although Christianity was at first a sect within Judaism, Paul's denial of the relevance of the Jewish community and the law made it into a revolutionary movement relative to its Israelitic background.[14]

For considerably more than half a century Marxism was a movement in stark opposition to the institutionalized regimes of the Western world in which it arose. The Russian Revolution created a situation in certain respects comparable to that of Christianity after Constantine, though with extraordinary complications that cannot be entered into here. In the non-Communist world, which includes countries with strong traditions of democratic socialism like Great Britain and the Scandinavian countries, Marxian socialism must still be regarded as in a certain rather fundamental sense alienated from the main institutionalized social structure.

When we come to the recent contemporary and short-run prospective situation in the Western non-Communist world, and particularly the United States, I think it is legitimate to speak of a fundamentally new phase in the development of the Western religious tradition.[15] The most salient feature of this situation is the emergence of a movement that resembles early Christianity in its emphasis on the theme of love. Although this theme has never been absent from the older branches of Christianity, both Catholic and Protestant, there are several things that are new about the contemporary movement. In the first place, it is clearly focused at a this-worldly rather than a transcendental level. Its field of application and institutionalization is clearly what Christian tradition defines as secular society. In this respect it is a legitimate heir of the versions of Protestantism that attempted to establish a kingdom of God on earth and of both versions of the modern civil religion to which I have referred.

Second, it is, in a sense that was not true of the Christian predecessor movements, relatively nontheistic. I use this term as a conscious alternative to "atheistic." This theme certainly has something to do with the this-worldliness of the movement, since there is in it no equivalent to the gospel conception expressed in the famous statement "In my Father's house are many mansions." In this statement, of course, the Father's house has generally been interpreted to refer to heaven, that is, the other world which the redeemed souls of the dead would enter and in which they would enjoy eternal life. In the new religion of love, if I may use that term, there is no "Father's house" separable from this world – that is, the concrete human condition – to be entered only after death. Indeed, a major problem for this new orientation is the interpretation of the meaning of death, about which I will have something to say before I conclude.

The nontheistic feature of the new religious tendency permits its followers to seek a rapprochement with some of the great Oriental religions, notably those in the Hindu-Buddhist tradition. Many proponents of the contemporary counterculture have been fascinated by these Oriental religions, and both Hinduism and Buddhism – certainly the classical Brahminism that historically underlies both of them – are devoid of the specific kind of theism that has characterized the Judeo-Christian and, of course, the Islamic traditions.

A rather prominent part in the new religious movements has been taken by people involved in the so-called counterculture. This movement is strongly colored by a sense of alienation from much of the current industrial and even incipiently postindustrial society. In this respect it resembles some of the movements deriving from the influence of Rousseau in the Enlightenment and after the French Revolution, and also the movement of Marxian socialism within the developing industrial society.

Proponents of the counterculture have made much use of Marxian rhetoric, especially with respect to the class struggle and the upgrading of disadvantaged sectors of society in the name of egalitarian values. I think, however, that there is in the counterculture a major shift of emphasis from the kind of relatively orthodox Marxism that was most influential in establishing the Communist states in Eastern Europe, especially the Soviet Union. Perhaps the most important difference is that in the newer movements it is difficult to impute a clear doctrine of historical materialism. One wing of the Neo-Marxian movement is almost obsessively concerned with the alleged power of the capitalist system,[16] but other wings use the Marxian rhetoric to express their alienation from the established institutional order. With their more or less revolutionary stance, they tend to grasp at almost any way of expressing this alienation. As a conceptual system, however, their position can only dubiously be called Marxist in the traditional sense.

Common to all the radical traditions, from Rousseau on, has been the idealization of a state of relatively spontaneous community solidarity. Although Marx's principal works were written before that of Tönnies, the latter's formulation of the concept *Gemeinschaft* has been exceedingly important to the relevant discussions.[17] Marxists, with their eschatological orientation, have always drawn a sharp dichotomy between the capitalist system, with its economic and power interests, and communism, with its spontaneous solidarity, projecting the realization of communism into the future. The new movements also idealize a society free of economic and power interests, free of coercion and even of rationally oriented discipline, achieving spontaneous solidarity in ways often governed by the imperative of love. There is probably more of a disposition, however, to see the realizability of such a society in the present or the quite immediate future. Furthermore, that society is even less institutionalized than the classical Marxian conception of the communist utopia. The more radical elements of the counterculture come very close to principled anarchism.

In the United States and other countries, there have been numerous attempts to set up what in a sense are experimental living groups, or communes, organized on this kind of ideal basis.[18] There seem to be three important points about the commune movement which pose certain problems about the institutionalization of a larger and more successful movement of religiously oriented change. The first is the fact that communes have established such order as they have only for rather small numbers of people, usually living in a state of considerable segregation from the mainstream of modern society. Many of them have avoided urban communities and established themselves in rural areas where they can cultivate extremely simple life styles. I have the impression, though I do not think the field has been quite adequately surveyed, that the rate of failure is extremely high in such groups. They have been organized on widely varying principles; some, for example, have insisted on mutual sexual access of all members to each other, notably those of opposite sex, while others have permitted relatively exclusive sexual relations confined to particular pairs. There are also variations in the degree to which individual participants are required to give up all personal property or personal claim to money earned outside the commune to the common needs of the commune. Perhaps the most striking structural development, however, seems to be that a disproportionate number of those communes that have achieved a certain stability and viability have accepted a quasi-dictatorial pattern of leadership on the part of one dominant leader. It seems that the achievement of a fully participatory democracy on the part of the members is very rare and difficult. It should also be kept in mind that, relative to the total population, commune memberships have been highly selective. They have consisted primarily of young people of about college or more-or-less immediately post-college ages. They conspicuously lack the middle- and older-aged components which any general population necessarily includes. There have been small children involved with a wide variety of arrangements for their belongingness and care. I have the impression that the fate of children in the commune constitutes a very difficult problem, and that there have been many failures in this respect.

To have any chance of influencing the religious orientation of a large proportion of the population, a movement of religious innovation will have to meet conditions that have not been met by the small-scale communal experiments I have very briefly referred to. What can be said about the kinds of conditions that will be necessary and the prospect of their actualization?

In the "effervescent" phase of the modern New Left countercultural move-ment, there has been a very strong stress on the liberation of the erotic compon-ent and its generalization outside the conventional marriage context. Janet Giele has suggested that an important process of differentiation has indeed been occurring among the relatively new generations as part of the "sexual revolu-tion."[19] The principal new note seems to be the establishment, within the participant groups, of the legitimacy of overt heterosexual relations before and even outside of marriage, provided that two conditions are fulfilled. The clearer one is that the parties should have, as Dr. Giele puts it, "affection for each other," that is to say, that their erotic relationship should not be confined to the generation of organic pleasure. Closely linked to this and a very important item but somewhat more vaguely felt is the criterion of a certain commitment to relative durability of the relationship. Casual one-night stands are not given a very high mark for legitimacy.

I would like to attempt to carry the analysis one step further by introducing the important concept "affect." Affect may be defined as a generalized symbolic medium of interchange at the level of the general system of action.[20] I use the concept in a sense closely related to Freud's use of it in his *Interpretation of Dreams*,[21] but – in a way not suggested by Freud – anchored at what I would technically call the level of the social system. This is to say, it is a medium particularly functioning in the area of mediating relations of solidarity. Freud quite correctly emphasized in his own analysis its bearing on the relation of sexual partners, especially importantly in marriage. I would carry this forward to the views of David Schneider of sexual intercourse as a primary *symbol* and not the primary bond of the solidarity of marriage partners. Seen in this context, affect is not in the first instance primarily a psychological medium but rather one whose primary functional significance is social and cultural.

Its relation to eroticism seems to me to be that of a generalized medium to what I have sometimes called its security base. A ready example is the role of certain precious metals as a security base for money. At certain stages gold functions both as a commodity and as a form of money. It is a boundary entity from this point of view. But in modern monetary systems only the tiniest fraction of the actual circulating medium of exchange consists of gold. On the other hand, until at least very recently, a "gold standard" meant the interchange-ability of nonmetalic money with gold. This is by and large no longer the case. I suggest that in at all diffuse and enduring relations of human solidarity which involve an erotic element the situation is similar to that of the involvement of gold in a monetary system. Where, that is to say, there is an erotic component, the organic aspect is not the only meaning of erotic pleasure; it is also a symbol of a noneerotic aspect of the relationship, the one that Janet Giele calls affection. As I have pointed out elsewhere,[22] mutual erotic attraction has one particularly severe limitation as the basis of the kind of solidarity that can involve large numbers of people over long periods of time – in which I would include specifically transgenerational periods. This derives from the simple fact that erotic stimulation is a matter of organic body relatedness and requires access to the body of the partner. This is clearly most readily attainable in the dyadic relationship of which the prototype has become marriage. Some approximation to its meaningfulness can be attained in wider groups – "group sex," for example, has developed certain attractions. The group in such a case, however, cannot be a very extensive one because of the inherent limitations on the universalization of bodily contact among large numbers of people, and the attenuation of solidary relationships.

Given these considerations, I think it follows that some transcending of the consideration of erotic pleasure in defining the mediation and bonding of solidarity is a fundamental functional imperative for large communities. Freud provided a psychological reference for this transformation in his famous concept of sublimation. The main purport of this crucial concept is that what in its genetic origin may have been a purely erotic basis of attachment can be and frequently is transformed to a level of generality that omits the erotic component or reduces it to purely symbolic status. In this statement I mean the term "symbolic" to signify something that is expressively meaningful but, as such, does not play a determinative role.

It seems to me that what in a religious or quasi-religious context we tend to refer to as love can be interpreted in more technical sociological jargon as a bond of solidarity between persons as individuals and involving their mutual identity as members of a collective entity which is mediated not by accessibility to mutual erotic pleasure but by a more generalized accessibility to an "attitudinal" entity, which I call affect. Without some such mechanism I cannot see how secularized "love solidarity" of large communities can be sociologically possible. It seems to me it is clearly impossible if the positive condition is mutual erotic concern of every member with every other.

Such solidarity, of course, involves multiple levels in the general system of action. Affect as I understand it, since it is a medium at the general level of action, is not specifically internal to the social system, but mediates between the social system and the other components of the general system, notably the personality of the individual on the one side, and the cultural system on the other. Insofar then as the new religious tendency wishes to make the pattern of mutual love salient, I think it is particularly bound to the effective operation of the medium of affect. It should, however, be kept clearly in mind that affect in my present sense is a *medium* of interchange and not the primary bond of solidarity itself. I mean this in a sense parallel to that in which money is a medium operating in a market system of economic exchange. But such solidarity as participants in such a market system are able to achieve is not a function only of their monetary dealings and the interests associated with them.

The question therefore arises of what other than affect – or love – is a functional requirement of the viability and stability of large-scale community structures characterized at the social system level by the kind of solidarity which the proponents of the love doctrine clearly have in mind. I raise this question on the assumption that the Puritan pattern has in fact prevailed in the sense that spiritual solidarity – which may be defined as religiously motivated love – cannot be projected into a transcendental world, but must somehow be defined and institutionalized as part of the empirically given system of human action – social, cultural, psychological, and otherwise. In that sense, but only in that sense, it must be a "secular" phenomenon.

I think the key term here is "institutionalization." One way of stating what I have in mind involves the familiar concept "spontaneity." By its radical proponents, spontaneity seems to connote the "giving" of oneself in what I define as a love relationship without any expectation of reciprocity of any sort. To be "pure" such giving should indeed be explicitly defined as independent of any expectations of reciprocity. In marginal human conditions instances of this type surely do occur. Yet I think we are entitled to be highly skeptical that they can be stabilized and generalized to constitute a major movement that can shape civilizational futures. The reciprocity of giving, however, cannot be posited only on the giving relationship itself with no pattern of the definition of mutual obligation and no supplementation by other factors in the determination of social relationships.

In the Christian tradition, the love of Christians for one another and for the church was considered not to be totally spontaneous but a matter of obligation. Fulfillment of this obligation was a condition of acceptability in the church and in the religious orders as a full Christian, and failure in fulfillment of this obligation defined unacceptable behavior. In other words, one could not love or not love according to momentary whim; religiously acceptable love had to have the quality of diffuseness and enduringness of which Schneider speaks in the context of modern marriage. The regulation and in a certain sense assurance of such reciprocity seems to me the only basis on which involvement of a generalized medium of the character which I assert to be that of affect is functionally significant.

For the regime of love to be stable, it must institutionalize the expectation of both diffuse and enduring ties. This in my opinion transforms it from a matter of simple encounter between persons into a nexus of solidarity in the institutionalized sociological sense of that term.

Solidarity in this sense, however, is *never* a function of a single variable, but always involves a combination of essential factors. I conceive these factors to operate at both the level of the general system of action and that of the social system. At the level of general action, in addition to affective attraction itself, I feel that absolute necessities are, first, the kind of personal motivational commitment that, following Freud, I call the cathexis of social objects, and second, a component transcending the mutual attraction of individuals for each other, affirming allegiance to a much more broadly defined order which I would define as a moral order. Without attachment beyond the level of motivational self-interest to other objects and without commitment to participate in a moral order, a community that uses the primary symbol of love cannot be an authentically stable community. If these components, other than what are sometimes thought of as affective ties taken alone, are essential to the stabilization of a love-dominated community at the general action level, namely, the cathexis of objects and the commitment to a moral order, there is a further set of such conditions at the social system level. The two most important of these I conceive to be, first, responsiveness to appropriate leadership initiative in defining the obligations, rights, and tasks of any such collectivity, including those applicable to its nonleader members, and second, what I have called the valuation or the commitment to valued association, which I consider to be a specification of a commitment to a moral order.[23] Hence I very specifically assert the Durkheimian position that not only is a religious entity a moral community but it must for viability extend this community aspect to meet the exigencies of stability on a social level.[24]

Finally, I would also include in this set of conditions that there should be an adequate rational component. Many of the counter culture people who have functioned as the spearhead of the movements I have been discussing have stood in sharp reaction against the whole rationalistic cognitive tradition of Western society. In my view this reaction has been pressed too far; if what they advocate were in fact fully implemented, it would produce a drastically unstable orientation.[25] There must be a major component of rationality at at least two levels in a viable "religion of love." The first of these must be at the level of belief in the more or less traditional religious sense. It is not possible to have a system of spontaneous sentiments which are not regulated by the cognitive discipline of beliefs. Beliefs, of course, need not be rigid as they have been in some religious systems. On the other hand, the cognitive questions about who we are, where we belong in the universe, what we are doing and expected to do, cannot be left without any cognitive response. It is clearly not sufficient to say that people should "do their own thing" in the sense of whatever they have a momentary impulse to do.

This component of rationalization, however, must extend beyond the cultural level to the social. The general purport of such a requirement is that persons who share what is in some sense a common religious orientation – for example, as defined by mutual love – must have some cognitively intelligible definition of what this entails with respect to their own conduct and their expectations of reciprocal conduct from each other and from others with whom they interact. This seems to me to be a profound meaning of Durkheim's dictum that a religion constitutes not only a moral community but one which may be called, as he put it, a "church." A church is an institutionalized social organization of human participants. To be a viable collective entity it must have rules – rules that can be communicated and understood in cognitive terms. It cannot be a community within which "anything goes," and this way of putting it has not only moral but also cognitive implications.

The Expressive Revolution

It is altogether possible that a new religious movement of far-reaching importance will follow the kinds of beginnings I have sketched above. If this does occur, it will be a major aspect of what I would call the expressive revolution. It would result in a tilting of the previous balance between the rational-cognitive components of our cultural orientation and the modes of its institutionalization in favor of the affective-expressive emphasis relative to the cognitive-rationalistic emphasis. As such, it would inevitably include a value change, but not a drastically revolutionary repudiation of the society's previous value system. The primary change would be in the relative standing of different components of the inherited value system.

One way of formulating this point is in terms of an interpretation of the frequent allegation that the Protestant ethic is dead.[26] In my opinion the Protestant ethic is far from dead. It continues to inform our orientations to a very important sector of life today as it did in the past. We do value systematic rational work in "callings," and we do so out of what is at some level a religious background. In my opinion the instrumental apparatus of modern society could not function without a generous component of this kind of evaluation. This, however, is not to say that systematic rational work is the only thing we value. In a certain sense we have always valued solidary human relationships, community in some sense, and love relationships. I suggest that the expressive revolution is bringing about an enhanced valuation of this latter set of components of the value system.

The counterculture version, with its exclusive emphasis on pure expressiveness and pure love and glorification of the totally autonomous self, seems to me to be definitely not viable as a cultural and social phenomenon. But to say this is not to say that the counterculture is not a symptom of a profound change which is already under way. Indeed, I think it is.

There is a negative as well as a positive sense in which the counterculture may be interpreted as a harbinger. This is that it is a reaction against certain aspects of the rationalistic and utilitarian individualism of the recent phases of development of American society and industrial societies generally. This reaction has been spearheaded particularly in the student movement of recent years, but if it is confined to the student generation it cannot take hold as a major transformation of the cultural-religious situation of the society as what we might call a new version of the civil religion. For that to happen it must involve a much broader band of the age structure than the student population.

The Watergate scandal and the whole complex of activities associated with the Nixon administration which have so preoccupied the American public in the last year or two represent the kind of individualistic corruption well suited to serve as the negative target of a movement of resuscitation. I think this movement must point in the direction of a lessening of the stress on self-interest in the traditional utilitarian sense, of a strong reinforcement of the affective solidarity – that is, love – of individuals for each other, and of revival of the sense of collective solidarity which was an essential part of the original Puritan ideal.

A further important point needs to be made about the contemporary situation. Certainly for American conditions I would add to the other nonaffective components of a viable new religious movement that it should fit with a pluralistic social ethic and social structure and should not manifest the monolithic characteristics either of the community characterized in Rousseau's thinking by the General Will or the community posited by Marxian socialism. There is a certain sense in which this condition is both over- and underemphasized in the counterculture.[27] One might say that in such circles there is an utter horror of any requirements of doctrinal conformity, although pragmatically within such groups severe pressures to peer conformity often actually operate. To have a serious chance to be widely institutionalized, such a movement in my opinion must be in some basic sense compatible with continued allegiance to Catholic, Protestant, and Jewish religious commitments, to secular humanism, and also to a tentative and exploratory set of allegiances to Oriental religions, notably in the Hindu–Buddhist complex. This religious pluralism, or extended ecumenism, if the term is appropriate, seems to me the only possible system that would be congruent with the structural pluralism of American society and the relation of that to its emerging pattern of individualism.

Let me make a very brief comment on this emerging pattern. I have in a number of places referred to the conception of "institutionalized individualism" by deliberate contrast with the utilitarian version. In the pattern of institutionalized individualism the keynote is not the direct utilitarian conception of "the rational pursuit of self-interest" but a much broader conception of the self-fulfillment of the individual in a social setting in which the aspect of solidarity, as I have discussed it, figures at least as prominently as does that of self-interest in the utilitarian sense. I have a profound conviction that, unlike the Marxian solution to the problems of industrial society, the sacrifice of individualism is not indicated, is not necessary, and would be particularly inappropriate to American conditions. Specifically, I think that the kinds of restrictions on individual freedom, particularly in the cultural sphere, which have been conspicuously manifested in the Soviet Union, even very recently, constitute a danger of a quite different kind from the one that I think is developing in this society. That is to say, I expect that the new religion of love will manifest a strong individualistic emphasis, that people will love as individuals, and that they will form attachments of love to other objects also with a very high valence attached to the individuality of the object.

The above is about as circumstantial an account as is yet feasible of the kind of movement that I think has already occurred in an incipient form and has a chance of very significant further development in the American situation. I would emphasize its basic continuity with the American civil religion as this has been outlined by Bellah, but I would also emphasize the emergence of new emphases and new components into salience. Finally, however, I wish to insist very strongly that "love is not enough." If the movement is to be viable and to have a major transforming effect on the culture and society, it must incorporate conditions other than the mutual love of participants.

To recapitulate what I said above, the new religious movement will have to have a political component in the sense of adequately effective leadership. Second, there will have to be a commitment widely shared in the movement to a pattern of moral order to what I have called "valued association." Third, and by no means least important, there will have to be a cognitive-rational component – that is to say, at the religious level a belief system and at the level of moral implication a rationally defensible ethic. This, in my opinion, will articulate with the famous Protestant ethic, but will not be identical with the version that has been historically operative and has attracted the greatest attention. Let me repeat, however, that I do not for a moment think that the Protestant ethic is dead.

Finally, I am very strongly of the opinion that the new religion, precisely because it will be in a certain historic sense a secular religion, must achieve, if it is to be viable, a special and new level of integration with the secular society in which it comes to be institutionalized. This requirement clearly includes integration with the rational-technological aspect of that society, which is said by so many proponents of the counterculture to be an intolerable feature of modern industrial society. To me it is inconceivable that modern industrial society is to be abolished. It can be modified and transformed, but I would follow Marx's profound insight in saying that the "productive forces" which have created an industrial society will remain indispensable to human welfare and it is the most drastically fatal kind of romanticism to advocate their destruction.

Notes

1 Talcott Parsons, Renée C. Fox, and Victor M. Lidz, "The 'Gift of Life' and Its Reciprocation," *Social Research*, XXXIX (Autumn 1972), 367–415. See also Talcott Parsons, "Belief, Unbelief, and Disbelief," in Rocco Caporale and Antonio Grumelli, eds, *The Culture of Unbelief* (Berkeley: University of California Press, 1971), pp. 207–45.

2 Marcel Mauss, *The Gift*, translated by Ian Cunnison (Glencoe, IL: Free Press, 1954).

3 See Edmund Leach, *Genesis as Myth and Other Essays* (London: Jonathan Cape, 1969), and Kenneth Burke, *The Rhetoric of Religion* (Boston: Beacon Press, 1961).

4 Cf. Matilda W. Riley, Marilyn Johnson, and Ann Foner, eds, *Aging and Society*, vol. III: *A Sociology of Age Stratification* (New York: Russell Sage Foundation, 1972).

5 David M. Schneider, *American Kinship: A Cultural Account* (Englewood Cliffs, NJ: Prentice-Hall, 1968).

6 Max Weber, "Basic Sociological Terms," in his *Economy and Society*, edited by Guenther Roth and Claus Wittich (New York: Bedminster Press, 1968).

7 Max Weber, *The Protestant Ethic and the Spirit of Capitalism*, translated by Talcott Parsons (New York: Charles Scribner's Sons, 1958).

8 Weber, *The Protestant Ethic and the Spirit of Capitalism*, p. 121.

9 Peter L. Berger, *The Sacred Canopy* (Garden City, NY: Doubleday, 1967).

10 Robert N. Bellah, *Beyond Belief: Essays on Religion in a Post-Traditional World* (New York: Harper & Row, 1970).

11 Seymour M. Lipset, *The First New Nation* (New York: Basic Books, 1963).

12 Seymour M. Lipset, personal communication. For a more general discussion of Marx, see Seymour M. Lipset, "Issues in Social Class Analysis," in his *Revolution and Counterrevolution*, rev. edn (Garden City, NY: Doubleday Anchor Books, 1970), and Reinhard Bendix and Seymour M. Lipset, "Karl Marx's Theory of Social Classes," in Bendix and Lipset, eds, *Class, Status and Power*, 2nd edn (New York: Free Press, 1966), pp. 6–11.

13 Perry Miller, *Errand into the Wilderness* (Cambridge: Harvard University Press, 1956).

14 Talcott Parsons, "Christianity," in David L. Sills, ed., *International Encyclopedia of the Social Sciences* (New York: Macmillan and Free Press, 1968), II, 425–47. See also Arthur D. Nock, *St. Paul* (New York: Harper & Bros, 1938).

15 The following statement is a revised version of the material presented in the last section of my article "Belief, Unbelief, and Disbelief."

16 See Herbert Gintis, "Radical Analysis of Welfare Economics and Individual Development," *Quarterly Journal of Economics*, LXXXVI (November 1972), 572–99.

17 Ferdinand Tönnies, *Community and Society*, translated and edited by Charles P. Loomis (New York: Harper & Row, 1963).

18 On communes, see Rosabeth Kanter, *Commitment and Community: Communes and Utopias in Sociological Perspective* (Cambridge: Harvard University Press, 1972) and *Communes: Social Organization of the Collective Life* (New York: Harper & Row, 1973). See also Jesse R. Pitts, "Survey Essay on Communes," *Contemporary Sociology*, II (July 1973), 351–9.

19 Janet Zollinger Giele, "Changes in the Modern Family: Their Impact on Sex Roles," *American Journal of Orthopsychiatry*, XLI (October 1971), 757–66.

20 See Talcott Parsons and Gerald M. Platt, *The American University* (Cambridge: Harvard University Press, 1973), especially chs 4 and 8.

21 Sigmund Freud, *The Interpretation of Dreams*, vols IV–V of the *Standard Edition of the Complete Psychological Works of Sigmund Freud*, translated by James Strachey in collaboration with Anna Freud (London: The Hogarth Press and the Institute of Psychoanalysis, 1958). See also Talcott Parsons, "*The Interpretation of Dreams* by Sigmund Freud," *Daedalus*, CIII (Winter 1974), 91–6.

22 Parsons, "Belief, Unbelief, and Disbelief."

23 See the categories developed in "Technical Appendix: Some General Theoretical Paradigms," in Parsons and Platt, *The American University*, pp. 423–47.

24 Émile Durkheim, *The Elementary Forms of the Religious Life*, translated by Joseph W. Swain (New York: Free Press, 1965).

25 See David Martin, "The Naked Person," *Encounter*, XL (June 1973), 12–20.

26 This has been most recently asserted with no qualifications in Daniel Bell, *The Coming of Post-Industrial Society* (New York: Basic Books, 1973).

27 See Robert K. Merton, "Insiders and Outsiders: A Chapter in the Sociology of Knowledge," *American Journal of Sociology*, LVIII (July 1972), 9–47; reprinted in Robert K. Merton, *The Sociology of Science*, edited by Norman W. Storer (Chicago: University of Chicago Press, 1973).

Bibliography of Talcott Parsons

1928 "Capitalism" in Recent German Literature: Sombart and Weber, I, *Journal of Political Economy*, 36: 641–61.

1929 "Capitalism" in Recent German Literature: Sombart and Weber, II, *Journal of Political Economy*, 37: 31–51.

1930 Translation of *The Protestant Ethic and the Spirit of Capitalism* by Max Weber, with a foreword by R. H. Tawney (reprint edn 1948). London: Allen & Unwin.

1931 Wants and Activities in Marshall, *Quarterly Journal of Economics*, 46: 101–40.

1932 Economics and Sociology: Marshall in Relation to the Thought of His Time, *Quarterly Journal of Economics*, 46: 316–47.

1933a Malthus, *Encyclopedia of the Social Sciences*, vol. 10, New York: Macmillan, 68–9.

1933b Pareto, *Encyclopedia of the Social Sciences*, vol. 11, New York: Macmillan, 576–8.

1934a Service, *Encyclopedia of the Social Sciences*, vol. 13, New York: Macmillan, 672–4.

1934b Samuel Smiles, *Encyclopedia of the Social Sciences*, vol. 14, New York: Macmillan, 111–12.

1934c Society, *Encyclopedia of the Social Sciences*, vol. 14, New York: Macmillan, 225–31.

1934d Thrift, *Encyclopedia of the Social Sciences*, vol. 14, New York: Macmillan, 623–6.

1934e Some Reflections on "The Nature and Significance of Economics," *Quarterly Journal of Economics*, 48: 511–45.

1934f Sociological Elements in Economic Thought, I, *Quarterly Journal of Economics*, 49: 414–53.

1935a Sociological Elements in Economic Thought, II, *Quarterly Journal of Economics*, 49: 645–67.

1935b The Place of Ultimate Values in Sociological Theory, *International Journal of Ethics*, 45: 282–316.

1935c H. M. Robertson on Max Weber and his School, *Journal of Political Economy*, 43: 688–96.

1936a Pareto's Central Analytical Scheme, *Journal of Social Philosophy*, 1: 244–62.

1936b On Certain Sociological Elements in Professor Taussig's Thought, *Explorations in Economics: Notes and Essays Contributed in Honor of F. W. Taussig*, Jacob Viner (ed.), New York: McGraw-Hill, 352–79.

1937a *The Structure of Social Action: A Study in Social Theory with Special Reference to a Group of Recent European Writers*, New York: McGraw-Hill (reprint edn New York, Free Press, 1949).

1937b Education and the Professions, *International Journal of Ethics*, 47: 365–9.

1938a The Role of Theory in Social Research, *American Sociological Review*, 3 (1): 13–20. [Address presented to the 1937 annual meeting of the Society for Social Research at the University of Chicago.]

1938b The Role of Ideas in Social Action, *American Sociological Review*, 3: 652–64. [Address written for a session on the problem of ideologies at the December 1937 annual meeting of the American Sociological Society, Atlantic City, NJ. Reprinted in *Essays in Sociological Theory*, 1949, 1954.]

1939a The Professions and Social Structure, *Social Forces*, 17 (May): 457–67. [Address written for a session on the problems of ideologies at the 1938 annual meeting of the American Sociological Society, Detroit (December). Reprinted in *Essays in Sociological Theory*, 1949, 1954.]

1939b Comte, *Journal of Unified Science*, 9: 77–83.

1940a Analytical Approach to the Theory of Social Stratification, *American Journal of Sociology*, 45: 841–62. [Reprinted in *Essays in Sociological Theory*, 1949, 1954.]

1940b The Motivation of Economic Activities, *Canadian Journal of Economics and Political Science*, 6: 187–203. [Public lecture at the University of Toronto. Reprinted in *Essays in Sociological Theory*, 1949, 1954; *Human Relations in Administration: The Sociology of Organization*, Robert Dubin (ed.), New York: Prentice-Hall (1st edn, 1951); and *Essays in Sociology*, C. W. M. Hart (ed.), Toronto: University of Toronto Press, 1940.]

1942a Max Weber and the Contemporary Political Crisis, *Review of Politics*, 4: 61–76, 155–72. [Reprinted in *Politics and Social Structure*, 1969.]

1942b The Sociology of Modern Anti-Semitism, *Jews in a Gentile World*, J. Graeber and Stuart Henderson Britt (eds), New York: Macmillan, 101–22.

1942c Age and Sex in the Social Structure of the United States, *American Sociological Review*, 7: 604–16. [Address presented to the annual meeting of the American Sociological Society, New York, (December) 1941. Reprinted in *Essays in Sociological Theory*, 1949; *Sociological Analysis: An Introductory Text and Case Book*, Logan Wilson and William Kolb under the editorship of Robert K. Merton, New York: Harcourt, Brace, 1949; and *Personality in Nature, Society, and Culture*, Clyde Kluckhohn and Henry A. Murray (eds), New York: Alfred A. Knopf, 1948, 1st and 2nd edns.]

1942d Propaganda and Social Control, *Psychiatry*, 5 (4): 551–72. [Reprinted in *Essays in Sociological Theory*, 1949, 1954.]

1942e Democracy and the Social Structure in Pre-Nazi Germany, *Journal of Legal and Political Sociology*, 1: 96–114. [Reprinted in *Essays in Sociological Theory*, revised edn, 1954; and *Politics and Social Structure*, 1969.]

1942f Some Sociological Aspects of the Fascist Movements, *Social Forces*, 21 (2): 138–47. [Presidential address presented at the 1942 annual meeting of the Eastern Sociological Society. Reprinted in *Essays in Sociological Theory*, revised edn, 1954.]

1943 The Kinship System of the Contemporary United States, *American Anthropologist*, 45: 22–38. [Reprinted in *Essays in Sociological Theory*, 1949.]

1944 The Theoretical Development of the Sociology of Religion, *Journal of the History of Ideas*, 5: 176–90. [Originally written to be read at the Conference on Methods in Science and Philosophy, New York, (November) 1942. Reprinted in *Essays in Sociological Theory*, 1949; and *Ideas in Cultural Perspective*, Philip Wiener and Aaron Noland (eds), New Brunswick, NJ: Rutgers University Press, 1962.]

1945a The Present Position and Prospects of Systematic Theory in Sociology, *Twentieth Century Sociology* (*A Symposium*), Georges Gurvitch and Wilbert E. Moore (eds), New York: Philosophical Library. [Reprinted in *Essays in Sociological Theory*, 1949, 1954.]

1945b The Problem of Controlled Institutional Change: An Essay on Applied Social Science, *Psychiatry*, 8: 79–101. [Prepared as an appendix to the *Report of the Conference on Germany after World War II*. Reprinted in *Essays in Sociological Theory*, 1949.]

1945c Racial and Religious Differences as Factors in Group Tensions, *Unity and Difference in the Modern World*, Lyman Bryson, Louis Finkelstein, and Robert M.

MacIver (eds), New York. [Approaches to National Unity, Fifth Symposium. Conference on Science, Philosophy and Religion in Their Relation to the Democratic Way of Life, held at the Men's Faculty Club of Columbia University, September 7–11, 1944. Reprinted in 1971 by Kraus Reprint Co., New York.]

1946a   The Science Legislation and the Role of the Social Sciences, *American Sociological Review*, 11 (6): 653–66.

1946b   Population and Social Structure, *Japan's Prospect*, Douglas G. Haring (ed.), Cambridge, MA: Harvard University Press, 87–114. [This book was published by the staff of the Harvard School for Overseas Administration. Reprinted in *Essays in Sociological Theory*, revised edn, 1954.]

1946c   Some Aspects of the Relations between Social Science and Ethics, *Social Science*, 22: 213–17. [Address presented to the 1946 annual meeting of the American Association for the Advancement of Science, Boston (December).]

1947a   Certain Primary Sources and Patterns of Aggression in the Social Structure of the Western World, *Psychiatry*, 10: 167–81. [Prepared for the Conference on Science, Philosophy and Religion at its September 1946 meeting in Chicago: also published in the volume issued by the Conference. Reprinted in *Essays in Sociological Theory*, 1949; and *Crisis and Continuity in World Politics* (2nd edn), G. Lanyi and W. McWilliams (eds), New York: Random House (1973), 220–3.]

1947b   Introduction to *Max Weber: The Theory of Social and Economic Organization* (co-edited and translated with A. M. Henderson), New York: Oxford University Press. [The Introduction was reprinted in *Essays in Sociological Theory*, 1949, 1954.]

1947c   Note on the Science Foundation Bill in the 80th Congress, *American Sociological Review*, 12 (1–6): 601–3.

1948a   Sociology, 1941–1946 (co-authored with Bernard Barber), *American Journal of Sociology*, 53: 245–57.

1948b   The Position of Sociological Theory, *American Sociological Review*, 13: 156–71. [Address presented to the 1947 annual meeting of the American Sociological Society, New York City (December). Reprinted in *Essays in Sociological Theory*, 1949.]

1949a   *Essays in Sociological Theory Pure and Applied*, New York: Free Press [revised edns 1954, 1964.]

1949b   The Rise and Decline of Economic Man, *Journal of General Education*, 4: 47–53.

1949c   Social Classes and Class Conflict in the Light of Recent Sociological Theory, *American Economic Review*, 39: 16–26. [Address presented to the annual meeting of the American Economics Association, (December) 1948. Reprinted in *Essays in Sociological Theory*, revised edn, 1954.]

1949d   *The Structure of Social Action*, New York: Free Press. (Reprint edn.)

1950a   The Prospects of Sociological Theory, *American Sociological Review*, 15 (1): 3–16. [Presidential address presented to the annual meeting of the American Sociological Society, New York City, (December) 1949. Reprinted in *Essays in Sociological Theory*, revised edn, 1954.]

1950b   Psychoanalysis and the Social Structure, *Psychoanalytic Quarterly*, 19: 371–84. [Substance of this paper was presented at the May 1948 annual meeting of the American Psychoanalytic Association, Washington, D.C. Reprinted in *Essays in Sociological Theory*, revised edn, 1954.]

1950c   The Social Environment of the Educational Process, *Centennial*, Washington, D.C., American Association for the Advancement of Science: 36–40. [Address presented to the AAAS Centennial Celebration, (September) 1948.]

1951a   *The Social System*, New York, Chicago: Free Press. (New edn edited by Bryan S. Turner, London: Routledge, 1991.)

1951b   *Toward a General Theory of Action* (co-authored with Edward A. Shils), Cambridge, MA: Harvard University Press. [Reprinted by Harper Torchbooks, New York, 1962.]

1951c   Graduate Training in Social Relations at Harvard, *Journal of General Education*, 5: 149–57.

1951d   Illness and the Role of the Physician: A Sociological Perspective, *American Journal of Orthopsychiatry*, 21: 452–60. [Address presented to the annual meeting of the American Orthopsychiatry Association in Detroit. Reprinted in *Personality in Nature, Society, and Culture* (2nd edn), Clyde Kluckhohn, Henry A. Murray, and David M. Schneider (eds), New York: Alfred A. Knopf, 1953.]

1952a   The Superego and the Theory of Social Systems, *Psychiatry*, 15: 15–25. [Substance of this paper was presented at the 1951 meeting of the Psychoanalytic Section of the American Psychiatric Association in Cincinnati, (May) 1951. Reprinted in *Social Structure and Personality*, 1964; and *Working Papers in the Theory of Action* (2nd edn), Talcott Parsons, Robert F. Bales, and Edward A. Shils (eds), New York: Free Press, 1953, 1967.]

1952b   Religious Perspectives in College Teaching: Sociology and Social Psychology, *Religious Perspectives in College Teaching*, Hoxie N. Fairchild (ed.), New York: Ronald Press.

1952c   A Sociologist Looks at the Legal Profession, *Conference on the Profession of Law and Legal Education*, Conference Series Number II, Chicago Law School, University of Chicago: 49–63. [Address presented to the first Symposium at the Fiftieth Anniversary Celebration of the University of Chicago Law School (December). Reprinted in *Essays in Sociological Theory*, 1954.]

1953a   *Working Papers in the Theory of Action* (in collaboration with Robert F. Bales and Edward A. Shils), New York, Chicago: Free Press. (Reprint edn, 1967.)

1953b   Psychoanalysis and Social Science with Special Reference to the Oedipus Problem, *Twenty Years of Psychoanalysis*, Franz Alexander and Helen Ross (eds), New York: W. W. Norton and Company, 186–215. [Substance of this paper was presented to the Twentieth Anniversary Celebration of the Institute for Psychoanalysis, Chicago, (October) 1952.]

1953c   A Revised Analytical Approach to the Theory of Social Stratification, *Class, Status, and Power: A Reader in Social Stratification*, Reinhard Bendix and Seymour M. Lipset (eds), New York: Free Press, 92–129. [Reprinted in *Essays in Sociological Theory*, 1954.]

1953d   Illness, Therapy, and the Modern Urban American Family (co-authored with Renée C. Fox), *Journal of Social Issues*, 8: 31–44. [Reprinted in *Patients, Physicians, and Illness*, E. Gartly Jaco (ed.), New York: Free Press, 1958.]

1953e   Some Comments on the State of the General Theory of Action, *American Sociological Review*, 18 (6) (December): 618–31.

1954a   The Father Symbol: An Appraisal in the Light of Psychoanalytic and Sociological Theory, *Symbols and Values: An Initial Study* (13th Symposium of the Conference on Science, Philosophy and Religion), Lyman Bryson, Louis Finkelstein, Robert M. MacIver, and Richard McKeon (eds), New York: Harper & Row, 523–44. [Substance of this paper was presented to the annual meeting of the American Psychological Association, Washington, D.C. (September). Reprinted in *Social Structure and Personality*, 1964.]

1954b   *Essays in Sociological Theory* (revised edn), New York, Chicago: Free Press.

1954c   Psychology and Sociology, *For a Science of Social Man*, John P. Gillin (ed.), New York: Macmillan, 67–102.

1954d   The Incest Taboo in Relation to Social Structure and the Socialisation of the Child, *British Journal of Sociology*, 5 (2) (June): 101–17.

1955a   *Family, Socialization, and Interaction Process* (co-authored with Robert F. Bales, James Olds, Morris Zelditch, and Philip E. Slater), New York: Free Press.

1955b   "McCarthyism" and American Social Tension: A Sociologist's View, *Yale Review* (Winter): 226–45. [Reprinted as Social Strains in America: A Postscript, *The Radical Right*, Daniel Bell (ed.), New York: Anchor Books, 1964.]

1956a   *Economy and Society* (co-authored with Neil J. Smelser), New York: Free Press. [Reprinted 1965.]

1956b   A Sociological Approach to the Theory of Organizations, I, *Administrative Science Quarterly* (June): 63–85. [Reprinted in *Structure and Process in Modern Societies*, 1960.]

1956c   A Sociological Approach to the Theory of Organizations, II, *Administrative Science Quarterly* (September): 225–39. [Reprinted in *Structure and Process in Modern Societies*, 1960.]

1957a   The Distribution of Power in American Society, *World Politics*, 10 (October): 123–43. [Reprinted in *Structure and Process in Modern Societies*, 1960.]

1957b   Malinowski and the Theory of Social Systems, *Man and Culture*, Raymond Firth (ed.), London: Routledge & Kegan Paul, 53–70.

1957c   Man in his Social Environment – As Viewed by Modern Social Science, *Centennial Review of Arts and Sciences*, 1 (1): 50–69.

1957d   The Mental Hospital as a Type of Organization, *The Patient and the Mental Hospital*, Milton Greenblatt, Daniel J. Levinson, and Richard H. Williams (eds), New York: Free Press, 108–29.

1958a   Authority, Legitimation, and Political Action, *Nomos 1. Authority*, C. J. Friedrich (ed.), Cambridge, MA: Harvard University Press, 197–221. [Reprinted in *Structure and Process in Modern Societies*, 1960.]

1958b   The Definitions of Health and Illness in the Light of American Values and Social Structure, *Patients, Physicians, and Illness*, E. Gartly Jaco (ed.), New York: Free Press, 165–87. [Reprinted in *Social Structure and Personality*, 1964.]

1958c   Social Structure and the Development of Personality: Freud's Contribution to the Integration of Psychology and Sociology, *Psychiatry*, 21 (November): 321–40. [Reprinted in *Social Structure and Personality*, 1964.]

1958d   General Theory in Sociology, *Sociology Today*, Robert K. Merton, Leonard Broom, and Leonard S. Cottrell, Jr. (eds), New York: Basic Books, 3–38.

1958e   Some Ingredients of a General Theory of Formal Organization, *Administrative Theory in Education*, Andrew W. Halpin (ed.), Midwest Administration Center, University of Chicago. [Reprinted in *Structure and Process in Modern Societies*, 1960.]

1958f   Some Reflections on the Institutional Framework of Economic Development, *The Challenge of Development (A Symposium)*, Jerusalem: Hebrew University, 107–36. [Reprinted in *Structure and Process in Modern Societies*, 1960.]

1958g   Some Trends of Change in American Society: Their Bearing on Medical Education, *Journal of the American Medical Association*, 167 (1): 31–6. [Reprinted in *Structure and Process in Modern Societies*, 1960.]

1958h   The Pattern of Religious Organisation in the United States, *Daedalus* (Summer): 65–85. [Reprinted in *Structure and Process in Modern Societies*, 1960.]

1958i   The Concepts of Culture and of Social System (co-authored with A. L. Kroeber), *American Sociological Review*, 23 (5) (October): 582–3. [Reprinted in *Ideas of Culture: Sources and Uses*, Frederick Gamst and Edward Norbeck (eds), New York: Holt, Rinehart & Winston, 1976.]

1958j   Some Highlights of the General Theory of Action, *Approaches to the Study of Politics*, Roland Young (ed.), Evanston: Northwestern University Press. [A paper originally presented at the Conference on Analytic Systems, Northwestern University, June 14–17.]

1958k   A Short Account of My Intellectual Development, *Alpha Kappa Delta*, Claremont: Pomona College, 3–12.

1959a   An Approach to Psychological Theory in Terms of the Theory of Action, *Psychology: A Study of A Science*, vol. 3, Sigmund Koch (ed.), New York: McGraw-Hill, 612–711.

1959b   The Principal Structures of Community: A Sociological View, *Community*, C. J. Friedrich (ed.), New York: Liberal Arts Press, 152–79. [Reprinted in *Structure and Process in Modern Societies*, 1960.]

1959c   "Voting" and the Equilibrium of the American Political System, *American Voting Behavior*, Eugene Burdick and Arthur Brodbeck (eds), New York: Free Press, 80–120.

1959d   Comment on American Intellectuals: Their Politics and Status, *Daedalus*, 88 (3): 493–5.

1959e   Durkheim's Contribution to the Theory of Integration of Social Systems, *Émile Durkheim, 1858–1917: A Collection of Essays, with Translations and a Bibliography*, Kurt H. Wolff (ed.), Columbus: Ohio State University Press, 118–53.

1959f   Some Problems Confronting Sociology as a Profession, *American Sociological Review*, 24 (4) (August): 547–59.

1959g   The School Class as a Social System: Some of its Functions in American Society, *Harvard Educational Review* (Fall): 297–318. [Reprinted in *Social Structure and Personality*, 1964; *Education, Economy and Society*, A. H. Halsey, Jean Floud, and Arnold C. Anderson (eds), New York: Free Press, 1961; and in *Socialization and Schools*, Reprint Series No. 1, compiled from the *Harvard Educational Review*, 1972: 69–90.]

1959h   An Approach to the Sociology of Knowledge, *Proceedings of the Fourth World Congress of Sociology*, Milan, Italy, vol. 4 (September): 25–49.

1959i   A Rejoinder to Ogles and Levy, *American Sociological Review*, 24 (2): 248–50.

1959j   Foreword to *The Chinese Family in the Communist Revolution* by C. K. Yang, Massachusetts: Technology Press, v–vii.

1960a   Mental Illness and "Spiritual Malaise": The Roles of the Psychiatrist and of the Minister of Religion, *The Ministry and Mental Health*, Hans Hofmann (ed.), New York: Association Press. [Reprinted in *Social Structure and Personality*, 1964.]

1960b   *Structure and Process in Modern Societies*, New York: Free Press.

1960c   In Memoriam: "Clyde Kluckhohn, 1905–1960", *American Sociological Review*, 25 (4) (August): 960–2.

1960d   Comment on: *The Mass Media and the Structure of American Society* (co-authored with Winston White), *Journal of Social Issues*, 16 (3): 67–77.

1960e   Pattern Variables Revisited: A Response to Robert Dubin, *American Sociological Review*, 25 (4) (August): 467–83.

1960f   Toward a Healthy Maturity, *Journal of Health and Human Behavior*, 1 (3) (Fall): 163–82. [Reprinted in *Social Structure and Personality*, 1964.]

1960g   Social Structure and Political Orientation: A Review of *Political Man*, by Seymour M. Lipset, and *The Politics of Mass Society*, by William Kornhauser, *World Politics*, 13 (October): 112–28.

1960h   Review Article of *Max Weber: An Intellectual Portrait*, by Reinhard Bendix, *American Sociological Review*, 25 (5) (October): 750–2.

1960i   The Physician in a Changing Society, *What's New*, 220: 11–12.

1961a   *Theories of Society* (2 vols) (co-edited with Edward Shils, Kaspar D. Naegele, and Jesse R. Pitts), New York: Free Press.

1961b   Some Principal Characteristics of Industrial Societies, *The Transformation of Russian Society: Aspects of Social Change since 1861*, Cyril E. Black (ed.), Cambridge, MA: Harvard University Press, 13–42.

1961c   The Link Between Character and Society (co-authored with Winston White), *Culture and Social Character*, S. M. Lipset and Leo Loewenthal (eds), New York: Free Press, 89–135. [Reprinted in *Social Structure and Personality*, 1964.]

1961d   The Contribution of Psychoanalysis to the Social Sciences, *Science and Psychoanalysis*, 4. [Reprinted in *Psychoanalysis and Social Process*, J. H. Masserman (ed.), New York: Grune & Stratton, 28–38.]

1961e   The Cultural Background of American Religious Organization, *Proceedings of the Conference on Science, Philosophy and Religion*.

1961f   The Point of View of the Author: A Critical Examination, *The Social Theories of Talcott Parsons*, Max Black (ed.), Englewood Cliffs, NJ: Prentice-Hall, 311–63.

1961g   Order and Community in the International Social System, *International Politics and Foreign Policy*, James N. Rosenau (ed.), New York: Free Press, 120–9.

1961h   Polarization of the World and International Order, *Preventing World War III*, Quincy Wright, William M. Evan, and Morton Deutsch (eds), New York: Simon & Schuster, 310–31. [Also in the *Berkeley Journal of Sociology*, 1961, 6 (1): 147–50.]

1961i   Some Considerations on the Theory of Social Change, *Rural Sociology*, 26 (3) (September): 219–39.

1961j   A Sociologist's View, *Values and Ideals of American Youth*, Eli Ginzberg (ed.), New York: Columbia University Press, 271–87.

1961k   The Cultural Background of Today's Aged, *Politics of Age*, Wilma Donahue and Clark Tibbitts (eds) (The Proceedings of the Michigan University Conference on Aging).

1961l   Comment on: "Preface to a Metatheoretical Framework for Sociology," by Llewellyn Gross, *American Journal of Sociology*, 68 (2): 136–40.

1961m   In Memoriam: Alfred L. Kroeber, 1876–1960, *American Journal of Sociology*, 67 (6) (May): 616–17.

1961n   Comment on: "Images of Man and the Sociology of Religion," by William Kolb, *Journal for the Scientific Study of Religion*, 1 (1) (October): 22–9.

1961o   Clyde Kluckhohn, Anthropologist, *Science*, 144.

1962a   Foreword to Herbert Spencer, *The Study of Sociology*, Ann Arbor: University of Michigan Press.

1962b   In Memoriam: Clyde Kay Maben Kluckhohn, 1905–1960 (co-authored with Evon Z. Vogt), *American Anthropologist*, 64 (1), pt. I (February): 140–61. [Reprinted as the Introduction to a new edition of Clyde Kluckhohn, *Navajo Witchcraft*, Boston: Beacon Press.]

1962c   Comment on: "The Oversocialized Conception of Man," by Dennis Wrong, *Psychoanalysis and Psychoanalytic Review* (Summer).

1962d   Review of *Law and Social Process in United States History*, by James Willard Hurst, *Journal of the History of Ideas*, 23 (4) (October–December): 558–64.

1962e   The Aging in American Society, *Law and Contemporary Problems*, 27 (1) (Winter): 22–35.

1962f   The Law and Social Control, *Law and Sociology: Exploratory Essays*, William M. Evan (ed.), New York: Free Press, 56–73.

1962g   In Memoriam: Richard Henry Tawney, 1880–1962, *American Sociological Review*, 27 (December): 888–90.

1962h   Review of *Reason in Society: Five Types of Decision and Their Social Conditions*, by Paul Diesing, *Industrial and Labor Relations Review*, 16 (4): 630–1.

1962i   Considerazioni Teoriche Intorno Alla Sociologia Della Medicina (Theoretical Considerations on the Sociology of Medicine), Estratto dai *Quaderni di Sociologia*, 11 (3) (July–September): 243–79.

1962j   The Cultural Background of American Religious Organization, *Ethics and Bigness: Scientific, Academic, Religious, Political, and Military*, Harlan Cleveland and Harold D. Lasswell (eds), New York: Conference on Science, Philosophy, and Religion in Their Relation to the Democratic Way of Life, 141–67.

1962k   Youth in the Context of American Society, *Daedalus*, 91 (1) (Winter): 97–123. [Reprinted in *Youth: Change and Challenge*, Erik H. Erikson (ed.), New York: Basic Books, 1963; and *Social Structure and Personality*, 1964. Also appears in a modified version in *Man in a World at Work*, 1964.]

1962l   Christianity and Modern Industrial Society, *Sociological Theory, Values and Sociocultural Change: Essays in Honor of Pitrim A. Sorokin*, Edward A. Tiryakian (ed.), New York: Free Press, 33–70.

1963a   Introduction to Max Weber, *The Sociology of Religion*, Boston: Beacon Press, xix–lxvii.

1963b   Social Strains in America: A Postscript, *The Radical Right*, Daniel Bell (ed.), New York: Doubleday Anchor Books, 231–8.

1963c   Social Change and Medical Organization in the United States: A Sociological Perspective, *Annals of the American Academy of Political and Social Science*, 346 (March): 21–33.

1963d   On the Concept of Influence, *Public Opinion Quarterly*, 27 (1) (Spring): 37–62. [Reprinted in *Sociological Theory and Modern Society*, 1967.]

1963e   On the Concept of Political Power, *Proceedings of the American Philosophical Society*, 107 (3) (June): 232–62. [Reprinted in *Sociological Theory and Modern Society*, 1967.]

1963f   Death in American Society (co-authored with Victor M. Lidz), *American Behavioral Scientist* (May). [Reprinted in *Essays in Self-Destruction*, Edwin Shneidman (ed.), New York: Science House, 1967.]

1963g   Old Age as Consummatory Phase, *Gerontologist*, 3 (2): 53–4.

1963h   The Intellectual: A Social Role Category, *On Intellectuals*, P. Rieff (ed.), Garden City: Anchor, 3–24.

1964a   Some Theoretical Considerations Bearing on the Field of Medical Sociology (written for a symposium that did not take place). [Published in *Social Structure and Personality*, 1964.]

1964b   *Social Structure and Personality*, New York: Free Press.

1964c   The Ideas of Systems, Causal Explanation, and Cybernetic Control in Social Science, *Cause and Effect*, Daniel Lerner (ed.), New York: Free Press. [Address presented at the Fourth Hayden Colloquium, Massachusetts Institute of Technology, 1964.]

1964d   Evolutionary Universals in Society, *American Sociological Review*, 29 (3) (June): 33–57. [Reprinted in *Essays on Modernization of Underdeveloped Societies*, A. R. Desai (ed.), Bombay: Thacker, 56–88.]

1964e   Sociological Theory, *Encyclopedia Britannica*.

1964f   Some Reflections on the Place of Force in Social Process, *Internal War: Basic Problems and Approaches*, Harry Eckstein (ed.), New York: Free Press, 33–70.

1964g   Levels of Organization and the Mediation of Social Interaction, *Sociological Inquiry*, 34 (2) (Spring): 207–20.

1964h   Die Juengsten Entwicklungen in Der Strukturell-Funktionalem Theorie, *Koelner Zeitschrift für Soziologie und Sozial-psychologie*, 16 (1): 30–49.

1964i   Youth in the Context of American Society, *Man in a World at Work*, Henry Borow (ed.), Boston: Houghton Mifflin, 237–56. [Modified version of an article previously written for *Daedalus*, 91 (1) (Winter 1962): 97–123.]

1964j   La Theorie de la Société, *Les Etudes Philosophiques, Perspectives sur la Philosophie Nord Americaine*, 3 (4): 537–47.

1964k   Commentary, *Crane Review*, 7 (2): 92–7. [Address presented to the First Crane Conference on the Ministry, (October) 1963.]

1964l   Rejoinder to Bauer and Coleman, *The Public Opinion Quarterly*, 27 (1) (Spring): 87–92.

1964m   The Sibley Report on Training in Sociology: On Eldridge Sibley, *The Education of Sociologists in the United States*, *American Sociological Review*, 29: 747–8.

1964n   Recent Trends in Structural-Functional Theory, *Fact and Theory in Social Science*, Earl W. Count and Gordon T. Bowles (eds), New York: Syracuse University Press, 140–58.

1965a   An American's Impression of Sociology in the Soviet Union, *American Sociological Review*, 30 (1) (February): 121–215.

1965b   Full Citizenship for the Negro American, A Sociological Problem, *Daedalus*, 94 (4) (Fall): 1009–54. [Reprinted in *The Negro American*, Talcott Parsons and Kenneth Clark (eds), Boston: Houghton Mifflin, 1966.]

1965c   Changing Family Patterns in American Society, *The American Family in Crisis*, Forest Hospital, Des Plaines, IL: Forest Hospital Publications, vol. 3, 4–10.

1965d   Evaluation and Objectivity in the Social Sciences: An Interpretation of Max Weber's Contributions, *International Journal of the Social Sciences*, 17 (1): 46–63. [Reprinted in *Sociological Theory and Modern Society*, 1967; and in *Max Weber and Sociology Today*, K. Morris (trans.), New York: Harper & Row, 1971. This address presented to the Weber Centennial, (April) 1964, was published first in German (*Wertgebundenheit und Objektivitat in den Sozialwissenschaften: Eine Interpretation der Beitrage Max Webers*) in *Max Weber und die Soziologie Heute*, Otto Stammer (ed.), Tübingen: Mohr, 39–64.]

1965e   Max Weber, 1864–1964, *American Sociological Review*, 30 (2) (April): 171–5.

1965f   Unity and Diversity in the Modern Intellectual Disciplines: The Role of the Social Sciences, *Daedalus*, 94 (1) (Winter): 39–65.

1966a   Youth Behavior and Values, *Needs and Influencing Forces*, E. Landy and A. Kroll (eds), Cambridge, MA: Harvard Graduate School of Education.

1966b   *Societies: Evolutionary and Comparative Perspectives*, Englewood Cliffs, NJ: Prentice-Hall.

1966c   The Political Aspect of Social Structure and Process, *Varieties of Political Theory*, David Easton (ed.), Englewood Cliffs, NJ: Prentice-Hall, 71–112.

1966d   *The Negro American* (co-edited with Kenneth Clark), Boston: Houghton Mifflin.

1966e   Die Bedeutung der Polarisierung für das Sozialsystem: Die Hautfarbe als Polarisierungsproblem, *Militanter Humanismus*, Alphons Silbermann (ed.), Frankfurt: Fischer.

1966f   Religion in a Modern Pluralistic Society, *Review of Religious Research*, 7 (3) (Spring): 125–46.

1967a   The Nature of American Pluralism, *Religion and Public Education*, Theodore Sizer (ed.), Boston: Houghton Mifflin.

1967b   Social Science and Theology, *America and the Future of Theology*, William A. Beardslee (ed.), Philadelphia: Westminister, 136–57.

1967c   *Sociological Theory and Modern Society*, New York: Free Press.

1967d   Death in American Society (co-authored with Victor M. Lidz), *Essays in Self-Destruction*, Edwin Shneidman (ed.), New York: Science House, 133–70.

1967e   Comment on "An Economist Looks at the Future of Sociology," by Kenneth Boulding et al. in *Sociology and Law*, William O. Douglas, Supreme Court, Washington, D.C.

1967f   Robert A. Nisbet, *The Sociological Tradition* (A Review Symposium) (co-authored with Morris Janowitz), *American Sociological Review*, 32 (4) (August): 638–43.

1968a   Components and Types of Formal Organization, *Comparative Administrative Theory*, Preston P. Le Breton (ed.), Seattle: University of Washington Press, 3–19.

1968b   Comment on: "The Future of the Nineteenth Century Idea of a University," by Sir Eric Ashby, *Minerva*, 6 (Spring): 267–71.

1968c   *American Sociology. Perspectives, Problems, Methods*, Talcott Parsons (ed.), New York: Basic Books.

1968d   Comment on: "Religion as a Cultural System," by Clifford Geertz, *The Religious Situation*, Donald R. Cutler (ed.), Boston: Beacon Press.

1968e   Christianity: Émile Durkheim: Interaction: Social Interaction: Vilfredo Pareto – Contributions to Economics: Professions: Systems Analysis: Social Systems: Utilitarians: Social Thought, *International Encyclopedia of the Social Sciences*, David L. Sills (ed.), New York: Macmillan and Free Press.

1968f   The Position of Identity in the General Theory of Action, *The Self in Social Interaction*, Chad Gordon and Kenneth J. Gergen (eds), New York: Wiley, 11–23.

1968g   *The American Academic Profession: A Pilot Study* (co-authored with Gerald M. Platt), Cambridge, MA: Multilith.

1968h   The Academic System: A Sociologist's View, *The Public Interest*, 13 (Fall): 173–95.

1968i   On the Concept of Value-Commitments, *Sociological Inquiry*, 38 (2) (Spring): 135–59. [Reprinted in *Politics and Social Structure*, 1969.]

1968j   Cooley and the Problem of Internalization, *Cooley and Sociological Analysis*, Albert J. Reiss, Jr. (ed.), Ann Arbor: University of Michigan Press, 48–67.

1968k   Sociocultural Pressures and Expectations, *Psychiatric Research Reports* (February). [A paper presented to the American Psychiatric Association.]

1968l   Order as a Sociological Problem, *The Concept of Order*, Paul G. Kuntz (ed.), Seattle: University of Washington Press, 373–84.

1968m   The Problem of Polarization on the Axis of Color, *Color and Race*, John Hope Franklin (ed.), Boston: Houghton Mifflin.

1968n   Considerations on the American Academic System (co-authored with Gerald M. Platt), *Minerva*, 6 (4) (Summer): 497–523.

1968o   Law and Sociology: A Promising Courtship? *The Path of the Law from 1967*, Harvard Law School Sesquicentennial Papers, Arthur E. Sutherland (ed.), Cambridge, MA: Harvard University Press.

1968p   The Disciplines as a Differentiating Force (co-authored with Norman Storer), *The Foundations of Access to Knowledge*, Edward B. Montgomery (ed.), Syracuse, Division of Summer Sessions, Syracuse University.

1968q   An Overview, *American Sociology*, Talcott Parsons (ed.), New York: Basic Books, 319–35.

1969a   Research with Human Subjects and the "Professional Complex," *Daedalus*, 98 (2) (Spring): 325–60. [Reprinted in *Action Theory and the Human Condition*, 1978.]

1969b   *Politics and Social Structure*, New York: Free Press.

1969c   On Stinchcombe's Conceptualization of Power Phenomena: A Review of *Constructing Social Theories*, by Arthur L. Stinchcombe, *Sociological Inquiry* (May): 226–31.

1969d   The Intellectual: A Social Role Category, *On Intellectuals*, Philip Rieff (ed.), New York: Doubleday, 3–26.

1970a   Some Problems of General Theory in Sociology, *Theoretical Sociology: Perspectives and Developments*, John C. McKinney and Edward A. Tiryakian (eds), New York: Appleton-Century-Crofts, 27–68.

1970b   Age, Social Structure, and Socialization in Higher Education (co-authored with Gerald M. Platt), *Sociology of Education*, 43 (1) (Winter): 1–37.

1970c   Decision-Making in the Academic System: Influence and Power Exchange (co-authored with Gerald M. Platt), *The State of the University: Authority and Change*, Carlos E. Kruythosch and Sheldon I. Messinger (eds), Beverly Hills: Sage Publications.

1970d   Theory in the Humanities and Sociology, *Daedalus*, 99 (2) (Spring): 495–523.

1970e   The Impact of Technology on Culture and Emerging New Modes of Behavior, *International Social Science Journal*, 22 (4): 607–27.

1970f   Equality and Inequality in Modern Society, or Social Stratification Revisited, *Sociological Inquiry*, 40 (2) (Spring): 13–72.

1970g   On Building Social Systems Theory: A Personal History, *Daedalus*. [Reprinted in *The Twentieth Century Sciences: Studies in the Biography of Ideas*, Gerald Holton (ed.), New York: Norton, 1972; and in *Social Systems and the Evolution of Action Theory*, 1977.]

1970h   Some Considerations on the Comparative Sociology of Education, *The Social Sciences and the Comparative Study of Educational Systems*, Joseph Fischer (ed.), Scranton: International Textbook.

1971a   *The System of Modern Societies*, Englewood Cliffs, NJ: Prentice-Hall. [Companion volume to *Societies: Evolutionary and Comparative Perspectives*, 1966.]

1971b   Kinship and the Associational Aspect of Social Structure, *Kinship and Culture*, Francis L. K. Hsu (ed.), Chicago: Aldine, 409–38.

1971c   Comparative Studies in Evolutionary Change, *Comparative Methods in Sociology*, Ivan Vallier (ed.), Berkeley: University of California Press, 97–139.

1971d   The Normal American Family, *Readings on the Sociology of the Family*, Bert N. Adams and Thomas Weirath (eds), Chicago: Markham, 53–66. [Reprinted from *Man and Civilization: The Family's Search for Survival*, Seymour M. Farber, Piero Mustacchi, and Roger H. L. Wilson (eds), New York: McGraw-Hill, 1965.]

1971e   Belief, Unbelief, and Disbelief, *The Culture of Unbelief: Studies and Proceedings from the First International Symposium on Belief*, Rocco Caporale and Antonio Grumelli (eds), Berkeley: University of California Press, 207–45.

1972a   Levels of Organization and the Mediation of Social Interaction: 23–35. Higher Education as a Theoretical Focus: 233–52. Commentary: 380–99. *Institutions and Social Exchange: The Sociologies of Talcott Parsons and George C. Homans*, Richard Simpson and Herman Turk (eds), Indianapolis: Bobbs-Merrill.

1972b   Higher Education and Changing Socialization (co-authored with Gerald M. Platt), *Aging and Society*, vol. 3: *A Sociology of Age Stratification*, Matilda White Riley, Marilyn Johnson, and Anne Foner (eds), New York: Russell Sage, 236–91.

1972c   Comment on: "Structural-Functionalism, Exchange Theory and the New Political Economy: Institutionalization as a Theoretical Linkage," by Terry Clarke, *Sociological Inquiry*, 42 (3–4): 299–308.

1972d   *Readings on Premodern Societies* (co-edited with Victor M. Lidz), Englewood Cliffs, NJ: Prentice-Hall.

1972e   Field Theory and Systems Theory: With Special Reference to the Relations Between Psychological and Social Systems, *Modern Psychiatry and Clinical Research:*

Essays in Honor of Roy R. Grinker, Sr., Daniel Offer and Daniel X. Freedman (eds), New York: Basic Books.

1972f   The Action Frame of Reference and the General Theory of Action Systems, *Classic Contributions to Social Psychology: Readings with Commentary*, Edwin P. Hollander and Raymond G. Hunt (eds), New York: Oxford University Press, 168–76. [Slightly abridged from *The Social System*, New York: Free Press (1951), 3–11, 15–19.]

1972g   The "Gift of Life" and Its Reciprocation (co-authored with Renée C. Fox and Victor M. Lidz), *Social Research*, 39 (3): 367–415. [Reprinted in *Death in American Experience*, Arien Mack (ed.), New York: Schocken (1973), 1–49.]

1972h   Review of *Scholarship and Partisanship*, by Reinhard Bendix and Guenther Roth, *Contemporary Sociology*, 1 (3): 200–3.

1972i   Culture and Social System Revisited, *Social Science Quarterly*, 53 (2) (September): 253–66. [Reprinted in *The Idea of Culture in the Social Sciences*, Louis Schneider and Charles Bonjean (eds), Cambridge: Cambridge University Press (1973), 33–46.]

1973a   Durkheim on Religion Revisited: Another Look at *The Elementary Forms of the Religious Life*: Beyond the Classics? *Essays in the Scientific Study of Religion*, Charles Y. Glock and Phillip E. Hammond (eds), New York: Harper Torchbooks, 156–80. [Reprinted in *Action Theory and the Human Condition*, 1978.]

1973b   *The American University* (co-authored with Gerald M. Platt and in collaboration with Neil J. Smelser), Cambridge, MA: Harvard University Press.

1973c   Clyde Kluckhohn and the Integration of Social Science, *Culture and Life: Essays in Memory of Clyde Kluckhohn*, Walter W. Taylor, John L. Fischer, and Evon Z. Vogt (eds), Carbondale: Southern Illinois University Press, 30–57.

1973d   The Bellah Case: Man and God in Princeton, New Jersey, *Commonweal*, 98 (11): 256–9.

1973e   Religious Symbolization and Death, *Changing Perspectives in the Scientific Study of Religion*, Allan W. Eister (ed.), New York: Wiley-Interscience, 217–26.

1973f   Some Reflections on Post-Industrial Society, *Japanese Sociological Review*, 24 (2): 109–13. [Address presented to the Japan Sociological Association (September).]

1973g   The Problem of Balancing Rational Efficiency with Communal Solidarity in Modern Society, *International Symposium on New Problems of Advanced Societies*, Tokyo: Japan Economic Research Institute, 9–14.

1973h   The Social Concept of the Present Civilization, *Tribuna Medica* (September): 19–20.

1973i   Review of *Sociology and Philosophy*, by L. T. Hobhouse, *Sociological Inquiry*, 43 (1): 85–7.

1973j   Review of *Capitalism and Modern Theory: An Analysis of the Writings of Marx, Durkheim, and Max Weber*, by Anthony Giddens, *American Political Science Review*, 67 (4): 1358–60.

1974a   *The Interpretation of Dreams*, by Sigmund Freud, *Daedalus*, 103 (1) (Winter): 91–6. [Reprinted in *Action Theory and the Human Condition*, 1978.]

1974b   The University "Bundle": A Study of the Balance Between Differentiation and Integration, *Public Higher Education in California: Growth, Structural Change, and Conflict*, Neil J. Smelser and Gabriel Almond (eds), Berkeley: University of California Press. [Reprinted in *Action Theory and the Human Condition*, 1978.]

1974c   Review of "A God Within," by Rene Dubos, *Commonweal*, 100 (2): 42–4.

1974d   The Institutional Function in Organization Theory, *Organization and Administrative Sciences*, 5 (1): 3–16. [Address presented at the Comparative Administrative Research Institute, Kent State University (May).]

1974e   The Life and Work of Émile Durkheim, *Sociology and Philosophy* by Émile Durkheim (reprint edn), New York: Free Press, xliii–lxiv.

1974f Review of *Ideology and Social Knowledge*, by Harold J. Bershady, *Sociological Inquiry*, 44 (3): 215–21. [Reprinted as part of ch. 6 in *Social Systems and the Evolution of Action Theory*, 1977.]

1974g Review of *Social Organization: A General Systems and Role Theory Perspective*, by Alvin L. Bertrand, *Social Forces*, 53 (1): 126–7.

1974h Comment on: "Current Folklore in the Criticisms of Parsonian Action Theory," by Turner and Beeghley, *Sociological Inquiry*, 44 (1): 55–8.

1974i Religion in Postindustrial America: The Problem of Secularization, *Social Research*, 41 (2) (Summer): 193–225. [Reprinted in *Social Research*, 51 (1–2) (Spring–Summer): 193–225.]

1974j Stability and Change in the American University, *Daedalus*, 103 (4) (Fall): 269–77.

1975a Pareto's Approach to the Construction of a Theory of the Social Systems. Rome: Accademia Nazionale dei Lincei. [Address presented at the International Conference on Vilfredo Pareto, (October) 1973.]

1975b The Present Status of Structural-Functional Theory in Sociology, *The Idea of Social Structure: Papers in Honor of Robert K. Merton*, Lewis A. Coser (ed.), New York: Harcourt Brace Jovanovich, 67–83. [Reprinted in *Social Systems and the Evolution of Action Theory*, 1977 (ch. 4).]

1975c The Sick Role and the Role of the Physician Reconsidered, *Millbank Memorial Fund Quarterly*, 53 (3) (Summer): 257–78. [Reprinted in *Action Theory and the Human Condition*, 1978 (ch. 1).]

1975d Social Structure and the Symbolic Media of Interchange, *Approaches to the Study of Social Structure*, Peter M. Blau (ed.), New York: Free Press, 94–120. [Reprinted in *Social Systems and the Evolution of Action Theory*, 1977 (ch. 9).]

1975e Some Theoretical Considerations on the Nature and Trends of Change of Ethnicity, *Ethnicity: Theory and Experience*, Nathan Glazer and Daniel P. Moynihan (eds), Cambridge, MA: Harvard University Press, 53–83. [Reprinted in *Social Systems and the Evolution of Action Theory*, 1977 (ch. 13).]

1975f Comment on: "Parsons' Interpretation of Durkheim," by Whitney Pope, and "Moral Freedom through Understanding in Durkheim," by Jere Cohen, *American Sociological Review*, 40 (1): 106–10.

1975g Comment on: "De-Parsonizing Weber. A Critique of Parsons' Interpretation of Weber's Sociology," by Cohen, Hazelrigg, and Pope, *American Sociological Review*, 40 (5) (October): 666–70.

1975h Comment on: "A Radical Analysis of Welfare Economics and Individual Development," by Herbert Gintis, *Quarterly Journal of Economics*, 89: 280–90.

1975i Comment on: "Parsons as a Symbolic Interactionist," by Jonathan Turner, *Sociological Inquiry*, 45 (1): 62–5.

1976a Some Considerations on the Growth of the American System of Higher Education and Research, *Culture and its Creators: Essays in Honor of Edward Shils*, T. N. Clark and J. Ben-David (eds), Chicago: University of Chicago Press, 266–84. [Reprinted in *Action Theory and the Human Condition*, 1978.]

1976b Clarence Ayers' Economics and Sociology, *Science and Ceremony: The Institutional Economics of Clarence E. Ayers*, William Breit and William Patton Culbertson, Jr. (eds), Austin: University of Texas Press, 175–9.

1976c Social Stratification: Professions, *Encyclopedia Italiana*, Vincenzo Cappelletti (ed.), Rome.

1976d Reply to Cohen, Hazelrigg, and Pope, with Special Reference to their Statement on the Divergence of Weber and Durkheim: A Critique of Parsons' Convergence Thesis, *American Sociological Review*, 41 (2) (April): 361–5.

1976e   A Few Considerations on the Place of Rationality in Modern Culture and Society, *Revue Européenne des Sciences Sociales et Cahiers Vilfredo Pareto* (special issue), 14 (38–9).

1976f   Vico and History, *Social Research*, 43 (4) (Winter): 881–5.

1976g   Social Science: The Public Disenchantment, *American Scholar*, 45 (4) (Autumn): 580–1.

1976h   Faculty Teaching Goals, 1968–73 (co-authored with Gerald M. Platt and Rita Kirshstein), *Social Problems*, 24 (2) (December): 298–307.

1976i   Afterword in *The Social Theories of Talcott Parsons: A Critical Examination*, Max Black (ed.), Carbondale: Southern Illinois University Press, 364–70.

1977a   *The Evolution of Societies* (edited, with an introduction, by Jackson Toby), Englewood Cliffs, NJ: Prentice-Hall.

1977b   *Social Systems and the Evolution of Action Theory*, New York: Free Press.

1977c   Retrospective Perspective: Alfred Schutz, Talcott Parsons, *Zur Theorie Sozialen Handelns, Ein Brietwechsel*, edited with an introduction by Walter M. Sprondel, Frankfurt am Main: Suhrkamp.

1977d   The Problem of Order in Society, and the Program of an Analytical Sociology, *American Journal of Sociology*, 83 (2) (September): 320–34.

1977e   Two Cases of Social Deviance: Addiction to Heroin, Addiction to Power (co-authored with Dean R. Gerstein), *Deviance and Social Change*, Edwin Sagarin (ed.), Beverly Hills: Sage Publications, 19–57.

1977f   Roberto Mangabeira Unger, "Law in Modern Society," *Law and Society Review*, 12 (1), (Fall): 145–9.

1977g   The Institutionalization of Belief, *Sociological Analysis*, 38 (20) (Summer): 137–9.

1977h   Law as an Intellectual Stepchild, *Sociological Inquiry*, 47 (3–4): 11–58.

1978a   Health and Disease: A Sociological and Action Perspective, *Encyclopedia of Bioethics*, New York: Free Press. [Reprinted in *Action Theory and the Human Condition*, 1978 (ch. 3).]

1978b   Death in the Western World, *Encyclopedia of Bioethics*, New York: Free Press. [Reprinted in *Action Theory and the Human Condition*, 1978 (ch. 14).]

1978c   *Action Theory and the Human Condition*, New York: Free Press.

1978d   Epilogue to *The Doctor–Patient Relationship in the Changing Health Scene*, Eugene B. Gallagher (ed.). [Proceedings of an international conference sponsored by the John E. Fogarty Center for Advanced Study in the Health Sciences, Bethesda, Maryland (April 26–28). Washington, D.C.: Government Printing Office.]

1978e   Action, Symbols, and Cybernetic Controls, *Towards the Sociology of Symbolic Structures*, Ino Rosi (ed.).

1978f   Toward a Redefinition of Action Theory: Paying the Cognitive Element its Due, *American Journal of Sociology*, 83 (6) (May): 1317–49.

1978g   Undergraduate Teaching Environments: Normative Orientations to Teaching among Faculty in the Higher Education System (co-authored with Gerald M. Platt and Rita Kirshstein), *Sociological Inquiry*, 48 (1): 3–21.

1979a   The Symbolic Environment of Modern Economies, *Social Research*, 46 (3) (Autumn): 436–53. [Originally written for a Japanese journal whose English title is *Contemporary Economics*.]

1979b   Émile Durkheim Today (co-authored with Harry Alpert, Werner J. Cathman, Lewis A. Coser, Ferdinand Kolegar, Dominick La Capra, Steven Lukes, Terry Nichols Clark, Neil J. Smelser, and Ernest Wallwork), *Research in Sociology of Knowledge, Sciences and Art*, 2: 123–53.

1979c   Religious and Economic Symbolism in the Western World, *Sociological Inquiry*, 49 (2–3): 1–48.

1980a   A Postscript to the Sociology of Modern Anti-Semitism, *Contemporary Jewry*, 5 (1) (Spring–Summer): 31–8.

1980b   On Theory and Metatheory, *Humboldt Journal of Social Relations*, 7 (1) (Fall–Winter): 5–16.

1980c   The Circumstances of My Encounter with Max Weber, *Sociological Traditions from Generation to Generation: Glimpses of the American Experience*, Robert K. Merton and Matilda White Riley (eds), New Jersey: Ablex, 37–43.

1981a   Revisiting the Classics Throughout a Long Career, *The Future of the Sociological Classics*, Buford Rhea (ed.), London: Allen & Unwin, 183–94.

1981b   Letter to Edward Tiryakian, *Sociological Inquiry*, 51 (1): 35–6.

1981c   The Sociological Import of a Metaphor: Tracking the Source of Max Weber's Iron Cage (co-authored with Edward Tiryakian), *Sociological Inquiry*, 51 (1): 27–33.

1986   *Aktor, Situation und normative Muster. Ein Essay zur Theorie sozialen Handelns*, Harald Wenzel (ed.), Frankfurt: Suhrkamp.

1989   A Tentative Outline of American Values, *Theory, Culture and Society*, 6 (4) (November): 577–612. [Reprinted in R. Robertson and B. S. Turner (eds), *Talcott Parsons: Theorist of Modernity*, London: Sage (1991), 37–65.]

1990   A Prolegomena to a Theory of Social Institutions (co-authored with Charles Camic, James S. Coleman, and Jeffrey C. Alexander), *American Sociological Review*, 55 (3) (June): 319–33.

1991   The Integration of Economic and Sociological Theory: The Marshall Lectures (Introduction by Richard Swedberg), *Sociological Inquiry*, 61 (1) (Winter): 10–59.

Selected Bibliography (in English) on the Sociology of Talcott Parsons

Adriaansens, H. P. M. (1980) *Talcott Parsons and the Conceptual Dilemma*. London: Routledge & Kegan Paul.

Alexander, J. C. (1984) *Theoretical Logic in Sociology*, vol. 4: *The Modern Reconstruction of Classical Thought: Talcott Parsons*. London: Routledge & Kegan Paul.

Black, M. (ed.) (1961) *The Social Theories of Talcott Parsons*. Englewood Cliffs, NJ: Prentice-Hall.

Bourricaud, F. (1981) *The Sociology of Talcott Parsons*. Chicago and London: University of Chicago Press.

Buxton, W. (1985) *Talcott Parsons and the Capitalist Nation-State: Political Sociology as a Strategic Vocation*. Toronto: University of Toronto Press.

Camic, C. (ed.) (1991) *Talcott Parsons: The Early Essays*. Chicago and London: University of Chicago Press.

Gerhardt, U. (ed.) (1993) *Talcott Parsons on National Socialism*. New York: Aldine de Gruyter.

Gouldner, A. W. (1970) *The Coming Crisis of Western Sociology*. New York: Basic Books.

Grathoff, R. (ed.) (1978) *The Theory of Social Action. The Correspondence of Alfred Schutz and Talcott Parsons*. Bloomington: Indiana University Press.

Hamilton, P. (1983) *Talcott Parsons*. London: Tavistock.

Holmwood, J. (1996) *Founding Sociology? Talcott Parsons and the Idea of General Theory*. London and New York: Longman.

Holton, R. J. and Turner, B. S. (1986) *Talcott Parsons on Economy and Society*. London: Routledge & Kegan Paul.

Levine, D. N. (1980) *Simmel and Parsons: Two Approaches to the Study of Society*. New York: Arno Press.

Loubser, J. J., Baum, R. C., Effrat, A., and Lidz, V. M. (eds) (1976) *Explorations in General Theory in Social Science. Essays in Honor of Talcott Parsons*. New York: Free Press, 2 vols.

Menzies, K. (1976) *Talcott Parsons and the Social Image of Man*. London: Routledge & Kegan Paul.

Mitchell, W. C. (1967) *Sociological Analysis and Politics: The Theories of Talcott Parsons*. Englewood Cliffs, NJ: Prentice-Hall.

Robertson, R. and Turner, B. S. (1991) *Talcott Parsons: Theorist of Modernity*. London: Sage.

Rocher, G. (1974) *Talcott Parsons and American Sociology*. London: Nelson.

Savage, S. P. (1981) *The Theories of Talcott Parsons: The Social Relations of Action*. London: Macmillan.

Wearne, B. C. (1989) *The Theory and Scholarship of Talcott Parsons to 1951*. Cambridge: Cambridge University Press.

Chronology of the Life of Talcott Parsons

1902	Born in Colorado Springs, Colorado
1920	Graduated from Horace Mann High School
	Entered Amherst College, Massachusetts
1923	Parsons converts to "institutional economics"
1924–5	Graduate study with Richard H. Tawney at the London School of Economics, England
1925	Doctoral thesis on the concept of capitalism in recent German literature as part of the Dr. Phil. at Heidelberg, Germany
1926	Seminar with Karl Jaspers on Kant's *Critique of Pure Reason*
1927–31	Became economics instructor at Harvard University
	Married Helen B. Walker
	Awarded D.Phil. for the thesis "The Concept of Capitalism in the Theories of Max Weber and Werner Sombart"
	Conceived the idea of translating Max Weber's *Die Protestantische Ethik und der Geist des Kapitalismus*
1931–6	Instructor, Department of Sociology at Harvard
1936	Promoted to assistant professor of sociology
1939	Promoted to associate professor of sociology
1940–1	Correspondence between Parsons and Alfred Schutz
1942	President of the Eastern Sociological Society
1944	Chair of the Department of Sociology at Harvard
1946	Entered into formal psychoanalytic training as a Class C Candidate at the Boston Psychoanalytic Institute
1946–56	Chairman of the Department of Social Relations at Harvard
1948	Membership of the Executive Committee of the Russian Research Centre (RRC) at Harvard
	Travels to Germany to study research opportunities for RRC
1949	President of the American Sociological Association
1953–4	Visiting professor of social theory at the University of Cambridge, England
	Delivered Marshall Lectures sponsored by the Department of Economics
1964	Parsons delivered his lecture on "Value-freedom and Objectivity" at the centenary of Weber's birth for the German Sociological Association at Heidelberg
	Invited to USSR by the Soviet Academy of Sciences to give a series of lectures on American sociology
1967	President of the American Academy of Arts and Sciences
1973	Retirement
1979	Died in Munich, Germany

Index